MW01596011

# *Readings for the 21st Century*

## *Tomorrow's Issues for Today's Students*

*Third Edition*

**William Vesterman**
*Rutgers University*

**Josh Ozersky**
*University of Notre Dame*

ALLYN AND BACON

BOSTON   LONDON   TORONTO   SYDNEY   TOKYO   SINGAPORE

*Editor in Chief, Humanities:* Joseph Opiela
*Editorial Assistant:* Kate Tolini
*Editorial Production Service:* York Production Services
*Cover Administrator:* Linda Dickinson
*Manufacturing Buyer:* Megan Cochran

**Library of Congress Cataloging-in-Publication Data**

Readings for the 21st century : tomorrow's issues for today's students
/ [compiled by] William Vesterman, Josh Ozersky. — 3rd ed.
    p.  cm.
  ISBN 0-205-19803-1
  1. College readers.  2. Twenty-first century—Problems, exercises,
etc.  3. Readers—Twenty-first century.  4. English language—
Rhetoric.  I. Vesterman, William, 1942– .  II. Ozersky, Josh.
PE1417.R418   1996
428.6—dc20                                       96-15116
                                               CIP

**CREDITS**

Angelou, Maya. "The Arc of the Moral Universe Is Long, but It Bends Toward Justice," reprinted by permission from *New Perspectibes Quarterly,* Winter 1992.

*Credits continued on page 441, which constitutes an extension of the copyright page.*

Printed in the United Sates of America

10  9  8  7  6  5  4  3  2  1     01  00  99  98  97  96

# CONTENTS

Contents    vii

# PREFACE

$R$*eadings for the 21st Century,* third edition, updates once more a collection of essays grouped around a general theme—the rapidly approaching twenty-first century. The essays, arranged into ten chapters, focus on various aspects of the future that today's students must face. Most chapters has six essays (Chapter six has five, Chapters three and ten, seven) representing a variety of authors from many fields, disciplines, and professions whose writings display variations in style, length, level, and point of view. Each chapter begins with a classic essay by a well-known author, in order to provide a historical perspective on the theme. Aldous Huxley, Frederick Douglass, Elizabeth Cady Stanton, George Orwell, and Lewis Thomas are among these authors.

An implicit subtheme in every chapter is "The Future and You," and the critical apparatus of the book invites students to consider themselves in direct relation to the issues and problems that will face their generation in the 1990s and beyond. A brief headnote introduces each author and indicates the original source of publication. The book also provides questions for each essay on *Themes, Issues, and Ideas* and on *Writing Strategies and Techniques,* along with two *Suggestions for Writing.* At the end of every chapter, *Making Connections* asks students to look at two or more essays within the chapter. These questions may form the basis for longer research assignments on chapter themes. A *Rhetorical Table of Contents* and an *Index of Authors and Titles* complete the apparatus of the book. With lively classic and contemporary writing addressing a broad spectrum of life in the United States, the book is designed with the hope of directing today's students to develop thoughtful, informed, and articulate views on topics that will define their futures.

At the current rate, the 1990s will add a billion more people to the 5.2 billion now inhabiting the earth. Unless those rates diminish, this generation of students may witness a virtual tripling in the earth's population over the next one hundred years. Within this growing world, American power is shrinking. Born into a society that took its economic and political leadership for granted, the Millennial Generation will enter an increasingly powerful global economy. And as it comes to maturity, that generation will face this problem with its many difficult questions. How will the United States compete with a more unified Western Europe? With the rising status of Asia's Pacific Rim community? With the rapidly changing nations of Eastern Europe? What will be our new relations with Africa, the Mideast, and Latin America? Can we deal with a stubbornly high poverty rate at home? How healthy can the population *afford* to be in the year 2000? If people live longer, who will care for them and support them? How will we come to terms with other important social issues facing this country?

Some changes are virtually ensured. The United States will become an increasingly older nation with a racial and ethnic mixture whose diversity will be unparalleled in world history. White males will become a minority in the labor force and two-earner households will become the norm. A shortage of skilled technical workers will force government into efforts to improve education at all levels, while adults undergoing career changes may make up the majority of future college applicants.

For several generations now, the year 2000 has symbolized the future. For all of us, that future will arrive in just a few short years. But it is the Millennial Generation who must lead our country bravely into the twenty-first century. This book is an attempt, in some small way, to help that generation define the meaning of the twenty-first century.

## Acknowledgments

Many people have helped to bring this book to its present form. At Rutgers we thank Kelly Griffin, for research and suggestions. At Allyn and Bacon we thank my editor Joe Opiela, and his assistant Kate Tolini.

For advice in shaping the book we thank teachers at many schools: John Bayer, St. Louis Community College at Meramec; Kathleen Shine Cain, Merrimack College; C. Jariel Howard, Northeastern Illinois University; William Lutz, Rutgers University-Camden; Jean Reynolds, Polk Community College; Mark Rollins, Ohio State University; Robert Schwegler, University of Rhode Island; and Tom Zaniello, Northern Kentucky University. And lastly, Fr. Bill Miscamble at Notre Dame, David Ozersky, and, especially, Cynthia R. Kachelmyer.

# CHAPTER
# ONE

# *Social Issues for the Twenty-first Century*

*Human Values in Changing Times*

# THE PAST AS PROLOGUE

## *from Looking Back on the Spanish War*

*George Orwell*

> *George Orwell (1903–1950) was the pen name of Eric Blair, one of the great essayists in the English language. Although most famous for his novel* 1984, *Orwell spent much of his life writing essays and news reports. It fell to him to chronicle the rise of fascism in the twentieth century, a story he told unflinchingly throughout his career. Born in England and educated at Eton and Oxford, Orwell described himself as a child of the upper-lower-middle-class, and upon graduating began a career as a civil servant in India, then a British colony. Morally disgusted by his work there, he returned to Europe, where he lived as a penniless dishwasher in Paris and as a homeless tramp in England, so as to understand oppression from the other side. The experience stayed with him for the rest of his life, which he spent writing about politics and class in the most realistic way possible. His political education was capped by the Spanish Civil War, in which he fought on the side of the Republicans against the fascist leader Francisco Franco. His book* Homage to Catalonia *provides a fuller record than does the following essay, which was written from greater remove.*

I never think of the Spanish war without two memories coming into my mind. One is of the hospital ward at Lerida and the rather sad voices of the wounded militiamen singing some song with a refrain that ended—

> Una resolucion,
> Luchar hast' al fin!

Well, they fought to the end all right. For the last eighteen months of the war the Republican armies must have been fighting almost without cigarettes, and with precious little food. Even when I left Spain in the middle of 1937, meat and bread were scarce, tobacco a rarity, coffee and sugar almost unobtainable.

The other memory is the Italian militiaman who shook my hand in the guardroom, the day I joined the militia. I wrote about this man at the beginning of my book on the Spanish war, and do not want to repeat what I said there. When I remember—oh, how vividly!—his shabby uniform and fierce, pathetic, innocent face, the complex side-issues of the war seem to fade away and I see clearly that there was at any rate no doubt as to who was in the right. In spite of power, politics and journalistic lying, the central issue of the war was the attempt of people like this to win the decent life which they knew to be their birthright. It is difficult to think of this particular man's probable end without several kinds of bitterness. Since I met him in the Lenin Barracks he was probably a Trotskyist or an Anarchist, and in the peculiar conditions of our time, when people of that sort are not killed by the Gestapo they are usually killed by the G. P. U. But that does not affect the long-term issues. This man's face, which I saw only for a minute or two, remains with me as a sort of visual reminder of what the war was really about. He symbolises for me the flower of the European working class, harried by the police of all countries, the people who fill the mass graves of the Spanish battlefields and are now, to the tune of several millions, rotting in forced-labour camps.

When one thinks of all the people who support or have supported Fascism, one stands amazed at their diversity. What a crew! Think of a programme which at any rate for a while could bring Hitler, Petain, Montagu Norman, Pavelitch, William Randolph Hearst, Streicher, Buchman, Ezra Pound, Juan March, Cocteau, Thyssen, Father Coughlin, the Mufti of Jerusalem, Arnold Lunn, Antonescu, Spengler, Beverley Nichols, Lady Houston, and Marinetti all into the same boat! But the clue is really very simple. They are all people with something to lose, or people who long for a hierarchical society and dread the prospect of a world of free and equal human beings. Behind all the ballyhoo that is talked about "godless" Russia and the "materialism" of the working class lies the simple intention of those with money or privileges to cling to them. Ditto, though it contains a partial truth, with all the talk about the worthlessness of social reconstruction not accompanied by a "change of heart". The pious ones, from the Pope to the yogis of California, are great on the "change of heart", much more reassuring from their point of view than a change in the economic system. Petain attributes the fall of France to the common people's "love of pleasure". One sees this in its right perspective if one stops to wonder how much pleasure the ordinary French peasant's or workingman's life would contain compared with Petain's own. The damned impertinence of these politicians, priests, literary men, and what-not who lecture the working-class socialist for his "materialism"! All that the working-man demands is what these others would consider the indispensable minimum without which human life cannot be lived at all. Enough to eat, freedom from the haunting terror of unemployment, the knowledge that your children will get a fair chance, a bath once a day, clean linen reasonably often, a roof that doesn't leak, and short enough working hours to leave you with a little energy when the day is done. Not one of those who preach against "materialism" would consider life livable without these things. And how easily that minimum could be attained if we chose to set our minds to it for only twenty years! To raise the standard of living of the whole world to that of Britain would not be a greater undertaking than the war we have just fought. I don't claim, and I don't know who does, that that would solve anything in itself. It is merely that privation and brute labour have to be abolished before the real problems of humanity can be tackled. The major problem of our time is the decay of the belief in personal immortality, and it cannot be dealt with while the average human being is either drudging like an ox or shivering in fear of the secret police. How right the working classes are in their "materialism"! How right they are to realise that the belly comes before the soul, not in the scale of values but in point of time! Understand that, and the long horror that we are enduring becomes at least intelligible. All the considerations that are likely to make one falter—the siren voices of a Petain or of a Gandhi, the inescapable fact that in order to fight one has to degrade oneself, the equivocal moral position of Britain, with its democratic phrases and its coolie empire, the sinister development of Soviet Russia, the squalid farce of left-wing politics—all this fades away and one sees only the struggle of the gradually awakening common people against the lords of property and their hired liars and bumsuckers. The question is very simple. Shall people like that Italian soldier be allowed to live the decent, fully human life which is now technically achievable, or shan't they? Shall the common man be pushed back into the mud, or shall he not? I myself believe, perhaps on insufficient grounds, that the common man will win his fight sooner or later, but I want it to be sooner and not later—some time within the next hundred years, say, and not some time within the next ten thousand years. That was the real issue of the Spanish war, and of the last war, and perhaps of other wars yet to come.

## Themes, Issues, and Ideas

1.  Orwell ends this selection by saying that the "real issue" of the Spanish war would also be the real issue of wars to come. Does this conclusion seem to be true to you? Does it apply to other wars that you know of?

2.  How, according to Orwell, might the "siren voice" of a Gandhi "make one falter"?

3.  Orwell makes a list of what he considers "the indispensable minimum without which human life cannot be lived at all." Is there anything that you would add to this list? Anything you would take away?

## Writing Strategies and Techniques

1.  Orwell's style does not leave much room for disagreement with his ideas. Does this persuade you, or do you feel in some way bullied? Describe your reaction to his style. Then, describe your reaction to the content of his essay.

2.  Orwell tends not to get very deeply into facts and figures in his work. What is the effect of this?

3.  Often in his writing Orwell will seem to overflow, to rhetorically pound his fist on the desk or slap his forehead. When do such moments occur in the essay, and how do they affect you? How calculated do you think this device is on Orwell's part?

# Suggestions for Writing

1. Orwell writes with a very oral, forceful style. What sort of person do you imagine speaking when you read this essay? Describe the views that person might hold on other subjects besides politics.

2. Orwell makes a list of disparate people who supported fascism. Look up these people in an encyclopedia and make a list of their equivalents today. Is there anything that would unite your list?

# Crackdown

## Treating the Symptoms of the Drug Problem

*James Q. Wilson and*
*John J. DiIulio, Jr.*

*Crime and drugs—two separable but related matters—are among the gravest social issues American society faces in the 1990s. The recent advent of crack— smokable cocaine available in small and relatively low-priced units—has intensified national concern. Some aspects of the issues and projections for their future are given in this essay (first published in* The New Republic*) by two political scientists. The authors also cover the background and many of the arguments, both pro and con, on the growing controversy over legalizing drugs.*

*James Q. Wilson has long been among the most lucid and frequent commentators on problems of crime in the United States. The author of many articles and books, he is Collins Professor of Management and Public Policy at the University of California at Los Angeles. Recently he has coauthored* Crime and Human Nature. *John J. DiIulio, Jr., teaches politics at Princeton University. His most recent book is* Governing Prisons.*

Accor ding to the projections, crime was supposed to be under control by now. The postwar baby-boom generation, which moved into its crime-prone years during the early 1960s, has grown up, yielding its place to the (proportionately) less numerous baby-bust generation. With relatively fewer 18-year-olds around, we should all be walking safer streets.

And in fact for most people crime *has* gone down. The Census Bureau's victimization surveys tell us that between 1980 and 1987 the burglary rate declined by 27 percent, the robbery rate by 21 percent. Despite what we hear, 3,000 fewer murders were committed in 1987 than in 1980. Even in some big cities that are in the news for the frequency with which their residents kill each other, the homicide rate has decreased. Take Los Angeles: Despite freeway shootings and gang warfare, there were 261 fewer murders in 1987 than in 1980, a drop of more than 20 percent.

But in specific enclaves the horror stories are all too true. In south central Los Angeles, in much of Newark, in and around the housing projects of Chicago, in the South Bronx and Bedford-Stuyvesant sections of New York, and in parts of Washington, D.C., conditions are not much better than they are in Beirut on a bad day. Drugs, especially crack, are sold openly on street corners; rival gangs shoot at each other from moving automobiles; automatic weapons are carried by teenagers onto school playgrounds; innocent people hide behind double-locked doors and shuttered windows. In Los Angeles there is at least one gang murder every day, Sundays included. A ten-foot-high concrete wall is being built around the junior high school one of us attended, in order, the principal explained, to keep stray bullets from hitting children on the playground.

The problem is drugs and the brutal struggles among competing gangs for control of the lucrative drug markets. The drug of choice is crack (except in Washington, where it is PCP). The crack craze has led to conditions far worse than were found in these same neighborhoods a decade or so ago, when heroin was the preferred drug. The reasons for the change are not reassuring.

Crack is a stimulant; heroin is a sedative. Crack produces exceptional euphoria; heroin produces, after a quick "rush," oblivion. Crack (and PCP) addicts are often stimulated to acts of violence and daring that make them dangerous to themselves as well as to others; heroin addicts are rarely violent when high—the drug even depresses the sexual drive.

Crack is marketed by competitive distribution systems, some of whose members are fighting—literally—to establish monopoly control. Heroin (at least on the East Coast) was marketed in a criminal environment dominated by established monopolies that were well equipped, in muscle and in political connections, to protect their market shares with a minimum of random violence.

Crack users have no attractive chemical alternative. The drug is far more rewarding than any substitute. Heroin users who had progressed to the point where they wanted nothing but relief from the pains of withdrawal and the diseases caused by intravenous injection could take oral methadone. The heroin substitute, though addictive, required no injections, prevented withdrawal pains, and (in the correct dosages) produced little or no "high."

In short, certain neighborhoods of our larger cities are being ravaged by a drug that consumers find more alluring than heroin, that stimulates rather than sedates its users, that suppliers must use violence to sell, and that therapists are at a loss to manage by chemical means.

Attempting to suppress the use of drugs is very costly. Some people therefore conclude that we must eliminate all the costs of law enforcement by repealing the laws that are being enforced. The result would be less crime, fewer and weaker gangs, and an opportunity to address the public health problems in a straightforward manner.

But legalizing drugs would also entail costs. Those costs are hard to measure, in part because they are to a large degree moral and in part because we have so little experience with legalized drugs.

There is an obvious moral reason for attempting to discourage drug use: The heavy consumption of certain drugs ravages human character. These drugs—principally heroin, cocaine, and crack—are for many people powerfully reinforcing. The pleasure or oblivion they produce leads many users to devote their lives to seeking pleasure or oblivion, and to do so regardless of the cost in ordinary human virtues, such as temperance, duty, and sympathy. The dignity, autonomy, and productivity of users is at best impaired, at worst destroyed.

Some people think society has no obligation to form and sustain the character of individuals. Libertarians would leave all adults free to choose their own habits and seek their own destiny so long as their behavior did not cause any direct harm to others. But most people, however willing they may be to tolerate human eccentricities and support civil liberties, act as if they believe that government, as the agent for society, is responsible for helping to instill certain qualities in the citizenry. This was the original reason for mandatory schooling. We not only want to train children to be useful, we want to train them to be decent. It is also the reason that virtually every nation that has been confronted by a sharp increase in addiction to any psychoactive substance, including alcohol, has enacted laws designed to regulate or suppress its use.

Great Britain once allowed physicians to prescribe opiates for addicts. The system worked reasonably well so long as the addicts were middle-class people who had become hooked as a consequence of receiving painkillers in hospitals. But when thrill-seeking youth discovered heroin, the number of addicts increased *40-fold,* and so Britain ended the prescription system. It was replaced at first with a system of controlled dispensation from government clinics, and then with a system of substituting methadone for heroin coupled with the stringent enforcement of the laws against the latter.

Even if we were to decide that the government had no responsibility for character formation and should regulate only behavior that hurts other people, we would still have to figure out what to do about drug-dependent people—because such dependency does hurt other people. A heroin addict dreamily enjoying his euphoria, a crack smoker looking for the next high, a cocaine snorter eager for relief from his depression—these users are not likely to be healthy people, productive workers, good parents, reliable neighbors, attentive students, or safe drivers. Moreover, some people are harmed by drugs that they have not chosen to use. The babies of drug-dependent women suffer because of their mothers' habits. We all pay for drug abuse in lowered productivity, more accidents, higher insurance premiums, bigger welfare costs, and less effective classrooms.

The question is whether the costs of drug use are likely to be higher when the drug is illegal or when it is legal. In both cases society must pay the bill. When the drug is illegal, the cost consists of the law enforcement costs (crime, corruption, extensive and intrusive policing), the welfare costs (poorer health, lost wages, higher unemployment benefits, more aid to families with dependent children, and various treatment and prevention programs), and the moral costs (debased and degraded people). If the drug were legal, the bill would consist primarily of the welfare costs and the moral costs. And there would still be law enforcement costs: the costs of enforcing tax collection if the drugs were sold, or of preventing diversion if the drugs were distributed through the health care system, and the costs in either case of keeping the drugs out of the hands, lungs, and veins of minors. Legalization without some form of regulation is inconceivable; the more stringent the regulation, the higher the law enforcement bill.

Which scenario will be costlier? The answer chiefly depends on how many people will use the drug. We have a rough idea of how many people regularly use heroin and cocaine despite its illegality. How many will regularly use it under the legal scenario?

No one really knows, but it will almost surely be many more than now. The free market price of cocaine is probably no more than 5 percent of its present black market price. Even allowing for heavy taxes, Stanford's John Kaplan has estimated that the free market price would be no more than 20 percent of what it now costs. The consumption of a widely desired, pleasure-inducing substance without question will increase dramatically if the price is cut by 80 percent to 95 percent.

Moreover, the true price of the drug is the monetary cost plus the difficulty and inconvenience of the search for it and the risk associated with consuming a product of unknown quality. Though drugs are sold openly on the streets of some communities, for most people—especially for novice, middle-class users—they are hard to come by and often found only in threatening surroundings. Legalization will make the drug more attractive, even if the price actually rises, by reducing the costs of searching for it, negotiating a transaction, and running the risk of ingesting a dangerous substance. The combined effect of lowered market prices and lowered transaction costs will be very great.

Just how great cannot be known without trying it. And one cannot try it experimentally, for there is no way to run a meaningful experiment. The increase in use that would occur if people in one neighborhood or patients at one clinic were allowed to buy the drug at its market cost can give us no reliable information on how many people would use the drug if it were generally available. And the experiment would have irreversible effects. Moreover, as the British experience showed, there is no such thing as "controlled distribution." Inevitably there will be massive leaks of government-supplied drugs into the black market.

We already have the "benefits" of one quasi-experiment. So long as cocaine was available only in its relatively expensive powdered form, its use was pretty much concentrated among more affluent people. But with the invention of crack, which can be sold in single low-priced doses rather than by the high-priced gram, cocaine use increased sharply.

We believe that the moral and welfare costs of heavy drug use are so large that society should continue to enforce the laws against its use for the sake of keeping the number of users as small as possible. But we recognize that by adopting this position, we are placing a heavy burden on those poor communities where drug use is endemic. We are allowing these neighborhoods to be more violent than they would be if the drug were legal. Since we do not live in such communities, we must ask ourselves whether our preferences can be justified to people who do.

The answer to that question is given by the testimony of those who live in the midst of the problem. They want drugs kept illegal. They say so and their representatives in Congress say so. We hope that our libertarian critics will not accuse the people of Watts, Anacostia, and the South Bronx of suffering from false consciousness on this matter. These people know what drug use is and they don't like it.

But if drugs are to be kept illegal, we have a special responsibility to prevent the streets of inner-city neighborhoods from being controlled by those who seek to profit from the trade. We have not done a very good job of this.

In some places there may not be enough police. In others the cops are just badly used, as when the focus is on making a case against "Mr. Big," the local drug kingpin. There are two things wrong with this. First, nothing is easier than replacing Mr. Big; indeed, often the police get evidence on him from tips supplied by his would-be replacement. Meanwhile the distribution of drugs goes on unabated. Second, arresting Mr. Big does nothing to improve the lives of the decent people in the neighborhood who want the drug dealers off the street.

Many cities, notably New York, have recognized this and are concentrating on street-level dealers. The NYPD has wrested control from the drug dealers in parts of the Lower East Side, all of Washington Square Park, much of West 107th Street, and other places. But they have done so at a cost, what Aric Press of *Newsweek* calls the criminal justice equivalent of bulimia. The police go on an arrest binge, and then, "overwhelmed and overfed, the rest of the system—prosecutors, defenders, judges, and jailers—has spent its days in an endless purge, desperately trying to find ways to move its population before it gets hit with another wave tomorrow." The purgatives included granting early release to some inmates and trying to shift other city prisoners to state penitentiaries; pressuring the governor to authorize the appointment of more judges while encouraging faster plea bargaining to clear the crowded dockets; and building "temporary" holding facilities for new arrestees.

The District of Columbia has begun to enter the bulimia phase. The number of people going through the criminal justice system on drug charges has exploded. Between 1983 and 1987 drug arrests increased by 45 percent, drug prosecutions by over 500 percent, drug convictions by over 700 percent. Clearly judges and prosecutors were starting to get tough. But until very recently, the toughness stopped at the jailhouse door. As recently as 1986, only 7 percent of the adults arrested on drug charges—and only 20 percent of those convicted on such charges—were sent to the city's principal correctional facility at Lorton. Then, suddenly, the system lurched into overdrive. Between 1986 and 1987 the number of drug incarcerations more than doubled, so that by the end of the year an adult arrested on a drug charge had a one-in-five chance of going to jail, and one convicted on such a charge had a one-in-two chance of winding up at Lorton.

This means that, until very recently, the price of drug dealing in Washington has been quite low. Those who say that "law enforcement has failed" should remember that until the last two years it was barely tried. Police Chief–designate Isaac Fulwood says that the same dealer may be arrested eight or nine times in the space of a few weeks. The city has been operating a revolving-door criminal justice system.

One reason for the speed with which the door revolves is that in Washington, as in most parts of the country, the prisons are jammed full. Another factor is that professional drug dealers know they can get a favorable plea bargain if they threaten to make the system give them a full trial, replete with every conceivable motion. The mere threat of such a demand is ordinarily enough to ensure that an attractive bargain is offered.

How can an overtaxed system help protect people in the drug-ridden neighborhoods? Building more conventional prisons is part of the answer, but that takes a lot of time, and no one wants them in their back yard. The goal is to take drug dealers off the streets for a longer period than the time it takes to be booked and released. One step is to ensure that no good arrest is washed out for want of prosecution because of a shortage of judges, prosecutors, and public defenders. These are not cheap, but candidates for these posts are more readily available than vacant lots on which to build jails.

Nevertheless, prisons are still needed and can be had, provided we are willing to think of alternatives to conventional holding tanks. One is to reserve regular prison space for major traffickers and to use parts of present (or all of former) military camps as boot camps for lower-level dealers. At these minimum-security camps, inmates would receive physical training, military discipline, and drug-abuse treatment, all under the direction of military personnel and with the aim of preparing them for a life that would combine, to the extent possible, the requirement of regular drug tests and the opportunity for gainful employment.

Meanwhile, the chances of released inmates rejoining old gangs can perhaps be reduced by enforcing a law, such as the one recently passed in California, that makes mere membership in certain gangs illegal and attaches civil or criminal penalties to parents who knowingly allow their children to join them.

Critics of punishment object that (1) incarceration is not a deterrent, either because young drug dealers are not "rational" or because drug trafficking is so lucrative as to make short stays behind a fence worth it; and that (2) the only true solution to the drug problem is to reduce the demand for drugs by education and treatment. We are tempted to respond to these views by pointing out that, insofar as we can tell, each is wrong in whole or in substantial part. Instead, let's assume that these views are entirely correct. They are also irrelevant.

At this stage, we are not trying to deter drug sales or reduce drug use. All we wish to do is to reassert lawful public control over public spaces. Everything else we may wish to achieve—reducing the demand for drugs, curing the users of drugs, deterring the sale of drugs—can only be done after the public and the police, not the dealers and the gangs, are in charge of the neighborhoods. In the short run, this can be done by repeatedly arresting every suspected dealer and user and sending them through the revolving door. If we cannot increase the severity of the penalties they face, we can at least increase the frequency with which they bear them. In police terms, we want to roust the bad guys.

After the bad guys find they are making repeated trips to the same prison camps, the decent people of the neighborhood must form organizations willing and able to work with the police to keep the bad guys from regaining control of the streets. The Kenilworth-Parkside area of Washington shows what can be done. A few years ago this neighborhood, the site of a public housing project, was an open-air drug market that spawned all manner of crime. In 1982 a tenants' committee led by Kimi Gray formed a corporation and assumed control of the housing project. Though the residents were primarily unwed mothers living on welfare, over the next five years their association collected the rents, ran the buildings, enforced school attendance on the children, and got rid of the addicts. In 1988 the association signed a contract to purchase the project from the government.

A key to the Kenilworth-Parkside group's accomplishment lies in its cooperation with the police. Gray and her colleagues set up neighborhood watch groups, held police-community meetings, and helped the police find and arrest drug dealers and street criminals.

Much is made these days of "community-oriented" policing. Both of us have written favorably about it and the problem-solving, police-neighborhood collaboration that lies at its heart. But the success stories are always in communities in which the people are willing to step forward and the police are willing to meet them halfway. Where open-air drug markets operate every night, where Uzi-toting thugs shoot rivals and bystanders alike, it is a brave or foolhardy resident who will even testify against a criminal, much less lead an anticrime crusade. But once the police have shown that they can control the streets, even if the dealers they have chased off spend only brief (albeit frequent) periods in prison camp, there is an opportunity to build new partnerships.

The drugs-crime problem ultimately will be solved only when the demand for drugs is dramatically reduced. Though it is necessary to make major investments in overseas crop eradication, the interdiction of international drug shipments, and the control of our borders, there is scarcely an experienced law enforcement officer in the country who does not believe that controlling the sources of supply is much more than a holding operation.

How do we reduce demand? We do not know. Realizing that is the beginning of wisdom. The greatest mischief is to assume that the demand for drugs will decline only when there is less racism and poverty, better schools and more jobs, more religion, and better-quality television.

Recall how the heroin epidemic finally ended. At one time the number of new addicts seemed to be rising exponentially despite the ending of the Turkish supply of illicit opium and the breaking up of the French processing laboratories. Now we have a fairly stable number of confirmed addicts whose ranks seem not to be increasing and may be decreasing. This was accomplished by three things: death, testing, and methadone.

Youngsters who were ready to ignore the lectures of their teachers or the blandishments of public-service television commercials were not so ready to ignore the testimony of their everyday experiences. Heroin addicts were dying from drug overdoses, dirty needles, and personal neglect. Doing heroin no longer seemed as glamorous as it did when one first heard about it from jazz musicians and big-time crooks.

The military began a rigorous program of testing, which continues to this day. There were sanctions attached to being found out—often a delay in being returned home, possibly military punishment, and probably a dishonorable discharge. Drug use in the military dropped dramatically, and has stayed low.

Heroin addicts who were burned out by their long and increasingly unsatisfying bout with the drug often turned to methadone as a way of easing the pain and stabilizing their lives. If they stayed with it, they had a good chance of benefiting from the counseling and training programs made available to them.

These three prevention measures are not likely to be as effective with cocaine and crack addicts. Some users are dying from these drugs, but smoking crack still seems to many users to be far more exciting and much less dangerous than injecting heroin. In time, enough people will ruin their lives so that even the fantastic high that crack produces will begin to seem unattractive to potential users. But that time is not here yet.

Testing works, but only if it is done rigorously and with real consequences, ranging from immediate counseling to discharge or punishment. As yet few civilian institutions seem prepared (or able) to do what the armed forces did. It is hard enough for private employers to test, and they are not subject to the search-and-seizure provisions of the Fourth Amendment. Opposition from employee groups and civil libertarians shows little sign of abating. Some government agencies are testing, but they are doing so gingerly, usually by limiting tests to workers such as prison guards and customs agents, who are in obviously sensitive positions. It is hard to imagine many schools adopting a testing program, though some are trying.

And there is no cocaine equivalent for methadone, though science may yet find one.

That doesn't leave much: some school-based drug-education programs that look promising but have not (as yet) proved their efficacy, and many treatment programs that can have some success—provided the patient is willing to stay in them.

"Willing": That is the key. Heavy drug use is an addiction about which we have, in other contexts, already learned a great deal. Fifty years ago we knew as little about dealing with alcoholism as we now know about cocaine abuse. Today we know enough about alcoholism to realize the key steps to coping with it.

First and foremost: Addicts will not get better until they first confront the fact that they are addicts. Alcoholics Anonymous knows this full well, making it the cornerstone of its Twelve Steps. The families of alcoholics are taught that they did not cause and can neither control nor cure the addictive behavior—the disease—of the alcoholic. The deaths of others and an inescapable testing program can help provoke among drug users what the destruction of the lives of alcoholics sometimes stimulates—a recognition that they are powerless in the face of the drug and that they need the help of others like themselves.

Among the heroin treatment programs that have worked, even without methadone, are those that have involved some aspect of confrontation. Therapeutic communities provide this, but they tend to reach relatively few people. The civil commitment program (technically, Civil Addict Program) in California reached more. It worked this way: An addict (usually arrested by the police) was incarcerated for a brief period, followed by release into the community under instructions to report regularly for a urine test. A parolee with a dirty urine test was reincarcerated on the original charge.

Douglas Anglin and William McGlothlin at UCLA were able to compare the drug use of two similar groups—one that had been sent through the Civil Addict Program and another that had been sent to it but was quickly released from its testing requirements through some legal error made in the commitment proceedings. Those who went through the full program reduced their narcotic use and criminality over a five-year–follow-up period at a rate three times greater than the control group.

This raises the possibility that frequent drug testing, backed up by the revocation of parole or of probation for those who fail, may help produce (out of either fear or growing self-awareness) that willingness to confront the fact of addiction that is the prerequisite of successful treatment. Though experts disagree about the role of coercion in treatment programs, an impressive number of studies suggest that cocaine-using arrestees will rarely volunteer for treatment unless they are subject to considerable legal pressure.

Harry Wexler and Douglas Lipton, two experienced drug researchers, have summarized what they have learned about intervening with drug offenders this way: "The criminal justice system must frequently and systematically supervise cocaine-heroin users so that they have less time for crime and drug use." This means urine testing as a condition of probation or parole.

The advocates of treatment and prevention sometimes argue as if these programs can be made to work under wholly voluntary arrangements, provided enough treatment slots are available. Indeed, the helping atmosphere makes treatment seem preferable to the callous toughness of law enforcement strategies. This is sometimes true, but for the majority of addicts it is a serious error, akin to thinking that alcoholics will follow their doctors' advice, if there are enough doctors around. Alcoholics need some measure of coercion; AA supplies it, through the peer pressure generated at regular meetings of other alcoholics. Cocaine users will require even more pressure because coke is far more pleasure-giving than alcohol.

Much of what we have said here will seem pointless to those who still believe that every social problem must be viewed as an indictment of society and its failure to eliminate the "root causes" of its ills. But when it comes to addictive behaviors, the symptoms *are* the causes. We do not know why some people try cocaine and then drop it, others try it and abuse it, and still others do not try it at all. We do not know the answers to those questions with respect to alcohol abuse either, and we have been studying that "symptom" pretty seriously for the last half century. What we do know is that addiction is a self-sustaining reaction that spreads as the addictive drug becomes more easily available.

We must begin with the facts, not with theories. The facts are these: Some parts of our cities are being destroyed by gangs competing for the right to destroy lives by selling drugs. Those gangs have to be defeated, even if it means hiring more judges and building more correctional facilities. After that we can help communities reorganize themselves so that the good people control the streets and the teachers, doctors, and scientists have a chance to find out what will prevent another addictive epidemic from breaking out when some chemist discovers a drug that is even cheaper and more euphoria-inducing than crack. And that last event, we can be certain, will happen.

## Themes, Issues, and Ideas

1.  Besides the cost of drugs to users, the authors are also concerned with the costs society incurs when drug abuse is prevalent. What are the three kinds of costs mentioned? Would these costs increase or decrease with legalization?

2.  Are the authors of this essay more concerned with helping addicts toward recovery or with helping neighborhoods become safer? How do they defend their position? Do you agree? Explain your answer.

3.  The authors claim that people who live among drug users are against legalization and that "since we do not live in such communities, we must ask ourselves whether our preferences can be justified to people who do." What do you think of this argument? What might the authors say to the objection that if public opinion decides the issue, we need polltakers rather than policy experts?

## Writing Strategies and Techniques

1.  The authors speculate on two remedies for the drug problem: legalization and law enforcement. In what differing ways do they organize their arguments on each topic? In what way is each method of organization similar?

2.  How do the authors deal with the objection that these remedies only cure the "symptoms" and not the "root causes" of the problem?

## Suggestions for Writing

1.  Where do you stand on the issue of legalizing drugs? Write an essay in which you express your views, being sure to take into account the evidence and arguments Wilson and DiIulio offer.

2.  Write an essay in which you analyze the differing ways Wilson and DiIulio address the two issues of helping addicts and helping neighborhoods.

# Living In "Apocutopia"

## Travis Charbenau

*As the millennium approaches, a number of differing perspectives are competing for space. Noted futurist Travis Charbenau considers two of the most extreme, and considers a more common view of the coming age as a time for us to reconsider our materialism, and so step aside from the extremes of millennialism to a better, saner future.*

At the close of the first millennium, hermits descended from the hills to warn, "The end is nigh!" As we near the conclusion of the second millennium, we may be forgiven for wondering if the medieval eccentrics were guilty only of hasty judgment. The entire twentieth century seems like a runaway locomotive bearing down on the year 2000 and freighted with cataclysms—world war, technology run amok, omens of nuclear Armageddon, environmental collapse, economic decline, and global overpopulation. There is certainly something apocalyptic about starting a new thousand-year cycle.

At the same time, the phrase "ushering in the millennium" promises something distinctly utopian. Alternating with humanity's pessimism is the "hope that springs eternal," and we look with excitement and anticipation to life in the next century—just as our predecessors did during the *fin de siècle* of the 1890s. Back then, the promise that technology would create heaven on earth was still shiny and new. Over the past 100 years, despite having been badly "Frankensteined" several times, we remain enthralled by the promise of a twenty-first century we long ago populated with marvels: robots, helicars, and world peace.

Clearly, our two eternally opposed views of the future—apocalyptic and utopian—will go at one another as never before in the current *fin de millénium* decade, making for a uniquely paradoxical era that may be called "apocutopia."

Still, what's so magical about the mere turning of a calendar page? Do such anachronistic and superstitious attitudes about time really matter? All of us can remember being asked on various birthdays, "Well, how does it *feel* to be 14 (or 35 or 77)?" What a dumb question!

Or is it?

How we *feel* about the twenty-first century matters a great deal. How we feel has mattered ever since the Industrial Revolution enabled us to begin shaping the planet to our own ends. Our power has grown so exponentially in recent years that how we feel about the twenty-first century could determine whether there will even *be* one.

The most recent change of any strong apocalyptic character is the still-volatile collapse of communism. A utopian idea from the Bible to the Bolsheviks, communism as we know it has been a flop. Yet even as so many gloat over the apocalyptic collapse of communism, the more honest may admit to sharing the same utopian goal as the Biblical and Bolshevik communists of yore: a better life—and better and better and better. If we are even more honest, we'll admit to having already adopted various forms of governmental social engineering that are socialism in all but name. And if we are more honest still, we'll admit that our real challenge has never come from some variation in economic theology. The real challenge of apocutopia consists of pausing long enough in our gloating to seriously redefine things like "better," "progress," and even "utopia," to get away from our hopelessly barbaric, truly anachronistic appetite for "More stuff!"

"More stuff!" failed the communists—and they didn't even produce much of it. "More stuff!" will similarly preclude any sort of sustainable future everywhere that "More stuff" prevails as the definition of progress—*especially* in places that have too much stuff already.

The Club of Rome's 1972 *Limits to Growth* study was not an invitation to dis-invent the Industrial Era, but to join "in understanding and preparing for a period of great transition—the transition from growth to global equilibrium." In the cancer patient, this would be called the transition from metastasis to stasis.

And that might be as good a working definition of "utopia" as we may realistically expect to encounter right now. I personally find it rather appealing.

Whether we are frightened or hopeful pessimistic or optimistic, conservative or liberal, the apocutopian nineties are a period of thoughtful ferment—a time for ideas that will help us make that "great transition" redefining progress from the brutish and untenable "more stuff" to the civilized and supportable "enough stuff." That would *truly* "usher in the millennium."

## Themes, Issues, and Ideas

1. Do you agree with Charbenau's characterization of the two schools of millennial thought? What might some alternative examples be?

2. Consider the connection Charbenau makes between communist millennialism and the credo of "more stuff." Is it a valid one? Why or why not?

3. Compare Charbenau's vision of the millennium with those he describes. Do you find it more appealing? More likely?

## Writing Strategies and Techniques

1. Many essays about the future begin by describing the past. What do you think of this strategy? Is it effective? Why or why not?

2. In the middle of the essay, Charbenau has placed a one-sentence paragraph. Why is it so short? What effect does this have? Why does he place it where it is?

## Suggestions for Writing

1. Write an essay describing your view of the millennium. Try not to take any of the positions Charbenau describes (e.g., utopian, apocalyptic, materialist).

2. Write an essay describing an alternative millennium to the one Charbenau describes.

# Invasion of the Body Snatchers

## Fetal Rights vs. Mothers' Rights

### Ronni Sandroff

*Abortion is one of the issues that have been raised as a result of the clash between the constantly improving technology available to modern medicine and the slowly changing traditional views of human rights. What happens to human rights originally formulated to safeguard human "individuals" in the case of pregnant women, who may be viewed as physically representing more than one individual? Society continues to agonize over this general question and its growing number of particular implications.*

*In an essay originally published in* Vogue *magazine, Ronni Sandroff takes us through part of the legal and ethical maze by reporting on both the case histories of ordinary people and the arguments marshaled by experts who often disagree among themselves.*

The baby and mother were almost certain to die unless a cesarean section was performed. But the mother was part of a small fundamentalist sect that prohibited surgery. And she was surrounded by family members who told her, "You can't have a cesarean section. Even if the baby dies, it's OK."

It was not OK with the doctor in charge, Mary Jo O'Sullivan, M.D., professor of obstetrics and gynecology at the University of Miami School of Medicine. "The baby's head was way too large. Without a c-section the only way to get the baby out would be to wait until it died and take it apart, piece by piece. I just couldn't do that. Nor was anyone else at the hospital willing to do it."

Dr. O'Sullivan finally took the matter to court, petitioning for the right to override the mother's decision. The court ordered a cesarean, but Dr. O'Sullivan was still uncomfortable about forcing surgery.

"To my surprise, when I showed the patient the court order, she seemed relieved that the decision was out of her hands," says Dr. O'Sullivan.

The story had a happy ending—mother, baby, and doctor are doing fine—but cases like this are causing alarm among civil libertarians and feminists. "The courts have no business in the delivery room," insists George Annas, professor of Health Law at Boston University School of Public Health. "Competent adults have the right to refuse even lifesaving treatment."

And it's irrelevant that, in this case, the mother turned out to be grateful to have the court decide, says Nancy Milliken, M.D., who recently cowrote a critique of cases of court-ordered surgery in the *Journal of the American Medical Association:* "Individuals can't have it both ways. We can't say: we want the right to make our own health decisions and then turn around and expect the doctor to *make us* do what's good for us."

Though the number of court-ordered cesareans is small, each one symbolizes a disturbing trend—the encroachment on the rights of the pregnant woman; the view of her as the "jar" or "container" of the next generation. In Wisconsin, for example, a sixteen-year-old pregnant girl was held in detention for her "lack [of] motivation or ability to seek prenatal care." In Michigan and Illinois, courts have permitted the child to sue its mother for damaging it during pregnancy. And, in a number of states, legislation has been introduced to expand the laws on child abuse to cover the fetus. This would permit after-the-fact prosecution of women who do anything during pregnancy (smoke, drink, use drugs, refuse treatment) that damages the offspring.

Public support for measures of this kind is surprisingly strong. A recent Gallup poll found that almost half of those surveyed agreed that a woman should be legally liable for damaging her child by drinking or smoking during pregnancy. People were about equally split on whether a woman should be held liable for refusing a cesarean.

Doctors are no more in agreement than the general public. The reason for the dissension is that our technological prowess has leapt ahead of our ethical and legal thinking. In the past, obstetricians had one patient: the mother. But new technology has opened up a much greater window on what's going on with the fetus throughout gestation.

"We're now taking care of premature infants at twenty-six, twenty-seven, twenty-eight weeks," explains Dr. Milliken. "So we're starting to devise treatments for fetuses as separate patients."

But the interests of the fetus are sometimes in conflict with the interests or desires of the mother—if a mother disagrees with medical advice or is reckless about how her actions affect the unborn child. In these cases, who is to defend the "rights" of the fetus?

Most experts hold that its physical location makes it impossible for a fetus to have rights: An unborn child cannot be treated without invading the body of its mother and severely affecting her freedom of movement, privacy, and health. Until a baby is born, they argue, it has no more independent rights than any other organ in the mother's body.

"On the one hand the interest in fetal rights is new," says Lynn Paltrow, staff counsel for the American Civil Liberties Union Reproductive Freedom Project. "On the other, it is simply a reflection of a historical trend to limit women's rights based on their reproductive ability."

Today, the question is whether our new understanding of gestation creates a need for special legislation to protect the interests of the fetus. The legions of infants born deformed, mentally retarded, or addicted to drugs are a burden to society as a whole as well as the individual parents.

John A. Robertson, a law professor at the University of Texas at Austin who did some of the earliest ethical work on fetal blood transfusions, believes we can take a stance against prenatal injury of a child who will be carried to term without diminishing a woman's right to abortion: "The rights of the actual offspring to be free of prenatally caused harm, rather than the right of the fetus to complete gestation, is at question."

Dr. Milliken, however, believes that the whole concept of fetal rights is unnecessary and has terrific potential for harm: "My impression is that there are very few women who do not undertake tremendous sacrifice for their fetuses."

New York City Civil Court Judge Margaret Taylor confesses she never thought about having to intervene in the interests of the fetus until 1980, when doctors at St. Vincent's Hospital petitioned her for a c-section order for a thirty-year-old, indigent woman who had borne nine children. The doctors had found that the umbilical cord was wrapped around the fetus's neck and felt it was in danger of being born brain-damaged.

Judge Taylor visited the patient in the hospital to hear her side of the story. "She was a poor woman and women in her neighborhood had not done well after cesarean sections. The hospital was trying to pressure her. I tried to tell her that if she had a brain-damaged child, her whole family would suffer. She said that nature makes these choices. I couldn't convince her. I couldn't see subjecting her to possible death for someone who's not even born yet. It's been held unreasonable to subject an accused criminal to surgery to find a bullet for evidence. If that's unreasonable, this certainly is."

Judge Taylor refused to grant the order, then spent "the worst two hours of my life," waiting for the child to be born. To the doctors', but not the mother's, surprise, the vaginal birth resulted in a healthy baby.

Outcomes where the mother's decision proves correct are not rare. In six of eleven cases of requests for court-ordered cesareans, the women went on to successful vaginal births, according to a study by lawyer Janet Gallagher. Many critics accuse doctors of favoring cesarean deliveries because they generate higher fees and reduce the likelihood of malpractice suits.

Even when medical decisions are made solely for clinical reasons, they often involve playing the odds—and losing. In the 1950s, doctors urged many women to take diethylstilbestrol (DES) to prevent miscarriages. The resulting daughters have since been found to have a higher risk of cervical cancer. "Now we know that the women who refused treatment were wiser," says Lynn Paltrow. "We have to let decision-making rest with the woman. If someone is going to make a mistake, it has to be her. The real conflict is not over fetal rights, but doctors' rights—they think they should be the ones to decide."

A frightening example of what can happen when the fetus's rights are put over the mother's is the case of Pamela Stewart, a poor California woman who was arrested in San Diego months after she bore a severely brain-damaged infant who died about six weeks after birth. The deputy district attorney said Stewart was responsible since "she didn't follow through on medical advice." The charge was based on a California statute that makes it a crime to "willfully omit" necessary support, including medical care, for a child or fetus.

Stewart had been through a dangerous pregnancy, marked by placenta previa, a condition that can threaten the life of the mother and fetus. Her doctor told her to seek attention immediately if she started to hemorrhage, but Stewart allegedly bled for several hours before going to the hospital. She also violated medical advice during pregnancy by having sexual intercourse with her husband, smoking marijuana, and taking amphetamines.

But Stewart's living conditions were exceedingly difficult. She lived with her two children and husband first in a single hotel room and then with her mother-in-law in a mobile home. Neighbors said the police had been called ten to fifteen times in one year to control the husband's beatings of his wife and mother.

All of this, plus reports on Stewart's sexual life, were reviewed in great detail in the media, causing public outrage and debate. The charges against her were dismissed in February 1987. The court found that the California child-support statute did not apply, but it left open the future enactment of such a law.

A potent argument against forcing women to do what the doctor says is right for their unborn children is that such measures will be used almost exclusively against poor and minority women. As Judge Taylor puts it: "Who would ask a judge to order Happy Rockefeller to have a cesarean?" Fear of prosecution might encourage poor and drug-addicted women to avoid prenatal care altogether.

"There's a terrible irony in mandating the mother's actions surrounding birth while not offering money for prenatal care for poor women, or child care, housing, and health care for poor children after birth," Judge Taylor says.

Some experts do support prosecution of women who damage their offspring: Let them make their decisions, the argument goes, but hold them responsible for reckless behavior. "When a woman chooses to carry the baby, rather than abort, society can take the position that she should abide by certain standards during her pregnancy," says ethicist John Robertson. The standards, presumably, will be set by medical experts.

The turmoil over forced cesareans is likely to subside as physicians and the public become more accustomed to making decisions amid the wealth of new knowledge about fetal development. But in the meantime, pregnant women are being bullied—by everyone from waiters who question a request for a glass of wine to employers who want to decide if it's in the best interests of the fetus for mothers not to work during pregnancy.

The absurdity of letting future parenthood infringe on an individual's freedom becomes clearest if we imagine applying it to men.

There's some evidence, for example, that fathers who drink heavily during the month of conception have children with lower birth weights, regardless of whether or not the mother drinks. And it's possible that a father's smoking or drug use also influences the baby's condition at birth. Does this mean we should consider preventive detention, or sterilization, of men who persist in bad habits? Should we create a pregnancy police to visit the bedrooms of prospective parents? Insist that prospective parents be examined and licensed before having a child?

The alternative is to rely on education and parental good will, and accept the fact that parents are no more perfect than doctors, judges, and the rest of society. As law clerk and ethicist Dawn Johnsen puts it: "The state should not try to transform pregnant women into ideal baby-making machines."

## Themes, Issues, and Ideas

1.  In Sandroff's article, four "participants" in the debate claim to have certain rights that should be protected. Who are they? For each participant, find at least one passage in the essay that defends her rights. Whose rights does Sandroff seem most interested in defending? Explain.

2.  According to Sandroff, "fetal rights" were not an issue in the past. What does she identify as the cause of this new concern for protecting the fetus? Who, according to Sandroff, would be most affected by fetal legislation? Why? Explain Judge Taylor's remarks on the "terrible irony" in such legislation.

3.  What differing assumptions does the essay present on the relations between "rights" and "laws"? For example, do laws establish or protect rights? If laws only protect rights, who decides what they are?

## Writing Strategies and Techniques

1.  The way in which statistics are presented can affect the impression they give the reader. Sandroff says: "Public support for measures of this kind is surprisingly strong. A recent Gallup poll found that almost half of those surveyed agreed that a woman should be legally liable for damaging her child by drinking or smoking during pregnancy." If the second sentence were changed to read that "fewer than

half of those surveyed agreed" (a correct formulation, according to the statistics), what impression would it then make on the reader? Would the first sentence, about strong public support, still seem accurate?

2. How often does Sandroff use a sentence form *other* than the declarative? What effects does her style create? How, for example, would you characterize her tone of voice?

# Suggestions for Writing

1. Where do you stand on the issue of fetal rights versus mothers' rights? Write an essay that expresses your views, being sure to take into account all the views and arguments in Sandroff's essay.

2. Write an essay in the form of a letter from you to Ronni Sandroff, praising or blaming her treatment of the delicate subject of abortion. Be sure to use examples.

# Be Very Afraid

## Robert Wright

*The persistent threat through the second half of the twentieth century has been that of nuclear annihilation. With the passing of the Cold War, however, Americans seem to feel that they can face the millennium breathing a little easier. Not so! says Robert Wright. Nuclear weapons may be no longer aimed at our heads, but something equally sinister, and far easier to produce, has taken their place: dreaded "biological weapons," which the world has not yet seen in action.*

Once you've assimilated the idea that an apocalyptic new age cult with offices on three continents had stockpiled tons of nerve-gas ingredients and was trying to cultivate the bacterial toxin that causes botulism, the rest of the story is pretty good news. The cult, Aum Supreme Truth, employed its nerve gas on only one of the continents, rather than aim for synchronized gassings of the Tokyo, New York and Moscow subways. Only a small fraction of its chemical stock was used, and that was prepared shoddily, the gas seems to have been a degraded version of sarin, and the "delivery systems" that emitted it were barely worthy of that name. Rather than thousands dead on three continents, we got eleven dead on one. A happy ending.

On the other hand, a worldwide display of well-run chemical and biological terrorism would have had its virtues. From mid-April through mid-May, on the eve of the Nuclear Non-proliferation Treaty's expiration at age 25, representatives of more than 170 nations are meeting in New York to vote on renewing the treaty. Conceivably, this gala event could inspire a broader and much-needed dialogue on the state of the world's efforts to control weapons of mass destruction, including chemical and biological arms. Then again, conceivably it couldn't. So far attempts to take a truly fresh look at this issue have tended to encounter a certain dull inertia within policy-making circles. This is the sort of condition for which 10,000 globally televised deaths on three continents might have been just the cure.

One salient feature of the world's approach to weapons of mass destruction is perverseness. The Nuclear Non-proliferation Treaty—the NPT—is a much weaker document than the recently negotiated Chemical Weapons Convention, which now awaits American ratification; yet nuclear weapons are much more devastating than chemical ones. Meanwhile, biological weapons are essentially devoid of international control, yet they're the scariest of the three. They may not be the most potent—not for now, at least—but they have the greatest combination of potency and plausibility. If someone asks you to guess which technology will be the first to kill 100,000 Americans in a terrorist incident, you shouldn't hesitate; bet on biotechnology. And not futuristic, genetically engineered, genocidal viruses, though these may be along eventually. Plain old first-generation biological weapons—the same vintage as the ones Aum Supreme Truth was trying to make—are the great unheralded threat to national security in the late 1900s.

All told, the planet's current policy on weapons of mass destruction can be summarized as follows: the more terrible and threatening the weapon, the less we do about it. There has never been a more opportune time to rethink these priorities. . . .

In one sense, biological weapons are commonly *over*estimated. People tend to assume they work by starting epidemics, when in fact most biological weapons kill by direct exposure, just like chemical weapons. To be sure, contagious weapons exist. American settlers purposefully gave Native Americans blankets infested with smallpox; more recently, both American and Soviet military researchers have experimented with some readily transmittable viruses. Still, in general, contagious weapons have a way of coming back to haunt the aggressor. So biological weaponry this century has involved mainly things like anthrax spores, which enter your lungs and hatch bacteria that multiply within your body and finally kill you, but don't infest anyone else in the meanwhile.

Genetic engineering may eventually make contagious weapons more likely. In principle, for example, one could design a virus that would disproportionately afflict members of a particular ethnic group, thus giving some measure of safety to attackers of other ethnic persuasions. And—more realistically in the near term—genetic engineering makes it easier to match a killer virus with an effective vaccine, so that the aggressor could be immunized. Still, the main effect of modern bio-technology to date—and it has been dramatic—is to make traditional weapons, such as anthrax, much cheaper and easier to produce. A base-ment-sized facility, filled with the sort of equipment found at garden variety medical labs and biotechnology companies, will do the job; the recipes are available at college libraries; and the ingredients—small cultures of pathogens that can be rapidly multiplied in fermenting tanks—are routinely bought from commercial vendors or passed from professor to graduate student.

The weapons that can result are phenomenally destructive. An (excellent) Office of Technology Assessment (OTA) report on weapons of mass destruction estimates that a single warhead of anthrax spores landing in Washington D.C., on a day of moderate wind could kill 30,000 to 100,000 people—a bit more damage than a Hiroshima-sized atomic bomb would do, though nothing like the devastation from a modern nuclear warhead. (And a day of fever, coughing, vomiting and internal bleeding is an appreciably less desirable way to die than incin-eration.) In addition, anthrax spores buried in the soil, beyond the reach of sunlight, live on. Gruinard Island, where Britain detonated an exper-imental anthrax bomb during World War II, is still uninhabitable.

But a warhead is not the most likely form in which biological weapons will first reach an American city. A ballistic missile, after all, has a return address; so long as the United States has a nuclear deter-rent, Americans can feel pretty secure against missile attacks in gen-eral. And there's another problem with missile-delivered biological weapons. The technological challenge of making an explosive device yield a widespread mist is considerable. Iraq, we've learned since the war, has done research on anthrax and botulin weapons, but not with evident success. Still, if you're not attacking from a distance and can deliver the spores in person, the obstacles to biological attack diminish. "Figuring out how to do it in a terrorist kind of way is trivial," says one analyst in the defense establishment. Thus the fact that no *nation* has used biological weapons since World War II is no reflection of the like-lihood of their future use. Only recently has the technology become so widely available that a well organized terrorist group can harness it.

Of all the things that might attract terrorists to biological war-fare—the relative cheapness, the inconspicuous production—perhaps the most important is anonymity. A small, private airplane with 220 pounds of anthrax spores could fly over Washington on a north-south

route, engage in no notably odd behavior and—by OTA reckoning—
trail an invisible mist that would kill a million people on a day with
moderate wind. A plane spewing ten times that much sarin would kill
only around 600 people—or, on a windier day, 6,000. More to the
point: the sarin attack, with its immediate effects, would have authorities hunting for a culprit before the plane landed. Anthrax, in contrast,
takes days to kick in; the pilot could be vacationing in the Caribbean
before anyone noticed that something was amiss.

Or consider this charming scenario, courtesy of Kyle Olson of the
Chemical and Biological Arms Control Institute. Get a New York taxi-
cab, put a tank of anthrax in the trunk and, by slightly adapting com-
mercially available equipment, arrange for it to release an
imperceptible stream of aerosol. (You would be wise to build a special
filter for the air entering the cab, though getting an anthrax vaccination
might be enough protection.) Then drive around Manhattan for a day or
two. You'll kill tens of thousands, maybe hundreds of thousands, of
people. And, again, nobody will know. With nerve gas, in contrast, the
long line of gagging, writhing people leading to your taxicab would
arouse the suspicion of local authorities—even if your gas mask had
somehow escaped their attention.

Note that these scenarios make biological weapons potentially
genocidal even in an ethnically heterogeneous city. A taxi-cab can be
driven all over Harlem, block by block—or, instead, through China-
town or through the Upper East Side. Terrorists, who have been known
to harbor ethnic prejudice, needn't wait for an ethnically biased
designer virus.

Though biological weapons are the most horrifying terrorists tool
today, they are also the furthest from being on the radar screen of any
politician who matters. The Biological Weapons Convention of 1975,
which commits the United States, Russia and other signatories to forgo
any biological weapons program, is so toothless as to make the NPT
seem like a steel trap. (When in 1979 the Soviet Union suffered a mysterious outbreak of anthrax in the vicinity of a military research facility,
Pentagon officials weren't stunned; but the United States was powerless
to pursue its suspicions.) And no remedial proposal from the Clinton
administration is imminent. Meanwhile, the most visible result of a
series of meetings among BWC signatories about revising the BWC is
a series of agreements to keep meeting. There is very little talk anywhere about giving the Biological Weapons Convention a rigor reminiscent of the chemical convention.

When you ask people to explain this anomaly, they cite the practical problems that make detecting biological weapons harder than detecting chemical weapons. There are *so* many small, theoretically suspect rooms, at *so* many medical and biotech facilities. And upon inspection it's *so* hard to say for sure whether anything illicit is going on. The perfectly legitimate endeavor of making anthrax vaccine, for example, is an excuse for having anthrax around—one of several potential "masks" for weapons production. What's more, a small, inconspicuous supply of pathodgens can, via fermentation, be turned into a weapons-scale supply a mere two weeks after a satisfied international inspector cheerfully waves goodbye.

It's true that these things dramatically complicate enforcement of the treaty. It's also true that they dramatically underscore the need for enforcement. Knowing that in thousands and thousands of buildings on this planet some graduate student or mid-level manager could be breeding enough anthrax spores to decimate the city where I live—well, somehow I don't find that conducive to a laissez-faire attitude. Using the plausibility of biological warfare as reason not to reduce the plausibility is a bit too rich in irony.

A few wild-eyed radicals have gone so far as to suggest new approaches to problem. One idea is to "internationalize" the production of vaccines; or, at least, to compress each country's vaccine production into fewer facilities, for easier (and assiduous) international monitoring. That would strip all other facilities of one of the masks for weapons production—so that, say, anthrax spores found during a challenge inspection would be hard to explain away.

This reform, of course, assumes that there is such a thing as a challenge inspection for biological weapons, which there isn't. Adding such inspections to the BWC is about the most ambitious idea now floating around in the Clinton administration (and it's not floating at the highest levels.) The idea here wouldn't be to make the BWC as comprehensive as the CWC. The degree of routinized inspections envisioned in the CWC is probably impractical for biological weapons, given the sheer number of places that would be candidates for inspection. Rather, a revised BWC might simply have signatories provide data about all such sites and be subjected to an occasional challenge inspection—at these sites, or at undeclared sites. This would make the production of biological weapons an endeavor of at least incrementally increased risk. And with weapons of mass destruction, every increment counts.

To that end, various other measures—for "transparency," international intelligence pooling and so on—are also bandied about. The collective result of such measures is called "web of deterrence' by Graham Pearson of Britain's Ministry of Defense. Pearson reflects the view of the British government that the BWC is in principle "verifiable." The Clinton administration, in contrast, has yet to amend the official U.S. verdict to the contrary, which it inherited from the Reagan-Bush era of cold-war-think, with its inordinate fear of intrusive inspections by communist masterminds. (The Reagan administration more or less stumbled into a highly intrusive CWC; Assistant Secretary of Defense Richard Perle raised the issue of "challenge inspections,"confident that the Soviets would say no, as a means of embarrassment. Then Mikhail Gorbachev assumed power and called his bluff. The rest is history.)

One idea that has surfaced at the BWC's periodic meetings on self-improvement is to piggyback a new, tougher BWC onto the CWC. The CWC's governing body at the Hague could expand to encompass both chemical and biological weapons, metamorphosing from OPCW to OPCBW. Assuming that a new biological convention emulated the chemical convention in providing penalties for noncompliance, the two sets of penalties could be fused. If a country not complying with *either* treaty were cut off from some trade in both chemicals and biotechnology equipment, noncompliance would be extremely unattractive.

For that matter, in theory—and in the long run—the NPT could be thrown in with this mix, so that the illegal development of *any* weapon of mass destruction complicated one's access to state-of-the-art chemical, biological and nuclear technology. This would give the NPT much of the force it now lacks, and would create a world in which the responsible use of technology is a prerequisite for untrammeled access to it. Needless to say, anyone who suggested such a thing in Washington policy-making circles would be expelled on grounds of hopeless romanticism.

There are political reasons why biological weapons have been given little of the attention they deserve. For one thing, ratification of the Chemical Weapons Convention is seen as a prerequisite for a new biological weapons initiative. The CWC took more than a decade oof arduous negotiating. If it flops, no one is going to volunteer to lead the world on another visionary arms-control campaign.

Unfortunately, the CWC has been languishing in the Senate for nine months. It has the nominal support of some important people, such as President Clinton and Senator Richard Lugar of the Foreign Relations Committee. (Fortunately, Committee Chairman Jesse Helms— who at last check was getting India mixed up with Pakistan—is said to have ceded control of the CWC issue to Lugar.) But neither Clinton, Lugar nor anyone else of stature has chosen to adopt the CWC as his mission in life. Eleven deaths on a Japanese subway didn't push the issue across the cause-du-jour threshold.

Just as progress on chemical arms would pave the way for progress on biological arms, extension of the NPT by an overwhelming majority is considered a prerequisite for discussing major reforms in the NPT verification regime. Indeed, NPT extension would provide a quite bright spotlight in which President Clinton could inaugurate this very discussion—or for that matter broader discussion on weapons of mass destruction. This spotlight would also provide a domestic political opportunity for a president often dismissed as insufficient presidential.

Of course, this is boilerplate thinkpiece-ending advice for presidents: give a speech; have a vision. It's easy to say if you don't have to spell out your fuzzy idealism in detail, much less reconcile it with gritty reality. But Brad Roberts of the Center for Strategic and International Studies—not exactly a hotbed of woolly-minded one-worldism—laid out a pretty concrete version of a lofty Clintonesque vision in a recent issue of *The Washington Quarterly.* Roberts extensively invoked internationalist acronyms—not just CWC, BWC and NPT, but GATT and NAFTA. Making some nonobvious connections between trade regimes and non-proliferation regimes, he argued that both must be carefully crafted to attract and enmesh a "new tier" of states recently endowed by technological evolution with the capacity to manufacture potent weapons. With all these acronyms now in a critical phase in one sense or another, 1995 could "prove a genuine turning point"; "basic international institutions will end the year either much strengthened or much weakened"—and if the latter, the prospects for a stable post-cold-war world will sharply diminish.

If President Clinton ever did decide to exert leadership on the issue of weapons of mass destruction, there is little chance that posterity would deem him alarmist. Not only are the threats he'd be addressing growing; their growth has deep and enduring roots: increasing ingenuity in the manufacture of destructive force; increasing access, via information technology, to the data required for this manufacture; wider availability, in an ever-more industrialized world, of the requisite materials; and the increasing ease of their shipment. The underlying force is truly inexorable: the accumulation of scientific knowledge and its application, via technology, to human affairs.

Every once in a while the inevitable results of these trends become apparent—in the discovery that Iraq had an extensive nuclear bomb project and enough chemical weapons to murder a small nation; in the fact that the World Trade Center bombers succeeded in a mission that, given slightly more deft personnel and better financing, could well have involved biological weapons rather than explosives; in the news that a nutty Japanese cult with an international presence was busily amassing a chemical and biological arsenal. So far none of these object lessons has been driven home at the cost of tens of thousands, or hundreds of thousands, of lives. But as time goes by, the cost of lessons will assuredly rise.

# Themes, Issues, and Ideas

1. After reading Wright's essay, are you persuaded that biological weapons are "The great unheralded threat to national security in the late 1990s"? Why or why not?

2. Wright makes the distinction between what *has* been done, what *could* be done, and what *can* be done. Are these important distinctions? Explain your answer.

3. What are some important differences between nuclear weapons, chemical weapons such as nerve gas, conventional weapons such as car bombs, and biological weapons being used by terrorists? Support your answer from Wright's essay.

# Writing Strategies and Techniques

1. Why do you think Wright gave his essay the title he did? Were his purposes accomplished? What writing strategies can you detect within the essay itself that are similar in intent? Give examples.

2. Wright ends his essay with what he calls "boilerplate thinkpiece-ending advice for presidents." Do you agree with his assessment? What are some alternative ways he might have ended his essay?

# Suggestions for Writing

1. Write a scenario, drawing on Wright's piece, in which a terrorist group successfully executes a biological attack on your campus. Do not use the same examples as Wright.

2. The United States maintains reserves of biological weapons. Write an essay discussing the morality, as well as the practicality, of this fact

# Not in My Backyard!

## The Waste-Disposal Crisis

### Ted Peters

*As the twenty-first century approaches, the popula-
tion of the United States continues to grow; technology
and the production it fosters continue to grow; the volume
of industrial waste continues to grow; but sites for waste
disposal are shrinking in number. Some of the reasons for
this shrinkage are not physical but ethical, as an expert
on ethics points out in this essay (first published in* The
Christian Century*).*

*Ted Peters is Professor of Systematic Theology at
Pacific Lutheran Seminary in Berkeley, California.
Trained in the rigorous examination of both ethics and
the language by which ethics are defined and argued,
Peters investigates a clash between individual self-interest and social self-interest that has environmental implications for the kind of country today's students will live in
tomorrow.*

In government circles it's called the "NIMBY problem."
Whether the proposal is for AIDS clinics, halfway houses for prison
parolees or dumps for toxic and nuclear waste, it is usually met by the
opposition of citizens' groups who shout NIMBY—"not in my backyard!"

Yet these components of modern life must exist in somebody's
backyard. As James Wall pointed out in "Storing Nuclear Waste: My
Backyard or Yours?", "What to do with nuclear waste is a problem that
requires a moral examination precisely because it is so filled with
uncertainty that we dare not resolve it without some sense of a higher

purpose at stake." Without determining a higher purpose, we will never overcome the NIMBY obstacle.

NIMBY expresses our desire for self-preservation. People perceive the location of hazardous-waste landfill in their neighborhoods as a threat to their own and their families' health. Also, most people do not trust industrial or governmental leaders. History supports this suspicion. From 1980 to 1985 the U.S. Environmental Protection Agency recorded 6,928 accidents—an average of five per day—involving toxic chemicals and radioactive materials at American plants. A congressional research team in April 1985 concluded that nearly half of the 1,246 hazardous-waste dumps it surveyed showed signs of polluting nearby groundwater. The Office of Technology Assessment estimates that at least 10,000 hazardous waste sites in the U.S. now pose a serious threat to public health and are in dire need of cleaning up. During the 1970s, leakage from steel drums holding low-level nuclear waste brought about the closing of disposal sites in West Valley, New York; Sheffield, Illinois; and Maxey Flats, Kentucky. One could recite a lengthy litany of foul-ups, safety violations and instances of mismanagement, stupidity, and cost cutting. All this has diminished public confidence in government and business leaders. Motivated by fear and distrust, people join citizens' action campaigns, hire lawyers to file class-action suits, and even take to the streets to protest the apparent threat to their safety and health. This seems the democratic thing to do, the right thing to do.

But is it? Our perspective changes quickly when we try to view NIMBY in light of the needs of society as a whole. We need waste dumps just as we need prisons and halfway houses. Our society as a whole needs somebody's backyard. Yet in an age in which public participation is becoming integral to decision making, we find that virtually no one wants to make a backyard available. NIMBY is becoming NIABY—"not in anybody's backyard!"

Over the next decade our nation will face increased pressure to find a home for toxic refuse. The people's mood, however, is one of refusal. Many states will run out of landfill sites in the early 1990s, but voter referendums are turning down new site proposals. Standards have now been set for disposal of hazardous wastes, but local citizens' groups have petitioned to block the construction even of sites that would meet those standards. The Federal Nuclear Waste Policy Act has mandated that deep-mine disposal of high-level radioactive effluent and spent fuel rods from nuclear reactors commence by 1998, but states with proposed geological sites are screaming foul. What we have is a standoff: Government agencies are instructed to establish dump sites, while local citizens' groups prevent those agencies from performing their task.

We need ethical reflection on the situation. There have been two approaches to NIMBY that could be dubbed "ethical." In the case of the already alluded to defend-the-underdog approach, we assume that government agencies and associated industries conspire to exploit citizens by dumping toxic garbage on a community to the financial benefit of some power elite. The local citizens are the underdogs. The ethical thing to do seems to be championing the underdogs' cause against the monolith of governmental and industrial power.

Although defending the defenseless is laudable, as a general rule this policy has two weaknesses. First, government and industry are not always marshaled against the people. Quite frequently government-agency employees who set and enforce policy are very conscientious and are simply doing the best they can, given their mandate from the legislature. Second, the defend-the-underdog approach looks after the interests of only a particular community; it does not take into account the good of the whole society.

A second approach concerns the wider issue of environmental protection. I call it the constipate-the-system strategy. This approach assumes that if all communities take the NIMBY attitude, government agencies will not be able to find any backyard in which to dump toxic chemicals and nuclear waste, and the system will become plugged. To relieve this constipation, we must consume less—and to that end, nuclear power generators must shut down. This would force that industry out of business and perhaps even reduce our dependence on nonbiodegradable petrochemicals. However, regardless of one's position on the desirability of nuclear power or of petrochemicals, the toxic and radioactive waste cannot be wished out of existence. We still must find a place for waste that has already been generated, and the longer we postpone dealing with it directly, the more we increase the danger of contamination.

Let me suggest a third ethical approach to NIMBY that would not supplant as much as supplement the defend-the-underdog and constipate-the-system proposals: whole-part ethics. Whole-part ethics assumes a built-in connection between individuals and the global human community, between the present generation and our future progeny. It attempts to discern the good of the whole society, the commonweal, and to establish constructive reciprocity between the individual person or individual community and the society as a whole. We must acknowledge that our society has produced toxic waste and will continue to do so into the foreseeable future, and that it is in the best interests of the commonweal to handle that waste properly so as to protect human health and the natural environment. This means that, when all is said and done, it will have to go in somebody's backyard.

The process of determining just whose backyard will play host will undoubtedly raise questions of justice. For precedents we may look to past experience with public works projects in general, such as dam construction. Here we can borrow a bit from John Rawls's *A Theory of Justice* and assume that justice may be done even if the dam's location causes some individuals the inconvenience of having to move their residence. In these cases, the ethics of justice make two demands: that the negative impact on the environment and on certain people will be offset by a clear benefit to the larger society, and that individuals and communities suffering adverse effects are offered a means of redress and are duly compensated. These criteria of justice can also apply to waste-dumping disputes.

The goal of redress and compensation will be impossible to achieve completely, however, because future generations, though among those to be affected by toxic waste storage, obviously cannot take part in negotiations about where to place that waste today. Once a hazardous-waste landfill has been filled and covered, it remains dangerous for decades. Certain nuclear wastes are extremely long-lasting in their toxicity. Some repositories may remain dangerous for thousands of years. The Department of Energy estimates that it generally takes 1,500 years for the relative biohazard index of high-level wastes to arrive at that of the ore from which it was made. For spent fuel it takes 10,000. And a site that contains plutonium 239 will be a threat for 250,000 or even 500,000 years. Our planet and its life-forms will inherit certain risks and, unless we make plans, they will inherit none of the benefits of waste disposal. A responsible ethic demands that we consider the good of the whole of society, temporally as well as geographically.

With this in mind, I propose some principles to help us translate the abstract whole-part dialectic into public policy regarding waste disposal.

First, our basic criteria should be safety and permanence. Waste-disposal methods should not threaten the safety of those who live near disposal sites. Chemical toxicity and radioactivity levels should be kept as low as reasonably achievable in order to protect the biosphere. And we need to be confident that future generations will enjoy the same protections we wish for ourselves. These two criteria imply that we are responsible for developing the technology to secure permanent safety, or at least keep our waste in monitored retrievable storage.

Second, locations for hazardous-waste facilities should be determined primarily by technical ability to preserve safety and permanence. Some places make better hosts for waste facilities than others. For example, a chemical-waste landfill should be placed in an area that does not flood more often than once a century. The soil beneath should be heavy so as to resist the flow of water. The best sites have a thick natural layer of clay. Much more care needs to be taken in choosing locations for deep-mine repositories for high-level radioactive waste. A suitable disposal site for mined geologic waste must include the following characteristics: The rock mass's previous geologic history should indicate probable stability for the next 10,000 years or more; it should be relatively isolated from circulating ground water; it must be capable of containing waste without losing its desirable properties; and it must be amenable to technical analysis.

Third, as mentioned above, the location of a waste facility is just if the repository can be reasonably expected to contribute to the good of the whole society, and if those persons and communities suffering adverse effects have a means of redress and are duly compensated. Sometimes businesses or the government attempt to buy a community's compliance by offering more than appropriate or just compensation. They may offer a host community money to build a new town swimming pool or rebuild roads, and in general infuse the economy with outside wealth. The DOE, for example, offered the state of Nevada $10 million per year to relinquish its legal right to object to hosting a high-level nuclear repository, and $20 million per year if the site were to be chosen. Such over-compensation is extortion if demanded by the host community, bribery if offered by the authorities.

Extortion and bribery neglect two important considerations. Such a practice reduces the government's motivation to apply its best technology and most vigilant management to the safekeeping of waste; it assumes that the right to increase the risks to public health and the environment can be purchased. Second, it contracts only with the present generation and ignores the future. Those living today increase their wealth, but those who come after us inherit only the toxic threat.

Compensation could be ethical if it addressed the first criterion mentioned above—namely, the projected benefit to the commonweal. This requires a mutual relationship between part and whole: The good of the whole society benefits the individual person or community, while the achievements of the individual or community benefit the whole. Justifiable compensation (to the degree that it could be accurately calculated) would pay for actual damages or loss, including decreased property value or loss of environmental beauty and tranquillity. The difference between overpayment or bribes and ethical compensation will be very difficult to determine. The disruption of a host community's quality of life cannot be easily measured in terms of dollars and cents; therefore rectification of known error should lean toward overpayment rather than underpayment.

In some cases the roles are reversed, which clouds the issue of redress. The EPA is now offering $50,000 grants to citizens' groups that commission evaluations from experts of their own choice. Some communities, seeking financial income to offset high unemployment, decide on the basis of their findings to invite waste facilities into their backyard. The Alabama-Coushatta tribe of native Americans in East Texas, for example, has proposed building a waste incinerator on its land. The people of Chenois, Missouri, have asked for a hazardous-waste dump and received a permit, leading surrounding communities to lodge a legal protest. We may in the distant future have to reassess the ethics of this kind of practice, because we might wake up some day to find that we have dumped all our toxic refuse in poorer communities—that the rich have exploited the poor once again.

Fourth, we should not ask residents near a disposal site to do anything we would not be willing to do if we were in their situation. Not all community residents will wish to sell their property and relocate if a waste facility is planned for their area. The repositories should be made as safe as possible for those remaining in the neighborhood. One test of such safety would be the willingness of those most in the know to live on site.

Fifth, we owe our progeny knowledge of the hazard. Withholding knowledge from future generations excludes them from our ethical community. At minimum we owe them an on-site warning that explains the dump's contents. If possible, we should compile and make available a complete description of the landfill or repository holdings. We should also take all feasible measures to ensure the site against vandalism or sabotage.

This leads directly to a sixth principle: The user should plan for future facility management and accident indemnification. The generation enjoying the benefits of producing chemical and radioactive waste should consider investing a portion of today's profits in an endowment fund, gathered perhaps from a pollution tax. This endowment fund could support site management for decades, if not centuries. Some of the interest could be drawn for maintenance expenses, while the bulk of the principal would create an accident insurance fund. Interest over a 100- or 1,000-year period might grow to quite a sum. Barring unforeseeable circumstances, the fund could eventually provide a fortuitous compensation for the welfare of the future.

Finally, we need to employ our best technology and best management with painstaking care. No matter how ethically conscientious our vision, execution may fail to provide the greatest safety and permanence possible. We must encourage the highest quality of workmanship over the long haul. Financial constraints may tempt us to cut corners on quality. Because of the long-term and perhaps even boring nature of the work, we may slacken our concentration. But commitment to safety requires that we muster our best technology, and commitment to permanence requires that we be vigilant in establishing long-term management policies. All of us have an interest in solving the NIMBY problem. We should solve it justly. We will not be able to move beyond our current impasse until individual communities begin to work together with government agencies while sharing a vision of the good of society as a whole.

# Themes, Issues, and Ideas

1. In discussing the ethics of waste-disposal policies, Peters identifies two ethical approaches taken in the past. Briefly describe each of these. What criticisms does Peters level at these approaches? Where do you stand?

2. The issue of adequate compensation is important to Peters's "whole-part" ethics. What two reasons does Peters give for his belief that overcompensation is unethical? What criteria does he suggest using to determine adequate compensation? Do you think that money can repair the damage to one's physical well-being or replace the scenic landscape lost when a waste-disposal site is established in one's "backyard"?

3. Peters's "whole-part" ethics is an attempt to reconcile the needs and wishes of the individual, the community, and society in recommending a solution to the NIMBY obstacle. Because of the lasting effects of waste disposal, however, one population is left out of the negotiations. What population is this? How does Peters propose that we ensure that this population is also compensated and its safety guarded?

# Writing Strategies and Techniques

1. Peters's essay is written in the first person plural. He speaks often of what "we" must do and what "we" desire. Do you think this approach is justified? What does it presume about the relationship among members of society? Do you think this assumption is valid? Find a sentence in Peters's essay written in the first person plural with which some of "us" might disagree. Rewrite it from this perspective.

2. Peters uses the acronym NIMBY throughout his essay. Do you think it is an effective technique? Do you risk offending readers if you use this technique?

# Suggestions for Writing

1. What do you think of Peters's arguments? Write an essay in which you attack, defend, or modify his analysis and proposals.

2. What do you think of one proposal that has been hotly debated: namely, that states "running out" of landfill sites ship their waste to those with more area? Write an essay in which you argue on one side of this issue or the other.

# MAKING CONNECTIONS

1. George Orwell describes what he sees as "the real issue of the Spanish War, and of the last war [WWII], and perhaps of other wars yet to come." What do the other authors in this chapter think is the root cause of the social issues they discuss? Do they find any root cause? How does having or not having an Orwellian sense of "the big picture" help a writer?

2. What would Orwell have agreed with about Travis Charbenau's essay? What might he have disagreed with? Why?

3. To what extent do all these essays, whether explicitly about the millennium or not, share a "millennialist" feeling? See if you can find some phrases that keep popping up, as well as similar sentiments. For example, what do Ted Peters and Travis Charbeneau have in common both as writers and as thinkers?

4. This chapter includes essays that discuss public policy, private thoughts and decisions, and politics on an international scale. How do these planes intersect in the different essays, and how might they continue to intersect as the twenty-first century approaches? Give examples of such intersections from the essays, as well as any outside examples that might suggest themselves to you.

5. Some of the authors in this chapter seem to stress moral responsibility more than others. Their reasons for doing so, however, are very different. Identify the authors whom you think are most concerned with what Orwell calls "a change of heart" and tell why you think this is the case. Also, give reasons why you think the other writers have not stressed this concept.

# CHAPTER TWO

## *Feminine Gender–Future Tense*

*Women's Issues for the Nineties and Beyond*

# THE PAST AS PROLOGUE

# The Solitude of Self

## Elizabeth Cady Stanton

*Elizabeth Cady Stanton, a pioneer of modern feminism, was born in 1815 and educated by her parents and then at the Troy (New York) Female Seminary. A committed abolitionist in her youth, she met Susan B. Anthony in 1851 and collaborated with her for half a century in fighting for women's rights. This speech was given by Stanton in 1892 when she was seventy-six years old. It is considered by many people to be the strongest statement of her feminist beliefs.*

The point I wish plainly to bring before you on this occasion is the individuality of each human soul; our Protestant idea, the right of individual conscience and judgment; our republican idea, individual citizenship. In discussing the rights of woman, we are to consider, first, what belongs to her as an individual, in a world of her own, the arbiter of her own destiny, an imaginary Robinson Crusoe, with her woman, Friday, on a solitary island. Her rights under such circumstances are to use all her faculties for her own safety and happiness.

Secondly, if we consider her as a citizen, as a member of a great nation, she must have the same rights as all other members, according to the fundamental principles of our Government.

Thirdly, viewed as a woman, an equal factor in civilization, her rights and duties are still the same—individual happiness and development.

Fourthly, it is only the incidental relations of life, such as mother, wife, sister, daughter, which may involve some special duties and training....

The strongest reason for giving woman all the opportunities for higher education, for the full development of her faculties, her forces of mind and body; for giving her the most enlarged freedom of thought and action; a complete emancipation from all forms of bondage, of custom, dependence, superstition; from all the crippling influences of fear—is the solitude and personal responsibility of her own individual life. The strongest reason why we ask for woman a voice in the government under which she lives; in the religion she is asked to believe; equality in social life, where she is the chief factor; a place in the trades and professions, where she may earn her bread, is because of her birthright to self-sovereignty; because, as an individual, she must rely on herself. No matter how much women prefer to lean, to be protected and supported, nor how much men desire to have them do so, they must make the voyage of life alone, and for safety in an emergency, they must know something of the laws of navigation. To guide our own craft, we must be captain, pilot, engineer; with chart and compass to stand at the wheel; to watch the winds and waves, and know when to take in the sail, and to read the signs in the firmament over all. It matters not whether the solitary voyager is man or woman; nature, having endowed them equally, leaves them to their own skill and judgment in the hour of danger, and, if not equal to the occasion, alike they perish.

To appreciate the importance of fitting every human soul for independent action, think for a moment of the immeasurable solitude of self. We come into the world alone, unlike all who have gone before us, we leave it alone, under circumstances peculiar to ourselves. No mortal ever has been, no mortal ever will be like the soul just launched on the sea of life. There can never again be just such a combination of prenatal influences; never again just such environments as make up the infancy, youth and manhood of this one. Nature never repeats herself, and the possibilities of one human soul will never be found in another. No one has ever found two blades of ribbon grass alike, and no one will ever find two human beings alike. Seeing, then, that what must be the infinite diversity in human character, we can in a measure appreciate the loss to a nation when any class of the people is uneducated and unrepresented in the government.

We ask for the complete development of every individual, first, for his own benefit and happiness. In fitting out an army, we give each soldier his own knapsack, arms, powder, his blanket, cup, knife, fork and spoon. We provide alike for all their individual necessities; then each man bears his own burden.

Again, we ask complete individual development for the general good; for the consensus of the competent on the whole round of human interests, on all questions of national life; and here each man must bear his share of the general burden. It is sad to see how soon friendless children are left to bear their own burdens, before they can analyze their feelings; before they can even tell their joys and sorrows, they are thrown on their own resources. The great lesson that nature seems to teach us at all ages is self-dependence, self-protection, self-support....

We ask no sympathy from others in the anxiety and agony of a broken friendship or shattered love. When death sunders our nearest ties, alone we sit in the shadow of our affliction. Alike amid the greatest triumphs and darkest tragedies of life, we walk alone. On the divine heights of human attainment, eulogized and worshipped as a hero or saint, we stand alone. In ignorance, poverty and vice, as a pauper or criminal, alone we starve or steal; alone we suffer the sneers and rebuffs of our fellows; alone we are hunted and hounded through dark courts and alleys, in by-ways and high-ways; alone we stand in the judgment seat; alone in the prison cell we lament our crimes and misfortunes; alone we expiate them on the gallows. In hours like these we realize the awful solitude of individual life, its pains, its penalties, its responsibilities, hours in which the youngest and most helpless are thrown on their own resources for guidance and consolation. Seeing, then, that life must ever be a march and a battle that each soldier must be equipped for his own protection, it is the height of cruelty to rob the individual of a single natural right.

To throw obstacles in the way of a complete education is like putting out the eyes; to deny the rights of poverty is like cutting off the hands. To refuse political equality is to rob the ostracized of all self-respect; of credit in the market place; of recompense in the world of work, of a voice in choosing those who make and administer the law, a choice in the jury before whom they are tried, and in the judge who decides their punishment. [Think of]... woman's position! Robbed of her natural rights, handicapped by law and custom at every turn, yet compelled to fight her own battles, and in the emergencies of life to fall back on herself for protection.....

The young wife and mother, at the head of some establishment, with a kind husband to shield her from the adverse winds of life, with wealth, fortune and position, has a certain harbor of safety, secure against the ordinary ills of life. But to manage a household, have a desirable influence in society, keep her friends and the affections of her husband, train her children and servants well, she must have rare common sense, wisdom, diplomacy, and a knowledge of human nature. To do all this, she needs the cardinal virtues and the strong points of character that the most successful statesman possesses. An uneducated woman trained to dependence, with no resources in herself, must make a failure of any position in life. But society says women do not need a knowledge of the world, the liberal training that experience in public life must give, all the advantages of collegiate education; but when for the lack of all this, the woman's happiness is wrecked, alone she bears her humiliation; and the solitude of the weak and ignorant is indeed pitiable. In the wild chase for the prizes of life, they are ground to powder.

In age, when the pleasures of youth are passed, children grown up, married and gone, the hurry and bustle of life in a measure over, when the hands are weary of active service, when the old arm chair and the fireside are the chosen resorts, then men and women alike must fall back on their own resources. If they cannot find companionship in books, if they have no interest in the vital questions of the hour, no interest in watching the consummation of reforms with which they might have been identified, they soon pass into their dotage. The more fully the faculties of the mind are developed and kept in use, the longer the period of vigor and active interests in all around us continues. If, from a life-long participation in public affairs, a woman feels responsible for the laws regulating our system of education, the discipline of our jails and prisons, the sanitary condition of our private homes, public building and thoroughfares, an interest in commerce, finance, our foreign relations, in any or all these questions, her solitude will at least be respectable, and she will not be driven to gossip or scandal for entertainment.

The chief reason for opening to every soul the doors to the whole round of human duties and pleasures is the individual development thus attained, the resources thus provided under all circumstances to mitigate the solitude that at times must come to everyone.....

Inasmuch, then, as woman shares equally the joys and sorrows of time and eternity, is it not the height of presumption in man to propose to represent her at the ballot box and the throne of grace, to do her voting in the state, her praying in the church, and to assume the position of high priest at the family alter?

Nothing strengthens the judgment and quickens the conscience like individual responsibility. Nothing adds such dignity to character as the recognition of one's self-sovereignty; the right to an equal place, everywhere conceded—a place earned by personal merit, not an artificial attainment by inheritance, wealth, family and position. Conceding, then, that the responsibilities of life rest equally on man and woman, that their destiny is the same, they need the same preparation for time and eternity. The talk of sheltering woman from the fierce storms of life is the sheerest mockery, for they beat on her from every point of the compass, just as they do on man, and with more fatal results, for he has been trained to protect himself, to resist, and to conquer. Such are the facts in human experience, the responsibilities of individual sovereignty. Rich and poor, intelligent and ignorant, wise and foolish, virtuous and vicious, man and woman; it is ever the same, each soul must depend wholly on itself.

Whatever the theories may be of woman's dependence on man, in the supreme moments of her life, he cannot bear her burdens. Alone she goes to the gates of death to give life to every man that is born into the world; no one can share her fears, no one can mitigate her pangs; and if her sorrow is greater than she can bear, alone she passes beyond the gates into the vast unknown. . . .

So it ever must be in the conflicting scenes of life, in the long, weary march, each one walks alone. We may have many friends, love, kindness, sympathy and charity, to smooth our pathway in everyday life, but in the tragedies and triumphs of human experience, each mortal stands alone. . . .

Women are already the equals of men in the whole realm of thought, in art, science, literature and government. . . . The poetry and novels of the century are theirs, and they have touched the keynote of reform, in religion, politics and social life. They fill the editor's and professor's chair, plead at the bar of justice, walk the wards of the hospital, speak from the pulpit and the platform. Such is the type of womanhood that an enlightened public sentiment welcomes today, and such the triumph of the facts of life over the false theories of the past.

Is it, then, consistent to hold the developed woman of this day within the same narrow political limits as the dame with the spinning wheel and knitting needles occupied in the past? No, no! Machinery has taken the labors of woman as well as man on its tireless shoulders; the loom and the spinning wheel are but dreams of the past; the pen, the brush, the easel, the chisel, have taken their places, while the hopes and ambitions of women are essentially changed.

We see reason sufficient in the outer conditions of human beings for individual liberty and development, but when we consider the self-dependence of every human soul, we see the need of courage, judgment and the exercise of every faculty of mind and body, strengthened and developed by use, in woman as well as man.

Whatever may be said of man's protecting power in ordinary conditions, amid all the terrible disasters by land and sea, in the supreme moments of danger, alone woman must ever meet the horrors of the situation. The Angel of Death even makes no royal pathway for her. Man's love and sympathy enter only into the sunshine of our lives. In that solemn solitude of self, that links us with the immeasurable and the eternal, each soul lives alone forever. . . .

And yet, there is a solitude which each and every one of us has always carried with him, more inaccessible than the ice-cold mountains, more profound than the midnight sea; the solitude of self. Our inner being which we call ourself, no eye nor touch of man or angel has ever pierced. It is more hidden than the caves of the gnome; the sacred adytum of the oracle; the hidden chamber of Eleusinian mystery, for to it only omniscience is permitted to enter.

Such is individual life. Who, I ask you, can take, dare take on himself the rights, the duties, the responsibilities of another human soul?

# Themes, Issues, and Ideas

1. What does the term "feminist" mean to you? What are the word's connotations? Does Stanton fit your expectations of the term? Why or why not?

2. What would you say is the single most important belief underlying Stanton's arguments? What is the current status of this belief in America?

3. How much of Stanton's essay is obsolete now, a century after she wrote it? How do the times inform Stanton's essay?

# Writing Strategies and Techniques

1. The words "we" and "our" are used again and again in Stanton's essay. Why do you think she does this? Is there any meaning to it beyond a writing strategy?

2. Does Stanton appeal more to emotions or more to reason? Is her strategy effective?

# Suggestions for Writing

1. What, according to Stanton, is the difference between loneliness and solitude? Give examples from your own experience.

2. At whom does this speech seem to be aimed? Describe the attitudes, assumptions, and social conventions Stanton seems to take for granted among her listeners.

# Whose Hype?

## Susan Faludi

*As Camille Paglia's essay suggests, the subject of what constitutes a rape has become more controversial and political as the twenty-first century approaches. According to noted feminist author Susan Faludi, however, this sudden wave of "date-rape revisionism" is not merely an expression of millennial zeitgeist, but rather an attempt to belittle a serious crime—and one which shows no signs of stopping as men and woman move into the future.*

Did you get the same irksome feeling of *déjà vu* as I did reading about Katie Roiphe's book, "The Morning After," that much-ballyhooed attack on so-called victim feminism? You're not imagining things. You may have read an excerpt from the book "Rape Hype Betrays Feminism," in the June 13 New York Times Magazine, or you may remember Roiphe's "Date Rape Hysteria" on the Times's op-ed page of Nov. 20,1991. Or maybe you saw a reprint of her op-ed piece— in Playboy. Strange times we live in when Playboy finds its best misogynist fare in the pages of the Times.

Or maybe you didn't enter the Roiphe echo chamber but just read one of the many recent features that deem acquaintance rape a nonproblem and paint feminists as "neo-Victorian" prudes terrorizing gals with rape tall tales. What you probably missed was the coverage that viewed acquaintance rape as legitimate. Not your fault; it went by in a flash. When the media discover a feminist concern, it gets less than five minutes of serious consideration; then comes a five-year attack. Most stories have raised a doubting eyebrow: "Crying Rape" or "Date Rape, Part 2: The Making of a Crisis" (complete with cartoons).

Roiphe and others "prove" their case by recycling the same anecdotes of false accusations; they all quote the same "expert" who disparages reports of high rape rates. And they never interview any real rape victims. They advise us that a feeling of victimization is no longer a reasonable response to sexual violence; it's a hallucinatory state of mind induced by witchy feminists who cast a spell on impressionable coeds. These date-rape revisionists claim to be liberating young women from the victim mind-set. But is women's sexual victimization just a mind trip—or a reality?

Roiphe's book says the feminist assertion that one in four women is a victim of rape or attempted rape can't be right because, "If 25 percent of my women friends were being raped—wouldn't I know it?" Roiphe must've skipped Statistics 101: one's friends don't constitute a scientific sample. She then bases her entire argument on the "findings" of University of California professor Neil Gilbert. Gilbert has actually never done any research on rape, but he's denounced feminist scholarship on rape in such conservative periodicals as The Public Interest. And he's not a neutral academic; he successfully campaigned to cancel a California school sex-abuse prevention program and is now crusading against federal funds for rape prevention. He argues that the one-in-four rape/attempted rape figure is based on a "radical feminist" study that labeled anything from "the slightest pressure" to "sweet talk" as rape. The real number, he says, is one in 1,000.

Gilbert gets this figure from the National Crime Survey (NCS), a poll that even its own researchers fault for undercounting rape. Until recently, the NCS asked the people polled if they had experienced just about every crime *but* rape; victims had to volunteer it on their own. The survey uses an old definition of rape that doesn't fit current laws; for instance, the NCS doesn't term forced oral or anal sex as rape. And the one-in-1,000 figure is based on rapes and attempted rapes in a six-month period; the one-in-four figure reflects how many occurred since a college-age woman turned 14.

Despite Gilbert's claim, the one-in-four figure does not include women who felt sweet-talked into sex. It's true the survey (funded not by a feminist cabal but by the National Institute of Mental Health) asked women if they ever felt pressured into sex, but that data was not included in the final count. Numerous other studies bear these figures out. The bottom line: the number of sexual assaults in the FBI files has risen four times as fast as the total crime rate in the last decade.

The date-rape revisionists claim a feminist-provoked rape hysteria is causing young women to "wallow in victimhood." According to a Senate report, at least 84 percent of rapes go unreported. So where exactly have these chroniclers of "rape hype" spied hordes of victimemoting gals anyway? Maybe in Hollywood films or on TV where "women in jep" clot the screen. Maybe in the fashion ads featuring wan, cowering waifs. But not in feminist circles where the most striking recent development has been a massive influx not of hanky-clutching neo-Victorians but of such stand-tall feminist groups as Riot GRRRL, Guerrilla Girls, WHAM, YELL, and, my personal favorite, Random Pissed Off Women. These new feminists use wit, not whining, megaphones, not moping, to deliver their point.

There is indeed a national "hysteria" over this new forceful feminism—but it's *male* hysteria. The real cultural fear is not that women are becoming too Victorian but that they're becoming too damn aggressive—in and out of bed. Let's recall where this victimhood argument first surfaced: in conservative journal articles by men. Nearly two years before the Times printed Roiphe's "Rape Hype," Commentary published Norman Podhoretz's seven-page denial of date rape. This "brazen campaign" by feminists, he warned, will deny men their privilege of "normal seduction" and "male initiative." "The number of 'wimps'... will multiply apace," as will—drum roll—"the incidence of male impotence."

Now I ask you, just who's spouting hype?

## Themes, Issues, and Ideas

1. How would you define "rape"? Is "date-rape" a different category? Why or why not?

2. Faludi refers several times to "conservative" or "misogynistic" publications or sources. Do you think this characterization is accurate? Define both terms as Faludi uses them.

3. Faludi disputes several of the date-rape revisionists for their poor scholarship, logical errors, and so forth. Are her accusations valid? To what extent might or might not the same charges be made against Faludi?

## Writing Strategies and Techniques

1. How would you characterize Faludi's overall tone? Is it effective?

2. The issue with which Faludi is concerned is far from an abstract one. How does Faludi bring across a sense of specifically *moral* urgency?

# Suggestions for Writing

1. Write an essay comparing Camille Paglia's essay with Susan Faludi's, paying attention both to style and content.

2. What is your definition of rape? Explain your answer.

# Why Mothers Should Stay Home

## Deborah Fallows

*In this essay Deborah Fallows uses the evidence of her own life to argue for "the radical middle" position on the issue of working versus full-time mothers. Fallows believes that "the choice is not to be either a career woman or a dumb housewife." She attempts to show how neither stereotype does justice to the possibilities available for women who want to raise their own children.*

*Deborah Fallows was raised in Ohio and educated at Radcliffe College and the University of Texas, where she earned a doctorate in linguistics. She worked as a research linguist and as an assistant dean at Georgetown University before deciding to stay at home with her two children. She describes the reasons for making her choice in an essay first published in* Washington Monthly *magazine.*

About eighteen months ago, when our first son was three years old and our second was about to be born, I decided to stop working and stay at home with our children. At the time, I wrote an article about the myth of the superwoman, saying that contrary to the prevailing notion of the day, it was not possible to be both a full-time career woman and a full-fledged mother. I said that while everyone recognizes the costs a stay-at-home mother pays in terms of power, prestige, money, and advancement in traditional careers, we are not always aware of or do not so readily admit what a full-time working woman loses and gives up in terms of mothering.

I've been at home with our children for almost a year and a half now, and I've learned a number of things about my choice. My convictions about the importance of mothering, which were based more on intuition than experience at the time, run even deeper and stronger. Nothing means more to me now than the hours I spend with my children, but I find myself coping with a problem I hadn't fully foreseen. It is the task of regearing my life, of learning to live as a full-time mother without a professional career but still with many of the interests and ambitions that I had before I had children. And this is the hard part. It means unraveling those long-held life plans for a certain kind of career and deciding which elements are possible to keep and which I must discard. Perhaps even more important, it means changing the way I've been taught to think about myself and value the progress of my life.

My mother became a mother in 1946; she had gone to college, studied music, and worked for a year at her father's office. Then she married and had my sister by the time she was twenty-two. She wasn't expected to have a career outside the home, and she didn't. When I was growing up, the only mothers who worked were those who, as we whispered, "had to." Even the high-school teachers, who we recognized probably weren't doing it just for the money, were slightly suspect.

But between my mother's time and our own, the climate of opportunity and expectations for women started to change. Betty Friedan and *The Feminine Mystique* came between all of those mothers and all of us daughters. The small town in northern Ohio where I grew up was not exactly a hotbed of feminist activity, but even there the signals for young women were changing in the mid-sixties. We were raised with a curious mixture of hope of becoming homecoming queen and pressure to run for student council president. When I was eleven, the mothers in our neighborhood bundled off their awkward, preadolescent daughters to Saturday morning charm classes, where we learned how to walk on a straight line, one foot directly in front of the other, and the proper way to don a coat. We all felt a little funny and humiliated, but we didn't say anything. By the time we were seventeen, we were May Queens, princesses, head drum majorettes, and cheerleaders, but we were also class valedictorians, editors of the school paper and yearbook, student directors of the school band, and candidates for six-year medical programs, Seven Sisters colleges, and honors programs at the Big Ten universities. I admit with some embarrassment that my two most thrilling moments in high school were being chosen for the homecoming court and being named first-chair trumpet in the concert band.

*This* was the way we were supposed to achieve—to be both beautiful and brilliant, charming and accomplished. It was one step beyond what our mothers did: We were aiming to be class presidents, not class secretaries; for medical school, not nursing school; we were building careers, not just jobs to tide us over before we landed husbands and started raising babies.

When I made my decision to stop working and stay home with our children, it was with a mixture of feelings. Part was defiance of the background I've just described—how could feminism dare tell me that I couldn't choose, with *pride,* motherhood alone? Part was anxiety—how could I keep some grasp on my extra-mothering self, on the things I had really enjoyed doing before I had children? I didn't want to become what the world kept telling me housewives are—ladies whose interests are confined to soap operas and the laundry. Certainly I knew from my own mother and from other women who had spent their middle years as full-time mothers that it was possible to be a thoughtful and sensitive person and still be a mother. But I didn't know how, and I didn't know where to turn to ask. Even my mother didn't have the answers. She was surprised when I told her I wanted to stop working and stay home with my kids. "You young women seem to handle everything so easily, so smoothly," she told me. "I never knew you were so torn between being a mother and being a professional."

The arrival of children in a woman's late twenties or early thirties can be handy, of course, because it means you can finish your education and start a career before taking "time out" to start your family. But it's also awkward.

At my tenth college reunion last June, I found that many of my friends had just become partner or vice-president of one thing or another, doctor-in-charge of some ward, tenured professor, editor-in-chief, and so forth. In these moments, I feel as if everyone is growing up around me. My reactions, though human, are not altogether pretty. I feel sorry for myself—there but for two small children go I. I feel frustrated in being passed over for things I know I could handle as well as or better than the next person. I feel anxious, wondering if I am going to "lose my touch," get rusty, boring, old, trivial too quickly. And I am afraid that in putting aside my professional ambitions just now, I may be putting aside forever the chance to attain the levels I once set for myself.

All of us, I think, spend time once in a while pondering the "what ifs" of our lives, and we all experience momentary pangs of self-pity over the course we've taken. I know I'm not an exception to this, but I also know that when I add up the pluses and minuses my choice was right for me, and it might be right for other women.

## The Importance of "Quantity" Time

The first adjustment on that first morning that I dressed for motherhood rather than for success was to believe intellectually in what I felt emotionally: that it was as important, as worthy for me to spend my time with my small children as to study, do research, try cases, or invest a bank's money. Furthermore, I had to believe it was worth it to the children to have me—not someone else—there most of the time. There are a thousand small instances I have witnessed over the past year and a half that illustrate this feeling. One that stays in my mind happened last summer.

I had just dropped off our older son at the morning play camp at the neighborhood school. I was about to drive off when a little boy about eight years old burst out of the school and ran down the front steps in tears. His mother was on her way down the walk and of course she saw him. She led him over to the steps, took his hands in hers, looked him directly in the eyes, and talked with him softly but deliberately for a few minutes, calming him down so he could go back inside happily and she could go on her way. What I recognized in that instant was something I'd been trying to put my finger on for months. I'd witnessed dozens of similar events, and when a child was simply overwhelmed by something, and I knew there was a difference—a distinct difference in the way parents respond at such moments from the way I had seen baby-sitters or maids act, however loving and competent they may have been. Parents seem to have some combination of self-assurance, completeness, deliberateness, and consistency. If that boy had been my son, I would have wanted to be with him, too.

Perhaps this one episode was no more important than the many reprimands or comforts I give my children during the day. But the more I'm around my children, the more such instances I happen to see and deal with. Perhaps a thousand of these episodes add up to the values and security I want to give my children.

I spend a lot of time with my children at playgrounds. We often go out on nice afternoons when our older son gets home from school, sampling new ones or returning to old favorites. I particularly like playgrounds because of the balance they afford: They encourage the kids to strike out on their own but let me be there as a fallback. I've watched my older son in his share of small fistfights and scuffles, and I have been able to let him fight without intervening. He knows I'm there and runs back as often for protection as for nice things like a "Mom, see what I can do." Or our younger son toddles toward the big slide and needs me to follow him up and hold him as we slide down together. After so many hours, we've developed a style of play. I think my children know what to expect of me and I have learned their limits. I've watched the styles of many mothers and children, and you often can see, after a time, a microcosm of their lives together. I've also seen plenty of children there with full-time maids. The maids have their own styles, which usually are different from the mothers'. I've never seen a maid slide down a slide with her small charge, but I have seen plenty scold children for climbing too high on the jungle gym, and I've seen plenty step in to stop the sandfights before anyone gets dirty or hurt. There's a reason for this, of course: A maid has a lot to explain if a youngster arrives home with a bloody nose, but a mother doesn't. Sometimes, I think, the nose is worth the lesson learned from it, yet that is something only a parent—not a maid or baby-sitter—can take the responsibility to decide.

It has taken me a few years to realize I have very high standards for my role as a mother. I don't have to be a supermom who makes my children's clothes (I really can't sew), who does all the volunteer work at school (I do my share), or who cooks gourmet meals (we eat a lot of hamburgers). But I have to be around my children—a lot. I have to know them as well as I possibly can and see them in as many different environments and moods as possible in order to know best how to help them grow up—by comforting them, letting them alone, disciplining and enjoying them, being dependable but not stifling. What I need with them is time—in quantity, not quality.

I'm not talking about being with my children every minute of the day. From the time they were several months old, we sent them out for short periods to the favorite neighborhood baby-sitter's. By the time he was two and a half, our older son was in a co-op nursery school (my husband and I would take turns doing parent duty for the seventeen kids); now he's in pre-kindergarten for a full school day. These periods away from me are clearly important for my sanity, as well as for my children's socialization, their development of trust in people, and their ability to experience other ways of living. But there is a big difference between using childcare from 8 to 6, Monday through Friday, and using a baby-sitter or a nursery school three mornings a week.

I realize that not everyone enjoys the luxury of choice. Some of my female friends work because it's the only way to make ends meet. But I think a lot of people pretend they have less room for choice than they really do. For some women, the reason may be the feeling—which is widespread among men—that their dignity and success are related to how much money they earn. For others, there is a sense of independence that comes with earning money that is hard to give up. (I know that I felt freer to buy things, especially for myself, or spend money on baby-sitters when I was contributing to the family income.) And still others define "necessities" in an expensive way: I've heard more than one woman say she "has to work" to keep up payments on the second house. Such a woman is the parallel to the government appointee who "has to resign" from his post to return to his former profession because he "can no longer afford government service."

Even though some women do have a choice, I am not suggesting that all the responsibility for home and children should lie with the mother. While my husband and I are an example of a more traditional family, with a bread-winning father, a full-time mother, and two children, he shares with me many of the family responsibilities: night-tending, diapering, bathing, cooking, and playtime. A woman's decision to stay home or work is, at worst, a decision made by herself and, at best, a decision made with her spouse.

But with all these qualifications noted, I still know that my own choice is to stay with my children. Why does this seem to be at odds with the climate of the times, especially among certain feminists? I think it is because of a confused sense of ambition—based, in turn, on a mistaken understanding of what being a housewife or mother actually means.

While the world's idea of the comparative importance of career and motherhood may have changed a good deal since my mother's time, the general understanding of what motherhood means for those who choose it has not changed or advanced. And that may be the real problem for many women of my generation: Who can blame them for shying away from a commitment to full-time motherhood if they're told, despite raising children, that motherhood is a vapid life of chores, routines, and TV? I couldn't stand motherhood myself if that were true. One of my many discoveries as a mother is that motherhood requires not the renunciation of my former ambitions but rather their refinement.

Even for those who intend to rush straight back to work, motherhood involves some interruption in the normal career plan. Separating people, even temporarily, from their professional identities, can help them see the difference between the ambition to *be*—to have an impressive job title to drop at cocktail parties—and the ambition to *do* specific things that seem satisfying and rewarding. The ambition to be is often a casualty of motherhood; the ambition to do need not be.

I see many of my friends intensely driven to keep doing things, to keep involved in their former interests, or to develop entirely new ones that they can learn from and grow with. In the free time they manage to set aside—thanks to baby-sitters, co-op babycare, naptimes, grandmothers' help, and husbands like mine who spend a lot of time with the children—they are thinking and doing.

Women I have talked to have described how, after some months or years of settling into motherhood, their sense of what work is worth, and what they're looking for in work, has greatly changed. They are less tolerant, more selective, more demanding in what they do. One woman said that before she had children she would focus on a "cause," and was willing to do just about anything as her job toward that cause. Now she's still interested in advancing the cause, but she has no patience for busywork. In the limited time she can spare from her family, she wants to do things that really count, work in areas where her efforts make a difference. I'm not suggesting narcissism here but a clearer focus on a search for some long-range goal, some tangible accomplishment, a feeling so necessary during the season of child raising when survival from one end of the day to the other is often the only achievement.

Each one's search is different, depending on factors like her husband's job (if she has a husband) and the extent of his role as a caretaker, her children's needs, her family's financial situation, and her personal lifestyle.

One of my friends had taught English in public high schools for the last ten years. She was the kind of teacher you remember fondly from your own childhood and hope your kids are lucky enough to have because she's dedicated, demanding, and creative. She expanded her subject to include other humanities, keeping herself several steps ahead of her students by reading and studying on her own, traveling to see museums and exhibits firsthand, collecting slides and books as she goes. She has a new baby daughter now and has stopped working to stay home with her child. She's decided to go back to school next fall, taking one or two courses at a time, to pursue a master's in fine arts—a chance to study formally what she's mostly taught herself and to return to her job someday with an even better background and more ideas for her teaching.

Going to school can be perfect for new mothers, as many in my own mother's generation found. It requires very little time away from home, which means cutting down on time away from the children as well as on child-care costs. It can be cheap, as with my friend, who can attend a virtually tuition-free state university. You can pace your work to suit demands at home by carefully choosing the number of courses you take and the type of work required. And it's physically easy but intellectually challenging—the complement to the other demands of the early years of mothering.

Other mothers I know do different things with their time. One friend, formerly a practicing lawyer and now a full-time mother, volunteers some of her time to advising the League of Women Voters on legal matters. Another, formerly a producer at a big radio station, now produces her own shows, albeit at a slower pace. A third quit her job to raise her daughter but spends a lot of time on artistic projects, which she sells.

But if there's no real blueprint for what a modern mother should be, you wouldn't know it from what comes through in the media. On the "Today Show" last summer, for instance, Jane Pauley interviewed Felice Schwartz, the president of Catalyst, an organization that promotes career development for women. They were discussing women's changing life-styles. Ms. Schwartz said that now women are going back to work full-time four months after having children, while fifteen years ago they were taking twenty years off to have them. "Isn't that fantastic progress?" she said. Fantastic it certainly is; progress it is not, except toward the narrowest and least generous notion of what achievement means for women or for humanity. Progress such as this is a step not toward "liberation" but toward the enslavement to career that has been the least attractive aspect of masculine success.

What it is really like to be a mother today seems to be a secret that's kept from even my contemporaries who may be considering motherhood themselves. At a dinner recently, I sat near a young woman about my age, a New York television producer and recently appointed

White House fellow. She and my husband and I were having a conversation about bureaucracy and what she found new or interesting or surprising about it in her new position. After several minutes, she turned away from my husband to me directly and said, "And how old are your children, Debbie?" It wasn't the question—not at all—but the tone that was revealing, the unattractive, condescending tone I've heard many older people use with youngsters, or doctors with patients. If I'd had her pegged as a fast-track superachiever, she had me pegged as little mother and lady of the house.

Hurt and anger were the wrong feelings at a moment like that, although I felt them. Instead, I should have felt sorry for her, not because of her own choice but because she had no sense that a choice exists—waiting to be made by women like her and like me. The choice is *not* to be either a career woman or a dumb housewife. The issue is one that she, a woman at the age when careers take off and childbearing ability nears its eleventh hour, should be sensitive to and think about.

# Themes, Issues, and Ideas

1. Fallows says that her decision to stay at home was made with mixed feelings. What are these feelings and how does she describe coming to terms with them?

2. What does Fallows see as the principal difference between her life as a mother and her mother's life?

3. What does Fallows mean by "quantity time"? What other reasons does she give in favoring part-time work over part-time mothering?

# Writing Strategies and Techniques

1. How does Fallows confront the points of view of those who have not made her decision? How does she blend reasoned arguments with anecdotes from her own life?

2. Whom does Fallows seem to be addressing? That is, where does she seem to be addressing young women who have perhaps not yet formed an opinion on the issue, and where does she seem to speak to women who already have careers and children? How do you decide on her imagined audience in each case?

# Suggestions for Writing

1. Write a response to Fallows as it might be written by one of the types of women she imagines in her essay; for example, the "fast-track superachiever."

2. Write an essay describing your own views as a man or a woman on the proper role for mothers of young children.

# Shake the Universe

## Madeleine L'Engle

*Madeleine L'Engle is probably the most well-known for her classic science-fiction novel* A Wrinkle in Time *(1962). She is the author of thirty-nine books, both fiction and nonfiction, the most recent of which,* Certain Women, *was published in 1992. In this essay she considers her gender in the largest context—that of the natural order of things in the universe.*

Last May I visited a 5000-year-old village near Xian, China. It had recently been discovered and excavated, and a roof and walls had been put around the entire village in order to protect it. Although it was a "primitive" village, the mud dwelling houses were solid and far more comfortable habitations than many I've seen in the barrios and *favelos* of South America, or in our own North American inner cities, for that matter. Research showed the village to have been originally that of a matriarchal society, agrarian and peaceable. At the grave site the head women of the tribe were buried in the center, with the men on either side, along with artifacts that appeared to be musical instruments, as well as cooking vessels beautified with artistic designs. These seemed to indicate a society dominated by women, a society concerned with music and art, with the expression of pattern and order.

A thousand or so years later, this society had shifted to a partriarchy: the head man was buried in the center of the grave, with his women on either side of him, along with primitive instruments of war.

It is a bit simplistic to say that when women guide the way of life society is peaceable, and there is time for music and beauty and things of the spirit; and that when men are in charge there is war, and the tribal dances become war dances rather than patterns of beauty in appreciation of the loveliness of nature—the sun by day, the moon and the stars by night.

Simplistic or not, that is the basic pattern throughout history.

So part of the calling of women as we move out of the last years of the 20th century and into the 21st is to revive a spirituality of creativity that is not afraid of the strange beauty of the underwater world of the subconscious and to help men out of the restricted and narrow world of provable and limited fact in which society has imprisoned them.

My role as a feminist is not to compete with men in their world—that's too easy, and ultimately unproductive. My job is to live fully as a woman, enjoying the whole of myself and my place in the universe.

Throughout the past several centuries, women have been allowed to remain in touch with the intuitive, the nurturing, the numinous—the spiritual, if you will—whereas men have been forced to limit themselves to the rational (which is not very rational, after all), and are offering their children and grandchildren a planet raped by war, stupidity, and greed.

This is a masculine point of view against which I have consciously rebelled since I was 12 years old and sent to an English boarding school where we were taught all the masculine virtues: be brave; do not cry; do not show emotions; be morally virtuous; do it yourself; never ask for help; be good and obedient and the world will be perfect. It didn't take much imagination to see that the world that was the outcome of these masculine virtues was anything but perfect. Hitler was already in power. In England we saw the great arms of the antiaircraft lights sweeping the sky as Britain prepared for war.

It was easy for me to rebel because I was clumsy at sports, daydreamed during class, wrote stories when I should have been doing homework. But I did learn one valuable lesson from that school in the spring of the year when we were given little garden plots to cultivate. We were allowed to bring the produce of our gardens in for tea, so most of the kids planted lettuce and tomatoes and radishes and watercress and cucumbers. My garden partner and I planted poppies, nothing but poppies. Our illegal reading had included *Bull-Dog Drummond* and *Fu Manchu,* from which we learned that opium comes from poppies, and that opium gives one beautiful dreams. So we had poppy leaf sandwiches and poppy flower sandwiches and poppy seed sandwiches and went to bed with flashlights and dream books under our pillows.

We found out quickly that we didn't need our poppy sandwiches for our dreams; but what we were doing, intuitively rather than consciously, was rebelling against the fragmented, basically masculine world of the adults. We were allowed no time for daytime dreaming. Daydreaming was suspect. If I locked myself in what at that school was known as The James for five minutes of privacy, after two minutes would come a knock and a sharp British voice: "Madaleen, what are you doing in there?" If we wanted privacy, it was assumed that it was for some nasty, perverse reason. So we had to make use of our night-time dreams. With our dream books we were trying to reconcile intellect and intuition, conscious and subconscious minds. In our youth and naïveté we were struggling toward what I believe to be truly feminine spirituality.

It is not coincidence that the root word for heal, health, whole, and holy, is hale, as in "hale and hearty." If we are healed we are healthy; if we are healthy we are whole; if we are whole we are holy—that is all being holy means. And in our own blundering way my garden partner and I were struggling to be holy. The worst thing you could call anybody at that school was "pi," short for pious, and I am still suspicious of piosity. Holiness is something else again.

How do we become, much less remain, whole and holy in a world that tears and fragments?

When my husband of 40 years died six months ago, it was as though I had been amputated or split in two. But death—unless it is murder, accident, suicide—is not an unnatural part of the whole journey of life. Death cannot take away anything that two lovers have had. Grief can be acute, and yet clean.

It is my blessing to have living with me in my apartment in New York my 17-year-old granddaughter, a freshman in college, and an 18-year-old friend of hers from high school. We have got into the delightful habit of having multigenerational dinner parties about every other week. A Sunday ago we ranged in age from eight months all the way up to me, with at least one person representing every decade in between. This Sunday we'll drop down to four months for the youngest. Then we jump to nine years, 13 years, 17, two 18s, five young men and women in their twenties, two in their thirties; two in their forties. (Do we have anybody in the fifties this time? I'm not sure.) And up to Madeleine and the sixties. These evenings have somehow or other been generated spontaneously, and they are full of good conversation, and often music if we have performers among the group. Nobody pays any attention to how old anybody is. There is certainly no attempt to try to have as many men as women, or vice versa. I do the cooking; the kids do the cleaning up. There is an amazing kind of wholeness and laughter and livingness that, to me, at this period of my life, is an icon of feminine spirituality.

Thus feminine spirituality must seek wholeness, holiness. Women have made great strides in this century. My grandmother was a suffragist, and now we take the vote for granted. Of course we can and do compete in the world of business, government, medicine. Less obvious but more important is the fact that now most women nurse their babies; in 1947 I had to fight for my right to nurse my first baby.

I went to a small village and an old-fashioned general practitioner to have my second baby, because I wanted my husband with me, and I wanted to deliver my child by natural childbirth. Remember that at that time most obstetricians were men. I, listening to my body, knew what was natural and easiest; male doctors did not. Childbearing in this century was a sterile and lonely business until women raised their voices. Today, natural childbirth with the father participating in the marvelously creative act of birth is becoming the normal procedure. In 2002 I hope that men will play an even more active part in the process of birth and the nurturing of children, touching the baby as it emerges into the world, being in fact midhusbands.

At the time of my marriage in 1946, I was working in the theater and had published two novels, so my husband more or less knew what he was getting, and that he was expected to do his share of the housework and taking care of the children. My husband was an artist, an actor; I doubt if I'd have made it for 40 years with a man in the business world. Today the sharing of household duties is becoming more and more the norm regardless of a man's occupation.

This change to "what comes naturally" in our domestic arrangements reflects a change in our spirituality that is a turning away from the rational and explicable to a new understanding of paradox and contradiction in our expressions of the meaning of life. The women mystics, who had been carefully swept under the carpet by a patriarchal church, are being rediscovered. There is 14th-century Julian of Norwich, who saw the entire universe in "the quantity of an hazelnut," and Hildegard of Bingen, an abbess in the Middle Ages who likened herself to "a feather on the breath of God."

Women are being ordained in the Episcopal Church, and there is much heated discussion of such a breakthrough in the Roman Catholic Church; and I have met several women rabbis. Far more important than the fact of ordination (no small triumph) is that these women are given the opportunity to free the churches and temples from a narrow vision of creation and our place in it, and that they may reveal a Creator who is—as I heard a friend say recently—exquisite. Suddenly the word burst open for me: ex–quisite—that which is on the other side of and outside the question.

How many people visualize God as looking like Moses—long beard, white nightgown—and Moses in a bad temper, at that? Male. Chauvinist. Punitive.

I want a Creator who is exquisite.

When we human beings opened the Pandora's box of the atom, a completely new vision of the universe was revealed, a universe that burst forth from a sub-subatomic particle (as physicist Stephen Hawking sees it) into all the countless galaxies exploding farther and farther into space. This universe is totally interdependent: nothing happens in isolation, and nothing can be observed objectively because to observe something is to change it. In an article on astrophysics, I came across the phrase "the butterfly effect," and what is meant by this is that if a butterfly should happen to fly into my office and somehow be hurt, the effect of that accident would be felt in galaxies billions of light-years away.

The universe as the physicists see it is also a world of randomness, of chance, which seems to upset some people. But if we lived in a determined universe, we would have no free will, no share in the writing of the story. I am far happier in an indeterminate universe than a determined one; it offers far more possibilities for spiritual growth and development.

To live in an open and undetermined universe with courage and grace seems to me to epitomize feminine spirituality, and it is the way we are going to go if we are to survive as a human race. We must stop reverting to the grave site with the man in the middle, his women on either side, along with the weapons of war. But unless we listen to our planet, unless we listen to our bodies, unless we listen to our spirits, society may plunge back to that world once again—autonomous, independent, destructive, and basically subhuman.

Feminine spirituality accepts interdependence, and is not threatened by questions that have no definitive answers. The world of sub-atomic particles is a world of paradox, of chance and pattern, randomness and purpose, the tangible and the mystical. It is a vision of creation that demands great courage, spiritual courage, a new kind of courage that women are going to have to be strong and patient enough to teach to men. To look at something is to change it. To hurt a butterfly is to shake the universe. To love is to be vulnerable. To attempt anything—music, love, art—is to risk failure, and that takes a kind of courage I believe to be uniquely feminine. This openness to change, interdependence, questions with no easy answers, vulnerability, and risk is the feminine spirituality that is desperately needed if the human race is to reach the year 2002.

## Themes, Issues, and Ideas

1. "To attempt anything is to risk failure, and that's a kind of courage I believe is uniquely feminine." What does L'Engle mean by this? On what is her observation based?

2. What is "their [men's] world," as L'Engle defines it? What are her attitudes to it? Are they the same as yours?

3. Do you agree that peace, courage, and a spiritual way of life are the result of women's controlling society, while war and cruelty is the result of men doing so? Is that, as L'Engle states, "the basic pattern throughout history"? What support for this view does L'Engle give?

## Writing Strategies and Techniques

1. Does the archeological example the essay opens with seem germane to L'Engle's subject? Why or why not?

2. How would you characterize L'Engle's writing? What seem to be her intents in writing this essay? Who would you guess the target audience was for this essay?

## Suggestions for Writing

1. Write a review of this essay in the style of Elizabeth Cady Stanton.

2. Write a play portraying one of the dinner parties L'Engle describes in her essay.

# It's a Jungle Out There, So Get Used to It!

## Camille Paglia

*Camille Paglia was until a few years ago an unknown professor of art history at the Philadelphia College of Art. Then, in 1990 her book* Sexual Personae: Art and Decadence from Nefertiti to Emily Dickinson *was published, and she achieved instant notoriety. Paglia's ideas, which are always controversial and incendiary, center around the natural sexual forces she believes are part of the human condition, and which are controlled and expressed through popular and serious art.*

*In "It's a Jungle Out There, So Get Used to It!" Paglia leaves her home ground of art history, and considers a much thornier question: What is rape, and what can be done about it? Paglia has alienated many feminists by her staunch opposition to the feminist critique of rape and sexuality. Here, she examines what she sees as the dynamics of campus rape, and how young women have been made vulnerable by misinformation.*

Rape is an outrage that cannot be tolerated in civilized society. Yet feminism, which has waged a crusade for rape to be taken more seriously, has put young women in danger by hiding the truth about sex from them.

In dramatizing the pervasiveness of rape, feminists have told young women that before they have sex with a man, they must give consent as explicit as a legal contract's. In this way, young women have been convinced that they have been the victims of rape. On elite campuses in the Northeast and on the West Coast, they have held consciousness-raising sessions, petitioned administrations, demanded inquests.

At Brown University, outraged, panicky "victims" have scrawled the names of alleged attackers on the walls of women's rest rooms. What marital rape was to the '70s, "date rape" is to the '90s.

The incidence and seriousness of rape do not require this kind of exaggeration. Real acquaintance rape is nothing new. It has been a horrible problem for women for all of recorded history. Once fathers and brothers protected women from rape. Once the penalty for rape was death. I come from a fierce Italian tradition where, not so long ago in the motherland, a rapist would end up knifed, castrated, and hung out to dry.

But the old clans and small rural communities have broken down. In our cities, on our campuses far from home, young women are vulnerable and defenseless. Feminism has not prepared them for this. Feminism keeps saying the sexes are the same. It keeps telling women they can do anything, go anywhere, say anything, wear anything. No, they can't. Women will always be in sexual danger.

One of my male students recently slept overnight with a friend in a passageway of the Great Pyramid in Egypt. He described the moon and sand, the ancient silence and eerie echoes. I will never experience that. I am a woman. I am not stupid enough to believe I could ever be safe there. There is a world of solitary adventure I will never have. Women have always known these somber truths. But feminism, with its pie-in-the-sky fantasies about the perfect world, keeps young women from seeing life as it is.

We must remedy social injustice whenever we can. But there are some things we cannot change. There are sexual differences that are based in biology. Academic feminism is lost in a fog of social constructionism. It believes we are totally the product of our environment. This idea was invented by Rousseau. He was wrong. Emboldened by dumb French language theory, academic feminists repeat the same hollow slogans over and over to each other. Their view of sex is naive and prudish. Leaving sex to the feminists is like letting your dog vacation at the taxidermist's.

The sexes are at war. Men must struggle for identity against the overwhelming power of their mothers. Women have menstruation to tell them they are women. Men must do or risk something to be men. Men become masculine only when other men say they are. Having sex with a woman is one way a boy becomes a man.

College men are at their hormonal peak. They have just left their mothers and are questing for their male identity. In groups, they are dangerous. A woman going to a fraternity party is walking into Test-osterone Flats, full of prickly cacti and blazing guns. If she goes, she should be armed with resolute alertness. She should arrive with girl-friends and leave with them. A girl who lets herself get dead drunk at a fraternity party is a fool. A girl who goes upstairs alone with a brother at a fraternity party is an idiot. Feminists call this "blaming the victim." I call it common sense.

For a decade, feminists have drilled their disciples to say, "Rape is a crime of violence but not of sex." This sugar-coated Shirley Temple nonsense has exposed young women to disaster. Misled by feminism, they do not expect rape from the nice boys from good homes who sit next to them in class.

Aggression and eroticism are deeply intertwined. Hunt, pursuit, and capture are biologically programmed into male sexuality. Genera-tion after generation, men must be educated, refined, and ethically per-suaded away from their tendency toward anarchy and brutishness. Society is not the enemy, as feminism ignorantly claims. Society is woman's protection against rape. Feminism, with its solemn Carry Nation repressiveness, does not see what is for men the eroticism or fun element in rape, especially the wild, infectious delirium of gang rape. Women who do not understand rape cannot defend themselves against it.

The date-rape controversy shows feminism hitting the wall of its own broken promises. The women of my '60s generation were the first respectable girls in history to swear like sailors, get drunk, stay out all night—in short, to act like men. We sought total sexual freedom and equality. But as time passed, we woke up to cold reality. The old dou-ble standard protected women. When anything goes, it's women who lose.

Today's young women don't know what they want. They see that feminism has not brought sexual happiness. The theatrics of public rage over date rape are their way of restoring the old sexual rules that were shattered by my generation. Because nothing about the sexes has really changed. The comic film *Where the Boys Are* (1960), the ultimate expression of '50s man-chasing, still speaks directly to our time. It shows smart, lively women skillfully anticipating and fending off the dozens of strategies with which horny men try to get them into bed. The agonizing date-rape subplot and climax are brilliantly done. The vic-tim, Yvette Mimieux, makes mistake after mistake, obvious to the other girls. She allows herself to be lured away from her girlfriends and into isolation with boys whose character and intentions she misreads. *Where the Boys Are* tells the truth. It shows courtship as a dangerous game in which the signals are not verbal but subliminal.

Neither militant feminism, which is obsessed with politically correct language, nor academic feminism, which believes that knowledge and experience are "constituted by" language, can understand pre-verbal or non-verbal communication. Feminism, focusing on sexual politics, cannot see that sex exists in and through the body. Sexual desire and arousal cannot be fully translated into verbal terms. This is why men and women misunderstand each other.

Trying to remake the future, feminism cut itself off from sexual history. It discarded and suppressed the sexual myths of literature, art, and religion. Those myths show us the turbulence, the mysteries and passions of sex. In mythology we see men's sexual anxiety, their fear of women's dominance. Much sexual violence is rooted in men's sense of psychological weakness toward women. It takes many men to deal with one woman. Woman's voracity is a persistent motif. Clara Bow, it was rumored, took on the USC football team on weekends. Marilyn Monroe, singing "Diamonds Are a Girl's Best Friend," rules a conga line of men in tuxes. Half-clad Cher, in the video for "If I Could Turn Back Time," deranges a battleship of screaming sailors and straddles a pink-lit cannon. Feminism, coveting social power, is blind to woman's cosmic sexual power.

To understand rape, you must study the past. There never was and never will be sexual harmony. Every woman must take personal responsibility for her sexuality, which is nature's red flame. She must be prudent and cautious about where she goes and with whom. When she makes a mistake, she must accept the consequences and, through self-criticism, resolve never to make that mistake again. Running to Mommy and Daddy on the campus grievance committee is unworthy of strong women. Posting lists of guilty men in the toilet is cowardly, infantile stuff.

The Italian philosophy of life espouses high-energy confrontation. A male student makes a vulgar remark about your breasts? Don't slink off to whimper and simper with the campus shrinking violets. Deal with it. On the spot. Say, "Shut up, you jerk! And crawl back to the barnyard where you belong!" In general, women who project this take-charge attitude toward life get harassed less often. I see too many dopey, immature, self-pitying women walking around like melting sticks of butter. It's the Yvette Mimieux syndrome: Make me happy. And listen to me weep when I'm not.

The date-rape debate is already smothering in propaganda churned out by the expensive Northeastern colleges and universities, with their overconcentration of boring, uptight academic feminists and spoiled, affluent students. Beware of the deep manipulativeness of rich students who were neglected by their parents. They love to turn the campus into hysterical psychodramas of sexual transgression, followed by assertions of parental authority and concern. And don't look for sexual enlightenment from academe, which spews out mountains of books but never looks at life directly.

As a fan of football and rock music, I see in the simple, swaggering masculinity of the jock and in the noisy posturing of the heavy-metal guitarist certain fundamental, unchanging truths about sex. Masculinity is aggressive, unstable, combustible. It is also the most creative cultural force in history. Women must reorient themselves toward the elemental powers of sex, which can strengthen or destroy.

The only solution to date rape is female self-awareness and self-control. A woman's number one line of defense is herself. When a real rape occurs, she should report it to the police. Complaining to college committees because the courts "take too long" is ridiculous. College administrations are not a branch of the judiciary. They are not equipped or trained for legal inquiry. Colleges must alert incoming students to the problems and dangers of adulthood. Then colleges must stand back and get out of the sex game.

# Themes, Issues, and Ideas

1.  What does Paglia say is the primary cause of rape? What, according to her, do feminists say is?

2.  According to Paglia, "[w]omen who do not understand rape cannot defend themselves against it." Why should this be true? Explain your answer.

3.  Common sense, prudence and caution, and self-awareness and self-control are what women need, according to Paglia, not "dumb French language theory" and "running to Mommy and Daddy on the campus grievance committee." What are the merits of this line of reasoning? What are its flaws? Write a balanced essay in which you neither support nor deny Paglia's points, but rather consider them in an objective way.

# Writing Strategies and Techniques

1.  What does Paglia accomplish by saying "dumb French language theory" instead of "post-structuralist discourse"?

2.  What is the effect of Paglia's first sentence? Do you feel when you are reading the essay that Paglia is really concerned with rape as a danger?

# Suggestions for Writing

1.  Write an essay in which you reply to Paglia without using or referring to any of the arguments she brings up in this reading.

2.  Write an essay agreeing or disagreeing with Paglia's description of men. Use examples from your own experience.

# Feminism—It's a Black Thang!

## bell hooks

*During the 1960s, two major social movements were at work: women's liberation and the civil rights struggle. To this day, bell hooks suggests, the progress of the two movements has stayed separate. In "Feminism— It's a Black Thang!" she suggests some good reasons for changing the status quo.*

*bell hooks is a cultural critic who is based in Ohio. Her books include* Black Looks: Race and Representation *(1992) and* Ain't I a Woman: Black Women and Feminism *(1981), among many others.*

It is obvious that most Black men are not in positions that allow them to exert the kind of institutionalized patriarchal power and control over Black women's lives that privileged white men do in this society. But it is undeniable that they do exert a lot of power over Black women and children in everyday life. Most of us are, however, reluctant to admit that male domination causes much of the gender conflict and pain experienced in Black women's lives.

Whether a man demands that "his" woman turn her signed pay-check over to him or forces his female companion to do the "wild thing" without a condom (because "the condom hurts" him), such assertions of power are sexist and abusive. And even if Black women do not have to face the sexist threats of male domination in the home, all too often when we walk down the streets, it is the brothers, not white men, who address us with sexual taunts. And if we do not respond, they become hostile and scream epithets at us like "Bitch, you think you too good to speak to me?" And when sexist incidents like this occur, Black women feel afraid—afraid that we may be hit, raped, robbed or some combination of the above.

Yet in spite of the fact that thousands of Black women are assaulted by Black males on the street or in the home every day, in most of these cases our male offenders do not believe that they've done anything wrong. Note recent conversations among Black folks about the Tyson case, where, by and large, men and women tend to see the woman as guilty, even though Tyson's own public history reveals him to be a man who has consistently abused women.

It is also no comfort to any of us that so much Black popular music—especially the growing subgenre of woman-hating rap—encourages Black males and every other listener to think there is nothing wrong with abusing women in general, and Black women in particular. That a Black male rap group like N.W.A. can become richer and even more famous than they already are by pushing woman-bashing lyrics is a sign of how dangerous these times are for women. And if any of us should think the boys are just having a little fun at our expense, we should take note of the fact that one of the group members is being sued for assaulting Black female television host Dee Barnes in an L.A. club. He has responded by bragging in *Rolling Stone:* "It ain't no big thing—I just threw her through a door." Let's face it, abusive Black male domination of Black women and children is so much a regular part of everyday Black life that most Black folks do not take it seriously.

Every Black person concerned about our collective survival must acknowledge that sexism is a destructive force in Black life that cannot be effectively addressed without an organized political movement to change consciousness, behavior and institutions. What we need is a feminist revolution in Black life. But to have such a revolution, we must first have a feminist movement.

Many Black folks do not know what the word *feminism* means. They may think of it only as something having to do with white women's desire to share equal rights with white men. In reality, feminism is a movement to end *all* sexism and sexist oppression. The strategies necessary to achieve that end are many. We need to find ways to address the specific forms that sexism takes in our diverse communities. We must start by educating our communities—at the grass-roots level—as to what sexism is, how it is expressed in daily life and why it creates problems.

Today many Black women and men are afraid that if we say that we support feminist movements, we will either be seen as traitors to the race or be privately or publicly humiliated by other Black people. In the past few months I have talked at colleges around the country where young Black men are physically threatening and even assaulting Black female students for criticizing and resisting Black male sexism, for starting Black female consciousness-raising support groups and even for taking women's studies classes.

A feminist movement that addresses the needs of Black women, men and children can strengthen our bonds with one another, deepen our sense of community and further Black liberation. We must not be afraid to create such a movement.

## Themes, Issues, and Ideas

1. The abuse that hooks describes black women as taking from black men is very dramatic and obvious. Why do you think it would need to be addressed only now, thirty years after the women's movement began to change American life?

2. Hooks talks about creating a "feminist movement that addresses the needs of Black women, men and children." What goals might such a movement have?

## Writing Strategies and Techniques

1. The essay begins with hooks speaking about black women and black men. Then she begins to use the first person ("Most of us . . ."). What purpose does this technique serve?

2. Throughout hooks's essay, "Black" is capitalized. What impact does this have, grammatically and politically?

3. Throughout her essay, hooks mixes an academic style ("The strategies necessary to achieve that end are many") with more down-to-earth idioms ("Let's face it . . . most Black folks do not take [abuse] seriously.") Why does she do this?

# Suggestions for Writing

1. Write an essay discussing some sexist elements of your own ethnic heritage, and how they might be addressed.

2. Do you think hooks is fair to black culture? Write an essay from the perspective of someone defending black culture.

# MAKING CONNECTIONS

1. Elizabeth Cady Stanton's sense of the possibilities of womanhood seems to differ greatly from Madeleine L'Engle's. What are some of the fundamental differences between both women? What seem to be assumptions they share, and what seem to be assumptions or beliefs which they do not?

2. For bell hooks, feminism is an empowering tool long resisted by black women. Would Camille Paglia agree with this interpretation? What is the difference between Paglia's and hooks's views of black womanhood? What are their differences concerning empowerment?

3. All the writers in this chapter in one way or another look toward the future. Write an essay that describes your own views on what women's lot might be in the twenty-first century.

4. Which of the authors in this chapter do you most admire as a writer? Which as a thinker? Compare two of the authors as writers and thinkers.

5. Who do you think does more for women: an idealistic feminist like Madeleine L'Engle or a practical pragmatist like Deborah Fallows? To what extent do they overlap? Are there other writers in this chapter who appear to be practical but are actually quite idealistic, or vice versa? Explain.

# CHAPTER THREE

## *The Millennial Melting Pot*

### *Race and Equality in America's Future*

# THE PAST AS PROLOGUE

## *The Ballot or the Bullet*

### *Malcolm X*

*Malcolm X was born Malcolm Little in 1925 in Omaha, Nebraska. After dropping out of high school, he was convicted of burglary at the age of 21 and sent to prison. There, he taught himself to read by copying the entire dictionary in longhand. While in prison he also converted to Islam, and upon his release adopted the name X to protest his legal status as the descendent of slaves. Malcolm X became a firebrand, and rivaled Martin Luther King, Jr., as a black leader. Militant and lucid, Malcolm possessed the religious austerity and conviction of a devoted Muslim. His appreciation of Islam as a world religion, among other things, led to his break with the Black Muslims, a radical organization. He was assassinated at the Audubon Ballroom in New York's Harlem on February 21, 1965.*

*The following excerpt is from Malcolm X's speech "The Ballot or the Bullet," which he delivered in early 1964.*

If we don't do something real soon, I think you'll have to agree that we're going to be forced either to use the ballot or the bullet. It's one or the other in 1964. It isn't that time is running out—time has run out! 1964 threatens to be the most explosive year America has ever witnessed. The most explosive year. Why? It's also a political year. It's the year when all of the white politicians will be back in the so-called Negro community jiving you and me for some votes. The year when all of the white political crooks will be right back in your and my community with their false promises, building up our hopes for a letdown, with their trickery and their treachery, with their false promises which they don't intend to keep. As they nourish these dissatisfactions, it can only lead to one thing, an explosion; and now we have the type of black man on the scene in America today—I'm sorry, Brother Lomax—who just doesn't intend to turn the other cheek any longer.

Don't let anybody tell you anything about the odds are against you. If they draft you, they send you to Korea and make you face 800 million Chinese. If you can be brave over there, you can be brave right here. These odds aren't as great as those odds. And if you fight here, you will at least know what you're fighting for.

I'm not a politician, not even a student of politics; in fact, I'm not a student of much of anything. I'm not a Democrat, I'm not a Republican, and I don't even consider myself an American. If you and I were Americans, there'd be no problem. Those Hunkies that just got off the boat, they're already Americans; Polacks are already Americans; the Italian refugees are already Americans. Everything that came out of Europe, every blue-eyed thing, is already an American. And as long as you and I have been over here, we aren't Americans yet.

Well, I am one who doesn't believe in deluding myself. I'm not going to sit at your table and watch you eat, with nothing on my plate, and call myself a diner. Sitting at the table doesn't make you a diner, unless you eat some of what's on that plate. Being here in America doesn't make you an American. Being born here in America doesn't make you an American. Why, if birth made you American, you wouldn't need any legislation, you wouldn't need any amendments to the Constitution, you wouldn't be faced with civil-rights filibustering in Washington, D.C., right now. They don't have to pass civil-rights legislation to make a Polack an American.

No, I'm not an American. I'm one of the 22 million black people who are the victims of Americanism. One of the 22 million black people who are the victims of democracy, nothing but disguised hypocrisy.

So, I'm not standing here speaking to you as an American, or a patriot, or a flag-saluter, or a flag-waver—no, not I. I'm speaking as a victim of this American system. And I see America through the eyes of the victim. I don't see any American dream; I see an American nightmare. . . .

Last but not least, I must say this concerning the great controversy over rifles and shotguns. The only thing that I've ever said is that in areas where the government has proven itself either unwilling or unable to defend the lives and the property of Negroes, it's time for Negroes to defend themselves. Article number two of the constitutional amendments provides you and me the right to own a rifle or a shotgun. It is constitutionally legal to own a shotgun or a rifle. This doesn't mean you're going to get a rifle and form battalions and go out looking for white folks, although you'd be within your rights—I mean, you'd be justified; but that would be illegal and we don't do anything illegal. If the white man doesn't want the black man buying rifles and shotguns, then let the government do its job. That's all. And don't let the white man come to you and ask you what you think about what Malcolm says—why, you old Uncle Tom. He would never ask you if he thought you were going to say, "Amen!" No, he is making a Tom out of you.

So, this doesn't mean forming rifle clubs and going out looking for people, but it is time, in 1964, if you are a man, to let that man know. If he's not going to do his job in running the government and providing you and me with the protection that our taxes are supposed to be for, since he spends all those billions for his defense budget, he certainly can't begrudge you and me spending $12 or $15 for a single-shot, or double-action. I hope you understand. Don't go out shooting people, but any time, brothers and sisters, and especially the men in this audience—some of you wearing Congressional Medals of Honor, with shoulders this wide, chests this big, muscles that big—any time you and I sit around and read where they bomb a church and murder in cold blood, not some grownups, but four little girls while they were praying to the same god the white man taught them to pray to, and you and I see the government go down and can't find who did it.

Why, this man—he can find Eichmann hiding down in Argentina somewhere. Let two or three American soldiers, who are minding somebody else's business way over in South Vietnam, get killed, and he'll send battleships, sticking his nose in their business. He wanted to send troops down to Cuba and make them have what he calls free elections—this old cracker who doesn't have free elections in his own country. No, if you never see me another time in your life, if I die in the morning, I'll die saying one thing: the ballot or the bullet, the ballot or the bullet.

If a Negro in 1964 has to sit around and wait for some cracker senator to filibuster when it comes to the rights of black people, why, you and I should hang our heads in shame. You talk about a march on Washington in 1963, you haven't seen anything. There's some more going down in '64. And this time they're not going like they went last year. They're not going singing "We Shall Overcome." They're not going with white friends. They're not going with placards already painted for them. They're not going with round-trip tickets. They're going with one-way tickets.

And if they don't want that non-nonviolent army going down there, tell them to bring the filibuster to a halt. The black nationalists aren't going to wait. Lyndon B. Johnson is the head of the Democratic Party. If he's for civil rights, let him go into the Senate next week and declare himself. Let him go in there right now and declare himself. Let him go in there and denounce the Southern branch of his party. Let him go in there right now and take a moral stand—right now, not later. Tell him, don't wait until election time. If he waits too long, brothers and sisters, he will be responsible for letting a condition develop in this country which will create a climate that will bring seeds up out of the ground with vegetation on the end of them looking like something these people never dreamed of. In 1964, it's the ballot or the bullet. Thank you.

# Themes, Issues, and Ideas

1. What is Malcolm X's attitude toward government and society?

2. What is the point of the phrase "the ballot or the bullet?" Why does Malcolm X repeat it several times throughout this selection?

3. Has Malcolm X's apocolyptic vision come true? Why or why not?

# Writing Strategies and Techniques

1. This reading was taken from a speech. How can you tell that this selection was meant for oral recitation?

2. How does Malcolm X use rhythm to add drama and emphasis to his message? Give examples.

## Suggestions for Writing

1. Write an essay comparing Malcom X's perspective with what you know of Martin Luther King's.

2. Do you consider yourself an American? What do you hold as the minimum definition of an "American?"

# "What Then Is an American?"

## Ali Ahmad

*Ali Ahmad is the pen name of a writer living in Cincinnati, Ohio. He was born in 1964 in Miami, Florida and attended public schools and then the University of Miami. His writing has usually in the past been on politics and political science, but he has not, previous to the writing of this essay, ever discussed his homosexuality in the context of American civics. This essay was commissioned especially for this volume.*

I am an American. I am gay. And I am Pakistani.

Do these three things seem ill-matched? They seemed that way to me when I was growing up, but I have hope that as America is changing, they may seem less unrelated to each other than they once did. I certainly hope so. Having three discrete identities is difficult enough; when the three all seem to exclude each other, the tension can be unendurable.

I am Paki; my father and mother are from the Moslem nation of Pakistan, which makes me a first-generation American. I am gay, which flies directly in the face of my parent's religious beliefs, and by extension, the Paki culture from which they come. (Pakistan was created specifically as a Moslem nation in 1947.) And finally, I am American. But what does that mean? I don't think it means gay; and I am sure it does not mean Moslem. And yet, this last and most confusing definition is the only one which offers me a real sense of hope.

Can being an American somehow reconcile the other three elements of my identity? That my parents will never know of my sexual orientation, I have resigned myself to. And that, for better or worse, I will never be steeped in Paki culture the way they are is a fait accompli also. But I still can be 100% American. Not Paki-American. Not Gay American. But American.

Because this name, this citizenship, this right is my own. It might not be a blank page, but unlike Pakistan, there is room to rewrite it. Americans, as the political scientist Hans Kohn once observed, had to define themselves from the outset by abstract notions. The founding fathers were all Englishmen by heredity and culture; so the only way to define Americanism was to commit its essence to high principles.

America has redefined itself time and time again. "What then is the American, this new man?" asked Crevocoeur in colonial times. As we approach the millennium, the time has come for a new redefinition. One that includes me, and those like me. Other definitions, like Gay and Paki, may contradict each other; but the only way to contradict American identity is by denying such principles as I have embraced my whole life long: life, liberty, and the pursuit of happiness; all men (and women) are created equal; one person, one vote; and freedom of action, speech, identity, and lifestyle.

I know that considering myself American does not automatically make me so to all my fellow citizens. But with all due respect, that is their problem.

This does not seem to be a good time to be redefining what may constitute an American. It's easier now to predicate my citizenship on being a taxpayer than a believer in American principles. But as the new millennium rolls around, I have a feeling that the crusty old verities of the Yankee Doodles are fading away. There is something neurotic and self-conscious about the way they wave the flag. They remind me of someone.

Myself.

And as the new millennium approaches, and any remnants of the old consensus scatter to the four winds, I expect (or at least hope) that Americans will find themselves in the opposite predicament of the founding fathers: unable to forge national identity out of heredity or environment because of the very *diversity* of the nation. And I expect (or at least hope) that they will find the same answer: that of American principles, as fixed and immovable as the society built on them is flexible and mutable.

# Themes, Issues, and Ideas

1. What is Ahmad's definition of an "American"? Is that your definition also? Why or why not?

2. Why does Ahmad say that Americans "will find themselves in the opposite predicament of the founding fathers"?

3. What is your ethnic background(s)? Do your identity as an ethnic and as an American ever conflict? Explain your answer.

# Writing Strategies and Techniques

1. Although Ali Ahmad is writing about what, for him, is a very emotional issue, would you say his tone is emotional? How would you characterize it?

2. Why does Ahmad begin his essay the way he does? What are the effects on the reader of his first paragraph.

# Suggestions for Writing

1. Write a short essay outlining the essential arguments Ahmad is making and demonstrating their logic or illogic?

# The Arc of the Moral Universe Is Long, but It Bends Toward Justice

## Maya Angelou

*Maya Angelou is a poet, playwright, and author of several autobiographical works including* I Know Why the Caged Bird Sings *and* The Heart of a Woman. *President Clinton selected her to compose a poem for his inauguration, which she read at the ceremony in January of 1993. She is currently the Z. Smith Reynolds Professor of American Studies at Wake Forest University and continues to maintain a place as one of the most celebrated women in American letters.*

*This essay was taken from a special issue of* New Perspectives Quarterly, *in which a number of black intellectuals were asked to comment on the racial climate of our times.*

Look at two fragments of American history: Selma 1965 and Los Angeles 1991. After the successful Selma march, President Johnson and key congressional leaders assured Dr. Martin Luther King that a strong voting rights bill would be enacted quickly. But first, marchers had to suffer the infamous attack by the police and state troopers at the Edmund Pettus Bridge, and bear the murders of several of their fellow civil rights marchers.

In the 26 years that have passed since Selma, one salient step has been taken: American politicians are no longer attacking black America by supporting discriminatory laws or heinous crimes like lynching or other types of murder. Today, the number of politicians who openly attack blacks seems to have diminished.

This is an enormous change, particularly when one considers that the actions of politicians reflect the desires of the people. I agree with philosophers from Euripides to Locke who say that people deserve the leaders they have. Americans deserved the politicians that gave them the police and state troopers in Selma. And we must see hope in the fact that those photographs coming out of Selma—of the police dog leaping toward the genitalia of the young black man—horrified a nation and provoked a change. Americans could have heard about the police brutality in Selma and not been so moved, but seeing it really embarrassed a large portion of the population—not all, but a large portion.

That event changed America, and the politicians that refused to change were taken out of office.

## Visual Aid: Fighting our Invisibility

For the most part, white Americans before Selma were not unlike Germans during the 1930s—both could still turn their heads and pretend not to see what was going on in their country. Jews and blacks were invisible, beaten members of society. By the 1940s in Germany, however, I don't believe any German was unaware of what was happening. In the US, until as late as 1957, for the most part, blacks were invisible and the cruelties foisted upon them were absolutely ignorable. Whites who did not consider themselves prejudiced did not think anything of sitting in the front of the bus and seeing the majority of people standing in the back because they were black.

Blacks in the US are no longer invisible. They have emerged, though not always positively, into the vision of whites. I say "not always positively" in the sense that a number of whites now see blacks, but only as a threat to their safety or their jobs. But at least they see them.

The young man who captured the beating of Rodney King on videotape is an embryonic historian. He, like the photographers in Selma, helped keep our plight in view; helped us fight our invisibility. The bestiality captured on film has affected all who would like to claim themselves apart from those baton-wielding police.

Without the film, we might have been able to deny our own bestiality, but seeing it allowed us to face our barbarism and run from it; to seek shelter in the horror we felt viewing that scene; to come closer to our own humanity.

## Slow vs. Fast Temperament

There is a natural, slow temperament in the body of those who are not themselves being harassed, imprisoned, segregated or abused. And there is a rapid temperament which inhabits those who are aware of social and political discrepancies, whether those discrepancies affect their own conditions or not. The fact that people become heros and she-roes can be credited to their ability to identify and empathize with "the other." These men and women could continue to live quite comfortably with their slow temperament, but they chose not to. They make the decision to be conscious of the other—the homeless and the hopeless, the downtrodden and oppressed. Heroism has nothing to do with skin color or social status. It is a state of mind and a willingness to act for what is right and just.

If we don't say enough about these heroes—those who went before us and acted in a heartful way—our young people will be discouraged from trying to do what is right. It is important to claim as part of our heritage the good actions and the victories they engendered.

Young black men and women in this country must see and understand that there have been changes since Selma or they will be hell-bent on their own suicide mission. We must have an answer when they say, "you mean to tell me that with the sacrifice of Martin Luther King and Malcolm X and Medgar Evers there *still* have been no changes? Well, then why the hell am I fighting?"

To contend that there have been no changes is as stultifying and crippling as saying that racism no longer exists and that if you're suffering, it's your fault.

## An American Martyr

I sympathize with Rodney King. But I will say this: Someone had to be Rodney King. Someone had to force us to begin the next phase of our national morality play. We have always needed martyrs. I am just sorry it was Rodney King.

However, I will not go so far as to say that this incident will herald a new era of national introspection. Unfortunately, we Americans do high-wire walking much better than we engage in introspection. Yet the distinct and powerful stench this incident has released over our collective self-image will not diminish quickly. It might even have the power to hold some of our viciousness, our bestiality, in check for a while.

Rodney King's isn't a story of an individual American being denied basic human rights but the story of America. It is the story of black and white and Asian and native American. The violence, the secret, furtive, collective, cave-man, good-old-boy, sexual—not just sensual, but sexual—violence is America.

When one notes that 57 percent of the white residents of Los Angeles polled responded that they were in support of the Los Angeles chief of police, they were responding in self-defense. These whites were not saying they were *for* the beating; they were saying they were for their protector. There is a difference. Their answer indicates that they are afraid to give away their mercenary. And Chief Gates, for them, is their mercenary. He is the person they have entrusted to protect their streets, their homes. Their response has nothing to do with perfidy. It has everything to do with self-defense.

I have little hope for any splendid, rapid rapprochement between the races. There is a large percentage of middle-class blacks and whites who are able to speak enough of the same language to communicate and even love each other. However, I am sorry to say that the unworking and working class of both races have not had the advantages of learning the language that could afford them the possibility of exchanging dialogue. Those unworking and working-class whites who think all they have is their skin color—no future, no career, no pride in past, no pride in present—will find the back of a black man or woman to give them a boost up. And a black man who has seen no kindness from whites and no effort from whites and no effort to include him in the larger polity will say, "there's nothing a white man can do but show me how far below him the black man is." This is the beginning of silence; a long and dangerous silence.

# Themes, Issues, and Ideas

1. What do you think Angelou means by slow and fast temperaments? Is this phrase a descriptive one? What do "slow" and "fast" refer to?

2. Angelou says that "I am sorry to say the unworking and working class of both races have not had the advantages of learning the language that could afford them the possibility of exchanging dialogue."

What language is it that Angelou is thinking of? Do you accept her statement that miscommunication is at the heart of racism?

3. "The violence, the secret, furtive, collective, cave-man, good-old-boy, sexual—not just sensual, but sexual—violence is America." What does this phrase mean? What are its basic premises? Do you agree?

## Writing Strategies and Techniques

1. The title of this essay is long and poetic. Do you think it fits the subject? What might an alternative title be? Do you think this essay would be served better by a brief, succinct title, or by a long poetic one such as the one Angelou has given it?

2. Angelou credits photojournalism with making America aware of its "bestiality." Can prose such as Angelou's help to accomplish the same task? Why or why not? What are some other artistic styles that might accomplish this?

## Suggestions for Writing

1. Write an essay in which you discuss the same issues as Angelou, but from a different perspective and in a different style. Imagine that your essay will be appearing next to hers in a national magazine.

2. Compare Maya Angelou's perspective to Malcolm X's. Which do you find more appealing? Which more accurate?

# Mother Tongue

## Amy Tan

*As different races mix and collide in the American melting pot, one of the most important issues is bound to be language. Traditionally, English has been the first mode of assimilation for immigrants to America, and in his this reading Amy Tan describes some of the differences between first- and second-generation Chinese-American's use of English. Is there really only one English, the English of the SATs? Tan suggests otherwise in "Mother Tongue."*

*Tan, born in 1952, is the author of* The Joy Luck Club, The Kitchen God's Wife, *and other stories of Chinese-American life.*

I am not a scholar of English or literature. I cannot give you much more than personal opinions on the English language and its variations in this country or others.

I am a writer. And by that definition, I am someone who has always loved language. I am fascinated by language in daily life. I spend a great deal of my time thinking about the power of language—the way it can evoke an emotion, a visual image, a complex idea, or a simple truth. Language is the tool of my trade. And I use them all—all the Englishes I grew up with.

Recently, I was made keenly aware of the different Englishes I do use. I was giving a talk to a large group of people, the same talk I had already given to half a dozen other groups. The nature of the talk was about my writing, my life, and my book, *The Joy Luck Club*. The talk was going along well enough, until I remembered one major difference that made the whole talk sound wrong. My mother was in the room. And it was perhaps the first time she had heard me give a lengthy speech, using the kind of English I had never used with her. I was saying things like, "The intersection of memory upon imagination" and

103

"There is an aspect of my fiction that relates to thus-and-thus"—a speech filled with carefully wrought grammatical phrases, burdened, it suddenly seemed to me, with nominalized forms, past perfect tenses, conditional phrases, all the forms of standard English I did not use at home with my mother.

Just last week, I was walking down the street with my mother, and I again found myself conscious of the English I was using, the English I do use with her. We were talking about the price of new and used furniture and I heard myself saying this: "Not waste money that way." My husband was with us as well, and he didn't notice any switch in my English. And then I realized why. It's because over the twenty years we've been together I've often used that same kind of English with him, and sometimes he even uses it with me. It has become our language of intimacy, a different sort of English that relates to family talk, the language I grew up with.

So you'll have some idea of what this family talk I heard sounds like, I'll quote what my mother said during a recent conversation which I videotaped and then transcribed. During this conversation, my mother was talking about a political gangster in Shanghai who had the same last name as her family's, Du, and how the gangster in his early years wanted to be adopted by her family, which was rich by comparison. Later, the gangster became more powerful, far richer than my mother's family, and one day showed up at my mother's wedding to pay his respects. Here's what she said in part:

"Du Yusong having business like fruit stand. Like off the street kind. He is Du like Du Zong—but not Tsung-ming Island people. The local people call putong, the river east side, he belong to that side local people. That man want to ask Zu Dong father take him in like become own family. Du Zong father wasn't look down on him, but didn't take seriously, until that man big like become a mafia. Now important person, very hard to inviting him. Chinese way, came only to show respect, don't stay for dinner. Respect for making big celebration, he shows up. Mean gives lots of respect. Chinese custom. Chinese social life that way. If too important won't have to stay too long. He come to my wedding. I didn't see, I heard it. I gone to boy's side, they have YMCA dinner. Chinese age I was nineteen."

You should know that my mother's expressive command of English belies how much she actually understands. She reads the *Forbes* report, listens to *Wall Street Week,* converses daily with her stockbroker, reads all of Shirley MacLaine's books with ease—all kinds of things I can't begin to understand. Yet some of my friends tell me they understand 50 percent of what my mother says. Some say they understand 80 or 90 percent. Some say they understand none of it, as if she were speaking pure Chinese. But to me, my mother's English is perfectly clear, perfectly natural. It's my mother's tongue. Her language, as I hear it, is vivid, direct, full of observation and imagery. That was the language that helped shape the way I saw things, expressed things, made sense of the world.

Lately, I've been giving more thought to the kind of English my mother speaks. Like others, I have described it to people as "broken" or "fractured" English. But I wince when I say that. It has always bothered me that I can think of no other way to describe it other than "broken," as if it were damaged and needed to be fixed, as if it lacked a certain wholeness and soundness. I've heard other terms used, "limited English," for example. But they seem just as bad, as if everything is limited, including people's perceptions of the limited English speaker.

I know this for a fact, because when I was growing up, my mother's "limited" English limited *my* perception of her. I was ashamed of her English. I believed that her English reflected the quality of what she had to say. That is, because she expressed them imperfectly her thoughts were imperfect. And I had plenty of empirical evidence to support me: the fact that people in department stores, at banks, and at restaurants did not take her seriously, did not give her good service, pretended not to understand her, or even acted as if they did not hear her.

My mother has long realized the limitations of her English as well. When I was fifteen, she used to have me call people on the phone to pretend I was she. In this guise, I was forced to ask for information or even to complain and yell at people who had been rude to her. One time it was a call to her stockbroker in New York. She had cashed out her small portfolio and it just so happened we were going to go to New York the next week, our very first trip outside California. I had to get on the phone and say in an adolescent voice that was not very convincing, "This is Mrs. Tan."

And my mother was standing in the back whispering loudly, "Why he don't send me check, already two weeks late. So mad he lie to me, losing me money."

And then I said in perfect English, "Yes, I'm getting rather concerned. You had agreed to send the check two weeks ago, but it hasn't arrived."

Then she began to talk more loudly. "What he want, I come to New York tell him front of his boss, you cheating me?"And I was trying to calm her down, make her be quiet, while telling the stockbroker, "I can't tolerate any more excuses. If I don't receive the check immediately, I am going to have to speak to your manager when I'm in New York next week." And sure enough, the following week there we were in front of this astonished stockbroker, and I was sitting there red-faced and quiet, and my mother, the real Mrs. Tan, was shouting at his boss in her impeccable broken English.

We used a similar routine just five days ago, for a situation that was far less humorous. My mother had gone to the hospital for an appointment, to find out about a benign brain tumor a CAT scan had revealed a month ago. She said she had spoken very good English, her best English, no mistakes. Still, she said, the hospital did not apologize when they said they had lost the CAT scan and she had come for nothing. She said they did not seem to have any sympathy when she told them she was anxious to know the exact diagnosis, since her husband and son had both died of brain tumors. She said they would not give her any more information until the next time and she would have to make another appointment for that. So she said she would not leave until the doctor called her daughter. She wouldn't budge. And when the doctor finally called her daughter, me, who spoke in perfect English—lo and behold—we had assurances the CAT scan would be found, promises that a conference call on Monday would be held, and apologies for any suffering my mother had gone through for a most regrettable mistake.

I think my mother's English almost had an effect on limiting my possibilities in life as well. Sociologists and linguists probably will tell you that a person's developing language skills are more influenced by peers. But I do think that the language spoken in the family, especially in immigrant families which are more insular, plays a large role in shaping the language of the child. And I believe that it affected my results on achievement tests, IQ tests, and the SAT. While my English skills were never judged as poor, compared to math, English could not be considered my strong suit. In grade school I did moderately well, getting perhaps B's, sometimes B-pluses, in English and scoring perhaps in the sixtieth or seventieth percentile on achievement tests. But those scores were not good enough to override the opinion that my true abilities lay in math and science, because in those areas I achieved A's and scored in the ninetieth percentile or higher.

This was understandable. Math is precise; there is only one correct answer. Whereas, for me at least, the answers on English tests were always a judgment call, a matter of opinion and personal experience. Those tests were constructed around items like fill-in-the-blank sentence completion, such as, "Even though Tom was _____, Mary thought he was _____." And the correct answer always seemed to be the most bland combination of thoughts, for example, "Even though Tom was shy, Mary thought he was charming," with the grammatical structure "even though" limiting the correct answer to some sort of semantic opposites, so you wouldn't get answers like, "Even though Tom was foolish, Mary thought he was ridiculous." Well, according to my mother, there were very few limitations as to what Tom could have been and what Mary might have thought of him. So I never did well on tests like that.

The same was true with word analogies, pairs of words in which you were supposed to find some sort of logical, semantic relationship—for example, "*Sunset* is to *nightfall* as _____ is to _____." And here you would be presented with a list of four possible pairs, one of which showed the same kind of relationship: *red* is to *stoplight, bus* is to *arrival, chills* is to *fever, yawn* is to *boring.* Well, I could never think that way. I knew what the tests were asking, but I could not block out of my mind the images already created by the first pair, "*sunset* is to *nightfall*"—and I would see a burst of colors against a darkening sky, the moon rising, the lowering of a curtain of stars. And all the other pairs of words—red, bus, stoplight, boring—just threw up a mass of confusing images, making it impossible for me to sort out something as logical as saying: "A sunset precedes nightfall" is the same as "a chill precedes a fever." The only way I would have gotten that answer right would have been to imagine an associative situation, for example, my being disobedient and staying out past sunset, catching a chill at night, which turns into feverish pneumonia as punishment, which indeed did happen to me.

I have been thinking about all this lately, about my mother's English, about achievement tests. Because lately I've been asked, as a writer, why there are not more Asian Americans represented in American literature. Why are there few Asian Americans enrolled in creative writing programs? Why do so many Chinese students go into engineering? Well, these are broad sociological questions I can't begin to answer. But I have noticed in surveys—in fact, just last week—that Asian students, as a whole, always do significantly better on math achievement tests than in English. And this makes me think that there are other Asian-American students whose English spoken in the home might also be described as "broken" or "limited." And perhaps they also have teachers who are steering them away from writing and into math and science, which is what happened to me.

Fortunately, I happen to be rebellious in nature and enjoy the challenge of disproving assumptions made about me. I became an English major my first year in college, after being enrolled as pre-med. I started writing nonfiction as a freelancer the week after I was told by my former boss that writing was my worst skill and I should hone my talents toward account management.

But it wasn't until 1985 that I finally began to write fiction. And at first I wrote using what I thought to be wittily crafted sentences, sentences that would finally prove I had mastery over the English language. Here's an example from the first draft of a story that later made its way into *The Joy Luck Club,* but without this line: "That was my mental quandary in its nascent state." A terrible line, which I can barely pronounce.

Fortunately, for reasons I won't get into today, I later decided I should envision a reader for the stories I would write. And the reader I decided upon was my mother, because these were stories about mothers. So with this reader in mind—and in fact she did read my early drafts—I began to write stories using all the Englishes I grew up with: the English I spoke to my mother, which for lack of a better term might be described as "simple"; the English she used with me, which for lack of a better term might be described as "broken"; my translation of her Chinese, which could certainly be described as "watered down"; and what I imagined to be her translation of her Chinese if she could speak in perfect English, her internal language, and for that I sought to preserve the essence, but neither an English nor a Chinese structure. I wanted to capture what language ability tests can never reveal: her intent, her passion, her imagery, the rhythms of her speech and the nature of her thoughts.

Apart from what any critic had to say about my writing, I knew I had succeeded where it counted when my mother finished reading my book and gave me her verdict: "So easy to read."

# Themes, Issues, and Ideas

1. Why does Tan think of her mother as a model reader? Do you think of a family member as a model reader? Do you have any model reader at all?

2. How many different kinds of English do you use in your daily life? What are the different strengths and weaknesses of these Englishes?

3. Is Tan's mother's English really as rich as Tan maintains, or is she being merely loyal and sentimental? Support your opinion with specific examples from the text and your own experience.

# Writing Strategies and Techniques

1. Why does Tan begin the way she does? Is her opening statement borne out by her essay? Describe the effect her prose has on her argument.

2. Describe the use of humor in "Mother Tongue."

# Suggestions for Writing

1. Write an essay about a friend or relative of yours who speaks in "broken" or "diluted" English.

2. Rewrite Tan's mother's story in three separate types of English, such as academic/intellectual English, "deadhead" English, black English, etc.

# Barrio Boy

## Ernesto Galarza

*Part of the ethnic identity comes from the areas immigrants live in: The more concentrated and isolated the area, the more cultural barriers arise. In "Barrio Boy," Ernesto Galarza describes what it was like to live in the Sacramento* barrio, *or ghetto, where he grew up.*

*Galarza graduated from Stanford and Columbia Universities in 1944, and then spent many years as a union organizer fighting for the rights of migrant workers. He taught elementary school and established some of the earliest programs in bilingual education. He published his autobiography in 1971, from which this reading is taken.*

We found Americans as strange in their customs as they probably found us. Immediately we discovered that there were no *mercados* and that when shopping you did not put the groceries in a *chiquihuite.* Instead everything was in cans or in cardboard boxes or each item was put in a brown paper bag. There were neighborhood grocery stores at the corners and some big ones uptown, but no *mercado.* The grocers did not give children a *pilón,* they did not stand at the door and coax you to come in and buy, as they did in Mazatlàn. The fruits and vegetables were displayed on counters instead of being piled up on the floor. The stores smelled of fly spray and oiled floors, not of fresh pineapple and limes.

Neither was there a plaza, only parks which had no bandstands, no concerts every Thursday, no Judases exploding on Holy Week, and no promenades of boys going one way and girls the other. There were no parks in the *barrio;* and the ones uptown were cold and rainy in winter, and in summer there was no place to sit except on the grass. When there were celebrations nobody set off rockets in the parks, much less on the street in front of your house to announce to the neighborhood that a wedding or a baptism was taking place. Sacramento did not have a *mercado* and a plaza with the cathedral to one side and the Palacio de Gobierno on another to make it obvious that there and nowhere else was the center of town.

It was just as puzzling that the Americans did not live in *vecindades,* like our block on Leandro Valle. Even in the alleys, where people knew one another better, the houses were fenced apart, without central courts to wash clothes, talk and play with the other children. Like the city, the Sacramento *barrio* did not have a place which was the middle of things for everyone.

In more personal ways we had to get used to the Americans. They did not listen if you did not speak loudly, as they always did. In the Mexican style, people would know that you were enjoying their jokes tremendously if you merely smiled and shook a little, as if you were trying to swallow your mirth. In the American style there was little difference between a laugh and a roar, and until you got used to them you could hardly tell whether the boisterous Americans were roaring mad or roaring happy. . . .

The older people of the *barrio,* except in those things which they had to do like the Americans because they had no choice, remained Mexican. Their language at home was Spanish. They were continuously taking up collections to pay somebody's funeral expenses or to help someone who had had a serious accident. Cards were sent to you to attend a burial where you would throw a handful of dirt on top of the coffin and listen to tearful speeches at the graveside. At every baptism a new *compadre* and a new *comadre* joined the family circle. New Year greeting cards were exchanged, showing angels and cherubs in bright colors sprinkled with grains of mica so that they glistened like gold dust. At the family parties the huge pot of steaming tamales was still the center of attention, the *atole* served on the side with chunks of brown sugar for sucking and crunching. If the party lasted long enough, someone produced a guitar, the men took over and the singing of *corridos* began.

In the *barrio* there were no individuals who had official titles or who were otherwise recognized by everybody as important people. The reason must have been that there was no place in the public business of the city of Sacramento for the Mexican immigrants. We only rented a corner of the city and as long as we paid the rent on time everything else was decided at City Hall or the County Court House, where Mexicans went only when they were in trouble. Nobody from the *barrio* ever ran for mayor or city councilman. For us the most important public officials were the policemen who walked their beats, stopped fights, and hauled drunks to jail in a paddy wagon we called *La Julia.*

The one institution we had that gave the *colonia* some kind of image was the *Comisión Honorífica,* a committee picked by the Mexican Consul in San Francisco to organize the celebration of the *Cinco de Mayo* and the Sixteenth of September, the anniversaries of the battle of Puebla and the beginning of our War of Independence. These were the two events which stirred everyone in the *barrio,* for what we were celebrating was not only the heroes of Mexico but also the feeling that we were still Mexicans ourselves. On these occasions there was a dance preceded by speeches and a concert. For both the *cinco* and the sixteenth queens were elected to preside over the ceremonies.

Between celebrations neither the politicians uptown nor the *Comisión Honorífica* attended to the daily needs of the *barrio.* This was done by volunteers—the ones who knew enough English to interpret in court, on a visit to the doctor, a call at the county hospital, and who could help make out a postal money order. By the time I had finished the third grade at the Lincoln School I was one of these volunteers. My services were not professional but they were free, except for the IOU's I accumulated from families who always thanked me with "God will pay you for it."

My clients were not *pochos,* Mexicans who had grown up in California, probably had even been born in the United States. They had learned to speak English of sorts and could still speak Spanish, also of sorts. They knew much more about the Americans than we did, and much less about us. The *chicanos* and the *pochos* had certain feelings about one another. Concerning the *pochos,* the *chicanos* suspected that they considered themselves too good for the *barrio* but were not, for some reason, good enough for the Americans. Toward the *chicanos,* the *pochos* acted superior, amused at our confusions but not especially interested in explaining them to us. In our family when I forgot my manners, my mother would ask me if I was turning *pochito.*

Turning *pocho* was a half-step toward turning American. And America was all around us, in and out of the *barrio.* Abruptly we had to forget the ways of shopping in a *mercado* and learn those of shopping in a corner grocery or in a department store. The Americans paid no attention to the Sixteenth of September, but they made a great commotion about the Fourth of July. In Mazatlàn Don Salvador had told us, saluting and marching as he talked to our class, that the *Cinco de Mayo* was the most glorious date in human history. The Americans had not even heard about it.

## Themes, Issues, and Ideas

1. What are some of the differences between Mazatlàn and Sacramento? How do the physical differences between the two cities reveal their differing cultural values?

2. Why do residents of the *barrio* feel isolated and alienated from the American culture around them?

3. What is the difference between *chicanos* and *pochos*? What seems to be the relationship between the two groups? What about the relationship between each group and the native Sacramentoans?

## Writing Strategies and Techniques

1. How do you feel about the narrator of this essay? Is his a sympathetic voice? Give examples to support your view.

2. Galarza uses the words "we" and "they" very often throughout his essay. To which group does he seem to assume his reader belongs?

## Suggestions for Writing

1. Write an essay about an experience in your childhood comparable to one in Galarza's. Have you ever experienced a cultural dislocation?

2. Respond to the implicit accusation that ends the essay.

# Tribes and Tribulations

## Jennifer Juarez Robles

*Jennifer Juarez Robles was born in 1957 in Emporia, Kansas. After graduating from the University of Kansas in 1986, she became an editorial writer for the* Minneapolis Star-Tribune, *writing about urban affairs and issues involving race and poverty. Of her desire to write this piece, which originally appeared in 1992 in the gay journal* The Advocate, *she says, "it had to do with the 500th anniversary of Columbus's arrival to the New World. It put to light the treatment of indigenous peoples by the Europeans, and how that struggle continues to this day. The religious element of the conquest tore apart Indian culture, and made gay people separate in a way they were not before. That is an element of Columbus's legacy."*

Like all such civic events, this year's Columbus Day parade in Chicago was led by a phalanx of community leaders, government officials, and political candidates. And, in keeping with the country's anti-incumbent mood, the huge crowd lining the route booed and jeered as soon as they saw the familiar faces. But when the onlookers spied the next parade entry, they fell silent.

Pressured by activists and politicians, parade organizers had invited the local American Indian Center to march in the event commemorating Columbus's stumbling upon Indian lands 500 years ago. And the indigenous delegation—small and proud—marched unsmilingly the full route.

It was a curious sight, and the group's participation was a bit of an anomaly in terms of Native American response to Columbus Day this year. But in its way it symbolized the diversity of responses to the quincentennial among American Indian groups—responses nearly as varied as Native American attitudes toward native gays. This year gay men and lesbians in the native community were integral to the October protests throughout the nation. In San Francisco, for example, a prominent American Indian lesbian community leader was the kickoff speaker at the city's main demonstration.

Native groups declared this year a time of unity across tribal and state boundaries and even across differences of sexual orientation. Benito Torres, spokesman for the League of Indigenous Sovereign Nations, an international native rights organization, says that in his group's demonstration at the United Nations building in New York, "there were gay groups working together with us from the beginning. I'm sure there were other gay and lesbian people who were present and in solidarity. We're all in the same boat."

For many Native Americans, this seemed only natural. By tradition, some Native American tribes have accorded positions of spiritual leadership to "two spirits"—the indigenous term for gays, meaning people with male and female spirits. For others, especially those who have experienced Native American homophobia in rural areas and on reservations, these anti-Columbus collaborations served as a sign of hope that they may yet have a place as open gays in their ethnic communities.

"All our people have been greatly involved in quincentennial efforts working side by side, but you won't see a banner that says GAY AND LESBIAN," says Angukcuaq (also known as Richard LaFortune), a two-spirit activist and director of training at the National Native American AIDS Prevention Center in Oakland, Calif. "Gay and lesbian Native Americans are doing quiet work within our communities because the communities are very homophobic."

Curtis Harris, a member of WeWah and BarCheAmpe, a New York two-spirit group, is more blunt. "In terms of educating the native community, we have a long way to go," he says. "There were factions of Native American groups [at Columbus Day demonstrations] who excluded our involvement. We know that many of the folks involved in these organizations have been virulently homophobic in the past. I find that oftentimes as a gay Indian man I'm rebuffed by Native Americans."

Angukcuaq says that because many Native Americans experience a mixture of both traditional values and Anglo teachings, attitudes toward gays and lesbians may be widely divergent from one community to the next. "There are men and women who are cross-dressing and

raising children and occupying positions of power, and everyone knows
about it," he explains. "There are 500 discrete native nations and cultures on this continent. There are many common denominators, and
there are many differences. It's going to be harder in redneck Wisconsin
to be openly two-spirit on a reservation. It depends on the community
and the pressure for assimilation."

U.S. representative Ben Nighthorse Campbell (D-Colo.), the only
Native American in Congress, has found his cosponsorship of the federal gay rights bill to be controversial among Native American constit-
uents. Campbell's support is unusual: Three of the most prominent
native civil rights groups—the American Indian Movement's International Indian Treaty Council, the Native American Rights Fund, and the
National Congress of American Indians, which represents about 25%
of the Indian and native Alaskan population—have no policy statement
on gay rights.

Campbell spokeswoman Carol Knight says the representative
"has taken some heat from tribal leaders who oppose gay rights,"
which, she says, is often based on ignorance about AIDS. "I'd venture
to guess that gay Native Americans are just now experiencing the backlash that white gay males felt in the early 1980s. We see a lot of hostil-
ity toward gay natives because of AIDS."

In an August meeting of the Navajo Nation council in Window
Rock, Ariz., Larry Curley, executive director of Navajo Nation health
services, drew fire when he proposed quarantining people with AIDS to
protect the general Navajo population, citing the Cuban policy of forcing people with HIV, the virus believed to lead to AIDS, to live in
restricted areas. Curley later retracted his comments under pressure
from the president of the Navajo Nation, which is one of the largest
tribal nations in the United States, comprising 200,000 people.

Melvin Harrison, president of the Navajo Nation AIDS Network,
a nonprofit educational and lobbying group, says, "Curley's comments
raised consciousness about AIDS and got people talking about the
issues. We still have a lot of work to be done. There's still a lot of denial
and bigotry out there."

Probably the most difficult place for Native Americans to be
openly gay is on reservations in rural areas. Susan Beaver, a Mohawk
lesbian who is executive director of Two-Spirited People of the First
Nations, a Toronto support and education group, testified in June about
discrimination on reservations before the Royal Commission on
Aboriginal Peoples, a Canadian government council. "We often grow

up without a language to describe ourselves: *Lesbian, gay,* or *queer* are used as curses and insults," Beaver said. "With the influence of the church and Europeans, two spirit is a tradition pushed so far away, only a few remember it, and even fewer honor it.

"Women are expected to marry a man or suffer the consequences of our willfulness," Beaver continued. "Two-spirited men know there is no room for their lives on the reserve. Your sexuality is not tolerated, and many men leave to find urban centers where they can express themselves. Many men live a dual life: Bisexuality on the reserve is more common than many think. If you are strong enough to be who you are, you are ridiculed, harassed, and only sometimes understood as again being 'different.' "

Tom Ledo, a Tlingit and Filipino gay man, knows firsthand the danger on reservations. Though openly gay in his job as HIV coordinator for San Diego's Indian Health Council, he isn't open about his sexuality when he visits reservations, about 50 miles north of San Diego.

"I've had tribal leaders tell me that they don't appreciate being around 'faggots,' " says Ledo, who heads the San Diego group Two-Spirited Nations of the Four Directions. "They tell me that if [gays] got AIDS, they deserve it. I'm outspoken about queer issues outside the reservation. But to be effective in my work, I need to talk to people about AIDS and their behavior. That's my priority. I try to work on their homophobia, but it's very hard."

"Unfortunately, there is a lot of hatred and ignorance about AIDS and two-spirited people," adds Avis Little Eagle, associate editor of the Rapid City, S. D., paper *Indian Country Today,* formerly the *Lakota Times.* Little Eagle concedes that many tribal leaders, particularly those in rural areas, often refuse to believe that homosexuality exists among their people. "They say they don't have any homosexuals in their tribes because they are traditional people," says Little Eagle. "We are from more isolated communities, so [gay issues] haven't hit us except in isolated incidents."

One of the incidents that Little Eagle recalls is the murder last fall of a gay man on the Pine Ridge reservation in southwestern South Dakota. Patrick Red Elk, a 30-year-old member of the Oglala tribe, was attacked on the reservation by three men who beat him with a football helmet and kicked him to death. The attackers were convicted of second-degree murder and sent to federal prison.

Assistant attorney general Robert Mandel, who handled the Pine Ridge case, remembers another assault there a few years ago in which two men attacked a gay man, fracturing his jaw. The assailants were convicted and sent to prison.

Mandel points out that the number of assaults generally on the reservation, where more than 15,000 people live, is significantly higher than that of South Dakota on the whole. "We get many assaults and murders there," he says, estimating that his office, which handles the Pine Ridge reservation exclusively, prosecutes about a hundred felonies per year.

"I have no doubt that there is violence and gay bashing on reservations," says Angukcuaq. "When you have a whole generation of people raised in Catholic boarding schools and you have homophobia inculcated in the community, then you put those people on reservations—which are very close-knit—there is going to be violence. Our people are being taught today that it's OK to beat up gays and lesbians.

"But violence on reservations and in urban communities is not confined to gay, lesbian, and bisexual people," Angukcuaq adds. "We cannot escape the violence."

Ironically, antigay attitudes aren't traditional, many two-spirit people argue. "Before, in our culture, two-spirited people were respected and honored, not ridiculed," says Little Eagle. "It's new now to see the younger generation ridicule gay people. Actually, it's foreign to our nation."

"In most native cultures, gay men and lesbians held positions as healers, visionaries, and teachers," explains Beaver. "They were the doctors and lawyers of native societies before the Europeans came. Tolerance used to be indigenous to our culture. We try to reclaim, against opposition from our own people, that we were the holy people, the special people."

In the clash between traditional acceptance and homophobia, many two spirits hope to lead tribal nations to greater cooperation and unity, seeing their role as a conduit of traditional Indian values.

"I've gone to the White River Apache reservation in Arizona to speak about homophobia," says Erna Pahe, a member of Gay American Indians, a San Francisco group, and the vice chair of the city's Board of Urban Indian Health. "They need Indians to go there and educate people. We have to tell them that we can't just throw away our kids if they're two-spirit. We can't afford to throw them off the reservations.

"Two spirits need to speak up and talk about ourselves," urges Pahe, who grew up on Navajo and Apache reservations in Arizona. "We can't afford to let the younger generation grow up thinking there's a group of people—two spirits—who don't know who they are or don't have anything to offer the tribe. That's the only way our people will understand. Two spirits have something to offer our people."

## Themes, Issues, and Ideas

1. There is a long history of problems facing Native Americans. Does Robles address these problems? What is not said—but implied—in her essay that a foreigner might miss?

2. According to some of the sources Robles quotes, "two spirits" were revered by many tribes. Do all of Robles's sources agree? How would you describe the range of opinion here about "two spirits?"

3. Gay people in white American society face many of the same problems as the gay Native Americans Robles describes. What do you think are the differences in the problems the two groups face?

## Writing Strategies and Techniques

1. Although this piece involves a great deal of reportage, it is clearly not "objective" journalism. How does the fact that it is written for a magazine called *The Advocate* inform its readers?

2. Robles uses the Native American entry in a Columbus Day parade to begin her story. How is this anecdote meaningful? Can you think of a better opening?

## Suggestions for Writing

1. Every ethnic group has a different attitude toward gays. Write an essay describing your own group's response. If you are Native American, write an essay responding to Robles's article.

2. Write an essay in which you take the view of one of the people in the piece who is described as being antigay. Discuss some of the problems you face as a heterosexual Native American. Try to keep the voice sane and sympathetic; don't impersonate a bigot.

# America as a Collage

## Ryzsard Kapuscinski

*Ryzsard Kapuscinski has spent most of the post–World War II years reporting on war and revolution in Africa, the Middle East, and Latin America. He has written a trilogy on dictators that covers Haile Selassi I of Ethiopia, Idi Amin of Uganda, and the last Shah of Iran. Being away from the United States frequently and being acquainted with social, ethnic, and racial conflicts in many cultures has given Kapuscinski a broader perspective on the social pressures facing the United States in the future. In this essay, commissioned by* The New Perspectives Quarterly, *Kapuscinski finds the changing composition of the American melting pot not a source of social problems but a sign of positive future and of the continuing vitality of the democratic experiment represented by the people and the government of the United States.*

T he mere fact that America still attracts millions of people is evidence that it is not in decline. People aren't attracted to a place of decline. Signs of decline are sure to be found in a place as complex as America: debt, crime, the homeless, drugs, dropouts. But the main characteristic of America, the first and most enduring impression, is dynamism, energy, aggressiveness, forward movement.

It is so hard to think of this nation in decline when you know that there are vast regions of the planet which are absolutely paralyzed, incapable of any improvement at all.

It is difficult for me to agree with Paul Kennedy's thesis in *The Rise and Fall of Great Powers* that America must inevitably follow historical precedent. That's the way history used to be—all powerful nations declined and gave way to other empires. But maybe there is another way to look at what is happening. I have a sense that what is going on here concerns much more than the fate of a nation.

It may be that the Euro-centered American nation is declining as it gives way to a new Pacific civilization that will include, but not be limited to, America. Historically speaking, America may not decline, but instead fuse with the Pacific culture to create a kind of vast Pacific collage, a mix of Hispanic and Asian cultures linked through the most modern communication technologies.

Traditional history has been a history of nations. But here, for the first time since the Roman Empire, there is the possibility of creating the history of a civilization. Now is the first chance on a new basis with new technologies to create a civilization of unprecedented openness and pluralism. A civilization of the polycentric mind. A civilization that leaves behind forever the ethnocentric, tribal mentality. The mentality of destruction.

Los Angeles is a premonition of this new civilization.

Linked more to the Third World and Asia than to the Europe of America's racial and cultural roots, Los Angeles and southern California will enter the twenty-first century as a multiracial and multicultural society. This is absolutely new. There is no previous example of a civilization that is being simultaneously created by so many races, nationalities, and cultures. This new type of cultural pluralism is completely unknown in the history of mankind.

America is becoming more plural every day because of the unbelievable facility of the new Third World immigrants to put a piece of their original culture inside of American culture. The notion of a "dominant" American culture is changing every moment. It is incredible coming to America to find you are somewhere else—in Seoul, in Taipei, in Mexico City. You can travel inside this Korean culture right on the streets of Los Angeles. Inhabitants of this vast city become internal tourists in the place of their own residence.

There are large communities of Laotians, Vietnamese, Cambodians, Mexicans, Salvadorans, Guatemalans, Iranians, Japanese, Koreans, Armenians, Chinese. We find here Little Taipei, Little Saigon, Little Tokyo, Koreatown, Little Central America, the Iranian neighborhood in Westwood, the Armenian community in Hollywood, and the vast Mexican-American areas of East Los Angeles. Eighty-one languages, few of them European, are spoken in the elementary school system of the city of Los Angeles.

This transformation of American culture anticipates the general trend in the composition of mankind. Ninety percent of the immigrants to this city are from the Third World. At the beginning of the twenty-first century, 90 percent of the world's population will be dark-skinned; the white race will be no more than 11 percent of all human beings living on our planet.

Something that can only be seen in America: In the manicured, landscaped, ultraclean high-technology parks of northern Orange County there is a personal computer company that seven years ago did not exist. There were only strawberry fields where the plant is. Now, there is a $500 million company with factories in Hong Kong and Taiwan as well.

The company was founded by three young immigrants—a Pakistani Muslim and two Chinese from Hong Kong. They only became citizens in 1984. Each individual is now probably worth $30 million.

Walking through this company we see only young, dark faces—Vietnamese, Cambodians, Laotians, Mexicans—and the most advanced technology. The culture of the work force is a mix of Hispanic-Catholic family values and Asian-Confucian group loyalty. Employment notices are never posted; hiring is done through the network of families that live in southern California. Not infrequently, employees ask to work an extra twenty hours a week to earn enough money to help members of their extended family buy their first home.

In Los Angeles, traditional Third World cultures are, for the first time, fusing with the most modern mentalities and technologies.

After decades of covering war and revolution in the Third World, I carry in my mind an image of crowds, tension, crisis. My experience has always been of social activity that leads to destruction, to trouble, to unhappiness. People are always trying to do something, but they are unable to. The intentions of people trying to make revolution are just and good, but suddenly, something goes wrong. There is disorganization, unending problems. The weight of the past. They cannot fulfill their objectives.

Usually, the contact between developed and underdeveloped worlds has the character of exploitation—just taking people's labor and resources and giving them nothing. And the border between races has usually been a border of tension, of crisis. Here we see a revolution that is constructive.

This Pacific Rim civilization being created is a new relationship between development and underdevelopment. Here, there is openness. There is hope. And a future. There is a multicultural crowd. But it is not fighting. It is cooperating, peacefully competing, building. For the first time in four hundred years of relations between the nonwhite Western world and the white Western world, the general character of the relationship is cooperation and construction, not exploitation, not destruction.

Unlike any other place on the planet, Los Angeles shows us the potential of development once the Third World mentality merges with an open sense of possibility, a culture of organization, a Western conception of time.

For the destructive, paralyzed world where I have spent most of my life, it is important, simply, that such a possibility as Los Angeles exists.

To adjust the concept of time is the most difficult thing. It is a key revolution of development.

Western culture is a culture of arithmetical time. Time is organized by the clock. In non-Western culture, time is a measure between events. We arrange a meeting at nine o'clock but the man doesn't show up. We become anxious, offended. He doesn't understand our anxiety because for him, the moment he arrives is the measure of time. He is on time when he arrives.

In 1924, the Mexican philosopher José Vasconcelos wrote a book entitled *La Raza Cosmica*. He dreamt of the possibility that, in the future, mankind would create one human race, a *mestizo* race. All races on the planet would merge into one type of man. *La raza cosmica* is being borne in Los Angeles, in the cultural sense if not the anthropological sense. A vast mosaic of different races, cultures, religions, and moral habits are working toward one common aim. From the perspective of a world submerged in religious, ethnic and racial conflict, this harmonious cooperation is something unbelievable. It is truly striking.

What is the common aim that harmonizes competing cultures in one place?

It is not only the better living standard. What attracts immigrants to America is the essential characteristic of American culture: the chance to try. There is a combination of two things that are important: culture and space. The culture allows you to try to be somebody—to find yourself, your place, your status. And there is space not only in a geographical sense, but in the sense of opportunity, of social mobility. In societies that are in crisis and in societies which are stagnant—or even in those which are stable—there is no chance to try. You are defined in advance. Destiny has already sentenced you.

Other countries, even if they are open like Great Britain or France, don't have this dynamic of development. There is no space for development. This is what unites the diverse races and cultures in America. If the immigrant to America at first fails, he always thinks, "I will try again." If he had failed in the old society, he would be discouraged and pessimistic, accepting the place that was given to him. In America, he's thinking, "I will have another chance, I will try again." That keeps him going. He's full of hope.

## Themes, Issues, and Ideas

1. Kapuscinski says that traditional history is the history of nations. What does he see as different about history in the future and how does he see America as uniquely suited to that future?

2. According to the author, Los Angeles is a symbol of the future. How does your knowledge of the Los Angeles riots of 1992, which took place after this essay was written, affect your reading of Kapuscinski's ideas?

3. How and why does the author distinguish between the social problems of other countries and those of the United States?

## Writing Strategies and Techniques

1. The author talks about large and complex issues in a causal and informal style. How is that style achieved? Point to some techniques; for example, word choice.

2. Los Angeles becomes a symbol of the future in the essay. What other symbols does the author evoke and what do they stand for?

# Suggestions for Writing

1.  Do you think it likely that the America of the future will be more influenced by Asia than by Europe? Write an essay in which you defend or disagree with the author on this issue.

2.  Pick something other than a city that symbolizes the American future for you. Using Kapuscinski's essay as a model, sketch out your views.

# MAKING CONNECTIONS

1.  Malcolm X has a much more direct style of addressing the issue of race than the more elevated perspective of Maya Angelou. Which is more appealing on an emotional level? Which on a practical level? Which on a political level? Explain your answer.

2.  What are some differences between Amy Tan's and Ali Ahmad's writing styles? How do some of these differences help or hinder each writer's argument?

3.  What are some of the differences and similarities between the different ethnic groups represented in this chapter—for example, between Malcolm X or Amy Tan's attitude toward assimilation, and Ali Ahmad and Maya Angelou's?

4.  Which do you find more suited to addressing the problem of racial inequality: an anecdotal essay like Amy Tan's or Ernesto Galarza's, or an ideological essay like Maya Angelou's? Why?

5.  After reading these selections, do you feel more optimistic or pessimistic about race relations in the twenty-first century? Explain your answer.

# CHAPTER FOUR

## *American Education for the Twenty-first Century*

*The Academy and the Workplace*

# Learning to Read and Write

## Frederick Douglass

*Frederick Douglass was the name chosen for himself by Frederick Augustus Washington Bailey, a slave on the eastern shore of Maryland who escaped his bondage and went on to become the first black abolitionist of national renown. His autobiography of 1845,* The Narrative of the Life of Frederick Douglass, an American Slave, *is one of the classics of world literature and reflects a mind whose intelligence and compassion, along with his shocking first-hand experience of slavery, combined to excite the imagination of Northern readers in the years before the Civil War. Before he could accomplish its writing, however, Douglass had to learn to read and write himself, in a place where such knowledge was forbidden to him. In the following selection from his autobiography, Douglass describes this struggle.*

I lived in Master Hugh's family about seven years. During this time, I succeeded in learning to read and write. In accomplishing this, I was compelled to resort to various stratagems. I had no regular teacher. My mistress, who had kindly commenced to instruct me, had, in compliance with the advice and direction of her husband, not only ceased to instruct, but had set her face against my being instructed by any one else. It is due, however, to my mistress to say of her, that she did not adopt this course of treatment immediately. She at first lacked the depravity indispensable to shutting me up in mental darkness. It was at least necessary for her to have some training in the exercise of irresponsible power, to make her equal to the task of treating me as though I were a brute.

My mistress was, as I have said, a kind and tender-hearted woman; and in the simplicity of her soul she commenced, when I first went to live with her, to treat me as she supposed one human being ought to treat another. In entering upon the duties of a slaveholder, she did not seem to perceive that I sustained to her the relation of a mere chattel, and that for her to treat me as a human being was not only wrong, but dangerously so. Slavery proved as injurious to her as it did to me. When I went there, she was a pious, warm, and tenderhearted woman. There was no sorrow or suffering for which she had not a tear. She had bread for the hungry, clothes for the naked, and comfort for every mourner that came within her reach. Slavery soon proved its ability to divest her of these heavenly qualities. Under its influence, the tender heart became stone, and the lamblike disposition gave way to one of tiger-like fierceness. The first step in her downward course was in her ceasing to instruct me. She now commenced to practise her husband's precepts. She finally became even more violent in her opposition than her husband himself. She was not satisfied with simply doing as well as he had commanded; she seemed anxious to do better. Nothing seemed to make her more angry than to see me with a newspaper. She seemed to think that here lay the danger. I have had her rush at me with a face made up of fury, and snatch from me a newspaper, in a manner that fully revealed her apprehension. She was an apt woman; and a little experience soon demonstrated, to her satisfaction, that education and slavery were incompatible with each other.

From this time I was most narrowly watched. If I was in a separate room any considerable length of time, I was sure to be suspected of having a book, and was at once called to give an account of myself. All this, however, was too late. The first step had been taken. Mistress, in teaching me the alphabet, had given me the *inch,* and no precaution could prevent me from taking the *ell.*

The plan which I adopted, and the one by which I was most successful, was that of making friends of all the little white boys whom I met in the street. As many of these as I could, I converted into teachers. With their kindly aid, obtained at different times and in different places, I finally succeeded in learning to read. When I was sent on errands, I always took my book with me, and by going one part of my errand quickly, I found time to get a lesson before my return. I used also to carry bread with me, enough of which was always in the house, and to which I was always welcome; for I was much better off in this regard than many of the poor white children in our neighborhood. This bread I used to bestow upon the hungry little urchins, who, in return, would give me that more valuable bread of knowledge. I am strongly tempted to give the names of two or three of those little boys, as a testimonial of the gratitude and affection I bear them; but prudence forbids;—not that it would injure me, but it might embarrass them; for it is almost an unpardonable offence to teach slaves to read in this Christian country. It is enough to say of the dear little fellows, that they lived on Philpot Street, very near Durgin and Bailey's ship-yard. I used to talk this matter of slavery over with them. I would sometimes say to them, I wished I could be as free as they would be when they got to be men. "You will be free as soon as you are twenty-one, *but I am a slave for life!* Have not I as good a right to be free as you have?" These words used to trouble them; they would express for me the liveliest sympathy, and console me with the hope that something would occur by which I might be free.

I was now about twelve years old, and the thought of being a *slave for life* began to bear heavily upon my heart. Just about this time, I got hold of a book entitled "The Columbian Orator." Every opportunity I got, I used to read this book. Among much of other interesting matter, I found in it a dialogue between a master and his slave. The slave was represented as having run away from his master three times. The dialogue represented the conversation which took place between them, when the slave was retaken the third time. In this dialogue, the whole argument in behalf of slavery was brought forward by the master, all of which was disposed of by the slave. The slave was made to say some very smart as well as impressive things in reply to his master—things which had the desired though unexpected effect; for the conversation resulted in the voluntary emancipation of the slave on the part of the master.

In the same book, I met with one of Sheridan's mighty speeches on and in behalf of Catholic emancipation: These were choice documents to me. I read them over and over again with unabated interest. They gave tongue to interesting thoughts of my own soul, which had frequently flashed through my mind, and died away for want of utterance. The moral which I gamed from the dialogue was the power of truth over the conscience of even a slaveholder. What I got from Sheridan was a bold denunciation of slavery, and a powerful vindication of human rights. The reading of these documents enabled me to utter my thoughts, and to meet the arguments brought forward to sustain slavery; but while they relieved me of one difficulty, they brought on another even more painful than the one of which I was relieved. The more I read, the more I was led to abhor and detest my enslavers. I could regard them in no other light than a band of successful robbers, who had left their homes, and gone to Africa, and stolen us from our homes, and in a strange land reduced us to slavery. I loathed them as being the meanest as well as the most wicked of men. As I read and contemplated the subject, behold! that very discontentment which Master Hugh had predicted would follow my learning to read had already come, to torment and sting my soul to unutterable anguish. As I writhed under it, I would at times feel that learning to read had been a curse rather than a blessing. It had given me a view of my wretched condition, without the remedy. It opened my eyes to the horrible pit, but to no ladder upon which to get out. In moments of agony, I envied my fellow-slaves for their stupidity. I have often wished myself a beast. I preferred the condition of the meanest reptile to my own. Any thing, no matter what, to get rid of thinking! It was this everlasting thinking of my condition that tormented me. There was no getting rid of it. It was pressed upon me by every object within sight or hearing, animate or inanimate. The silver trump of freedom had roused my soul to eternal wakefulness. Freedom now appeared, to disappear no more forever. It was heard in every sound, and seen in every thing. It was ever present to torment me with a sense of my wretched condition. I saw nothing without seeing it, I heard nothing without hearing it, and felt nothing without feeling it. It looked from every star, it smiled in every calm, breathed in every wind, and moved in every storm.

I often found myself regretting my own existence, and wishing myself dead; and but for the hope of being free, I have no doubt but that I should have killed myself, or done something for which I should have been killed. While in this state of mind, I was eager to hear any one speak of slavery. I was a ready listener. Every little while, I could hear something about the abolitionists. It was some time before I found what the word meant. It was always used in such connections as to make it an interesting word to me. If a slave ran away and succeeded in getting clear, or if a slave killed his master, set fire to a barn, or did any thing very wrong in the mind of a slaveholder, it was spoken of as the fruit of *abolition.* Hearing the word in this connection very often, I set about learning what it meant. The dictionary afforded me little or no help. I found it was "the act of abolishing"; but then I did not know what was to be abolished. Here I was perplexed. I did not dare to ask any one about its meaning, for I was satisfied that it was something they wanted me to know very little about. After a patient waiting, I got one of our city papers, containing an account of the number of petitions from the north, praying for the abolition of slavery in the District of Columbia, and of the slave trade between the States. From this time I understood the words *abolition* and *abolitionist,* and always drew near when that word was spoken, expecting to hear something of importance to myself and fellow-slaves. The light broke in upon me by degrees. I went one day down on the wharf of Mr. Waters; and seeing two Irishmen unloading a scow of stone, I went, unasked, and helped them. When we had finished, one of them came to me and asked me if I were a slave. I told him I was. He asked, "Are ye a slave for life?" I told him that I was. The good Irishman seemed to be deeply affected by the statement. He said to the other that it was a pity so fine a little fellow as myself should be a slave for life. He said it was a shame to hold me. They both advised me to run away to the north; that I should find friends there, and that I should be free. I pretended not to be interested in what they said, and treated them as if I did not understand them; for I feared they might be treacherous. White men have been known to encourage slaves to escape, and then, to get the reward, catch them and return them to their masters. I was afraid that these seemingly good men might use me so; but I nevertheless remembered their advice, and from that time I resolved to run away. I looked forward to a time at which it would be safe for me to escape. I was too young to think of doing so immediately; besides, I wished to learn how to write, as I might have occasion to write my own pass. I consoled myself with the hope that I should one day find a good chance. Meanwhile, I would learn to write.

The idea as to how I might learn to write was suggested to me by being in Durgin and Bailey's ship-yard, and frequently seeing the ship carpenters, after hewing, and getting a piece of timber ready for use, write on the timber the name of that part of the ship for which it was intended. When a piece of timber was intended for the larboard side, it would be marked thus—"L." When a piece was for the starboard side, it would be marked thus—"S." A piece for the larboard side forward, would be marked thus—"L. F." When a piece was for starboard side forward, it would be marked thus.—"S. F." For larboard aft, it would be marked thus—"L. A." For starboard aft, it would be marked thus—"S. A." I soon learned the names of these letters, and for what they were intended when placed upon a piece of timber in the ship-yard. I immediately commenced copying them, and in a short time was able to make the four letters named. After that, when I met with any boy who I knew could write, I would tell him I could write as well as he. The next word would be, "I don't believe you. Let me see you try it." I would then make the letters which I had been so fortunate as to learn, and ask him to beat that. In this way I got a good many lessons in writing, which it is quite possible I should never have gotten in any other way. During this time, my copy-book was the board fence, brick wall, and pavement; my pen and ink was a lump of chalk. With these, I learned mainly how to write. I then commenced and continued copying the Italics in Webster's Spelling Book, until I could make them all without looking on the book. By this time, my little Master Thomas had gone to school, and learned how to write, and had written over a number of copy-books. These had been brought home, and shown to some of our near neighbors, and then laid aside. My mistress used to go to class meeting at the Wilk Street meetinghouse every Monday afternoon, and leave me to take care of the house. When left thus, I used to spend the time in writing in the spaces left in Master Thomas's copy-book, copying what he had written. I continued to do this until I could write a hand very similar to that of Master Thomas. Thus, after a long, tedious effort for years, I finally succeeded in learning how to write.

# Themes, Issues, and Ideas

1. Douglass describes, midway through the selection, the unhappiness his brush with literacy caused him. Does this surprise you? Why or why not?

2. What seems to be Douglass' estimation of Master Hughes' wife? Does she seem more or less wicked than some of the other people in

the selection? Why does Douglass discuss her character to the extent he does?

3. Does the way in which Douglass learned to read and write have anything in common with the way you did? What do the differences and the similarities tell you?

## Writing Strategies and Techniques

1. Douglass frequently employs an ironic tone, e.g., "She at first lacked the depravity indispensable to shutting me up in mental darkness." Why does he do so? What is the effect on the reader?

2. To what extent are Douglass' arguments about slavery inserted into the tale of how he came to read and write?

## Suggestions for Writing

1. Write an essay in which you describe a way in which you could learn to read and write in circumstances like Douglass'.

2. Write an essay describing the kind of person Douglass seems to be, based on your reading of this selection. Use examples from the text to illustrate your observations.

# Telelearning: The Multimedia Revolution in Education

## William E. Halal and Jay Leibowitz

*As computer, fax, and other communications technologies have exploded in recent years, many educators have wondered how they will affect the classroom—an establishment basically unchanged since the beginning of the century. In this essay originally published in* The Futurist, *William E. Halal and Jay Leibowitz, two professors at George Washington University, suggest some of the ways in which "multimedia" may change the way we learn.*

In a complex world of constant change, where knowledge becomes obsolete every few years, education can no longer be something that one acquires during youth to serve for an entire lifetime. Rather, education must focus on instilling the ability to continue learning throughout life. Fortunately, the information-technology revolution is creating a new form of electronic, interactive education that should blossom into a lifelong learning system that allows almost anyone to learn almost anything from anywhere at anytime.

The key technology in future education is interactive multimedia—a powerful combination of earlier technologies that constitutes an extraordinary advance in the capability of machines to assist the educational process. Interactive multimedia combines computer hardware, software, and peripheral equipment to provide a rich mixture of text, graphics, sound, animation, full-motion video, data, and other information. Although multimedia has been technically feasible for many years, only recently has it become a major focus for commercial development.

Interactive multimedia systems can serve a variety of purposes, but their great power resides in highly sophisticated software that employs scientifically based educational methods to guide the student through a path of instruction individually tailored to suit the special needs of each person. As instruction progresses and intelligent systems are used, the system learns about the student's strengths and weaknesses and then uses this knowledge to make the learning experience fit the needs of that particular student. Interactive multimedia has several key advantages:

- Students receive training when and where they need it. An instructor does not have to be present, so students can select the time best suited to their personal schedules.

- Students can adjourn training at any point in the lesson and return to it later.

- The training is highly effective because it is based on the most-powerful principles of individualized learning. Students find the program interesting, so they stick with it. Retention of the material learned is excellent.

- The same videodisc equipment can be used to support a variety of training paths.

- Both the training and the testing are objectively and efficiently measured and tracked.

Educational systems of this type, offered by IBM under the product label *Ultimedia,* engage students in an interactive learning experience that mixes color movies, bold graphics, music, voice narration, and text; for instance, the program *Columbus* allows students to relive the great navigator's voyages and explore the New World as it looked when Columbus first saw it. The ability to control the learning experience makes the student an active rather than passive learner.

Other common systems include *Sim City, Carmen Sandiego,* and a variety of popular multimedia games created by Broderbund Software, one of the biggest companies in this new field. Rather than the old "drill and kill" forms of computerized instruction that bore students, this new form of "edutainment" is far more effective precisely because kids get totally immersed in an exciting learning experience. "They get so worked up they can hardly stand it," says the parent of a 4-year-old. "It's beyond question a more effective way to learn," says Warren Buckleit, a former teacher who is now editor of *Children's Software Revue*. "The computer gives control back to the kids."

A similar revolution is under way in training aimed at upgrading employee skills for more-complex, changing jobs. Literally millions of people are being trained quickly, effectively, and inexpensively using multimedia systems at companies such as Hewlett-Packard, Apple, Chrysler, Shell, Xerox, and Ford, as well as the U.S. government. "Multimedia is the preferred method of training," says Nancy Kenworthy at the International Training Company. Today these systems can often be accessed by employees through their own PCs, and they should eventually be constantly available from anywhere when an individual or group feels the need for some type of knowledge, instruction, and other form of help. The concept has been called "just-in-time learning."

Studies of these programs show that learning time is shortened by 50%, retention is increased by 80%, and costs are cut in half. Hewlett-Packard has used this approach to eliminate 90% of its former classroom training and Apple Computer has reduced its classroom training by 75%. The corresponding savings are so vast that most corporations should soon follow suit. "We aim to get [classroom instruction] down to zero as soon as the technology is ready," says Lucy Carter, a training director at Apple.

Classroom training will always be needed for some things, of course, but interactive multimedia training should become the common method for teaching employees how to use an organization's systems, acquire the skills needed to handle a new job, and brush up on the latest management methods.

Information networks will undoubtedly be built to provide multimedia instruction for schools and colleges around the world. Of course, these developments will require resolving difficult issues of bandwidth, cost feasibility, establishing common standards, and other complex issues. For example, compression and decompression techniques and standards for full-motion video still need to be developed. But the wholesale movement of America's largest corporations into this breach is a clear signal that multimedia is destined to find its way into society before the year 2000, and education will be a prime application.

## Knowledge-Based Systems

To make electronic education a reality, knowledge-based systems will be essential. A knowledge system is a computer program containing a body of knowledge and heuristics (rules based on the experience of an expert) that assist in understanding some field of study. A knowledge system can be thought of as an elementary form of artificial intelligence. Without knowledge systems, multimedia would be merely dumb though colorful presentations used strictly for entertainment.

Knowledge-based systems are developing rapidly, and in a decade or so they should be commonly used in elementary and secondary schools. Interactive videodisc technology is already being used to teach history, geography, science, and other subjects. Knowledge-based systems could be linked with videodisc technology to enhance classroom instruction by tutoring students. For example, an expert system could be constructed to conduct simulated chemistry experiments via videodisc technology to demonstrate the analytical process. An intelligent tutoring system can adjust its instruction to suit a student's level of understanding. Intelligent tutors are now used in teaching foreign languages, geography, and other subjects.

Intelligent tutoring systems should become common in schools soon after the year 2000 as supplements to teachers' instruction. Students will be able to explore almost any topic through richly detailed, fascinating arrays of intelligent multimedia computer programs, almost as if a wise scholar guided each student individually through the intricacies of the world.

Multimedia instructional systems are becoming powerful, user-friendly, and cheap— while schools, governments, and corporations are looking for better ways to educate people. So it is easy to envision these systems finding wide use in learning situations that occur throughout life: teaching well-defined subjects such as languages, math, and science; guiding technicians and mechanics through complex jobs; helping surgeons learn new operations; acting as automated sales offices where customers can get information; occupying registration booths where college students can conveniently register for classes; and performing countless other information-handling tasks. Already, the Marriott Corporation has installed kiosks at eight universities to interest graduating students in joining the company: An interactive program informs the student about the firm, outlines various career opportunities and salaries, and answers any questions they may have.

## Distance Learning

Interactive multimedia and knowledge-based systems offer great promise for conducting education over long distances. One application is home schooling. (About 1 million U.S. children now are being educated at home, compared with 49 million in public and private schools through the twelfth grade.) Personal computers, educational compact discs, on-line databases, and networks will make home schooling increasingly effective. The beneficiaries will include not simply those children whose parents opt for year-round home schooling, but also those who are homebound due to illness or bad weather and those with special learning needs that cannot be met in their school. The technologies can also be used to augment normal school education, somewhat like homework assignments.

Advances in telecommunications are also facilitating distance learning for adults who want to broaden their education by hooking up and tuning in to college degree programs. Adult distance learners typically receive college lectures via laptop computer and satellite or cable TV. Many universities are using distance learning quite effectively now, and the trend is growing dramatically. As more adults return to school and as middle managers get shuffled around in the turmoil of business restructuring, distance learning is a valuable alternative that should help these individuals pursue new career paths.

These technologies also fit in nicely with the rapid emergence of collaborative learning and group problem solving. "Groupware"—the use of information networks to form various group decision support systems—is poised to explode because it offers a convenient, powerful new form of working together in modern organizations. *Lotus Notes,* for instance, is now being used by several million employees who work together at a distance on consensus building, brainstorming, technical tasks, writing reports, or any other type of teamwork. As time moves on, the growth of networking will facilitate the wide use of these methods for collaborative working relationships of any type around the globe, forming a new type of organization that has been called the "virtual corporation."

Many people are rightly concerned that electronically mediated education will lack the human touch that is essential for true understanding. "There's no substitute for that immediate dialogue that occurs in a classroom," says Linda Pratt, professor of English at the University of Nebraska. Most of these concerns are normal, but unwarranted, fears concerning such a radically different mode of instruction. Anyone who has participated in computer conferencing or other interactive media knows that the intensity of relationships can be astounding. Even religious services are now commonly held over computer bulletin boards, and participants usually find the experience *more* profoundly spiritual than services in a church or temple!

As this technology improves, the "bandwidth" of clear, accurate, vivid information transmitted through electronic education should expand greatly to include almost all of the subtle visual and tonal cues that we rely on for communication. And, of course, few people would want to use telelearning alone for important matters such as understanding a difficult academic subject, so they will also seek out personal contacts to augment electronic education. Teachers will always play an essential role, but that role is changing to focus on the more-complex issues in learning that machines cannot deal with. Distance learning can be viewed as a vast increase in the range of instruction, permitting especially gifted lecturers to reach an almost limitless number of students around the world, while other teachers give the students individual assistance.

## The University of the Future

In the near future, ordinary PCs will be able to vividly explain and show students the answer to a question in full-motion, talking, color videographics instead of simple written text. Personal digital assistants will become book-sized electronic companions for communicating, computing, and performing endless other tasks. Keyboards will be replaced with voice-recognition systems, and language translation will be computerized. Virtual reality will eventually allow one to enter any world imaginable. Screens won't be just the size of a desk, but an entire wall, so images will become life-size. Miniaturization of hardware will continue to reduce the size of information technology such that powerful systems will be cheap and small enough to put in a pocket. Already, one can buy a briefcase that incorporates a computer, printer, fax, copier, and telephone, permitting instantaneous contact from anywhere.

If we hope to accommodate this flood of information that is now beginning to pour forth, universities will be forced to become far more electronic than ever before. However, the emphasis will change: "A primary focus for information technology...over the last decade was automating university administrative functions," said a 1992 report from the Higher Education Information Resources Alliance, a group of five professional university information associations. "The focus for the next decade will be on making strategic investments to improve academic productivity."

A major concern of the wired university should be electronic publication of scholarly journals, a cherished goal of researchers because it speeds the distribution of knowledge and reduces costs. Publishers, however, have been slow to embrace the concept because they are concerned that users would easily pirate copies of protected works using computer technology. But these issues will be resolved as methods are improved to protect information and to automatically charge users for their access to an electronic publication.

Journals are already being electronically transmitted to a limited extent, and this trend will continue. Harvard University has embarked on an eight-year, $20-million project to convert its books and journals to computerized storage. Elsevier Science Publishers is experimenting to make its journals available over computer networks. TULIP (The University Licensing Program) is believed to be the first attempt to provide published, copyrighted materials over the Internet. By roughly the year 2000, electronic scholarly journals are likely to be common, with hard copies being used for archival purposes.

As these trends reach a peak about the year 2000, universities may finally realize the enormous untapped potential of the information-technology revolution. Today's typical college classroom is archaic: The only thing that distinguishes it from the classroom of the medieval university is an overhead projector. In a decade or so, electronic, wired universities will likely be competing to tap the best minds around the world for ideas and knowledge, which will then be distributed to students, corporations, and other clients. Excellent professors might become international celebrities, sought after in a world that prizes understanding; conversely, students would have access to the wealth of knowledge growing exponentially as the Information Age gains speed.

## Caution Signs on the Electronic Highway

There is an inevitable downside to every technology, and one wonders what it will be for electronic education. Will students find themselves struggling with dumb machines to acquire knowledge once easily learned from caring teachers? Consider the battle now required to get an answer to some simple question from organizations that use automated touchtone answer systems. Will the sanctity of the classroom be lost as people get their instruction from distant locations over impersonal networks? Will disadvantaged members of society who cannot afford multimedia become an underclass of information have-nots?

Difficult questions of this type will rise as electronic education becomes dominant in all sectors of society over the coming years, so we should think carefully about how we want to use this powerful technology. What precautions and alternatives should be considered to avoid the dangers as the technologies race ahead?

Future developments are almost certain to surprise us to some extent. However, a few major features about the future of education are fairly clear:

First, it seems likely that educational institutions must be restructured to suit the different imperatives of an era that focuses on learning to learn. Just as business did not benefit from computerization until corporations were reengineered, education needs to be redesigned as well. "We're not going to see computers teaching kids until we restructure and reengineer the institution," says Michael Kirst former president of the California Board of Education and a professor at Stanford University.

Today's wave of interest in educational "choice" is rolling on in public schools because the entrepreneurial features of a market system are needed to provide the flexibility required by the Information Age. Students will then have to choose from various options to obtain the type of schooling they prefer or need. Adults may find distance learning more convenient, and some youngsters will use telelearning at home exclusively; others may prefer a more traditional education at a school or college campus, and many will want to supplement a campus approach with interactive multimedia and intelligent tutoring systems in their homes.

Whatever the form of education people choose and whatever the method of instruction, clearly the type of schools that educated youngsters in the past will soon be gone forever. For better or worse, an age of constant, turbulent change lies ahead, making continuous learning and scientific discovery a central challenge of modern societies. Education has not been one of the more powerful institutions in life, but schools may now gain increasing influence as they assume these greater responsibilities.

The key to unlocking the new possibilities is to envision modern education as an omnipresent activity. As the technology for acquiring and distributing knowledge permeates home, work, and all other locations, all social functions should be integrated into a seamless web of learning. Everyday living will then take place in an electronic school without walls.

## Themes, Issues, and Ideas

1. Does the idea of "telelearning" appeal to you? Do you think it would help your education? What is the relationship between the two above questions?

2. Find three places in the text where the conclusion does not necessarily follow from the premises.

3. What are some arguments you might make for education not being an "omnipresent . . . seamless web of learning"?

## Writing Strategies and Techniques

1. Describe the tone that Halal and Leibowitz take. Do they strike you as balanced in their judgment? Does their argument for telelearning raise any doubts in your mind? Give examples.

2. How do quotations function in this essay?

## Suggestions for Writing

1. Write an essay in which you take Halal and Leibowitz's argument to a ludicrous extreme.

2. Write a day in the life of a future student, as envisioned by Halal and Leibowitz.

# Will America Choose High Skills or Low Wages?

## Ira Magaziner and Hillary Rodham Clinton

*Ira Magaziner, at the time this essay was written, was president of SJS Inc., a public policy consulting firm. As this book goes to press, he is President Clinton's senior policy advisor on domestic affairs. Hillary Rodham Clinton, of course, is the wife of the current President of the United States as well as a long-time advocate of progressive public policy. In this proposal, Magaziner and Clinton point out some of the shortcomings of our current labor policy and go on to explain how they may be remedied. "High-performance" workers are the key, they claim, and the sooner we can produce a better, more highly motivated, highly skilled work force the sooner we will be able to compete with our international rivals.*

During the past two decades, the United States has watched as Singapore, Taiwan, and Korea grew from run-down Third World outposts to world premier exporters; as Germany, with one quarter of our population, almost equaled us in exports; as Japan became the world's economic juggernaut. During these transformations, America became the world's biggest borrower.

We have heard the excuses: The countries we beat in World War II are simply regaining their former places in the world. The Europeans and the Japanese are exploiting their low wages. Our competitors are class-ridden countries.

The truth is otherwise: Our former adversaries are doing far better in relation to us than they did before the war. A dozen nations now pay wages above ours. Our distribution of income is more skewed than any of our major competitors, and our poverty rate is much higher.

Our education statistics are as disappointing as our trade statistics. Our children rank at the bottom on most international tests—behind children in Europe and East Asia. Again, we heard the excuses: They have elite systems, but we educate everyone. They compare a small number of their best to our much larger average. The facts are otherwise: Many of the countries with the highest test scores have more of their students in school than we do.

We are not facing the facts about our future. What we are facing is an economic cliff—and the frontline working people of America are about to fall off.

## A Drop in Productivity

From the 1950s to the 1970s, America's productivity grew at a healthy pace. The nation was getting richer, and workers lived better on what they earned. Since then, the rate of increase in productivity has dropped dramatically. The distribution of income in the United States has been worsening. Those with college degrees are prospering, but frontline workers have seen the buying power of their paychecks shrink year after year. Since 1969, real average weekly earnings in the United States have fallen by more than 12 percent. And, during the past two decades, our productivity growth has slowed to a crawl. It now takes nearly three years to achieve the same productivity improvement we used to achieve in one year.

If productivity continues to falter, we can expect one of two futures. Either the top 30 percent of our population will grow wealthier while the bottom 70 percent becomes progressively poorer, or we all slide into relative poverty together.

If we are to avert catastrophe, we must make drastic improvements in our rate of productivity growth. But we cannot grow simply by putting more people to work. We must grow by having every American worker produce more. If we do not, our incomes will go into a free-fall with no end in sight.

## Going High Performance

We must work more productively and be more competitive. We cannot do this simply by using better machinery, because low-wage countries can use the same machines and still sell their products more cheaply than we can. Nor can we continue to organize work by breaking complex jobs into myriad simple rote tasks, because the world's best companies now use new high-performance work organizations, unleashing major advances in productivity, quality, variety, and speed of new product introductions.

Because most American employers organize work in a way that does not require high skills, they foresee no shortage of people who have such skills. With some exceptions, the education and skill levels of American workers roughly match the demands of their jobs. But if we want to compete more effectively in the global economy, we will have to move to high-performance work organizations.

To do this we must mobilize our most vital asset, the skills of our people—not just the skills of the 30 percent who will graduate with baccalaureate degrees from college, but those of the frontline workers—the bank tellers, farm workers, truck drivers, retail clerks, data entry operators, laborers, and factory workers.

We can do this only by reorganizing the way we work in our stores and factories, in our warehouses, insurance offices, government agencies, and hospitals. We can give our frontline workers much more responsibility, educate them well, and train them to do more highly skilled jobs.

If we do this, we can streamline work. We will need fewer supervisors, fewer quality checkers, fewer production schedulers, and fewer maintenance people, so organizations will become more efficient. Because they will be more efficient, they will be able to sell more. Because they will sell more, they can expand. Because they can expand, they can employ more people. Although each operation will require fewer people, society as a whole can increase employment and wages can go up.

## The Commission on the Skills of the American Workforce

With hopes of steering a new course for the U.S. before we face a crisis, the Commission on the Skills of the American Workforce came together in June 1989 to analyze the interplay between economic trends and population dynamics. The Commission included a research team of 23 loaned executives from companies, unions, industry associations, and the U.S. Department of Labor.

The team probed into several industries both in the United States and abroad and concentrated on major markets of several states. In total, the team interviewed more than 2,000 people at 550 firms and agencies and analyzed many government and private reports.

The Commission's findings on American industry, labor policy, and education pointed in one direction: Americans are unwittingly making a choice that most of us would not make were we aware of its consequences. It is a choice that will lead to an America where over 70 percent of our people will see their dreams slip away.

This choice is being made by companies that cut wages to remain competitive. It is being made by public school officials who fail to prepare our children to be productive workers. Ultimately, we are all making the choice by silently accepting this course.

We still have time to make the other choice, one that will lead us to a more prosperous future: we can opt for high skills rather than low wages. But to make this choice we must fundamentally change our approach to work and education.

## Problems and Solutions

The Commission set out to both identify the problems America faces and recommend feasible solutions. Based on its research, the Commission made several key recommendations for an education and training system.

*Problem 1:* Two factors stand in the way of producing a highly educated work force—we lack a clear standard of achievement and few students are motivated to work hard in school. One reason that students going right to work after school have little motivation to study hard is that they see little or no relationship between how well they do in school and what kind of job they can get after school.

*Recommendation:* A new educational performance standard should be set for all students, to be met at or around age 16. This standard should be established nationally and benchmarked to the highest in the world.

Students passing a series of performance-based assessments that incorporate this new standard would be awarded a Certificate of Initial Mastery. Possession of the certificate would qualify the student to choose among going to work, entering a college preparatory program, or studying for a Technological and Professional Certificate, described below.

*Problem 2:* More than 20 percent of our students drop out of high school—almost 50 percent in many of our inner cities. These dropouts go on to make up more than a third of our frontline work force. Turning our backs on those dropouts, as we do now, is tantamount to turning our backs on our future work force.

*Recommendation:* The states should take responsibility for assuring that virtually all students achieve the Certificate of Initial Mastery. Through new local employment and training boards, states, with federal assistance, should create and fund alternative learning environments for those who cannot attain the Certificate of Initial Mastery in regular schools.

All students should be guaranteed the educational attention necessary to attain the Certificate of Initial Mastery by age 16, or as soon as possible thereafter. Youth Centers should be established to enroll school dropouts and help them reach that standard.

*Problem 3:* Other industrial nations have multiyear career-oriented educational programs that prepare students to operate at a professional level in the workplace. America prepares only a tiny fraction of its non-college bound students for work. As a result, most flounder in the labor market, moving from low-paying job to low-paying job until their mid-20s, never being seriously trained.

*Recommendation:* A comprehensive system of technical and professional certificates should be created for students and adult workers who do not pursue a baccalaureate degree.

Technical and professional certificates would be offered across the entire range of service and manufacturing occupations. A student could earn the entry-level occupation certificate after completing a two- to four-year program of combined work and study. A sequence of advanced certificates could be obtained throughout one's career.

National committees of business, labor, education, and public representatives should be convened to define certification standards for two- to four-year programs of professional preparation in a broad range of occupations. These programs should combine general education with specific occupational skills and should include a significant work component.

*Problem 4:* The vast majority of American employers are not moving to high-performance work organizations, nor are they investing in training their nonmanagerial employees for these new forms of work organization. The movement to high-performance work organizations is more widespread in other nations, and training of frontline workers is commonplace.

*Recommendation:* We propose a system whereby all employers will invest at least 1 percent of their payroll for the education and training of their workers. We further recommend that public technical assistance be provided to companies, particularly small businesses, to assist them in moving to higher-performance work organizations.

*Problem 5:* The United States is not well organized to provide the highly skilled workers needed to support the emerging high-performance work organizations. The training system is fragmented with respect to policies, administration, and service delivery.

*Recommendation:* A system of employment and training boards should be established by federal and state governments, together with local leadership, to organize and oversee the new school-to-work transition programs and training systems.

We envision a new, more comprehensive system where skills development and upgrading for the majority of our workers becomes a central aim of public policy. The key to accomplishing these goals is finding a way to enable the leaders of our communities to take responsibility for building a comprehensive system that meets their needs. The local employment and training boards would serve as the vehicles for oversight and management of training and school-to-work transition programs, Youth Centers, and job information services.

## Implementing America's Choice

Since the release of the report in June 1990, the Commission has promoted awareness of the report's recommendations through speeches and briefing sessions with educators, business and labor leaders, government officials, and advocacy groups. As the report's findings have been disseminated, interest in implementing its recommendations has become widespread.

On the national level, key members of Congress, both Democrats and Republicans, have introduced the High Skills, Competitive Workforce Act of 1991 based on the Commission's recommendations. Without creating a needless new bureaucracy, this legislation (H.R. 3470 and S. 1790) goes a long way toward ensuring that U.S. businesses will remain competitive in the global marketplace and that American workers will continue to enjoy a high standard of living. The act supports national education and job-skill standards benchmarked to world-class standards. It provides grants to local communities to establish Youth Opportunity Centers aimed at bringing high school dropouts back into the education system to ensure that they, too, meet world-class standards. And the bill provides technical assistance to employers to help them train their frontline workers and make the shift to high-performance work organizations. To finance the training, the bill requires employers to invest at least 1 percent of payroll in training frontline workers or contribute to a national trust fund earmarked for training.

More than 20 states have expressed an interest in working with the Commission on implementation strategies. Oregon, Washington, New York, and Minnesota have already created legislative initiatives to implement the Commission's recommendations. And education groups are moving to do the same.

## New Standards for the Schools

Key national groups, including the President's Advisory Committee on Education, the governing board of the National Assessment of Educational Progress, and the National Education Goals Panel, have begun to advocate the development of an examination system consistent with the creation of a Certificate of Initial Mastery.

And recently, President Bush, in his education initiative, "America 2000," announced the development of a national examination system for the nation's K-12 school system. Numerous groups, including the New Standards Project, a partnership of the National Center on Education and the Economy and the Learning Research and Development Center of the University of Pittsburgh, have begun to develop a new student performance assessment system, putting into place the first steps to making this new system a reality.

## Recovering Our Dropouts

It will do no good to raise academic standards for school leavers if large numbers of high school students cannot meet them. The idea of Youth Centers, the Commission's strategy for recovering school dropouts and bringing them up to a high academic standard, is an essential component of the whole strategy for national human resource development.

The Commission is working closely with the William T. Grant Foundation's Commission on Work, Family, and Citizenship and others to develop a national network of Youth Centers. A bill has been submitted to the New York State legislature to create Youth Centers in that state. The Commission is also working to make information available to other states on the characteristics of successful alternative education programs for dropouts.

## Preparing Frontline Workers

Most employers in this country have never been seriously involved in setting industry standards for entry-level employment and have no established mechanisms for doing so. Neither do they have a tradition of offering formal, multiyear, on-the-job training programs to high school graduates.

Efforts are currently under way to change American employer attitudes and practices toward work force education. The U.S. Departments of Labor and Education are focusing on work force training and vocational education. The Department of Labor's Commission on Work-Based Learning serves as an advisory commission on workplace training and high-performance work organization.

The Commission on the Skills of the American Workforce plans to work with industry associations and key national business organizations to develop certification standards for their industries. This past summer, the Commission participated with the National Governor's Association and the National Council on Vocational Education in an NGA-sponsored conference on new forms of technical and professional preparation programs.

## Reorganizing Work

Setting standards must go hand-in-glove with a strategy to reorganize work. Under current forms of work organization, employers do not demand highly skilled workers. It is unlikely that this country will do what must be done about workers' skills unless there is a strong demand from business and industry for people with those skills. That will not happen until employers see the need to embrace high-performance forms of work organization.

The Commission has met with national business groups to begin a concerted campaign to promote an understanding of high-performance work organization. Plans are under way to develop an industry-led technical assistance network to help companies make the transition. Some companies will have the international resources to develop the necessary training programs to upgrade worker skills, while others will need outside consultation.

## Building a Comprehensive System

Without a coherent labor market system that embraces national, state, and local government, the Commission's other recommendations will be less effective. Therefore, the Commission has put forth a legislative proposal that we believe is a first step toward uniting disparate pieces of the nation's existing labor market programs. In addition, we plan to publish papers on the elements of the system we believe should be put in place—from postsecondary data systems to a reborn employment service. Then, we hope to convene a working group of state, federal, and national government leaders with business, labor, and education leaders to begin discussions in implementation.

## Leaping Ahead

The system we propose provides a uniquely American solution. Boldly executed, it has the potential not simply to put us on an equal footing with our competitors, but to allow us to leap ahead, to build the world's premier work force. In doing so, we will create a formidable competitive advantage.

The status quo is not an option. The choice is between becoming a nation of high skills or one of low wages. The choice is ours. It should be clear. It must be made.

## Themes, Issues, and Ideas

1. The logic of this essay is very tight, but does it allow for many obstacles? What stumbling blocks other than the ones mentioned might prevent American companies from adopting the authors' plan?

2. According to Magaziner and Clinton, by training its workers better and paying them more, America can turn its labor force around. Do you think this is true based on your own experience? Explain.

3. Is this essay directed only toward businesspeople, or does it have any importance for college students such as yourself? Explain your answer.

## Writing Strategies and Techniques

1. What can you say about the style that Magaziner and Clinton use? Does it fit the subject matter? Why do you think it was chosen by the authors?

2. The authors of this essay talk about training "frontline" workers better. Why do you think they use this term? What images does it suggest?

## Suggestions for Writing

1. Write a proposal for lower wages, written in as close an imitation of Magaziner and Clinton's style as you can manage.

2. Write an essay discussing the differences between abstract policy and actual reform, using this essay as an example.

# The Future of Work

## Robert B. Reich

*This essay provides a detailed survey on the future of those activities that your education will presumably prepare you for. Some occupations will expand in the future, others will almost disappear. Reich lays out the costs and benefits that each general career area provides. One drawback to planning, as the author establishes early in the essay, is that what is best known is what one should definitely not do to prepare for the work of tomorrow.*

*Reich wrote this essay for* Harper's *magazine while he was a professor of Political Economy at the John F. Kennedy School of Government at Harvard University. He is currently the U.S. Secretary of Labor.*

It's easy to predict what jobs you *shouldn't* prepare for. Thanks to the wonders of fluoride, America, in the future, will need fewer dentists. Nor is there much of a future in farming. The federal government probably won't provide long-term employment unless you aspire to work in the Pentagon or the Veterans Administration (the only two departments accounting for new federal jobs in the last decade). And think twice before plunging into higher education. The real wages of university professors have been declining for some time, the hours are bad, and all you get are complaints.

Moreover, as the American economy merges with the rest of the world's, anyone doing relatively unskilled work that could be done more cheaply elsewhere is unlikely to prosper for long. Imports and exports now constitute 26 percent of our gross national product (up from 9 percent in 1950), and barring a new round of protectionism, the portion will move steadily upward. Meanwhile, ten thousand people are added to the world's population every hour, most of whom, eventually, will happily work for a small fraction of today's average American wage.

This is good news for most of you, because it means that you'll be able to buy all sorts of things far more cheaply than you could if they were made here (provided, of course, that what your generation does instead produces even more value). The resulting benefits from trade will help offset the drain on your income resulting from paying the interest on the nation's foreign debt and financing the retirement of aging baby boomers like me. The bad news, at least for some of you, is that most of America's traditional, routinized manufacturing jobs will disappear. So will routinized service jobs that can be done from remote locations, like keypunching of data transmitted by satellite. Instead, you will be engaged in one of two broad categories of work: either complex services, some of which will be sold to the rest of the world to pay for whatever Americans want to buy from the rest of the world, or person-to-person services, which foreigners can't provide for us because (apart from new immigrants and illegal aliens) they aren't here to provide them.

Complex services involve the manipulation of data and abstract symbols. Included in this category are insurance, engineering, law, finance, computer programming, and advertising. Such activities now account for almost 25 percent of our GNP, up from 13 percent in 1950. They already have surpassed manufacturing (down to about 20 percent of GNP). Even *within* the manufacturing sector, executive, managerial, and engineering positions are increasing at a rate almost three times that of total manufacturing employment. Most of these jobs, too, involve manipulating symbols.

Such endeavors will constitute America's major contribution to the rest of the world in the decades ahead. You and your classmates will be exporting engineering designs, financial services, advertising and communications advice, statistical analyses, musical scores and film scripts, and other creative and problem-solving products. How many of you undertake these sorts of jobs, and how well you do at them, will determine what goods and services America can summon from the rest of the world in return, and thus—to some extent—your generation's standard of living.

You say you plan to become an investment banker? A lawyer? I grant you that these vocations have been among the fastest growing and most lucrative during the past decade. The securities industry in particular has burgeoned. Between 1977 and 1987, securities-industry employment nearly doubled, rising 10 percent a year, compared with the average yearly job growth of 1.9 percent in the rest of the economy.

The crash of October 1987 temporarily stemmed the growth, but by mid-1988 happy days were here again. Nor have securities workers had particular difficulty making ends meet. Their average income grew 21 percent over the decade, compared with a 1 percent rise in the income of everyone else. (But be careful with these numbers; relatively few securities workers enjoyed such majestic compensation. The high average is partly due to the audacity of people such as Henry Kravis and George Roberts, each of whom takes home a tidy $70 million per year.)

Work involving securities and corporate law has been claiming one-quarter of all new private sector jobs in New York City and more than a third of all the new office space in that industrious town. Other major cities are not too far behind. A simple extrapolation of the present trend suggests that by 2020 one out of every three American college graduates will be an investment banker or a lawyer. Of course, this is unlikely. Long before that milestone could be achieved, the nation's economy will have dried up like a raisin, as financiers and lawyers squeeze out every ounce of creative, productive juice. Thus my advice: Even if you could bear spending your life in such meaningless but lucrative work, at least consider the fate of the nation before deciding to do so.

Person-to-person services will claim everyone else. Many of these jobs will not require much skill, as is true of their forerunners today. Among the fastest growing in recent years: custodians and security guards, restaurant and retail workers, day-care providers. Secretaries and clerical workers will be as numerous as now, but they'll spend more of their time behind and around electronic machines (imported from Asia) and have fancier titles, such as "paratechnical assistant" and "executive paralegal operations manager."

Teachers will be needed (we'll be losing more than a third of our entire corps of elementary- and high-school teachers through attrition over the next seven years), but don't expect their real pay to rise very much. Years of public breast-beating about the quality of American education notwithstanding, the average teacher today earns $28,000— only 3.4 percent more, in constant dollars, than he or she earned fifteen years ago.

Count on many jobs catering to Americans at play—hotel workers, recreation directors, television and film technicians, aerobics instructors (or whatever their twenty-first century equivalents will call themselves). But note that Americans will have less leisure time to enjoy these pursuits. The average American's free time has been shrinking for more than fifteen years, as women move into the work force (and so spend more of their free time doing household chores) and as all wage earners are forced to work harder just to maintain their standard of living. Expect the trend to continue.

The most interesting and important person-to-person jobs will be in what is now unpretentiously dubbed "sales." Decades from now most salespeople won't be just filling orders. Salespeople will be helping customers define their needs, then working with design and production engineers to customize products and services in order to address those needs. This is because standardized (you can have it in any color as long as it's black) products will be long gone. Flexible manufacturing and the new information technologies will allow a more tailored fit—whether it's a car, machine tool, insurance policy, or even a college education. Those of you who will be dealing directly with customers will thus play a pivotal role in the innovation process, and your wages and prestige will rise accordingly.

But the largest number of personal-service jobs will involve health care, which already consumes about 12 percent of our GNP, and that portion is rising. Because every new medical technology with the potential to extend life is infinitely valuable to those whose lives might be extended—even for a few months or weeks—society is paying huge sums to stave off death. By the second decade of the next century, when my generation of baby boomers will have begun to decay, the bill will be much higher. Millions of corroding bodies will need doctors, nurses, nursing-home operators, hospital administrators, technicians who operate and maintain all the fancy machines that will measure and temporarily halt the deterioration, hospice directors, home-care specialists, directors of outpatient clinics, and euthanasia specialists, among many others.

Most of these jobs won't pay very much because they don't require much skill. Right now the fastest growing job categories in the health sector are nurse's aides, orderlies, and attendants, which compose about 40 percent of the health-care work force. The majority are women; a large percentage are minorities. But even doctors' real earnings show signs of slipping. As malpractice insurance rates skyrocket, many doctors go on salary in investor-owned hospitals, and their duties are gradually taken over by physician "extenders" such as nurse practitioners and midwives.

What's the best preparation for one of these careers?

Advice here is simple: You won't be embarking on a career, at least as we currently define the term, because few of the activities I've mentioned will proceed along well-defined paths to progressively higher levels of responsibility. As the economy evolves toward services tailored to the particular needs of clients and customers, hands-on experience will count for more than formal rank. As technologies and markets rapidly evolve, moreover, the best preparation will be through cumulative learning on the job rather than formal training completed years before.

This means that academic degrees and professional credentials will count for less; on-the-job training, for more. American students have it backwards. The courses to which you now gravitate—finance, law, accounting, management, and other practical arts—may be helpful to understand how a particular job is *now* done (or, more accurately, how your instructors did it years ago when they held such jobs or studied the people who held them), but irrelevant to how such a job *will* be done. The intellectual equipment needed for the job of the future is an ability to define problems, quickly assimilate relevant data, conceptualize and reorganize the information, make deductive and inductive leaps with it, ask hard questions about it, discuss findings with colleagues, work collaboratively to find solutions, and then convince others. And *these* sorts of skills can't be learned in career-training courses. To the extent they can be found in universities at all, they're more likely to be found in subjects such as history, literature, philosophy, and anthropology—in which students can witness how others have grappled for centuries with the challenge of living good and productive lives. Tolstoy and Thucydides are far more relevant to the management jobs of the future, for example, than are Hersey and Blanchard (*Management of Organizational Behavior,* Prentice Hall, 5th Edition, 1988).

# Themes, Issues, and Ideas

1. Many writers whose subject is the future have talked about the dangers of population increase to human well-being. Why does Reich conditionally say that the increase is *good* news? What are the conditions that will make the news good?

2. What type of occupations does Reich say will constitute America's major economic contribution to the world in the years to come? How many of the occupations he surveys fall into this area?

3. Reich says that among the most interesting and important jobs will be those now generally called "sales." What reasons does he give for this opinion? Do you agree with his view of "sales?" Why or why not?

# Writing Strategies and Techniques

1. Reich addresses students directly. What writing techniques does he use to maintain the sense of a specific and an immediate audience for his predictions?

2. Much of Reich's information is necessarily mathematical in form. How does he use humor to lighten the burden of factual content?

# Suggestions for Writing

1. Many people have shied away from sales and need to be sold on the idea as a career path. How does Reich sell his idea that sales will be a very important part of the future economy? Write an essay analyzing his persuasive techniques.

2. Though his subject is careers of the future, Reich deprecates the possibility or usefulness of any direct career training. Do you agree? Write an essay in which you attack, defend, or modify Reich's suggestions for an education suitable to the American future.

# Blowing Up the Tracks

## Patricia Kean

> *The practice of public school "tracking"—setting up classes for gifted, intermediate, and remedial students—has been around for the better part of a century. But according to Patricia Kean, tracking isn't all it's cracked up to be: It keeps "slower" students from receiving better grades, better education, and ultimately better jobs. Is there anything that can be done about tracking? What are its advantages, anyway? Patricia Kean, in an essay taken from the* Washington Monthly, *takes a fresh look at an old practice—and gives it an F.*
>
> *Kean taught grade school in Manhattan during the 1980s. She is now writing about education full-time.*

It's morning in New York, and some seventh graders are more equal than others.

Class 7–16 files slowly into the room, prodded by hard-faced men whose walkie-talkies crackle with static. A pleasant looking woman shouts over the din, "What's rule number one?" No reply. She writes on the board. "Rule One: Sit down."

Rule number two seems to be an unwritten law: Speak slowly. Each of Mrs. H's syllables hangs in the air a second longer than necessary. In fact, the entire class seems to be conducted at 16 RPM. Books come out gradually. Kids wander about the room aimlessly. Twelve minutes into class, we settle down and begin to play "O. Henry Jeopardy," a game which requires students to supply one-word answers to questions like: "O. Henry moved from North Carolina to what state—Andy? Find the word on the page."

The class takes out a vocabulary sheet. Some of the words they are expected to find difficult include popular, ranch, suitcase, arrested, recipe, tricky, ordinary, humorous, and grand jury.

Thirty minutes pass. Bells ring, doors slam.

Class 7–1 marches in unescorted, mindful of rule number one. Paperbacks of Poe smack sharply on desks, notebooks rustle, and kids lean forward expectantly, waiting for Mrs. H to fire the first question. What did we learn about the writer?

Hands shoot into the air. Though Edgar Allen Poe ends up sounding a lot like Jerry Lee Lewis—a booze-hound who married his 13-year-old cousin—these kids speak confidently, in paragraphs. Absolutely no looking at the book allowed.

We also have a vocabulary sheet, drawn from "The Tell-Tale Heart," containing words like audacity, dissimulation, sagacity, stealthy, anxiety, derision, agony and supposition.

As I sit in the back of the classroom watching these two very different groups of seventh graders, my previous life as an English teacher allows me to make an educated guess and a chilling prediction. With the best of intentions, Mrs. H is teaching the first group, otherwise known as the "slow kids," as though they are fourth graders, and the second, the honors group, as though they are high school freshmen. Given the odds of finding a word like "ordinary" on the SAT's, the children of 7–16 have a better chance of standing before a "grand jury" than making it to college.

Tracking, the practice of placing students in "ability groups" based on a host of ill-defined criteria—everything from test scores to behavior to how much of a fuss a mother can be counted on to make— encourages even well-meaning teachers and administrators to turn out generation after generation of self-fulfilling prophecies. "These kids know they're no Einsteins," Mrs. H said of her low-track class when we sat together in the teacher's lounge. "They know they don't read well. This way I can go really slowly with them."

With his grades, however, young Albert would probably be hanging right here with the rest of lunch table 7–16. That's where I discover that while their school may think they're dumb, these kids are anything but stupid. "That teacher," sniffs a pretty girl wearing lots of purple lipstick. "She talks so slow. She thinks we're babies. She takes a year to do anything." "What about the other one?" a girl named Ingrid asks, referring to their once-a-week student teacher. "He comes in and goes like this: Rail (pauses) road. Rail (pauses) road. Like we don't know what a railroad means!" The table breaks up laughing.

Outside the walls of the schools across the country, it's slowly become an open secret that enforced homogeneity benefits no one. The work of researchers like Jeannie Oakes of UCLA and Robert Slavin of Johns Hopkins has proven that tracking does not merely reflect differences—it causes them. Over time, slow kids get slower, while those in the middle and in the so-called "gifted and talented" top tracks fail to gain from isolation. Along the way, the practice resegregates the nation's schools, dividing the middle from the lower classes, white from black and brown. As the evidence piles up, everyone from the Carnegie Corporation to the National Governors Association has called for change.

Though some fashionably progressive schools have begun to reform, tracking persists. Parent groups, school boards, teachers, and administrators who hold the power within schools cling to the myths and wax apocalyptic about the horrors of heterogeneity. On their side is the most potent force known to man: bureaucratic inertia. Because tracking puts kids in boxes, keeps the lid on, and shifts responsibility for mediocrity and failure away from the schools themselves, there is little incentive to change a nearly century-old tradition. "Research is research," the principal told me that day, "This is practice."

## Back Track

Tracking has been around since just after the turn of the century. It was then, as cities teemed with immigrants and industry, that education reformers like John Franklin Bobbitt began to argue that the school and the factory shared a common mission, to "work up the raw material into that finished product for which it was best adapted." By the twenties, the scientific principles that ruled the factory floor had been applied to the classroom. They believed the IQ test—which had just become popular—allowed pure science, not the whims of birth or class, to determine whether a child received the type of education appropriate for a future manager or a future laborer.

It hasn't quite worked out that way. Driven by standardized tests, the descendants of the old IQ tests, tracking has evolved into a kind of educational triage premised on the notion that only the least wounded can be saved. Yet when the classroom operates like a battleground, society's casualties mount, and the results begin to seem absurd: Kids who enter school needing more get less, while the already enriched get, well, enricher. Then, too, the low-track graduates of 70 years ago held a distinct advantage over their modern counterparts: If tracking prepared them for mindless jobs, at least those jobs existed.

The sifting and winnowing starts as early as pre-K. Three-year old Ebony and her classmates have won the highly prized "gifted and talented" label after enduring a battery of IQ and psychological tests. There's nothing wrong with the "regular" class in this Harlem public school. But high expectations for Ebony and her new friends bring tangible rewards like a weekly field trip and music and computer lessons.

Meanwhile, regular kids move on to regular kindergartens where they too will be tested, and where it will be determined that some children need more help, perhaps a "pre-first grade" developmental year. So by the time they're ready for first grade reading groups, certain six-year-olds have already been marked as "sparrows"—the low performers in the class.

In the beginning, it doesn't seem to matter so much, because the other reading groups—the robins and the eagles—are just a few feet away and the class is together for most of the day. Trouble is, as they toil over basic drill sheets, the sparrows are slipping farther behind. The robins are gathering more challenging vocabulary words, and the eagles soaring on to critical thinking skills.

Though policies vary, by fourth grade many of these groups have flown into completely separate classrooms, turning an innocent three-tier reading system into three increasingly rigid academic tracks—honors, regular, and remedial—by middle school.

Unless middle school principals take heroic measures like buying expensive software or crafting daily schedules by hand, it often becomes a lot easier to sort everybody by reading scores. So kids who do well on reading tests can land in the high track for math, science, social studies, even lunch, and move together as a self-contained unit all day. Friendships form, attitudes harden. Kids on top study together, kids in the middle console themselves by making fun of the "nerds" above and the "dummies" below, and kids on the bottom develop behavioral problems and get plenty of negative reinforcement.

By high school, many low-track students are locked out of what Jeannie Oakes calls "gatekeeper courses," the science, math, and foreign language classes that hold the key to life after twelfth grade. Doors to college are slamming shut, though the kids themselves are often the last to know. When researcher Anne Wheelock interviewed students in Boston's public schools, they'd all insist they were going to become architects, teachers, and the like. What courses were they taking? "Oh, Keyboarding II, Earth Science, Consumer Math. This would be junior year and I'd ask, 'Are you taking Algebra?' and they'd say no."

## Black Marks

A funny thing can happen to minority students on the way to being tracked. Even when minority children score high, they often find themselves placed in lower tracks where counselors and principals assume they belong.

In Paula Hart's travels for The Achievement Council, a Los Angeles-based educational advocacy group, she comes across district after district where black and Latino kids score in the 75th percentile for math, yet never quite make it into Algebra I, the classic gatekeeper course. A strange phenomenon occurs in inner city areas with large minority populations—high track classes shrink, and low track classes expand to fit humble expectations for the entire school population.

A few years ago, Dr. Norward Roussell's curiosity got the better of him. As Selma, Alabama's first black school superintendent, he couldn't help but notice that "gifted and talented" tracks were nearly lily white in a district that was 70 percent black. When he looked for answers in the files of high school students, he discovered that a surprising number of low track minority kids had actually scored higher than their white top track counterparts.

Parents of gifted and talented students staged a full-scale revolt against Roussell's subsequent efforts to establish logical standards for placement. In four days of public hearings, speaker after speaker said the same thing: We're going to lose a lot of our students to other schools. To Roussell, their meaning was clear: Put black kids in the high tracks and we pull white kids out of the system. More blacks and more low-income whites did make it to the top under the new criteria, but Roussell himself was left behind. The majority-white school board chose not to renew his contract, and he's now superintendent in Macon County, Alabama, a district that is overwhelmingly black.

Race and class divisions usually play themselves out in a more subtle fashion. Talk to teachers about how their high track kids differ from their low track kids and most speak not of intelligence, but of motivation and "family." It seems that being gifted and talented is hereditary after all, largely a matter of having parents who read to you, who take you to museums and concerts, and who know how to work the system. Placement is often a matter of who's connected. Jennifer P., a teacher in a Brooklyn elementary school saw a pattern in her class. "The principal put all the kids whose parents were in the PTA in the top tracks no matter what their scores were. He figures that if his PTA's happy, he's happy."

Once the offspring of the brightest and the best connected have been skimmed off in honors or regular tracks, low tracks begin to fill up with children whose parents are not likely to complain. These kids get less homework, spend less class time learning, and are often taught by the least experienced teachers, because avoiding them can become a reward for seniority in a profession where perks are few.

With the courts reluctant to get involved, even when tracking leads to racial segregation and at least the appearance of civil rights violations, changing the system becomes an arduous local battle fought school by school. Those who undertake the delicate process of untracking need nerves of steel and should be prepared to find resistance from every quarter, since, as Slavin notes, parents of high-achieving kids will fight this to the death. One-time guidance counselor Hart learned this lesson more than a decade ago when she and two colleagues struggled to introduce a now-thriving college curriculum program at Los Angeles' Banning High. Their efforts to open top-track classes to all students prompted death threats from an unlikely source—their fellow teachers.

## Off Track Betting

Anne Wheelock's new book, *Crossing the Tracks,* tells the stories of schools that have successfully untracked or never tracked at all. Schools that make the transition often achieve dramatic results. True to its name, Pioneer Valley Regional school in Northfield, Massachusetts was one of the first in the nation to untrack. Since 1983, the number of Pioneer Valley seniors going on to higher education jumped from 37 to 80 percent. But, the author says, urban schools continue to lag behind. "We're talking about unequal distribution of reform," Wheelock declares. "Change is taking place in areas like Wellesley, Massachusetts and Jericho, Long Island. It's easier to untrack when kids are closer to one another to begin with."

It's also easier for educators to tinker with programs and make cosmetic adjustments than it is to ask them to do what bureaucrats hate most: give up one method of doing things without having another to put in its place. Tracking is a system; untracking is a leap of faith. When difficult kids can no longer be dumped in low tracks, new ways must be found to deal with disruptive behavior: early intervention, intensive work with families, and lots of tutoring. Untracking may also entail new instructional techniques like cooperative group learning and peer tutoring, but what it really demands is flexibility and improvisation.

It also demands that schools—and the rest of us—admit that some kids will be so disruptive or violent that a solution for dealing with them must be found *outside* of the regular public school system. New York City seems close to such a conclusion. Schools Chancellor Joseph Fernandez is moving forward with a voluntary "academy" program, planning separate schools designed to meet the needs of chronic troublemakers. One of them, the Wildcat Academy, run by a non-profit group of the same name, plans to enroll 150 students by the end of the year. Wildcat kids will attend classes from nine to five, wear uniforms, hold part-time jobs, and be matched with mentors from professional fields. Districts in Florida and California are conducting similar experiments.

Moving away from tracking is not about taking away from the gifted and talented and giving to the poor. That, as Wheelock notes, is "political suicide." It's not even about placing more black and Latino kids in their midst, a kind of pre-K affirmative action. Rather, it's about raising expectations for everyone. Or, as Slavin puts it: "You can maintain your tracking system. Just put everyone into the top track."

That's not as quixotic as it sounds. In fact, it's long been standard practice in the nation's Catholic schools, a system so backward it's actually progressive. When I taught in an untracked parochial high school, one size fit all—with the exception of the few we expelled for poor grades or behavior. My students, who differed widely in ability, interest, and background, nevertheless got Shakespeare, Thoreau, and Langston Hughes at the same pace, at the same time—and lived to tell the tale. Their survival came, in part, because my colleagues and I could decide if the cost of keeping a certain student around was too high and we had the option of sending him or her elsewhere if expulsion was warranted.

The result was that my honor students wrote elegant essays and made it to Ivy League schools, right on schedule. And far from being held back by their "regular" and "irregular" counterparts, straight-A students were more likely to be challenged by questions they would never dream of asking. "Why are we studying this?" a big-haired girl snapping gum in the back of the room wondered aloud one day. Her question led to a discussion that turned into the best class I ever taught.

In four years, I never saw a single standardized test score. But time after time I watched my students climb out of whatever mental category I had put them in. Tracking sees to it that they never get that chance. Flying directly in the face of Yogi Berra's Rule Number One, it tells kids it's over before it's even begun. For ultimately, tracking stunts the opportunity for growth, the one area in which all children are naturally gifted.

## Themes, Issues, and Ideas

1. Did you attend a school where tracking was used? If so, does Kean's critique seem true? If not, do you think your school would have been helped or hindered by tracking?

2. Public versus private education is a controversial issue now. Does this reading shed light on this issue for you? How so?

3. What are some benefits to tracking for students? What are some disadvantages? Answer the question for both "gifted" and "backward" students.

## Writing Strategies and Techniques

1. How does Kean get the reader on her side in the essay? What does she do, and not do, to persuade the reader?

2. What does Kean assume about the reader? Does your response, as a reader, justify these assumptions?

## Suggestions for Writing

1. Write an essay describing how tracking might work in another setting: college, home, work, etc.

2. Write an essay describing your own experience with the tracking system. Does it cause you to agree or disagree with Kean? Explain.

# Education—Less of It!

## Tertius Chandler

*The preceding essays in this chapter present wide-ranging disagreements, but they all share the view that more and perhaps different formal education is needed to meet the life awaiting us in the twenty-first century. The author of this essay has a different estimation of the benefits and limits of higher education. Although he acknowledges the common faith people place in education, he says, "I venture to wonder why."*

*Tertius Chandler was born near Boston in 1915 and graduated from Harvard University in 1937. He did graduate work at the University of California at Berkeley and has both given and taken courses throughout his lifetime. He has also washed "a few million dishes," edited two magazines, and run for Congress twice. This essay was first published in* The College Board Review.

Will Durant in his *Lessons of History* claimed that the greatest hope of the human race is increased education.

I venture to wonder why? School is unfree, rather like a jail with a term lasting twenty years, if you're able to stick the course. Childhood and youth are sacred times when innate curiosity is intense and health and zest tend to be strong. Those years are too important to be frittered away memorizing irrelevant trivia in herded mobs under the heavy hand of compulsion. Ben Franklin had just two years in school and flunked both times—yet he went on to make himself the ablest and best-rounded leader in our history. Pascal and Petrie had no schooling at all. So learning can occur outside school as well as in—perhaps even better, and especially now, when there are fine libraries open to all as well as television, bookstores, newspapers, and magazines. Think of the *National Geographic*!

Here on the other hand are arguments for education:

1. *Older people know more, so the young can learn from them.*
Parental teaching might be preferable (and does increasingly occur),
but in many families both parents are away at work. Anyway, teachers
are specialists in particular subjects. These arguments are valid, and, it
must be conceded, some learning does occur in schools.

2. *Money!* A school diploma is virtually useless on the job market, and so is a college degree. But school prepares for college, which
prepares for postgraduate school, which prepares for entry into well-
paid professions. In 1981 the average high school graduate made
$18,138, whereas the average for those with five or more years of col-
lege was $32,887. Lifetime earnings for the high school graduates aver-
aged $845,000, compared with $1,503,000 for five-year collegians.[1]
Yet an underlying flaw vitiates the comparison, for college draws people of higher intelligence and those from richer families. Their lifelong
earnings largely reflect these particular factors.

3. *The rah-rah spirit.* A person likes to say he or she has been to
such-and-such college. It's the "in" thing.

4. *High ambition.* In this country of open opportunity parents naturally push their children all they can. It is refreshing to recall, however,
that Washington, Lincoln, and Truman were among those who made it
to president without going to college—and they were unusually good
presidents.

5. *Culture.* The claim is often made that if culture wasn't rammed
into the young, they would never come to appreciate literature, art, and
fine music. Frankly, that's ridiculous.

6. *Meeting friends.* There are, of course, other places to meet
people, and most of them allow more leisure to enjoy the friendship.
Nevertheless it must be said that college is a fine place to make
interesting acquaintances. Students are easily met in the dining halls
and on campus. Eventually one may make friends even among the professors.

To sum up, education does pass on some learning and introduces
a person to many out-of-town folks, while being the only way to enter
some professions. But it takes a long, long time!

## Conditioned Robots

Raymond Moore observes that: "The biggest shortcoming of mass education is the fact that students end up completely turned off to learning."[2] Or as Bertrand Russell ruefully concluded: "We are faced with the paradox that education has become one of the chief obstacles of intelligence and freedom of thought."

The educational profession has become geared to the College Board examinations, which give it an awesome amount of rigidity. As a result, elective courses are rather few, and are becoming fewer even in college.

The number of school years is also prescribed. If a child masters mathematics in one year, so much the worse for him. Conversely, someone of low IQ has to suffer year after year with subjects that baffle him. Insofar as school is adjusted to anybody, it is adjusted to the mediocre student, and he, hopelessly unable to lead the class or win any prize, just drones on, loathing the whole procedure.

All that keeps the system from destroying the students altogether is that most of them instinctively rebel inwardly against it and cooperate only enough to get by, reserving as much energy and time as they can manage for other activities. Indeed, the most unruly boys in class sometimes tend to do better later on in life. Unfortunately some rebellious activities, such as smoking, heavy drinking, and fast driving, are not healthy, yet by a discreet degree of rebelliousness and shirking a boy can remain spiritually alive.

As Agatha Christie put it: "I suppose it is because nearly all children go to school nowadays, and have things arranged for them, that they seem so forlornly unable to produce their own ideas."[3]

Kahlil Gibran's great passage is relevant here: "Your children are not your children. They are the sons and daughters of life's longing for itself . . . you may give them your love but not your thoughts, for they have their own thoughts. You may house their bodies but not their souls. Their souls dwell in the house of tomorrow, which you may not visit, even in your dreams."

Gibran was not looking for conditioned robots.

## A Shorter School Year

Some sadist must have written the law requiring 180 annual school days. They begin in August, when berries are still ripening, and last into the sweltering heat of June. Fall and spring, by their nature gorgeous seasons, become fixed in young minds as symbols of the agony of school.

It was when I was about halfway through prep school that teachers thought up a way to cut into the summer vacation—our only prolonged free time. They began assigning compulsory reading of novels. This was a grief and an indignity I will not easily forget. I had been reading the finest sort of literature on my own in the summers. After that I read the minimum—and hated it. Liberty dies hard in the human soul.

Change should be in the other direction: toward less schooling.

## How Early?

Jean Piaget noticed stages in children's capacity to learn. To impose reading and mathematics on them before their minds are ready is to puzzle and torment them. School by its nature is force-feeding and, when children are very young, not only their bodies but also their feelings are very tender. To separate them from their parents and to inflict cold drill in seemingly pointless subjects on them can drive their feelings inward and make them feel unwanted and lonely, even in a crowded room. All this Piaget understood. Indeed, it is perfectly obvious.

But, Piaget added, give the students those same subjects a few years later, and they can grasp them rather quickly, because their minds have become equal to the techniques needed and because they have reached the stage where they can see a purpose in what they are doing.

Raymond Moore in his book *School Can Wait*[4] suggests delaying school to the age of eight or ten and in a recently published letter[5] opposes giving any exams before the age of ten. The idea is not new. A century ago Robert Owen withheld books from children in his famous school until their tenth year. Montessori, likewise, set the young to playing games. These are the real heroes for the cause of children.

## Puberty

School treats pupils alike year after year. Yet somewhere in their teens boys notice girls. They are never the same again. School carries on as if the children were still just that. In the school where I went, aside from a warning to "stay pure," nothing changed. The hard drill on useless scholasticism to get us into college continued. We were to think college and nothing but college so that success in life would be automatic.

I got the message. When I was seventeen I met a girl I liked on a ski trip. I deliberately dropped her and by a hard effort, managed to forget her, since I still had five years before I'd be clear of college (actually nine, but I didn't know about postgraduate study then). That was a romance that should have gotten off the ground and didn't. Looking back, I see that I could probably have worked in the girl's father's factory. The father and mother liked me. I was past the compulsory school-age, which was then sixteen in my state—but nobody told me things like that. College was a fixation for my parents and my teachers, and therefore for me, too.

I was not unique. Bernard DeVoto told us in a talk at Harvard around 1935, "No one marries his first love." He meant among the highly educated, for of course some dropouts do marry their first choice. It was, anyway, a chilling remark, an unpleasant commentary on how the educational system impacts on youth. The trade-off of love for a series of degrees is a poor deal.

Lately, private schools have done a sudden about-face and flung the boys and girls together. They are aroused to love earlier and so have longer to agonize. Education and puberty thus now clash head-on, but they still haven't come to terms.

## On Teaching English

English can be dropped altogether. Charles W. Eliot of Harvard and others put English into our schools in 1900 by making it a requirement for the College Board Examinations. Eliot's idea was that pupils can be compelled to present ideas clearly and to enjoy literature. He would drill these skills into them. The sheer quantity of disciplined effort would get results and turn our 18-year-olds into incisive, clear, witty writers.

The result of all this massive drill over nearly a century has been to make our youths somewhat duller than before. Our few famous writers now are notable for their gloom, their insobriety, and their utter inability to come up with answers to our problems. It would seem that English was made a required subject to no purpose whatsoever.

The correct way to teach English fundamentals—grammar, spelling, sentence structure—is to teach them as a part of other subjects.

That way, English has a chance of being interesting. Just in this way, one teaches the use of a hammer in the process of teaching carpentry; one does not take a special course in hammering. It would be fiendishly dull if one did.

## Mathematics

Ever since the Russians put Sputnik into orbit in 1957 there have been spasmodic efforts to increase the mathematics load of *all* U.S. schoolchildren, including future janitors, nurses, maids, and ditch diggers. While I respect those occupations, they do not require higher mathematics. Actually any useful computations for war or business will be made by a very few experts—perhaps by one-hundredth of 1 percent of the population—and they will be using computers.

Underwood Dudley of DePauw University, himself a mathematics teacher, believes that we teach mathematics not to solve problems or inculcate logical thinking but simply because we always have done so. As he puts it: "Practical? When was the last time you had to solve a quadratic equation? Was it just last week that you needed to find the volume of a cone? Isn't it a fact that you never need any mathematics beyond arithmetic?... Algebra? Good heavens! Almost all people never use algebra, ever, outside of a classroom."[6]

He rightly adds that mathematical talent is very easy to spot early in life. Surely he is right that a special annual test should be held to see which students should be allowed to take mathematics beyond arithmetic—as an honor, not a requirement! The motivated proud few would then accomplish more than the slave-driven multitude.

## Any School at All?

Once the need for school was clear. Back around 1800 schools were few and didn't take long, only four to six years. They taught basics and were almost the only place for the young to get books. Nowadays, alternative means of learning are plentiful. As already mentioned, they include public libraries, television, bookstores, newspapers, and magazines. These actually represent an overabundance.

If some state dropped schooling altogether, I wouldn't oppose it. (I would not wish this change to be imposed by the federal government however.)

## Self-Reliance

Adult life calls for decision making and responsibility. These arise naturally at home but not in the educational system, where teachers make the decisions. A student, moreover, is competing against all the others, a self-centered attitude he will have to drop when he goes on to a job or into marriage.

## Required Reading

In British colleges (but not schools!) the students pick their own reading. Here in the United States, students are told what to read and when to read it. Recoiling against this conformity, Professor Carl Sauer told us in his class at the University of California in 1939: "The required book list defeats its own purpose. Books should enable you to meet ideas, meet other personalities, if you like, appropriating from them what you can use, what you need. I don't think I remember a single thing I had to read as required reading for any professor in college. I think if I had had any share in the discovery of something, a few ideas would have stuck. . . . Doing things for instructors is basically not doing anything at all."

## Do Universities Broaden Minds?

Does university training help or hinder in developing intellectual capacity to do highly original work? Among highly creative modern thinkers the following were formally educated: Montesquieu, Jefferson, Goethe, Macaulay, Marx, Freud, Schweitzer, Proskouriakoff, Champollion, and Gandhi. These did not go to college: Voltaire, Hume, Owen, Austen, Balzac, Jairazbhoy, Gibran, Tolstoy, Twain, and Shaw.

Bright people can teach themselves. As Henry Adams said, "No one can educate anyone else. You have to do it for yourself." There should, of course, be equivalency exams for the self-taught, as well as on-the-job training, for most professions.

Some would claim that if the youthful were encouraged to act freely, their initiative would be too great; that they would go berserk. But I think not: Most would marry, others would travel, invent, and carry on original work on all sorts of lines. Early marriage could balance many of them so they could work better. It is worth remembering in this connection that among the young, idealism and faith are uncommonly strong.

Those destined for ordinary jobs don't need to learn anything taught in college, and many of them know it. They attend college because it's the thing to do. They tend to take "snaps" such as English literature or sociology. I see no objection to letting them enjoy themselves at private colleges if they want to.

Public universities should, I think, confine themselves to serious training. The number entering should be preset as in Sweden, so as to train the quantity of people needed to fit the estimated number of openings in each profession, always allowing for the rise of some persons via equivalency exams.

College represents now too much of a good thing. There are too many learned professors and section leaders to adjust to, too many books to hasten through at a set speed, too many years to plod away on the treadmill. A Ph.D. in history is now expected to take four to eight years—on top of the twelve in school and four in college. Perhaps, worst of all, the Ph.D. subject is deliberately kept small, so that the student will be able to claim mastery of something. Four to eight years of deliberate narrowing can have the effect of incapacitating him from ever taking a broad view of anything. The result of all this mental drill tends to be a mashed human, an eviscerated person. Only a very sturdy soul, such as a Freud or a Schweitzer, can come through all this and still retain the ability to think for himself. University study could, with no intrinsic loss, be shortened from eight years to four, and school could be limited to ages ten to fifteen.

These suggested reductions in compulsory education would have another powerful advantage: They might set our people's minds largely free, a result surely to be wished.

### References

1. *Digest of Education Statistics.* Washington, D.C.: National Center for Education Statistics, 1982. P. 181–82.
2. Raymond Moore, *Parent Educator & Family Report,* August 1984. P. 6.
3. Agatha Christie, *Autobiography.* New York: Doubleday, 1978. P. 59.
4. Raymond Moore, *School Can Wait.*
5. Raymond Moore, correspondence cited in *Parent Educator & Family Report,* January 24, 1985.
6. Underwood Dudley, article in *San Francisco Chronicle,* April 28, 1984.

# Themes, Issues, and Ideas

1. Chandler says of the years we normally spend in education: "Those years are too important to be frittered away memorizing irrelevant trivia in herded mobs under the heavy hand of compulsion." What examples and arguments does he offer to support his views?

2. How has your own education equipped you to judge Chandler's essay? Does your experience support or refute Chandler's claims?

3. Chandler argues that English courses should be dropped altogether. How do you feel about this? What arguments would you use to defend or refute Chandler on this issue?

# Writing Strategies and Techniques

1. How many famous people without formal education does Chandler name? How does he use them as examples? Does he suggest, for instance, that *not* going to school will make you famous?

2. Chandler lists six reasons in favor of education in the beginning of his essay. What would have been the effect if he had made his own points first?

# Suggestions for Writing

1. Beginning with a list of Chandler's arguments against formal education, write an essay defending education, using Chandler's essay as a model.

2. Write an essay that sketches out the ideal education for students (as Chandler would see it) from the time they begin school up to the age of twenty-one.

# MAKING CONNECTIONS

1. Robert Reich, Hillary Rodham Clinton, and Ira Magaziner are, unlike most of the authors in this book, now in a position to implement some of their ideas. Does this give their essays added weight? How does the fact that they may influence national policy change the way you read their work?

2. How might Patricia Kean respond to Clinton and Magaziner's or Chandler's views of education? How does the idea of tracking appear in some of the other essays in this chapter?

3. Compare Douglass' education experience with that Halal and Leibowitz describe in "Telelearning." Would Douglass have benefited from telearning? Why or why not?

4. Do you think writers like Tertius Chandler, or for that matter William Halal and Jay Leibowitz really seem to know what it's like to go to school in the 1990s? What could you tell them they missed in their essays? Would your comments change the essential content of their essays? Why or why not?

5. After reading these essays, combine the best ideas in each of them to create your own master plan for revitalizing American education. Support your selections with quotations from the readings and solid reasoning of your own.

# CHAPTER
# FIVE

## *American Life in the Age of the Internet*

# THE
# PAST AS
# PROLOGUE

## from *Media and the American mind*

### *Daniel Czitrom*

*Long before anyone had heard of the Internet or cyberspace, Americans had been enthralled by the possibilities of new communications media. In the 1960s, some will remember, Marshall McLuhan spoke of a "global village," where a transformed humankind would perceive the world differently. And as Daniel Czitrom, Professor of History at the Mount Holyoke College, points out, even before McLuhan, Americans had thrilled to the idea of a national community, bound by instantaneous, ubiquitous, and lightening-quick communications.*

"Canst thou send lightnings, that they may go, and say unto thee, Here we are?" (Job 38:35). This Biblical quotation, one of the impossibilities enumerated to convince Job of his ignorance and weakness, frequently prefaced nineteenth-century writings on the telegraph. It expressed well the sense of miracle that these works invariably sought to convey. As the most astounding product of electrical science, the telegraph promised miraculous consequences. T. P. Shaffner, historian and early telegraph booster, concluded a history of all the past forms of communication: "But what is all this to subjugating the lightnings, the mythological voice of Jehovah, the fearful omnipotence of the clouds, causing them in the fine agony of chained submission to do the offices of a common messenger—to whisper to the four corners of the earth the lordly behests of lordly man!"

While Shaffner and others seized upon the telegraph as a means of recasting all history in the terms of the growth of communication, some became intoxicated with what the telegraph would bring to the future. Always they spoke of a twin miracle: the grand moral effects of instantaneous communication and the wonderful mystery of the lightning lines themselves. "Universal communication" became the key phrase in these exhortations. The electric telegraph promised a unity of interest, men linked by a single mind, and the worldwide victory of Christianity. "It gives the preponderance of power to the nations representing the highest elements in humanity...It is the civilized and Christian nations, who, though weak comparatively in numbers, are by these means of communication made more than a match for the hordes of barbarism." Universal peace and harmony seem at this time more possible than ever before, as the telegraph "binds together by a vital cord all the nations of the earth. It is impossible that old prejudices and hostilities should longer exist, while such an instrument has been created for an exchange of thought between all the nations of the earth."

Just as the telegraph promised "a revolution in moral grandeur," the instrument itself seemed "a perpetual miracle, which no familiarity can render commonplace. This character it deserves from the nature employed and the end subserved. For what is the end to be accomplished but the most spiritual ever possible? Not the modification or transportation of matter, but the transmission of thought."

"The Telegraph" asserted the *New York Times* in 1858, "undoubtedly ranks foremost among that series of mighty discoveries that have gone to subjugate matter under the domain of mind." Not only did the new electrical technology further man's ability to conquer nature, it actually allowed him to penetrate it. By successfully liberating the subtle spark latent in all forms of matter, man became more godlike. "Piercing so the secret of Nature, man makes himself symmetrical with nature. Penetrating to the working of creative energies, he becomes himself a creator."

Underpinning the grand moral claims made on behalf of the telegraph lay a special understanding of an elusive term, *communication*. The word has had a complex history. Praisers of "universal communication" no doubt had in mind the most archaic sense of the word: a noun of action meaning to make common to many (or the object thus made common). The notion of common participation suggested communion, and the two words shared the same Latin root, *communis.* Sometime in the late seventeenth century the meaning was extended to include the imparting, conveying, or exchanging of information and materials. In this sense the means of communication also included roads, canals, and railroads. The telegraph thus split communication (of information, thought) from transportation (of people, materials). But the ambiguity between the two poles of meaning, between communication as a mutual process or sharing and communication as a one-way or private transmission, remained unresolved.

Those who celebrated the promise of universal communication stressed religious imagery and the sense of miracle in describing the telegraph. They subtly united the technological advance in communication with the ancient meaning of that word as common participation or communion. They presumed the triumph of certain messages; but they suggested too that the creation of a new communications technology itself, "the wonderful vehicle," was perhaps the most important message of all.

Henry Thoreau's sceptical view of the telegraph, one of very few pessimistic expressions on the subject, sought to deflate just such moral claims made on behalf of the new technology. In *Walden* (1854) he argued that the telegraph represented simply another illusory modem improvement rather than a positive advance, "an improved means to an unimproved end.... We are in great haste to construct a magnetic telegraph from Maine to Texas; but Maine and Texas, it may be, have nothing important to communicate.... We are eager to tunnel under the Atlantic and bring the old world some weeks nearer to the new; but perchance the first news that will leak through into the broad, flapping American ear will be that Princess Adelaide has the whooping cough." Thoreau was perhaps a bit churlish here, for Maine and Texas did indeed have a great deal to communicate. But the essence of that communication would not be the celestial commerce savored by both Thoreau and those who deemed the telegraph a sublime moral force.

For the telegraph promised to transform the earthly realms of politics and trade as well. The presumed annihilation of time and space held a special meaning for a country of seemingly limitless size. And here for the first time, one finds the repeated use of organic metaphor and symbol to describe how modem communication would change American life. As early as 1838, in trying to convince Congress to subsidize his work, Morse anticipated twentieth-century notions of the "global village." It would not be long, he wrote, "ere the whole surface of this country would be channelled for those *nerves* which are to diffuse, with the speed of thought, a knowledge of all that is occurring throughout the land; making, in fact, one *neighborhood* of the whole country."

# Themes, Issues, and Ideas

1. Why did the telegraph have the effect Czitrom describes? What features did the nineteenth century find particularly dazzling? Why?

2. Czitrom writes of "the triumph of certain messages." What might such messages consist of?

3. Why does Czitrom discuss the etymology of the word "communication?" Why is it relevant to his subject?

# Writing Strategies and Techniques

1. Much of Czitrom's history consists of direct quotation. Do you find this an effective way to relate history? Why or why not?

2. In what ways does Czitrom sum up the attitudes of the nineteenth century toward the telegraph in his own words, while at the same time distancing himself from them?

# Suggestions For Writing

1. Write an essay on the internet in terms similar to those Czitrom quotes.

2. Write an essay describing a middle position between Thoreau's skepticism and Shaffner's enthusiasm.

# Is There a There In Cyberspace?

## John Perry Barlow

*John Perry Barlow, a self-described "cognitive dissident," is probably best known for the songs he wrote for the Grateful Dead, such as "Cassidy" and "Estimated Prophet." Most of those songs were written during the seventeen years he lived on a Wyoming ranch, which he was forced to sell in 1988. It was that year that he began thinking and writing about the new frontier of cyberspace, and his experiences soon led him to found, with Mitchell Kapor, the Electronic Frontier Foundation, to which contributor Mike Godwin also belongs. He can be reached via e-mail at barlow@eff.org.*

I am often asked how I went from pushing cows around a remote Wyoming ranch to my present occupation (which *Wall Street Journal* recently described as "cyberspace cadet"). I haven't got a short answer, but I suppose I came to the virtual world looking for community.

Unlike most modern Americans. I grew up in an actual place, an entirely nonintentional community called Pinedale, Wyoming. As I struggled for nearly a generation to keep my ranch in the family, I was motivated by the belief that such places were the spiritual home of humanity. But I knew their future was not promising.

At the dawn of the 20th century, over 40 percent of the American workforce lived off the land. The majority of us lived in towns like Pinedale. Now fewer than 1 percent of us extract a living from the soil. We just became too productive for our own good.

Of course, the population followed the jobs. Farming and ranching communities are now home to a demographically insignificant percentage of Americans, the vast majority of whom live not in ranch houses but in more or less identical split-level "ranch homes" in more or less identical suburban "communities." Generica.

In my view, these are neither communities nor homes. I believe the combination of television and suburban population patterns is simply toxic to the soul. I see much evidence in contemporary America to support this view.

Meanwhile, back at the ranch, doom impended. And, as I watched community in Pinedale growing ill from the same economic forces that were killing my family's ranch, the Bar Cross, satellite dishes brought the cultural infection of television. I started looking around for evidence that community in America would not perish altogether.

I took some heart in the mysterious nomadic City of the Deadheads, the virtually physical town that follows the Grateful Dead around the country. The Deadheads lacked place, touching down briefly wherever the band happened to be playing. and they lacked continuity in time, since they had to suffer a new diaspora every time the band moved on or went home. But they had many of the other necessary elements of community, including a culture, a religion of sorts (which, though it lacked dogma, had most of the other, more nurturing aspects of spiritual practice), a sense of necessity, and, most importantly, shared adversity.

I wanted to know more about the flavor of their interaction, what they thought and felt, but since I wrote Dead songs (including "Estimated Prophet" and "Cassidy"), I was a minor icon to the Deadheads, and was thus inhibited, in some socially Heisenbergian way, from getting a clear view of what really went on among them.

Then, in 1987, I heard about a "place" where Deadheads gathered where I could move among them without distorting too much the field of observation. Better, this was a place I could visit without leaving Wyoming. It was a shared computer in Sausalito, California, called the Whole Earth 'Lectronic Link. or WELL. After a lot of struggling with modems, serial cables, init strings, and other computer arcana that seemed utterly out of phase with such notions as Deadheads and small towns. I found myself looking at the glowing yellow word "Login:" beyond which lay my future.

"Inside" the WELL were Deadheads in community. There were thousands of them there, gossiping, complaining (mostly about the Grateful Dead), comforting and harassing each other, bartering, engaging in religion (or at least exchanging their totemic set lists), beginning and ending love affairs, praying for one another's sick kids. There was, it seemed, everything one might find going on in a small town, save dragging Main Street and making out on the back roads.

I was delighted. I felt I had found the new locale of human community—never mind that the whole thing was being conducted in mere words by minds from whom the bodies had been amputated. Never mind that all these people were deaf, dumb. and blind as paramecia or that their town had neither seasons nor sunsets nor smells.

Surely all these deficiencies would be remedied by richer, faster communications media. The featureless log-in handles would gradually acquire video faces (and thus expressions), shaded 3-D body puppets (and thus body language). This "space" which I recognized at once to be a primitive form of the cyberspace William Gibson predicted his sci-fi novel *Neuromancer,* was still without apparent dimensions or vistas, But virtual reality would change all that in time.

Meanwhile, the commons, or something like it, had been rediscovered. Once again, people from the 'burbs had a place where they could encounter their friends as my fellow Pinedalians did at the post office and the Wrangler Cafe. They had a place where their hearts could remain as the companies they worked for shuffled their bodies around America. They could put down roots that could not be ripped out by forces of economic history. They had a collective stake. They had a community.

It is seven years now since I discovered the WELL. In that time, I co-founded an organization, the Electronic Frontier Foundation, dedicated to protecting its interests and those of other virtual communities like it from raids by physical government. I've spent countless hours typing away at its residents, and I've watched the larger context that contains it, the Internet, grow at such an explosive rate that, by 2004, every human on the planet will have an e-mail address unless the growth curve flattens (which it will).

My enthusiasm for virtuality has cooled. In fact, unless one counts interaction with the rather too large society of those with whom I exchange electronic mail, I don't spend much time engaging in virtual community at all. Many of the near-term benefits I anticipated from it seem to remain as far in the future as they did when I first logged in. Perhaps they always will.

Pinedale works, more or less, as it is, but a lot is still missing from the communities of cyberspace, whether they be places like the WELL, the fractious newsgroups of USENET, the silent "auditoriums" of America Online, or even enclaves on the promising World Wide Web.

What is missing? Well, to quote Ranjit Makkuni of Xerox Corporation's Palo Alto Research Center, "the *prāna* is missing," *prāna* being the Hindu term for both breath and spirit. I think he is right about this and that perhaps the central question of the virtual age is whether or not *prāna* can somehow be made to fit through any disembodied medium.

*Prāna* is, to my mind, the literally vital element in the holy and unseen ecology of relationship, the dense mesh of invisible life. on whose surface carbon-based life floats like a thin film. It is at the heart of the fundamental and profound difference between information and experience. Jaron Lanier has said that "information is alienated experience," and, that being true, *prāna* is part of what is removed when you create such easily transmissible replicas of experience as, say, the evening news.

Obviously a great many other, less spiritual, things are also missing entirely, like body language, sex, death, tone of voice, clothing, beauty (or homeliness), weather, violence, vegetation, wildlife, pets, architecture, music, smells, sunlight, and that ol' harvest moon. In short, most of the things that make my life real to me.

Present, but in far less abundance than in the physical world, which I call "meat space," are women, children, old people, poor people, and the genuinely blind. Also mostly missing are the illiterate and the continent of Africa. There is not much human diversity in cyberspace, which is populated, as near as I can tell, by white males under 50 with plenty of computer terminal time—great typing skills, high math SATS, strongly held opinions on just about everything, and an excruciating face-to-face shyness, especially with the opposite sex.

But diversity is as essential to healthy community as it is to healthy ecosystems (which are, in my view, different from communities only in unimportant aspects).

I believe that the principal reason for the almost universal failure of the intentional communities of the '60s and '70s was a lack of diversity in their members It was a rare commune with any old people in it, or people who were fundamentally out of philosophical agreement with the majority.

Indeed, it is the usual problem when we try to build something that can only be grown. Natural systems, such as human communities are simply too complex to design by the engineering principles we insist on applying to them. Like Dr. Frankenstein, Western civilization is now finding its rational skills inadequate to the task of creating and caring for life. We would do better to return to a kind of agricultural mind-set in which we humbly try to re-create the conditions from which life has sprung before. And leave the rest to God.

Given that it has been built so far almost entirely by people with engineering degrees, it is not so surprising that cyberspace has the kind of overdesigned quality that leaves out all kinds of elements nature would have provided invisibly.

Also missing from both the communes of the '60s and from cyberspace are a couple of elements that I believe are very important, if not essential, to the formation and preservation of real community: an absence of alternatives and a sense of genuine adversity, generally shared. What about these?

It is hard to argue that anyone would find losing a modem literally hard to survive, while many have remained in small towns, have tolerated their intolerances and created entertainment to enliven their culturally arid lives simply because it seemed there was no choice but to stay. There are many investments—spiritual, material, and temporal—one is willing to put into a home one cannot leave. Communities are often the beneficiaries of these involuntary investments.

But when the going gets rough in cyberspace, it is even easier to move than it is in the 'burbs, where, given the fact that the average American moves some 12 times in his or her life, moving appears to be pretty easy. You can not only find another bulletin board service (BBS) or newsgroup to hang out in, you can, with very little effort, start your own.

And then there is the bond of joint suffering. Most community is a cultural stockade erected against a common enemy that can take many forms. In Pinedale, we bore together, with an understanding needing little expression, the fact that Upper Green River Valley is the coldest spot, as measured by annual mean temperature, in the lower 48 states. We knew that if somebody was stopped on the road most winter nights, he would probably die there, so the fact that we might loathe him was not sufficient reason to drive on past his broken pickup.

By the same token, the Deadheads have the Drug Enforcement Administration, which strives to give them 20-year prison terms without parole for distributing the fairly harmless sacrament of their faith. They have an additional bond in the fact that when their Microbuses die, as they often do, no one but another Deadhead is likely to stop to help them.

But what are the shared adversities of cyberspace? Lousy user interfaces? The flames of harsh invective? Dumb jokes? Surely these can all be survived without the sanctuary provided by fellow sufferers.

One is always free to yank the jack, as I have mostly done. For me, the physical world offers far more opportunity for *prāna*-rich connections with my fellow creatures. Even for someone whose body is in a state of perpetual motion. I feel I can generally find more community among the still-embodied.

Finally, there is that shyness factor. Not only are we trying to build community here among people who have never experienced any in my sense of the term, we are trying to build community among people who, in their lives, have rarely used the word *we* in a heartfelt way. It is a vast club, and many of the members—following Groucho Marx—wouldn't want to join a club that would have them.

And yet. . . .

How quickly physical community continues to deteriorate. Even Pinedale, which seems to have survived the plague of ranch failures, feels increasingly cut off from itself. Many of the ranches are now owned by corporate types who fly their Gulfstreams in to fish and are rarely around during the many months when the creeks are frozen over and neighbors are needed. They have kept the ranches alive financially, but they actively discourage their managers from the interdependence my former colleagues and I require. They keep agriculture on life support, still alive but lacking a functional heart.

And the town has been inundated with suburbanites who flee here, bringing all their terrors and suspicions with them. They spend their evenings as they did in Orange County, watching television or socializing in hermetic little enclaves of fundamentalist Christianity that seem to separate them from us and even, given their sectarian animosities, from one another. The town remains. The community is largely a wraith of nostalgia.

So where else can we look for the connection we need to prevent our plunging further into the condition of separateness Nietzsche called sin? What is there to do but to dive further into the bramble bush of information that, in its broadcast forms, has done so much to tear us apart?

Cyberspace, for all its current deficiencies and failed promises, is not without some very real solace already.

Some months ago, the great love of my life, a vivid young woman with whom I intended to spend the rest of it, dropped dead of undiagnosed viral cardiomyopathy two days short of her 30th birthday. I felt as if my own heart had been as shredded as hers.

We had lived together in New York City. Except for my daughters, no one from Pinedale had met her. I needed a community to wrap around myself against colder winds than fortune had ever blown at me before. And without looking, I found I had one in the virtual world.

On the WELL, there was a topic announcing her death in one of the conferences to which I posted the eulogy I had read over her before burying her in her own small town of Nanaimo, British Columbia. It seemed to strike a chord among the disembodied living on the Net. People copied it and sent it to one another. Over the next several months I received almost a megabyte of electronic mail from all over the planet, mostly from folks whose faces I have never seen and probably never will.

They told me of their own tragedies and what they had done to survive them. As humans have since words were first uttered, we shared the second most common human experience, death, with an openheartedness that would have caused grave uneasiness in physical America, where the whole topic is so cloaked in denial as to be considered obscene. Those strangers, who had no arms to put around my shoulders, no eyes to weep with mine, nevertheless saw me through. As neighbors do.

I have no idea how far we will plunge into this strange place. Unlike previous frontiers, this one has no end. It is so dissatisfying in so many ways that I suspect we will be more restless in our search for home here than in all our previous explorations. And that is one reason why I think we may find it after all. If home is where the heart is, then there is already some part of home to be found in cyberspace,

So . . . does virtual community work or not? Should we all go off to cyberspace or should we resist it as a demonic form of symbolic abstraction? Does it supplant the real or is there, in it, reality itself?

Like so many true things, this one doesn't resolve itself to a black or a white. Nor is it gray. It is, along with the rest of life, black/white. Both/neither. I'm not being equivocal or wishy-washy hem We have to get over our Manichean sense that everything is either good or bad, and the border of cyberspace seems to me a good place to leave that old set of filters.

But really it doesn't matter. We are going there whether we want to or not. In five years everyone who is reading these words will have an e-mail address other than the determined Luddites who also eschew the telephone and electricity.

When we are all together in cyberspace we will see what the human spirit, and the basic desire to connect, can create there. I am convinced that the result will be more benign if we go there open-minded, open-hearted, and excited with the adventure than if we are dragged into exile.

And we must remember that going to cyberspace, unlike previous great emigrations to the frontier, hardly requires us to leave where we have been. Many will find, as I have, a much richer appreciation of physical reality for having spent so much time in virtuality.

Despite its current (and perhaps in some areas permanent) insufficiencies, we should go to cyberspace with hope. Groundless hope, like unconditional love, may be the only kind that counts.

## Themes, Issues, and Ideas

1. What are some ways in which Barlow defines a "community"? Do you accept this definitions?

2. Discuss the concept of *prāna* and how it might relate to electronic communications. What is Barlow's view of the question?

3. How much does Barlow's background affect his perspective, in your estimation? How might someone else, with another background, see things differently?

## Writing Strategies and Techniques

1. What is the basic structure of Barlow's essay? Is it autobiographical? Chronological? Analytic? How are the different aspects of his work bound to-gether?

2. Does Barlow's enthusiasm for (and reservations about) the Internet seem genuine? In what ways does he convey sincerity?

## Suggestions for Writing

1. Answer the question of Barlow's title. Is there a there in cyberspace? What is your definition of a community?

2. Find one sentence of Barlow's that seems particularly significant to you, and write a one-page essay discussing it.

# High-Tech Redlining

## Reginald Stuart

*We've all heard how the internet is changing society and will change more in the future in unforeseeable ways. But just who will it change for? Is everyone entering the information revolution together? In an essay excerpted from the African-American magazine* Emerge, *Reginald Stuart asks some questions about the internet revolution, and particularly in regard to a part of the population often ignored when computers are discussed.*

It is the world's most unusual highway, with no speed limits, no police and no need for gasoline gauges.

It's called the information superhighway, and already limited access ramps have been constructed. When completed, the information superhighway will be a pipeline through which nearly every form of communication conceivable will pass. You name it and the highway most likely will carry it: love letters, business mail, televised telephone calls, newspaper stories, radio and TV shows, movies, educational programs and even medical assistance.

Big predictions for something many Americans—especially African-Americans—have never heard of.

"This convergence of media will create one central nervous system of our society. African-Americans have a lot at stake," says Jeff Chester, executive director of the Washington–based Center for Media Education.

Just as many Black communities today bear the scars of the interstate highway system that slowly plowed through them a generation ago, Black Americans risk being road kill on the information superhighway.

"I see this as the civil rights issue and the economic rights issue of the 21st century," says Chester.

192

In the embryonic days of the now 40,000–mile–plus interstate highway system, there were many who doubted it ever would be built. Even fewer black people knew what the interstate was or understood its potential to redefine or even destroy entire communities. Now, amid the remnants of what used to be cohesive communities, more wish they had known about it or had listened to those who did.

In many respects, the scenario for the communications highway is evolving in much the same way. A handful of visionaries are working the halls of Congress to clear the legal obstacles to the convergence of communications technologies. In boardrooms across the nation, big ideas are being explored on how to pool big money to control positions in the information marketplace much as Holiday Inns and Exxon appeared to make it to every major interstate highway interchange and exit before the rest of the pack could read the maps.

Amid this activity, investors and controllers of the medium are viewing African-Americans as marginal players—only as consumers.

"African-Americans do not have to be road kill, but it is going to require a concerted effort," says Larry Irving, an assistant secretary at the United States Department of Commerce and director of the National Telecommunications Information Administration. Irving is at the core of the small group of people who really understand the information highway concept and its potential.

"We either have to get on it or be left behind," Irving says. "We have to get the technologies deployed in minority communities, make sure our children are technologically literate and seize the entrepreneurial opportunities."

Indeed, Irving, Vice President Gore and other promoters of the next generation of communications concede this idea has the potential of further separating America's haves and have-nots. But they say this is not their intent. "We want to make sure the on- and off-ramps get to everyone in this country," Irving says.

Things are off to a rocky start.

A coalition of groups following developments in Washington have accused the nation's telephone companies of "electronic redlining" in developing their plans for building a communications network for the superhighway. The Center for Media Education, the NAACP, the Office of Communication of the United Church of Christ, the Consumer Federation of America and the Council of La Raza, assert that minority communities are being bypassed and have asked the Federal Communications Commission to investigate; the phone companies strongly deny the claim.

To understand the information superhighway, one has to understand something called Internet. An easy way to do that is to talk to Sherman B. Ellegood, a 41-year-old computer program analyst at the Smithsonian Institution in Washington. Today, Ellegood, and increasingly his wife and children, can talk about Internet and the superhighway the way sports fans talk about their favorite pastimes. Internet allows computer users around the world to send short messages or encyclopedia-sized volumes of information to one another. It's done through a sophisticated interconnection of the world's telephone network.

"It puts a lot of people in touch with a lot of information," says Ellegood, who, with the push of a button on his home computer, sends simultaneous messages almost daily to his mother in Wilmington, Del., sister in California, brother in Richmond, Va., and sister in Saratoga, N.Y. "I can talk to them everyday with one swoop, one message, one local phone call."

Ellegood and fellow users connect with one computer network, which connects to another, then to another, making Internet a super bulletin board system. Today, there are some 13,000 types of services accessible through Internet, according to the National Science Foundation.

There also are many single commercial bulletin board systems in operation: CompuServe, America OnLine and Prodigy, to name a few. These on-line services can cost as little as $8.95 a month. They allow one to do such things as check on the latest news quotes, find the cheapest airline prices and book the seat, view the weather forecast and, of course, interact with other users.

Internet is the bulletin board of bulletin boards, a general purpose network for commercial operations such as CompuServe, non-commercial operations such as academia, area social clubs and nonprofit groups. Only a handful of the millions of Internet users pay for the access. Usually, an employer or school foots the bill as a routine business expense. Users get free access at work or at home through a code.

The U.S. Defense Department established Internet some 25 years ago as the Advanced Research Projects Agency (ARPA) network to help the communication among colleges doing government research. The government then set up a worldwide network for the institutions.

In the mid-1980s, the National Science Foundation set up a similar network for the academic community. It became so successful that in 1990, the government shut down the ARPA network. The NSF network became the catalyst for the establishment of numerous computer communications networks and eventually the vision of a super Internet called the information superhighway.

The invention of digital television in 1990, by General Instruments gave a whole new dimension to the possibilities of an electronic information superhighway. Through digital technology, voice, text and visual data can be converted to a common signal for transmission purposes and transformed back to voice, text or visuals for reception. The new communications industry would allow a convergence of computer, television, cellular telephone and satellite technologies to bring every conceivable bit of knowledge to anyone with a computer to access it.

The theory among electronic superhighway advocates is that something almost magical is about to happen: In the not too distant future, every home will have a computer and every person in the home will use it. Fiber optic cables capable of carrying huge volumes of information, from every television episode of *Fresh Prince of Bel Air* to every word in the Bible, will be commonplace in the poorest and wealthiest of neighborhoods. People will hook up to this fiber optic cable and through digital technology, receive communications from anyone at any time and in most any form (voice, text or visual). The knowledge will be there for the taking if you are part of the superhighway "in-crowd."

Ellegood is part of that "in-crowd." With their computers in tow, his children will be, too. But so far, they are among the relatively few in Black America. A 1989 report by the U.S. Census Bureau found computer use and ownership skyrocketing. But use and ownership by African–Americans was almost negligible.

The report said that 26.9 million, or 18.3 percent, of Whites used computers at home, while only 1.5 million, or 8.4 percent, of Blacks did the same.

On the eve of the dawn of the highway, Blacks are getting a late start. Among children, age 3 to 17, some 10.7 million, or 26.7 percent, of Whites used computers at home, compared with 806,000, or 10.6 percent, of Black children. Not good for the generation that will be looking for jobs in the next century when the highway may be plowing ahead at a steady clip.

In school, the number of children using computers rises significantly for both groups, but the gap is just as profound. Some 17.4 million White students, or 48.2 percent, used computers in schools in 1989. Only 2.4 million Black students, or 35.1 percent, were using computers at school.

The same report found most computer ownership at home was closely associated with household income (and education) levels, with 47.5 percent of households with annual incomes of $75,000 or more owning computers and 4.8 percent of households with incomes of $15,000 or less owning a computer.

To put that in context, nearly one-third of all Black Americans lived in poverty in 1990, according to the census bureau. The government defines poverty as a two-person household making $9,165 or less a year or a four-person household with an annual income of $13,924 or less. Not enough fuel here for competitively traveling the new highway.

"There's a whole lot of stuff out there we don't have," says Barbara Valerious, principal at Chicago High School for the Agricultural Sciences. The South Side school has one of the highest graduation rates of any school in the Windy City, and 95 percent of its graduates go to college (70 percent to four-year colleges).

But like most high schools in the nation, Chicago high has only a handful of computers—three to be exact—and only one is accessible to students.

Educators contend that any policy should ensure that each school in the country has computers to access the highway, lest their students be left behind. Librarians are making the case that certainly any policy would not neglect the needs of the nation's cash-strapped library systems.

Valerious, who knows few details of the superhighway, is optimistic. "Our kids sitting on the Southwest Side of Chicago are going to be touching the world," she predicts.

In the meantime, the big companies are keeping their eye on the dollar prize. The potential for making big money on the information highway with the right combination of forces and ideas has prompted more than a few breathtaking merger proposals. The largest was a proposal by Bell Atlantic, one of the seven Regional Bell Operating Companies spun off from AT&T a decade ago, to buy cable giant TCI for $26 billion.

Black companies, by and large, rarely talk of mergers and pooling capital, and when they do, it is more likely to be in the $26 million range.

In Washington power circles, less than half a dozen names come to mind as being in a position to bid for a piece of the action as investors or information suppliers: Don Barden, the Detroit area cable television operator; Robert Johnson, owner of Black Entertainment Television; and Percy Sutton, head of Inner City Broadcasting in New York.

"To become a player it is going to take tens of millions of dollars," says Irving of the Commerce Department. "It's a risk minority entrepreneurs cannot afford not to take if they are going to be a player in these technologies. They are going to have to consolidate resources and network with non-minorities."

Irving echoes other telecommunications veterans who warn against declaring the field essentially closed to all but the big cable and telephone companies. They note that there will be all sorts of niches to be filled and that African-Americans have the creative talents—if not the money—to make a way out of no way.

When the National Infrastructure Network debuted this time a year ago, it had two primary objectives: to eliminate barriers to competition between the telephone and cable companies so that their local service monopolies would give way to competition, and to give business more research and development tax breaks so the highway could evolve.

Woven through this agenda was the notion of extending so–called "universal service," to ensure that the new technology were available to everyone at affordable prices. It's the closest thing to an on- and off-ramp for Blacks along the highway. It was the universal service philosophy pursued by the federal government that ensured affordable telephone service would be within reach of every American.

In a relatively short time, the new information highway has become a lot of things to a lot of people. The cable companies deny that pending infrastructure legislation is a veiled attempt to allow them to compete with the phone companies. Local telephone companies deny they are riding the infrastructure bandwagon just to win relief from a 10-year-old court order that bars them from offering such profitable services as long distance and cable programs.

But the information superhighway steadily has begun to look more and more like a Christmas tree as highway legislation moves through Congress. To get the legislation passed, the Clinton administration and lawmakers pushing the legislation are entertaining all constituent ideas—the desires of educators and librarians, for example—to tack on their tree.

Some people believe there can be presents under the superhighway tree for African-Americans in the form of billions of dollars in savings on telephone and cable service costs. At least that's the argument they make on behalf of themselves and the seven Regional Bell Operating Companies.

Delores Davis-Penn is one such optimist. Her two trips this year to Washington to woo lawmakers were paid for by Southwestern Bell. Davis-Penn was armed with a report by Philadelphia-based PNR & Associates Inc., a telecommunications marketing research firm. It contends minorities would see a savings of $116 billion by the year 2003 on long distance charges alone if the regional phone companies were allowed to offer long distance to compete with AT&T and MCI.

The report says very little about the information highway. But the phone companies argue there can be no true highway if they are not allowed to travel it unfettered. Davis-Penn finds merit in their case and has become an advocate for them and, in the process, the new super-highway.

"If we take the attitude that we're going to bury our heads in the sand and say, 'This is something I don't understand so I'm not going to pay it any attention,' we're the losers," says Davis-Penn, who holds a doctorate in educational gerontology at the Cooperative Extension Service of Lincoln University in Columbia, Missouri.

Davis-Penn admits few people—Black, White, Yellow, Brown— know what she is talking about or what the new highway is. But there was a time not too long ago, she recalls, when the television set was new and nearly as strange.

"When television sets were first introduced, very few Blacks had television sets," recalls Davis-Penn. (Now, not only do they have them, most surveys show Blacks watch more television than any other demographic group.)

"Looking into the future, it is my belief that computers will become like television sets in our homes," says Davis-Penn. With that computer saturation comes the new highway, she explains, and with the new highway comes new job opportunities and new chances to create radio and television programming that is culturally sensitive to African-Americans.

Says Davis-Penn, "It requires creativity to push our people to accept the challenge."

# Themes, Issues,and Ideas

1. What is the difference between being viewed as a consumer, and being viewed as to a director?

2. What are some ways in which blacks or other minorities might be disenfranchised by the growth of the information superhighway? In what ways do the advantages of being white overlap with those of being on-line?

3. Stuart starts off his essay by an analogy with the national highway system. How does it affect communities? What are some other innovations that have had similar effects?

# Writing Strategies and Techniques

1. Is Stuart's use of statistics convincing? Why or why not?

2. Does Stuart give you information in this essay? Does he give you too much? How much would you give in an essay of comparable length on the same subject? Explain your answer.

# Suggestions for Writing

1. Write three examples of ways in which exclusion from the "information superhighway" can hurt a person in American society.

2. Dispute the conclusions Stuart derives from his statistics. What might be alternate explanations for them?

# Babes in the Net

## Sadie Plant

*"Is there a there in cyberspace?" asked John Perry Barlow in an earlier essay. In this essay by the British writer Sadie Plant, the question "who's who?" is at least as important. Why should the internet not change gender identities, Plant asks, when it is in the process of changing everything else? Identity—not social status or power—is the most radical of the changes that the cyber-age will bring.*

T he storm has broken in the past few months. Turn on the TV, and there's virtual reality, mulitmedia, the Net, computers, and video games. Go to the newsagents, and in between the top-shelf fantasies of *Digital Dreams* and the piles of highbrow papers you find a wealth of magazines devoted to the software and hardware of computing, telecommunications, games, new media arts, techno music, dance culture, and other cyberian interests. Suddenly, cyberspace is everywhere.

Though its arrival seems strangely abrupt, this cybernetic future has in fact been here for some time. It is more than a decade since the publication of William Gibson's *Neuromancer,* the novel that brought cyberspace to the street. The Internet is older still. Even the computer, still referred to as a "new technology," is only a little younger than the old, grey TV.

What is new, of course, is the ubiquity of things cyber, hyper, and virtual. And although it is fashionable to dismiss them all as simply matters of consumerist hype, even die-hard Luddites are beginning to realize the extent of the cultural changes they bring.

Work, play, art, science, literature, sex, education... digitisation leaves nothing untouched. Social relations are being transformed by the development of telecommuting, hypermedia systems. and a new world of on-line information. In particular, everything in the vicinity of sex, gender, and sexuality is being dramatically rewired.

Cyberspace brings unprecedented confusion to sexual—and all—identities. You can go on-line and be anyone. You can go on-line and be no one at all. As for where and when you are when you're connected to the global telecoms network, it's always difficult to say. Such deregulated possibilities have star appeal for women—and all those who've struggled within the straightjacket of identity.

Recent undoings of history, moreover, discover a close and long-standing interface between women and non-linear machines: women were at one time literally called computers, and now even the machines seem to be converging with the women who first programmed them. The centralized, top-down structures of the old serial systems are not subsumed by the smart speeds of parallel distributed processors with their lateral connections and intuitive leaps. The Net itself has no organizing core, but pulls itself together from the bottom-up, replicating networks and making connections, just as women have organized themselves.

It may be problematic to define these tendencies as positively feminine. But it is also clear that they go against everything dear to the heart of all power structures—and the phallic principles that keep them secure.

Even so, it it's now right-on to distrust the hype, it wasn't long ago that the politically correct believed computers to be somehow essentially male. Traditional feminists and misogynists alike have insisted that cyberspace does nothing to disturb the roots of patriarchal power, and there have indeed been some celebrated cases of virtual sexual harassment and other examples of boyish bad news. It certainly seems that male users of the Net still outnumber their female counterparts and, back on the top shelf, heterosex and computer games converge between the cover of *Digital Dreams* (and, of course, on its free CD). Teresa May and Vicky Lee meet Wake of the Ravager and Wrath of the Gods. Yet more toys for the same old boys: not much of a sexual politics here.

But facts and figures are as hard to ascertain as gender itself in the virtual world. And if women face the same old problems there as in their everyday lives, they are also, and increasingly, discovering new possibilities for work, play, and communication of all kinds in the spaces emergent from the telecoms revolution. As for politics, even those of the sexual variety, questions of the "what is to be done?" variety are no longer the only ones to rise. The digital revolution does a great deal more than rework the rules of social and familiar life. Complex dynamics, self-organising systems, non-linear processes, nano-technology, machine intelligence: the species that thought it was in control now find itself in a paradigm shift that undermines its role and destroys its separation from its own machines and from what it called nature.

If life itself is being re-engineered by computerised genetics and intelligent machines, modern conceptions of what it is to be human are hardly immune from the runaway effects of what were once believed to be simply the discoveries and inversions of man. And it always has been man, the male, who has circumscribed humanity. *Homo sapiens* has defined itself against a feminine considered too fluid, flexible and lacking in concentration to merit anything more than associate membership of the species. It is these women, however, who have the last laugh.

As intelligence becomes more valuable than strength, the strong sense of purpose and identity that once served the masculine so well becomes nothing more than a liability in a world of Net schizophrenia, self-organising systems, and emergent planetary intelligence. Girls are achieving more than boys at school, female skills and working patterns are reshaping the economic world. From Brazil to Bangladesh, women are escaping social control and men are running to catch them up.

In the face of such dramatic shifts, arguments about whether the Net or virtual reality allow more or less room for benign social orders lose clout; the telecoms revolution is no good for anyone concerned with such solely humanist affairs. While there are high hopes that new and improved social relations will begin to emerge on the Net, nothing is simply reproduced, least of all communities (you remember them— the social bonds that once kept women and immigrants at home). But it is the case that, by a suitably bottom-up and piecemeal process distributed far beyond the social world, the digital revolution is re-engineering the very conditions of patriarchy. Hooked up to the Net, the computerised economy and his new prostheses and implants, man loses his power and self-control as he becomes entangled with the machines. And *this* is what is doing the trick, opening new spaces for brand new girls and whatever post-human mutations may come.

While everyone gazes in the rear-view mirror, guarding the present as the reproduction of the past and hoping to legislate the future in advance, the sands of time are running into silicon, and Read Only Memory is coming to an end. Digitisation is traumatic for humans. Those with no identity to lose don't even need to adjust their sets

# Themes, Issues, and Ideas

1. Why does Plant maintain that women "have the last laugh" in cyberspace? Do you agree?

2. To what extent does Plant agree or disagree with traditional conceptions of gender? What are these conceptions?

3. "You can go on-line and be anyone. You can go on-line and be no one at all." Do you agree with this statement? To what extent does Plant's essay support or deny it?

# Writing Strategies and Techniques

1. Pick a phrase that strikes you as persuasive and/or original. Is it typical of Plant's writing style as a whole? Why or why not?

2. Does Plant seem brilliant and creative, or just verbose and ostentatious, to you—or something in-between? What are the points in her essay that are best, and worst, served by the over-the-top style of her prose?

# Suggestions for Writing

1. Write a diary-entry of a "post-human mutation" such as Plant suggests will be ushered into being by the internet.

2. Think of some examples of computer communications that seem exceptions to the trends Plant describes. Try to think of some that support these trends. Decide which list has the better claim, and discuss it in a short essay.

# from Silicone Snake Oil

## Clifford Stoll

*As you may have gathered from reading some of the other essays in this chapter, the advent of a "computer age" and its attendant changes is pretty much taken for granted these days. But although "cyberspace" may seem as inevitable at the millennia itself, not everyone is convinced. Science writer Clifford Stroll published the book-length 1995 essay from which this selection is taken.*

America Online, CompuServe, and public Free-nets, by making the networks easily accessible, have brought lots of newbies online. It's a young, mostly male population...informal surveys suggest that fewer than a quarter of all users are female.

Logged in, it's hard to tell who's who—some hide behind pseudonyms, others advertise their names directly. The Jane Fonda that's listed in a return address may well belong to some guy; another may simply be listed as K8366.

Since there's no identification required on the Internet, you can be as anonymous as you wish. You can change your name and identity as you please, and your location may be little more than a node.

You can invent a more confident persona, freed from shyness and physical limitations. A housewife in Boise, Idaho, gives herself the name Amazon Gal; a New York City teenager becomes Ranchhand. At this masquerade party, you truly don't know who you're associating with.

Anonymity and untraceability seem to bring out the worst in people. I'm hardly surprised to see online chat rooms labeled "Want MF for Affair" and "Teenage Confessional."

As my computer screen scrolls before me, I see each person with the same font, style, and packaging. In person, we'd sense a difference in clothing, facial expression, accent, and sex. All these disappear online.

Meet a bigot on the street who's shouting obscenities, and you get away from him fast. Should the same person post to net news, you'll read most of his message before going on to the next. Access to the network gives both audience and credibility to extreme opinions.

MUDs—Multi-User Dungeons—are interactive role games, played across the Internet. People connect to a distant computer, create their own characters, and interact with others by typing commands and comments. Nobody knows anybody else's identity; online persona is everything. We can step outside of traditional boundaries of social constraint, confide in strangers, and become intimate with utterly fictional characters.

Both in role-playing games and in chat rooms, the network presents an unreal world where you can appear to be anyone you wish. Adopt a friendly persona or that of a grinch. But you aren't who you pretend to be. Inside, you're still you.

Participants at this masked ball are free to talk about otherwise uncomfortable or verboten subjects. Popular discussion groups revolve around sex, bondage, and pornographic images.

All this from a decidedly unsexy medium. There's no possibility of physical intimacy; at best, only a hope that a correspondent might turn out to be as you imagine. Yet you may well be chatting with someone masquerading as a different sex and different age.

Tailoring a persona is an experience of otherness, a way to escape the here and now. I'll bet some bearded philosopher—Martin Buber, maybe—discussed how the authenticity of experience can diffuse alienation from our true selves. The separation between us, once imposed by circumstance, is now chosen by network addicts.

Yet for all these network creations, you have nothing physical invested. No matter where you appear to be, you are always in the same place. No matter how dangerous the situation seems, you're always safe. No matter how sensual the conversation feels, you cannot consummate the relationship. And no matter what persona you adopt, inside you're still you.

Computer networks isolate us from one another, rather than bring us together. We need only deal with one side of an individual over the net. And if we don't like what we see, we just pull the plug. Or flame them. There's no need to tolerate the imperfections of real people. It's the same intolerance found on the highway, where motorists direct intense anger at one another.

By logging on to the networks, we lose the ability to enter into spontaneous interactions with real people. Evening time is now spent watching a television or a computer terminal—safe havens in which to hide. Sitting around a porch and talking is becoming extinct, as is reading aloud to children.

The Internet puts me in touch with thousands of people across the country. But it's more important to spend time with my friends and neighbors. Karen Anderson, the penguin keeper at San Francisco's Steinhart Aquarium, puts it this way: "The people who are right close to me are the most important ones in my life. Why should I get excited about personal relationships on some computer network?"

Karen told me of the work of Dr. Luis Baptista, the curator of ornithology at the California Academy of Sciences. This guy knows his birds—he can whistle the songs of doves and sparrows. Jeez, he did his dissertation on the dialects of these birds.

Well, to see how birds learn songs, he raised white-crowned sparrows. When they left the nest, Dr. Baptista placed single fledglings in a special cage where they could see and hear an Asian strawberry finch. The young birds could also hear several dialects of their own sparrow songs in the same room, but they couldn't see those sparrows.

The fledgling sparrows didn't learn their own songs. Instead, they matured, singing the songs of the Asian finches with whom they socially interacted. And later, as parents, these sparrows taught their young to sing Chinese songs, too. Sparrows learn from living teachers, not from machines.

In the same way, the isolation of computers and online networks causes us to sing others' songs. Children, raised with less social interaction, adopt the ways of the first people they come in close contact with. It encourages a divorce from parental values and the dominance of peer culture. Kids that interact with computers rather than their parents miss out on the most important part of growing: being close to their families.

Think I'm exaggerating? One teenager in Berkeley began using a computer when he was three years old; today, he's utterly fluent in getting around the Internet, but can't converse with an adult. I know several computer wizards who can tell you details of their computer's disk cache, but don't know when their family immigrated to America. And I've met dozens of high school students who can proficiently use a word processor, but have never written a thank-you letter.

# Themes, Issues, and Ideas

1. What does Stoll see as the main disadvantage in computer users being able to hide or abstract their identity?

2. Do you find Stoll's examples convincing? Are the representative? Choose one or two and write a critique.

3. What do you think about Stoll's final point, about children (or sparrows) learning what they are exposed to? Is there anything unusual about the conclusions Stoll draws? Explain your answer.

# Writing Strategies and Techniques

1. How would you describe the style in which Stoll writes? Do you feel it is appropriate for the subject matter he discusses?

2. Stoll's arguments are orderly, but not linear—that is, he likes to make a series of short, self-contained arguments in a row. Why?

# Suggestions for Writing

1. "Yet for all these network creations, you have nothing physical invested. No matter where you appear to be, you are always in the same place.... [N]o matter what persona you adopt, inside you're still you." Write an essay agreeing or disagreeing with this statement, and using examples from outside Stoll's text.

2. Write a scenario between two people on the internet that either demonstrates or refutes Stoll's main points.

# ASCII Is Too Intimate

## Mike Godwin

> *In this essay from* Wired Magazine, *Mike Godwin discusses the question of whether ASCII (the computer word for the marks and letters on the basic typewriter keyboard) is really less communicative than other, more hi-tech, forms such as video graphics. Mike Godwin is the legal counsel for Electronic Frontier Foundation, the California organization of which "Is There a There in Cyberspace?" author John Perry Barlow is president. His internet address, should you wish to write him, is godwin@eff.org.*

You're a newcomer to the Internet, but you've learned the basics. So here you are, floating along in cyberspace, dropping the occasional bon mot or learned exposition into Usenet discussions and jetstreaming e-mail through T3 backbones. Suddenly, you jump back from your monitor with adrenalin nausea and the irrational sense that your eyebrows have been singed. You've been flamed!

Not to worry, your e-friends and e-mentors will assure you. Flaming (typically defined as the posting of e-mail or public messages designed to insult or provoke) is an occupational hazard of the Net. Mere text, they'll tell you, is too narrow a communications medium for human beings—it doesn't carry body language or emotional nuance—so misunderstandings are all too probable.

Sometimes they'll even go further: When the information superhighways are all built, they say, and when we're able to transmit live, full-motion video to each other, we will enter a Golden Age of Telepresence, and online misunderstandings will evaporate.

I'm here to tell you they're wrong. Wake up, online belle-lettrists everywhere—the Golden Age is already here, and flames are the proof.

The problem is not that ASCII is too restricted a medium—the problem, if anything, is that text says too much, and that the medium is too intimate! Flames are the friction that comes of minds rubbing too closely together.

Think about it for a minute. If you're face to face with someone, you're exposed to countless things over which the other person may have had no conscious control—hair color, say, or facial expressions. But when you're reading someone's posted ASCII message, *everything you see is a product of that person's mind.* As SNOW CRASH author Neal Stephenson has remarked, "There is something about the process of translating events into words that clarifies what is really going on and filters out the glamorous irrelevancies." The problem of flaming is not that we don't understand each other. It's that we understand each other all too well. We're mainlining each other's thoughts.

Before I became a lawyer, I was a graduate student of literature. And it's hard to read many of the classics of English literature without being overcome by the immense capability, of language to express emotional states, complex ideas, sensory experience, humor. In a way, text is almost *telepathic* in its power. Want to experience the thoughts of a truly alien mind? Try reading some Emily Dickinson or William Blake! You'll learn more about their souls in an hour's reading than you would in a week of video conferencing.

So you can imagine what I thought when I first read long-time Usenetter Chuq Von Rospach's advice to new users about the "need" for smileys. "Without the voice inflections and body language of personal communications," Von Rospach wrote back in 1984, "it is easy for a remark meant to be funny to be misinterpreted. Subtle humor tends to get lost, so take steps to make sure that people realize you are trying to be funny. The net has developed a symbol called the smiley face. It looks like ":-)" and points out sections of articles with humorous intent. No matter how broad the humor or satire, it is safer to remind people that you are being funny."

Safer? Tell it to S. J. Perelman, bub! Or Cynthia Heimel! Or Dave Barry, for Christ's sake! You don't see any of those folks using so-called "smileys." And, in fact, sometimes smileys are used to obscure meaning rather than to reveal it. Stephenson, who wrote an essay about the use of smileys for *The New Republic* a few months back, told me that "After I wrote the smiley piece I started noticing that people would say something intentionally obnoxious and then tack a smiley on at the end. They weren't afraid of being misunderstood—they were afraid of being correctly understood." Just so.

But flames aren't the only proof of ASCII's uncanny power. Just talk to a couple that's ever fallen in love online. In, uh, *face-to-face mode* (one hesitates to coin a term like "real reality"), these two people might never have broken the ice. But online they revealed their deepest secrets to each other and each discovered a kindred spirit. Even the often-disappointing first meetings of would-be online lovers tell you something of the power of text—it's those face-to-face distractions (his weight problem, say, or her acne) that prevent the union of those who otherwise might be soulmates.

This problem of too much sensory bandwidth is not a new one. Says John Schwartz, a WELL user who writes on science and technology issues for the *Washington Post:* "That part of the reason that filmmakers like Woody Allen or Steven Spielberg shoot their movies in black and white. When you narrow the bandwith, you focus the message." And Jerry Michalski of RELease 1.0 mentions a researcher who asked a child which she liked better, TV or radio. "Radio," she tells the researcher. "'Cause the pictures are better."

Electronic Frontier Foundation co-founder John Barlow came across a different take on this old problem when he saw a demonstration of a videoconferencing system. Feeling oddly disappointed by what he saw, Barlow asked the system's project director what was missing. The problem, said the director, a native of India, is that the system cannot transmit *"prāna."*

That is, it cannot transmit that almost mystical sense of life force or presence that one wants in a true meeting of minds. The problem, I submit, is that video is constantly reminding you that it *is* video—sophisticated TV viewers of the late 20th century have learned not to take video seriously, and to appraise it more for production values that for content. We no longer expect TV to tell us the truth—we expect it to entertain us. (If you doubt me, check the TV ads in any election year.) So when we see bosses or co-workers on video, earnestly trying to work through a meeting agenda, we can't help thinking that, well, this show ought to end after 13 weeks.

The language of Shakespeare, in contrast, admits no impediment to the marriage of true minds. It's no accident that users of the WELL tend to think of themselves as a "virtual community"—subjectively, at least, many of them feel more truly connected to each other than they do to their next-door neighbors. When I lost a major part of my household, including my library, countless fellow WELLbeings pitched in and sent me replacement volumes—a few books were more valuable than the ones I'd lost. I'm inclined to think they did this because they had a sense that they *knew* me from my postings. I wasn't a stranger, but, rather, a familiar person who happened to be in trouble. Yet the WELL is decidedly low-tech as far as user interfaces go; almost all communications there are in plain ol' ASCII.

It's a measure of how efficient ASCII is that one has been able for years to punt text versions of whole novels—HOWARDS END, for example, or THE REMAINS OF THE DAY—across the Net, and it's a rare novel that requires more than a standard floppy disk of storage. Yet it will be a long time before we can ship the movie versions of those books (which are often regarded as inferior to the texts) around so easily.

Of course, not everyone who uses text online is a Forster or an Ishiguro. "It takes some time to learn how to use text properly," Stephenson says, "I'm still learning every day—but once you've got the hang of it you can create extremely, complex webs of metaphors and allusions that deliver vast cognitive bandwidth over minimal informational bandwidths." But even the poorest writers manage to invest something of their souls in what they send out to the Net—it's not the kind of claim you can easily make about video.

So you can see why I'm somewhat sceptical about the wonders of the new broadband information highway that we've all begun reflexively to demand. As a practical matter, everyday folks prefer technologies like the camcorder, which allow you to just point and shoot, to technologies like desktop publishing, which require serious work if you're going to be any good at them. When everyone can send a memo or love letter in full-motion video, why take the trouble to learn to write well?

On the other hand, the inevitable irrelevancies and distractions that video will introduce into everyday communications may mean fewer flames and more online peace. By distracting net users from the irritating presence of other minds, video will have a placating effect—it'll be a digital Valium. And then, perhaps, the world of ASCII communications will become a preserve for the edgy exchanges of tense text maniacs. Like me.

# Themes, Issues, and Ideas

1. When Godwin writes of the "telepathic" nature of writing, what does he mean? What other technologies have you heard of or used that also seem "telepathic" somehow?

2. Have you ever seen a "smiley [:-)]? What do you think of them? Do you think it would prove helpful to you in your writing assignments for class? Why or why not?

3. Do you think that written communication is as direct a form of communication as Godwin seems to? Give three or four reasons for your answer.

# Writing Strategies and Techniques

1. Does Godwin's use of computer jargon-words such as "flame," "T-3 backbones," and "Usenet discussions" affect your opinion of him? Why does he only use those words conspicuously in the first paragraph?

2. What kind of people does Godwin quote? Who are his authorities— who provides his "expert testimony?" Why?

# Suggestions for Writing

1. Write an essay using not just ASCII, but also pictures, different kinds of typescript, and anything else you can think of to try and prove Godwin wrong.

2. Have the class make a list of kinds of information that are conveyed by the following media: ASCII, video, telephones, in-person contact, and another medium of the students' choice.

# MAKING CONNECTIONS

1. What connections can you draw between the nineteenth-century boosters of telegraphy Czitrom describes and some of the other writers in this chapter? What about the critics? Is there a twentieth century Thoreau to be found here?

2. Reginald Stuart is concerned about the internet for very different reasons than John Perry Barlow. What constitute these differences.

3. Compare Clifford Stoll's essay with Tertius Chandler's in Chapter Four. What would they agree on in each other's essays? Why?

4. Mike Godwin and Sadie Plant both think of the internet as a communications medium. In what important ways, however, do they differ in the way they characterize "cyberspace"?

5. Write an imaginary e-mail or hypertext conference in which all five authors discuss the future of the 1st Amendment in the age of the internet.

# CHAPTER SIX

## *American Life and Popular Culture*

### *Style and Substance in the Shape of Things to Come*

# THE PAST AS PROLOGUE

# A Eulogy for the Twentieth Century

## Tom Wolfe

*In his essay Tom Wolfe says that the particularly American contribution to the many innovations of the twentieth century was made in the area of "manners and mores," especially during the 1960s. Whether or not Wolfe is right in his assessment of the facts, he had good cause to know them, since it was in the 1960s that he and others began the kind of cultural reporting that quickly became known as the "New Journalism."*

*Wolfe was born in Richmond, Virginia, in 1931 and was educated at Washington and Lee University and at Yale University, where he took a Ph.D. in American Studies. He went on to work as a journalist, most notably for the* New York Herald Tribune. *With books like The* Kandy-Kolored Tangerine-Flake Streamline Baby *(1965) and The* Electric Kool-Aid Acid Test *(1968), he began paying attention to popular culture and American lifestyle in a new way, and has kept a keen eye on the American scene ever since. He added to this collection most recently with his novel on the boom years of Wall Street in the 1980s,* The Bonfire of the Vanities.

In 1968, in San Francisco, I came across a curious foot-
note to the psychedelic movement. At the Haight-Ashbury Free Clinic
there were doctors who were treating diseases no living doctor had ever
encountered before, diseases that had disappeared so long ago they had
never even picked up Latin names, diseases such as the mange, the
grunge, the itch, the twitch, the thrush, the scroff, the rot. And how was
it that they had now returned? It had to do with the fact that thousands
of young men and women had migrated to San Francisco to live com-
munally in what I think history will record as one of the most extraordinary religious experiments of all time.

The hippies, as they became known, sought nothing less than to
sweep aside all codes and restraints of the past and start out from zero.
At one point Ken Kesey organized a pilgrimage to Stonehenge with the
idea of returning to Anglo-Saxon civilization's point zero, which he fig-
ured was Stonehenge, and heading out all over again to do it better.
Among the codes and restraints that people in the communes swept
aside—quite purposely—were those that said you shouldn't use other
people's toothbrushes or sleep on other people's mattresses without
changing the sheets or, as was more likely, without using any sheets at
all or that you and five other people shouldn't drink from the same bot-
tle of Shasta or take tokes from the same cigarette. And now, in 1968,
they were relearning the laws of hygiene . . . by getting the mange, the
grunge, the itch, the twitch, the thrush, the scroff, the rot.

This process, namely the relearning—following a Promethean
and unprecedented start from zero—seems to me to be the leitmotif of
our current interlude, here in the dying years of the twentieth century.

Start from zero was the slogan of the Bauhaus School. The story
of how the Bauhaus, a tiny artists' movement in Germany in the 1920s,
swept aside the architectural styles of the past and created the glass-box
face of the modern American city is a familiar one, and I won't retell it.
But I should mention the soaring spiritual exuberance with which the
movement began, the passionate conviction of the Bauhaus's leader,
Walter Gropius, that by starting from zero in architecture and design
man could free himself from the dead hand of the past. By the late
1970s, however, architects themselves were beginning to complain of
the dead hand of the Bauhaus: the flat roofs, which leaked from rain
and collapsed from snow, the tiny bare beige office cubicles, which
made workers feel like component parts, the glass walls, which let in
too much heat, too much cold, too much glare, and no air at all. The
relearning is now under way in earnest. The architects are busy rum-

maging about in what the artist Richard Merkin calls the Big Closet. Inside the Big Closet, in promiscuous heaps, are the abandoned styles of the past. The current favorite rediscoveries: Classical, Secession, and Moderne (Art Deco). Relearning on the wing, the architects are off on a binge of eclecticism comparable to the Victorian period's a century ago.

In politics the twentieth century's great start from zero was one-party socialism, also known as communism or Marxism-Leninism. Given that system's bad reputation in the West today (even among the French intelligentsia), it is instructive to read John Reed's *Ten Days That Shook the World*—before turning to Solzhenitsyn's *Gulag Archipelago*. The old strike hall poster of a Promethean worker in a blue shirt breaking his chains across his mighty chest was in truth the vision of ultimate human freedom the movement believed in at the outset. For intellectuals in the West the painful dawn began with the publication of the *Gulag Archipelago* in 1973. Solzhenitsyn insisted that the villain behind the Soviet concentration-camp network was not Stalin or Lenin (who invented the term concentration camp) or even Marxism. It was instead the Soviets' peculiarly twentieth-century notion that they could sweep aside not only the old social order but also its religious ethic, which had been millennia in the making ("common decency," Orwell called it) and reinvent morality... here...now..."at the point of a gun," in the famous phrase of the Maoists. Today the relearning has reached the point where even ruling circles in the Soviet Union and China have begun to wonder how best to convert communism into something other than, in Susan Sontag's phrase, *successful fascism.*

The great American contribution to the twentieth century's start from zero was in the area of manners and mores, especially in what was rather primly called "the sexual revolution." In every hamlet, even in the erstwhile Bible Belt, may be found the village brothel, no longer hidden in a house of blue lights or red lights or behind a green door but openly advertised by the side of the road with a thousand-watt back-lit plastic sign: Totally All-Nude Girl Sauna Massage and Marathon Encounter Sessions InSide. Up until two years ago pornographic movie theaters were as ubiquitous as the 7-Eleven, including outdoor drive-ins with screens six, seven, eight stories high, the better to beam all the moist-ened folds and glistening nodes and stiffened giblets to a panting American countryside. Two years ago the pornographic theater began to be replaced by the pornographic videocassette, which could be brought into any home. Up on the shelf in the den, next to the set of *The Ency-*

*clopaedia Britannica* and the great books, one now finds the cassettes: *Shanks Akimbo, That Thing with the Cup.* My favorite moment in Jessica Hahn's triumphal tour of medialand this fall came when a 10-year-old girl, a student at a private school, wearing a buttercup blouse, a cardigan sweater, and her school uniform skirt, approached her outside a television studio with a stack of *Playboy* magazines featuring the famous Hahn nude form and asked her to autograph them. With the school's blessing, she intended to take the signed copies back to the campus and hold a public auction. The proceeds would go to the poor.

But in the sexual revolution, too, the painful dawn has already arrived, and the relearning is imminent. All may be summed up in a single term, requiring no amplification: AIDS.

The Great Relearning—if anything so prosaic as remedial education can be called great—should be thought of not as the end of the twentieth century but the prelude to the twenty-first. There is no law of history that says a new century must start ten or twenty years beforehand, but two times in a row it has worked out that way. The nineteenth century began with the American and French revolutions of the late eighteenth. The twentieth century began with the formulation of Marxism, Freudianism, and Modernism in the late nineteenth. And now the twenty-first begins with the Great Relearning.

The twenty-first century, I predict, will confound the twentieth-century notion of the Future as something exciting, novel, unexpected, or radiant; as Progress, to use an old word. It is already clear that the large cities, thanks to the Relearning, will not even look new. Quite the opposite; the cities of 2007 will look more like the cities of 1927 than the cities of 1987. The twenty-first century will have a retrograde look and a retrograde mental atmosphere. People of the next century, snug in their neo-Georgian apartment complexes, will gaze back with a ghastly awe upon our time. They will regard the twentieth as the century in which wars became so enormous they were known as World Wars, the century in which technology leapt forward so rapidly man developed the capacity to destroy the planet itself—but also the capacity to escape to the stars on spaceships if it blew. But above all they will look back upon the twentieth as the century in which their forebears had the amazing confidence, the Promethean *hubris,* to defy the gods and try to push man's power and freedom to limitless, godlike extremes. They will look back in awe . . . without the slightest temptation to emulate the daring of those who swept aside all rules and tried to start from zero.

Instead, they will sink ever deeper into their neo-Louis bergères, content to live in what will be known as the Somnolent Century or the Twentieth Century's Hangover.

## Themes, Issues, and Ideas

1. What cultural examples from the twentieth-century does Wolfe give of what he calls "starting from zero"? Can you think of others?

2. What does Wolfe mean by "the Great Relearning"? Why does he assign it to the twenty-first century rather than to the end of the twentieth century?

3. How, according to Wolfe, will twenty-first-century reality differ from what the twentieth century imagined it would be?

## Writing Strategies and Techniques

1. Wolfe's second sentence of his first paragraph and the last sentence of his second paragraph end with the same list of words. What effect does the repetition create?

2. Wolfe refers twice to Prometheus. How does Prometheus serve as a symbol in Wolfe's argument? (If you do not know the figure, look him up.)

## Suggestions for Writing

1. Wolfe calls his essay a "eulogy." Given his many criticisms of the period, do you think his title is an appropriate one? Write an essay in which you argue whether or not Wolfe's essay deserves its title.

2. Wolfe argues that "the twenty-first century will have a retrograde look and a retrograde mental atmosphere." Write an essay in which you (1) summarize Wolfe's arguments in support of this claim, and (2) attack, defend, or modify his contention with arguments and evidence of your own.

# Ice-T: Is the Issue Social Responsibility or Free Speech?

## Michael Kinsley/Barbara Ehrenreich

*Michael Kinsley is one of the most visible of political commentators. As the editor of the* New Republic, *he is one of the principal voices behind what is in many ways the leading moderate journal in America, and he regularly represents the left on CNN's* Crossfire.

*Barbara Ehrenreich is an accomplished essayist and social critic whose writings in* Time, Mother Jones, *and other magazines, along with her numerous books and appearances, place her in the cultural vanguard to the left of Kinsley.*

*Both Kinsley and Ehrenreich were invited by* Time *magazine to discuss the ramifications of Ice-T's controversial rap song* Cop Killer.

### Michael Kinsley:

How did the company that publishes this magazine come to produce a record glorifying the murder of police?

I got my 12-gauge sawed off
I got my headlights turned off
I'm 'bout to bust some shots off
I'm 'bout to dust some cops off ...
Die, Die, Die Pig, Die!

So go the lyrics to *Cop Killer* by the rapper Ice-T on the album *Body Count*. The album is released by Warner Bros. Records, part of the Time Warner media and entertainment conglomerate.

In a *Wall Street Journal* op-ed piece laying out the company's position, Time Warner Co-CEO Gerald Levin makes two defenses. First, Ice-T's *Cop Killer* is misunderstood. "It doesn't incite or glorify violence... It's his fictionalized attempt to get inside a character's head... *Cop Killer* is no more a call for gunning down the police than *Frankie and Johnny* is a summons for jilted lovers to shoot one another." Instead of "finding ways to silence the messenger," we should be "heeding the anguished cry contained in his message."

This defense is self-contradictory. *Frankie and Johnny* does not pretend to have a political "message" that must be "heeded." If *Cop Killer* has a message, it is that the murder of policemen is a justified response to police brutality. And not in self-defense, but in premeditated acts of revenge against random cops. ("I know your family's grievin'—f_____ 'em.")

Killing policemen is a good thing—that is the plain meaning of the words, and no "larger understanding" of black culture, the rage of the streets or anything else can explain it away. This is not Ella Fitzgerald telling a story in song. As in much of today's popular music, the line between performer and performance is purposely blurred. These are political sermonettes clearly intended to endorse the sentiments being expressed. Tracy Morrow (Ice-T) himself has said, "I scared the police, and they need to be scared." That seems clear.

The company's second defense of *Cop Killer* is the classic one of free expression: "We stand for creative freedom. We believe that the worth of what an artist or journalist has to say does not depend on pre-approval from a government official or a corporate censor."

Of course Ice-T has the right to say whatever he wants. But that doesn't require any company to provide him an outlet. And it doesn't relieve a company of responsibility for the messages it chooses to promote. Judgment is not "censorship." Many an "anguished cry" goes unrecorded. This one was recorded, and promoted, because a successful artist under contract wanted to record it. Nothing wrong with making money, but a company cannot take the money and run from the responsibility.

The founder of *Time*, Henry Luce, would snort at the notion that his company should provide a value-free forum for the exchange of ideas. In Luce's system, editors were supposed to make value judgments and promote the truth as they saw it. *Time* has moved far from its old Lucean rigidity—far enough to allow for dissenting essays like this one. That evolution is a good thing, as long as it's not a handy excuse for abandoning all standards.

No commercial enterprise need agree with every word that appears under its corporate imprimatur. If Time Warner now intends to be "a global force for encouraging the confrontation of ideas," that's swell. But a policy of allowing diverse viewpoints is not a moral free pass. Pro and con on national health care is one thing; pro and con on killing policemen is another.

A bit of sympathy is in order for Time Warner. It is indeed a "global force" with media tentacles around the world. If it imposes rigorous standards and values from the top, it gets accused of corporate censorship. If it doesn't, it gets accused of moral irresponsibility. A dilemma. But someone should have thought of that before deciding to become a global force.

And another genuine dilemma. Whatever the actual merits of *Cop Killer,* if Time Warner withdraws the album now the company will be perceived as giving in to outside pressure. That is a disastrous precedent for a global conglomerate.

The Time-Warner merger of 1989 was supposed to produce corporate "synergy": the whole was supposed to be more than the sum of the parts. The *Cop Killer* controversy is an example of negative synergy. People get mad at *Cop Killer* and start boycotting the movie *Batman Returns.* A reviewer praises *Cop Killer* ("Tracy Morrow's poetry takes a switchblade and deftly slices life's jugular," etc.), and *Time* is accused of corruption instead of mere foolishness. Senior Time Warner executives find themselves under attack for—and defending—products of their company they neither honestly care for nor really understand, and doubtless weren't even aware of before controversy hit.

Anyway, it's absurd to discuss *Cop Killer* as part of the "confrontation of ideas"—or even as an authentic anguished cry of rage from the ghetto. *Cop Killer* is a cynical commercial concoction, designed to titillate its audience with imagery of violence. It merely exploits the authentic anguish of the inner city for further titillation. Tracy Morrow is in business for a buck, just like Time Warner. *Cop Killer* is an excellent joke on the white establishment, of which the company's anguished apologia ("Why can't we hear what rap is trying to tell us?") is the punch line.

## Barbara Ehrenreich:

Ice-T's song *Cop Killer* is as bad as they come. This is black anger—raw, rude and cruel—and one reason the song's so shocking is that in postliberal America, black anger is virtually taboo. You won't find it on TV, not on the *McLaughlin Group* or *Crossfire,* and certainly not in the placid features of Arsenio Hall or Bernard Shaw. It's been beaten back into the outlaw subcultures of rap and rock, where, precisely because it is taboo, it sells. And the nastier it is, the faster it moves off the shelves. As Ice-T asks in another song on the same album, "Goddamn what a brotha gotta do/To get a message through/To the red, white and blue?"

But there's a gross overreaction going on, building to a veritable paroxysm of white denial. A national boycott has been called, not just of the song or Ice-T, but of all Time Warner products. The President himself has denounced Time Warner as "wrong" and Ice-T as "sick." Ollie North's Freedom Alliance has started a petition drive aimed at bringing Time-Warner executives to trial for "sedition and anarchy."

Much of this is posturing and requires no more courage than it takes to stand up in a VFW hall and condemn communism or crack. Yes, *Cop Killer* is irresponsible and vile. But Ice-T is as right about some things as he is righteous about the rest. And ultimately, he's not even dangerous—least of all to the white power structure his songs condemn.

The "danger" implicit in all the uproar is of empty-headed, suggestible black kids, crouching by their boom boxes, waiting for the word. But what Ice-T's fans know and his detractors obviously don't is that *Cop Killer* is just one more entry in pop music's long history of macho hyperbole and violent boast. Flip to the classic-rock station, and you might catch the Rolling Stones announcing "the time is right of violent revoloo-shun!" from their 1968 hit *Street Fighting Man.* And where were the defenders of our law-enforcement officers when a white British group, the Clash, taunted its fans with the lyrics: "When they kick open your front door/How you gonna come/With your hands on your head/Or on the trigger of your gun?"

"Die, Die, Die Pig" is strong speech, but the Constitution protects strong speech, and it's doing so this year more aggressively than ever. The Supreme Court has just downgraded cross burnings to the level of bonfires and ruled that it's no crime to throw around verbal grenades like "nigger" and "kike." Where are the defenders of decorum and social stability when prime-time demagogues like Howard Stern deride African Americans as "spear chuckers?"

More to the point, young African Americans are not so naive and suggestible that they have to depend on a compact disc for their sociology lessons. To paraphrase another song from another era, you don't need a rap song to tell which way the wind is blowing. Black youths know that the police are likely to see them through a filter of stereotypes as miscreants and potential "cop killers." They are aware that a black youth is seven times as likely to be charged with a felony as a white youth who has committed the same offense, and is much more likely to be imprisoned.

They know, too, that in a shameful number of cases, it is the police themselves who indulge in "anarchy" and violence. The U.S. Justice Department has received 47,000 complaints of police brutality in the past six years, and Amnesty International has just issued a report on police brutality in Los Angeles, documenting 40 cases of "torture or cruel, inhuman or degrading treatment."

Menacing as it sounds, the fantasy in *Cop Killer* is the fantasy of the powerless and beaten down—the black man who's been hassled once too often ("A pig stopped me for nothin'!"), spread-eagled against a police car, pushed around. It's not a "responsible" fantasy (fantasies seldom are). It's not even a very creative one. In fact, the sad thing about *Cop Killer* is that it falls for the cheapest, most conventional image of rebellion that our culture offers: the lone gunman spraying fire from his AK-47. This is not "sedition"; it's the familiar, all-American, Hollywood-style pornography of violence.

Which is why Ice-T is right to say he's no more dangerous than George Bush's pal Arnold Schwarzenegger, who wasted an army of cops in *Terminator 2*. Images of extraordinary cruelty and violence are marketed every day, many of far less artistic merit than *Cop Killer.* This is our free market of ideas and images, and it shouldn't be any less free for a black man than for other purveyors of "irresponsible" sentiments, from David Duke to Andrew Dice Clay.

Just, please, don't dignify Ice-T's contribution with the word sedition. The past masters of sedition—men like George Washington, Toussaint-Louverture, Fidel Castro or Mao Zedong, all of whom led and won armed insurrections—would be unimpressed by *Cop Killer* and probably saddened. They would shake their heads and mutter words like "infantile" and "adventurism." They might point out that the cops are hardly a noble target, being, for the most part, honest working stiffs who've got stuck with the job of patrolling ghettos ravaged by economic decline and official neglect.

There is a difference, the true seditionist would argue, between a revolution and a gesture of macho defiance. Gestures are cheap. They feel good, they blow off some rage. But revolutions, violent or otherwise, are made by people who have learned how to count very slowly to ten.

## Themes, Issues, and Ideas

1. Kinsley and Ehrenreich both address the issue of free speech. How do they differ on its application to *Cop Killer*? Do you find Kinsley's or Ehrenreich's perspective more convincing? Explain why.

2. Kinsley writes knowingly about mass media and big business. Do you find his authority pertinent to the discussion of *Cop Killer*? What seems to be Ehrenreich's field of expertise? Compare it to Kinsley's.

3. Ehrenreich brings up the names of "past masters of sedition," such as George Washington, Fidel Castro, and Mao Zedong. Do you agree with her labeling of these figures? Do you agree with her judgment of Ice-T?

## Writing Strategies and Techniques

1. Compare Kinsley's closing paragraph with Ehrenreich's. Which fits in better with the rest of each writer's essay? Which is more persuasive?

2. Kinsley maintains that Time Warner must accept responsibility for the records it produces, and brings *Time* magazine into his argument. Ehrenreich brings Kinsley in, implicitly, by mentioning *Crossfire,* a television show he is featured on. How do these strategies advance their arguments?

# Suggestions for Writing

1.  Write two short essays imitating Kinsley and Ehrenreich on opposite sides of an issue. If you want, imitate them as they might be if they switched positions on *Cop Killer.*

2.  *Cop Killer* is now over two years old. Rewrite this argument, updating the subject. Do not use rap music as a topic.

# Big Brother Is You, Watching

## Mark Crispin Miller

*Mark Crispin Miller is the author of* Boxed In: The Culture of Television, *as well as numerous essays on American popular culture and social history. He teaches film studies at Johns Hopkins University, and is currently at work on a book about the Gulf War. In the essay from which this selection is taken, Miller compares the world of George Orwell's* 1984 *to our own. In Orwell's novel, the superstate of Oceania is ruled by the tyrannical Inner Party, as symbolized by Big Brother: The slogan "Big Brother Is Watching You" appears everywhere, and the Thought Police are ever-alert for signs of discontent or nonconformity. Is this so in our time? asks Miller, and his answer may surprise you.*

Television's formal erasure of distinctness complements—or perhaps has actually fostered—a derisive personal style that inhibits all personality, a knowingness that now pervades all TV genres and the culture which those genres have homogenized. The corrosive irony emanating from the Oceanic elite has been universalized by television, whose characters—both real and fictional—relentlessly inflict it on each other and themselves, defining a negative ideal of hip inertia which no living human being is able to approach too closely. For example, in situation comedies or "sitcoms"—TV's definitive creation—the "comedy" almost always consists of a weak, compulsive jeering that immediately wipes out any divergence from the indefinite collective standard. The characters vie at self-containment, reacting to every simulation of intensity, every bright idea, every mechanical enthusiasm with the same deflating look of jaded incredulity. In such an atmosphere, those already closest to the ground run the least risk of being felled by the general ridicule, and so those characters most adept at enforcing the proper emptiness are also the puniest and most passive: blasé wives and girlfriends, and—especially—blasé children, who, like Parsons' daughter, prove their own orthodoxy by subverting their subverted parents.

Nearly all of TV's characters—on sitcoms and in "dramas," on talk shows and children's programs—participate in this reflexive sneering, and such contemptuous passivity reflects directly on the viewer who watches it with precisely the same attitude. TV seems to flatter the inert skepticism of its own audience, assuring them that they can do no better than to stay right where they are, rolling their eyes in feeble disbelief. And yet such apparent flattery of our viewpoint is in fact a recurrent warning not to rise above this slack, derisive gaping. At first, it seems that it is only those eccentric others whom TV belittles. Each time some deadpan tot on a sitcom responds to his frantic mom with a disgusted sigh, or whenever the polished anchorman punctuates his footage of "extremists" with a look that speaks his well-groomed disapproval, or each time Johnny Carson comments on some "unusual" behavior with a wry sidelong glance into our living rooms, we are being flattered with a gesture of inclusion, the wink that tells us, "*We* are in the know." And yet we are the ones belittled by each subtle televisual gaze, which offers not a welcome but an ultimatum—that we had better see the joke or else turn into it.

If we see the joke, however, we are nothing like those Oceanic viewers "shouting with laughter" at the sight of their own devastation. All televisual smirking is based on, and reinforces, the assumption that we who smirk together are enlightened past the point of nullity, having evolved far beyond whatever datedness we might be jeering, whether the fanatic's ardor, the prude's inhibitions, the hick's unfashionable pants, or the snob's obsession with prestige. Thus TV's relentless comedy at first seems utterly progressive, if largely idiotic, since its butts are always the most reactionary of its characters—militarists, bigots, sexists, martinets. However, it is not to champion our freedom that TV makes fun of these ostensible oppressors. On the contrary: Through its derision, TV promotes only *itself,* disvaluing not Injustice or Intolerance but the impulse to resist TV.

Despite the butt's broad illiberality, what makes him appear ridiculous in TV's eyes is not his antidemocratic bias but his vestigial individuality, his persistence as a self sturdy and autonomous enough to sense that there is something missing from the televisual world, and to hunger for it, although ostracized for this desire by the sarcastic mob that watches and surrounds him. Like Winston Smith, the butt yearns for and exemplifies the past that brought about the present, and which the present now discredits through obsessive mockery. Whether arrogantly giving orders, compulsively tidying up, or longing for the good old days when men were men, the butt reenacts the type of personality—marked by rigidity and self-denial—that at first facilitated the extension of high capitalism but that soon threatened to impede its further growth. And it is just such endless growth that is the real point and object of TV's comedy, which puts down those hard selves in order to exalt the nothingness that laughs at them. Whereas the butt, enabled by his discrete selfhood, pursues desires that TV cannot gratify, we are induced, by the sight of his continual humiliation, to become as porous, cool, and acquiescent as he is solid, tense, and dissident, so that we might want nothing other than what TV sells us. This is what it means to see the joke. The viewer's enlightened laughter at those uptight others is finally the expression of his own Oceanic dissolution, as, within his distracted consciousness, there reverberates TV's sole imperative, which once obeyed makes the self seem a mere comical encumbrance—the imperative of total consumption.

Guided by its images even while he thinks that he sees through them, the TV-viewer learns only to consume. That inert, ironic watchfulness which TV reinforces in its audience is itself conducive to consumption. As we watch, struggling inwardly to avoid resembling anyone who might stand out as pre- or non- or antitelevisual, we are already trying to live up, or down, to the same standard of acceptability that that TV's ads and shows define collectively: the standard that requires the desperate use of all those goods and services that TV proffers, including breath mints, mouthwash, dandruff shampoos, hair conditioners, blow-dryers, hair removers, eye drops, deodorant soaps and sticks and sprays, hair dyes, skin creams, lip balms, diet colas, diet plans, local frozen dinners, bathroom bowl cleaners, floor wax, car wax, furniture polish, fabric softeners, room deodorizers, and more, and more. Out of this flood of commodities, it is promised, we will each arise as sleek, quick, compact, and efficient as a brand-new Toyota; and in our effort at such self-renewal, moreover, we are enjoined not just to sweeten every orifice and burnish every surface, but to evacuate our psyches. While selling its explicit products, TV also advertises incidentally an ideal of emotional self-management, which dictates that we purge ourselves of all "bad feelings" through continual confession and by affecting the same stilted geniality evinced by most of TV's characters (the butts excluded). The unconscious must never be allowed to interfere with productivity, and so the viewer is warned repeatedly to atone for his every psychic eruption, like Parsons after his arrest for talking treason in his sleep: "'Thoughtcrime is a dreadful thing, old man,' he said sententiously. 'It's insidious...There I was, working away, trying to do my bit—never knew I had any bad stuff in my mind at all.'"

Thus, even as its programs push the jargon of "honesty" and "tolerance," forever counseling you to "be yourself," TV shames you ruthlessly for every symptom of residual mortality, urging you to turn yourself into a standard object wholly inoffensive, useful, and adulterated, a product of and for all other products. However, this transformation is impossible. There is no such purity available to human beings, whose bodies will sweat and whose instincts will rage—however expertly we work to shut them off. Even Winston Smith, as broken as he is at the conclusion, is still impelled by his desires, which the Party could not extinguish after all, since it depends on their distorted energy. For all its chilling finality, in other words, the novel's closing sentence is merely another of the Party's lies. What O'Brien cannot achieve through torture, we cannot attain through our campaigns of self-maintenance—no matter how many miles we jog, or how devotedly, if skeptically, we watch TV.

Like the Party, whose unstated rules no person can follow rigidly enough, TV demands that its extruded viewers struggle to embody an ideal too cool and imprecise for human emulation. And like Winston Smith, we are the victims of Enlightenment in its late phase, although it is the logic of consumption, not the deliberate machinations of some cabal, that has impoverished our world in the name of its enrichment. As the creatures of this logic, we have become our own overseers. While Winston Smith is forced to watch himself in literal self-defense, trying to keep his individuality a hard-won secret, we have been forced to watch ourselves lest we develop selves too hard and secretive for the open market. In America, there is no need for an objective apparatus of surveillance (which is not to say that none exists), because, guided by TV, we watch ourselves as if already televised, checking ourselves both inwardly and outwardly for any sign of untidiness or gloom, moment by moment as guarded and self-conscious as Winston Smith under the scrutiny of the Thought Police: "The smallest thing could give you

away. A nervous tic, an unconscious look of anxiety, a habit of mutter-
ing to yourself—anything that carried with it the suggestion of abnor-
mality, of having something to hide." Although this description refers to
the objective peril of life in Oceania, it also captures the anxiety of life
under the scrutiny of television. Of course, all televisual performers
must abide by the same grim advice or end up canceled; but TV's nervous viewers also feel themselves thus watched, fearing the same absolute exclusion if they should ever show some sign of resisting the
tremendous pressure.

Television further intensifies our apprehension that we are being
watched by continually assuring us that it already understands our
innermost fears, our private problems, and that it even knows enough
about our most intimate moments to reproduce them for us. The joy of
birth is brought to us by Citicorp, the tender concern of one friend for
another is presented by AT&T, the pleasures of the hearth are depicted
for us by McDonald's. And on any talk show or newscast, there might
suddenly appear the competent psychologist, who will deftly translate
any widespread discontent into his own antiseptic terms, thereby representing it as something well-known to him, and therefore harmless. As
we watch TV, we come to imagine that Winston Smith eventually discovers: "There was no physical act, no word spoken aloud, that they
had not noticed, no train of thought that they had not been able to infer."

Television is not the cause of our habitual self-scrutiny, however,
but has only set the standard for it, a relationship with a complicated
history. It is through our efforts to maintain ourselves as the objects of
our anxious self-spectatorship that we consummate the process of
American Enlightenment, whose project throughout this century has
been the complete and permanent reduction of our populace into the
collective instrument of absolute production. This project has arisen not
through corporate conspiracy but as the logical fulfillment, openly and
even optimistically pursued, of the imperative of unlimited economic
growth. Thus compelled, the enlightened captains of production have
employed the principles, and often the exponents, of modern social science, in order to create a perfect work force whose members, whether
laboring on products or consuming them, would function inexhaustibly
and on command, like well-tuned robots.

As the material for this ideal, Americans have been closely
watched for decades: in the factory, then in the office, by efficiency
experts and industrial psychologists; in the supermarkets, then throughout the shopping malls, by motivational researchers no less cunningly

than by the store detectives; in the schools, and then at home, and then in bed, by an immense, diverse, yet ultimately unified bureaucracy of social workers, education specialists, and "mental health professionals" of every kind. The psychic and social mutations necessarily induced by this multiform intrusion have accomplished what its first engineers had hoped for, but in a form, and at a cost, which they could never have foreseen: Americans—restless, disconnected, and insatiable—are mere consumers, having by now internalized the diffuse apparatus of surveillance built all around them, while still depending heavily on its external forms—TV, psychologistic "counseling," "self-help" manuals, the "human potential" regimens, and other self-perpetuating therapies administered to keep us on the job.

And so the project of industrial Enlightenment has only forced us back toward the same helpless natural state that Enlightenment had once meant to abolish. Both in America and in Oceania, the telescreens infantilize their captive audience. In *Nineteen Eighty-Four* and in 1984, the world has been made too bright and cold by the same system that forever promises the protective warmth of mother love, leaving each viewer yearning to have his growing needs fulfilled by the very force that aggravates them. So it is, first of all, with Orwell's famished hero. The figure who had slipped quickly into Victory Mansions, "his chin nuzzled into his breast," had tried unknowingly to transcend the Oceanic violence by mothering himself, but then ends up so broken by that violence that he adopts its symbol as his mother: "O cruel, needless misunderstanding!" he exults inwardly before the image of Big Brother's face. "O stubborn, self-willed exile from the loving breast!" And, as it is with Winston Smith in his perverted ardor, so it is with every vaguely hungry TV viewer, who longs to be included by the medium that has excluded everyone, and who expects its products to fulfill him in a way that they have made impossible.

What is most disconcerting, then, about the ending of *Nineteen Eighty-Four* is not that Winston Smith has now been made entirely unlike us. In too many ways, the ex-hero of this brilliant, dismal book anticipates those TV viewers who are incapable of reading it: "In these days he could never fix his mind on any one subject for more than a few moments at a time." At this moment, Winston Smith is, for the first time in his life, not under surveillance. The motto, "Big Brother Is Watching You," is now untrue as a threat, as it has always been untrue as an assurance. And the reason why he is no longer watched is that the Oceanic gaze need no longer see through Winston Smith, because he is no longer "Winston Smith," but "a swirl of gritty dust," as primitive and transparent as the Party.

As this Smith slumps in the empty Chestnut Tree, credulously gaping, his ruined mind expertly jolted by the telescreen's managers, he signifies the terminal fulfillment of O'Brien's master plan, which expresses the intentions not only of Orwell's fictitious Party, but of the corporate entity that, through TV, contains our consciousness today: "We shall squeeze you empty, and then we shall fill you with ourselves." The Party has now done for Winston Smith what all our advertisers want to do for us, and with our general approval—answer all material needs, in exchange for the self that might try to gratify them independently, and that might have other subtler needs as well. As a consumer, in other words, Orwell's ex-hero really has it made. "There was no need to give orders" to the waiters in the Chestnut Tree. "They knew his habits." Furthermore, he "always had plenty of money nowadays." In short, the Party has paid him for his erasure with the assurance, "We do it *all* for you." And so this grotesque before-and-after narrative ends satirically as all ads end in earnest, with the object's blithe endorsement of the very product that has helped to keep him miserable: "But it was all right, everything was all right, the struggle was finished. He had won the victory over himself. He loved Big Brother."

It is a horrifying moment; but if we do no more than wince and then forget about it, we ignore our own involvement in the horror and thus complacently betray the hope that once inspired this vision. Surely Orwell would have us face the facts. Like Winston Smith, and like O'Brien and the others, we have been estranged from our desire by Enlightenment, which finally reduces all of its proponents to the blind spectators of their own annihilation. Unlike that Oceanic audience, however, the TV viewer does not gaze up at the screen with angry scorn or piety, but—perfectly enlightened—looks down on its images with a nervous sneer which cannot threaten them and which only keeps the viewer himself from standing up. As you watch, there is no Big Brother out there watching you—not because there isn't a Big Brother, but because Big Brother is you, watching.

## Themes, Issues, and Ideas

1. Is the "reflexive sneering" Miller describes typical of TV? Give five examples from television of what you think Miller means, and five examples that attempt to refute Miller's view.

2.  What might be an example of a self "too hard and secretive for the open market"? Of a "butt"? Of TV "continually assuring us that it already understands our innermost fears, our private problems"?

3.  In what way is the Party's boast, "We will squeeze you empty, and then we shall fill you with ourselves" true of today's society, in Miller's view? Give examples.

# Writing Strategies and Techniques

1.  Miller uses many quotations in his essay, both from *1984* and from TV. What are the effect of these quotations on the essay? Do you find them disruptive? Convincing? Why does Miller use them so often?

2.  Does Miller impress you as someone familiar with popular culture, or as a professor in an ivory tower? Why?

# Suggestions for Writing

1.  Mark Miller has a very unusual view of television. Write an essay in which you describe three or four different ways of looking at TV. Explain which approach is closest to your own, and why.

2.  Write a defense of television that takes TV as seriously as this attack does.

# On "Junk Food for the Soul"

## In Defense of Rock and Roll

### Frank Zappa

*Allan Bloom's* The Closing of the American Mind
*(1987) attacked rock-and-roll music, among many other
things, as a "junk food for the soul," and claimed that it
was poisoning American lives now and through the foreseeable future. Famous rock artist Frank Zappa was born
in 1940 and made his reputation in the 1960s as a performer with the rock group The Mothers of Invention.
Both as a musician and during a late career as a political
and social commentator on television shows, Zappa
defended rock music, even appearing before Congress to
testify against Tipper Gore's Parents Music Resource
Center. Although also a composer of modern classical
music, Zappa relished his role as spokesman for rock, and
published this rebuttal of Bloom in* New Progressive
Quarterly. *Zappa died of cancer in 1994.*

## The Nature of Music

Music is the soul's primitive and primary speech . . . without articulate speech or reason. It is not only not reasonable, it is hostile to
reason. . . . Civilization . . . is the taming or domestication of the soul's
raw passions. . . . Rock music has one appeal only, a barbaric appeal,
to sexual desire—not love, not eros, but sexual desire undeveloped
and untutored . . .                                             —A. Bloom

This is a puff pastry version of the belief that music is the work of the Devil: that the nasty ol' Devil plays his fiddle and people dance around and we don't want to see them twitching like that. In fact, if one wants to be a real artist in the United States today and comment on our culture, one would be very far off the track if one did something delicate or sublime. This is not a noble, delicate, sublime country. This is a mess run by criminals. Performers who are doing the crude, vulgar, repulsive things Bloom doesn't enjoy are only commenting on that fact.

In general, anti-rock propositions began when rock n' roll began, and most of these were racially motivated. In the fifties, petitions were circulated which said, "Don't allow your children to buy Negro records." The petitions referred to the "raw unbridled passion" of screaming people with dark skin who were going to drive our children wild. Some things never go out of fashion in certain ideological camps. They are like tenets of the faith.

Music's real effect on people is a new field of science called psychoacoustics—the way an organism deals with wiggling air molecules. Our ears decode the wiggling air molecules, and that gives us the information of a particular musical sound. Our brain says, "This is music, this is a structure," and we deal with it based on certain tools we have acquired.

I personally make music because I want to ask a question, and I want to get an answer. If that question and answer amuse me, then statistically, there are a certain number of other people out there who have the same amusement factor. If I present my work to them, they will be amused by it, and we will all have a good time.

I need to be amused because I get bored easily and being amused entertains me. If I could be easily amused, like many people who like beer and football, I would never do anything because everything that would be beautiful for my life would already be provided by American television.

But beer and television bore me, so what am I going to do? I am going to be alive for X number of years. I have to do something with my time besides sleep and eat. So, I devise little things to amuse myself. If I can amuse somebody else, great. And if I can amuse somebody else and earn a living while doing it, that is a true miracle in the twentieth century!

## Music and the Dark Forces of the Soul

To Plato and Nietzsche, the history of music is a series of attempts to give form and beauty to the dark, chaotic, premonitory forces in the soul—to make them serve a higher purpose, an ideal, to give man's duties a fullness.          —A. Bloom

This is a man who has fallen for rock's fabricated image of itself. This is the worst kind of ivory tower intellectualism. Anybody who talks about dark forces is right on the fringe of mumbo jumbo. Dark forces? What is this, another product from Lucasfilm? The passions! When was the last time you saw an American exhibit any form of passion other than the desire to shoot a guy on the freeway? Those are the forces of evil as far as I am concerned.

If there are dark forces hovering in the vicinity of the music business, they are mercantile forces. We meet the darkness when we meet the orchestra committees, when we get in touch with funding organizations, when we deal with people who give grants and when we get into the world of commerce that greets us when we arrive with our piece of art. Whether it's a rock n' roll record or a symphony, it's the same machinery lurking out there.

The reason a person writes a piece of music has got nothing to do with dark forces. I certainly don't have dark forces lurking around me when I'm writing. If someone is going to write a piece of music, in fact they are preoccupied with the boring labor and very hard work involved. That's what's really going on.

## What Makes Music Classical

Rock music... has risen to its current heights in the education of the young on the ashes of classical music, and in an atmosphere in which there is no intellectual resistance to attempts to tap the rawest passions.... Cultivation of the soul uses the passions and satisfies them while sublimating them and giving them an artistic unity.... Bach's religious intentions and Beethoven's revolutionary and humane ones are clear enough examples.          —A. Bloom

This is such nonsense. All the people recognized as great classical composers are recognized at this point for two reasons:

One, during the time these composers were alive and writing they had patrons who liked what they did and who therefore paid them money or gave them a place to live so that the composers could stay alive by writing dots on pieces of paper. If any of the compositions these men wrote had not been pleasing to a church, a duke, or a king, they would have been out of work and their music would not have survived.

There is a book called *Grove's Dictionary of Music and Musicians,* with thousands of names in it. You have never heard of most of the people in that book, nor have you heard their music. That doesn't mean they wrote awful music, it means they didn't have hits.

So basically, the people who are recognized as the geniuses of classical music had hits. And the person who determined whether or not it was a hit was a king, a duke, or the church or whoever paid the bill. The desire to get a sandwich or something to drink had a lot to do with it. And the content of what they wrote was to a degree determined by the musical predilections of the guy who was paying the bill.

Today, we have a similar situation in rock n' roll. We have kings, dukes, and popes: the A&R guy who spots a group or screens the tape when it comes in; the business affairs guy who writes the contract; the radio station programers who choose what records get air play.

The other reason the classical greats survived is their works are played over and over again by orchestras. The reasons they are played over and over again are: (1) all the musicians in the orchestra know how to play them because they learned them in the conservatory; (2) the orchestra management programs these pieces because the musicians already know them and therefore it costs less to rehearse them; (3) the composers are dead so the orchestras pay no royalties for the use of the music.

Today, survivability is based on the number of specimens in the market place—the sheer numbers of plastic objects. Many other compositions from this era will vanish, but Michael Jackson's *Thriller* album will survive because there are 30 million odd pieces of plastic out there. No matter what we may think of the content, a future generation may pick up that piece of plastic and say, "Oh, they were like this."

I suppose somewhere in the future there will be other men like Bloom certifying that the very narrow spectrum of rock n' roll which survives composes the great works of the later half of the twentieth century.

## The Difference Between Classical Music and Rock n' Roll

Rock music provides premature ecstasy and, in this respect, is like the drugs with which it is allied.... These are the three great lyrical themes: sex, hate and a smarmy, hypocritical version of brotherly love.... Nothing noble, sublime, profound, delicate, tasteful or even decent can find a place in such tableaux.            —A. Bloom

Again, Bloom is not looking at what is really going on here. The ugliness in this society is not a product of unrefined art, but of unrefined commerce, wild superstition, and religious fanaticism.

The real difference between the classics and rock n' roll is mostly a matter of form. In order to say we have written a symphony, the design we put on a piece of paper has to conform to certain specifications. We have an exposition that lasts a certain amount of time, then modulation, development, and recapitulation. It's like a box, like an egg carton. We must fill all the little spaces in the egg carton with the right forms. If we do, we can call it a symphony because it conforms to the spaces in that box.

Compare that creative process to rock n' roll. If we want to have an AM hit record, we have another egg carton to fill. We have an intro, a couple of verses, a bridge, another verse, and then a fade out. All of which requires a "hook." That's a very rigid form. If we wander away from that form, our song's not going to go on the radio because it doesn't sound like it fits into their format.

Now, whether the person writing the song graduated from a conservatory or whether they came out of a garage, they know that in order to finish a piece they have to do certain things to make it fit into a certain form. In the classical period the sonata or a concerto or symphony had to be that certain size and shape or else the king was not going to like it. One could die. These were literally matters of life and death, but not in the way Bloom defines them.

## The Rock Business

The family spiritual void has left the field open to rock music.... The result is nothing less than parents' loss of control over their children's moral education at a time when no one else is seriously concerned with it. This has been achieved by an alliance between the strange young males who have the gift of divining the mob's emergent wishes—our versions of Thrasymachus, Socrates' rhetorical adversary—and the record-company executives, the new robber barons, who mine gold out of rock.—A. Bloom

There is some truth to that, but how did we get to this point and what do we do about it?

We got here because teenagers are the most sought-after consumers. The whole idea of merchandising the prepubescent masturbational fantasy is not necessarily the work of the songwriter or the singer, but the work of the merchandiser who has elevated rock n' roll to the commercial enterprise it is.

In the beginning, rock n' roll was young kids singing to other kids about their girlfriends. That's all there was. The guys who made those records came from Manual Arts High School. They went into a recording studio, were given some wine, $25, and a bunch of records when their song came out as a single—which made them heroes at school. That was their career, not, "Well, we're not going to sing until we get a $125 thousand advance."

Today, rock n' roll is about getting a contract with a major company, and pretty much doing what the company tells you to do. The company promotes the image of rock n' roll as being wild and fun when in fact it's just a dismal business.

Record companies have people who claim to be experts on what the public really wants to hear. And they inflict their taste on the people who actually make the music. To be a big success, you need a really big company behind you because really big companies can make really big distribution deals.

Even people who are waiting to go into the business know it's a business. They spend a great deal of time planning what they will look like and getting a good publicity photo before they walk in the door with their tape. And the record companies tend to take the attitude that it doesn't make too much difference what the tape sounds like as long as the artists look right, because they can always hire a producer who will fix up the sound and make it the way they want it—so long as the people wear the right clothes and have the right hair.

## Retaining Classical Music

Classical music is dead among the young.... Rock music is as unquestioned and unproblematic as the air the students breathe, and very few have any acquaintance at all with classical music.... Classical music is now a special taste, like Greek language or pre-Columbian archeology, not a common culture of reciprocal communication and psychological shorthand.                                    —A. Bloom

On this point, Bloom and I can agree, but how can a child be blamed for consuming only that which is presented to him? Most kids have never been in contact with anything other than this highly merchandised stuff.

When I testified in front of the Senate, I pointed out that if they don't like the idea of young people buying certain kinds of music, why don't they stick a few dollars back into the school system to have music appreciation? There are kids today who have never heard a string quartet; they have never heard a symphony orchestra. I argued that the money for music appreciation courses, in terms of social good and other benefits such as improved behavior or uplifting the spirit, is far less than the cost of another set of uniforms for the football team. But I frankly don't see people waving banners in the streets saying more music appreciation in schools.

When I was in school, we could go into a room and they had records there. I could hear anything I wanted by going in there and putting on a record. I won't say I enjoyed everything that was played for me, but I was curious, and if I had never heard any of that music I wouldn't know about it.

Once we're out of school, the time we can spend doing that type of research is limited because most of us are out looking for a job flipping hamburgers in the great tradition of the Reagan economic miracle. When all is said and done, that's the real source of America's barren and arid lives.

## Themes, Issues, and Ideas

1.  In his first paragraph, Zappa says, "Performers who are doing the crude, vulgar, repulsive things Bloom doesn't enjoy are only commenting on that fact." In context, how does his argument for art as "commentary" work? What do you think about it? Do you think vulgar language is needed to discuss vulgarity, for example?

2.  Zappa says that "the ugliness in this society is not a product of unrefined art, but of unrefined commerce, wild superstition, and religious

fanaticism." Where and how in his essay does he support these coun-terexplanations?

3. Zappa uses the word "boring" several times. As a writer, does he ever seem bored in his essay? Locate some moments where you feel *some* mood, then characterize the mood created by his style and the ways that style creates the mood.

## Writing Strategies and Techniques

1. What is the effect created by Zappa's attribution of quotations to "A. Bloom"? What other attributions would create different effects, for example, "Dr. Allan Bloom?"

2. Zappa seems to assume that some concepts are inherently ridiculous ("the nasty ol' Devil") and that some deserve more respect ("a new field of science called psychoacoustics"). Make a list of both kinds of concepts. What qualities seem to characterize each list?

## Suggestions for Writing

1. Zappa arranges his remarks around a series of quotations from Bloom, which he then comments on. Write an essay in which you do the same for Zappa. Quote some of his remarks and attack, defend, or modify them.

2. Until the very end Zappa seems to move toward a greater degree of agreement with Bloom's assessments, though he continues to dis-agree with Bloom's causal explanations. How do you stand? Write an essay in which you position yourself with respect to either Frank Zappa or Allan Bloom on the article's common issues.

# Box of Babel?

## Charles Oliver

*Television has long been seen as an engine of disorder, a "vast wasteland," a spoiler of children's minds. In recent years, the sexual and violent content of some shows has become a controversy of its own. But as Charles Oliver points out in this essay, television is not the monolithic force it has been made out to be, but an uncertain business, subject to the pressures of change and technology. Whether those changes will be good or bad is less certain than change itself according to Oliver.*

Who killed Laura Palmer? In 1990, this became the hottest television question since "Who shot J. R.?" But the two shows that spawned those questions couldn't have been more different. *Dallas* was just an old-fashioned soap opera—a genre that had been pioneered on radio back in the 1930s. It featured the usual cast of rich men, attractive mistresses, and alcoholic wives. Its plot elements were simply racier and more-upscale versions of what the soap operas of the '30s had used: adultery, family feuds, dishonest business deals.

But *Twin Peaks*.... Television hadn't seen anything quite like it before. A surreal examination of the sordid underbelly of small-town life, the show had as central characters a midget who talked backwards, a singing FBI agent, and a woman who carried a small log everywhere. A key plot element was the demonic possession of one of the town's residents.

For one brief moment, the avant-garde images of *Twin Peaks* creator David Lynch (previously best known for art-house films such as *Eraserhead* and *Blue Velvet*) dominated the mainstream. And although *Twin Peaks* mania lasted less than a television season, the show permanently altered the TV landscape, opening the way for other off-kilter shows such as *Northern Exposure* and *Picket Fences.*

In the 10 years separating the shooting of J. R. Ewing and the death of Laura Palmer, television had changed dramatically. Cable had finally come into its own, and Rupert Murdoch's Fox network had begun to establish itself as a force. Increasingly, the television-viewing audience had fragmented. In 1980, the big three networks had over 90 percent of all prime-time viewers; by 1990, they could get only 60 percent of the prime-time audience. More than half of all TV sets tuned in to find out who shot J. R. But only a quarter of all viewers watched the *Twin Peaks* episode that unmasked Laura Palmer's killer.

For 30 years or so, television defined a broad-based popular American culture. But beginning in the '80s, that culture began to break down, dividing into small subcultures, as technology, deregulation, and market demand made it increasingly difficult for the broadcast networks to attract a broad national audience. In turn each of these subcultures influences each other, producing a mainstream culture that is currently evolving at an ever more-rapid rate.

As television enters the 21st century, it offers a variety that viewers never could have imagined when they sat down to watch Jackie Gleason for the first time 45 years ago. The typical viewer has access to 30 channels today, compared to two or three in the early '50s. And these channels offer everything from music videos to soft-core sex films to classic movies.

This diversity has provoked a backlash. On the right, cultural conservatives such as Michael Medved decry the sex, sin, and violence that television brings into their homes. On the left, the type of intellectual who in the '50s complained about television creating a bland, homogenized popular culture now argues that TV is offering too much variety. "Whatever its failings, a mass medium creates a sense of community," writes Ken Auletta in *Three Blind Mice*. "[T]he public has an investment in the larger public purpose a network can perform. . . ." Each side overstates the dangers of diversity and ignores the benefits from an expanding television universe.

In many ways television is beginning to resemble radio, with a multiplicity of channels serving a large number of specialized tastes. And we can see the future of television by looking at the past of radio. What is particularly interesting about the history of radio is that the musical genres it fostered did not exist in isolation; each form influenced the others, producing new forms of entertainment. And the technology of radio brought the sounds of these diverse musical forms into millions of homes, enhancing and speeding up this process of evolution.

In the '20s and '30s, the CBS and NBC radio networks established themselves as media of mass national culture. Each night families gathered to listen to shows such as *Amos'n'Andy* or *The Fred Allen Show*. Radio was the primary source for news. Along with motion pictures, it determined American tastes in music and drama. And radio helped create a national music—a jazz-based "pop" that appealed to all ages, regions, and races. 'Me networks banned songs that were racy or that might offend some segment of their audience, and they black-listed controversial artists.

But beginning in the late '40s, technological innovation and changes in federal regulations quickly ended the networks' cultural dominance, much as 40 years later similar changes would cripple the broadcast television networks. The biggest change was the introduction of commercial television broadcasting. TV quickly became *the* medium of national mass culture. By 1955, over half of all U.S. homes had a television. Families that had previously listened to network dramas and variety shows quickly abandoned radio for similar shows done on television. According to the A. C. Nielsen Co., the average family's daily radio listening dropped by 50 percent between 1948 and 1956. from 4.4 hours to 2.2 hours.

But even as radio's national audience was deteriorating, the FCC was licensing new radio stations at an unprecedented rate . There were 973 radio stations in 1945. By 1950, that number had increased to 2,867; by 1960, there were 4,306 radio stations in the United States.

With the national radio audience dead. radio in the '40s and '50s began to go after niche audiences, bringing new sounds out of urban bars and country honky-tonks. Country music had been on some Southern radio stations for decades, but the many new low-power stations serving rural communities quickly established country as their format. This exposed country artists to millions of more listeners and spurred record sales to new highs. Moreover, this music defied the norms of the dominant "Pop" culture. While Frank Sinatra was singing about broken hearts and Bing Crosby was crooning love songs, country artists like Hank Williams were singing earthy songs about adulterous affairs and getting drunk.

Similarly, in Northern cities, radio stations went after a black audience by playing rhythm & blues, the down-and- dirty cousin of jazz. Again, this music explicitly violated the norms of mass culture. Songs such as "Baby (You've Got What It Takes)" and "Roll with Me Henry" were full of sexual energy. But programmers didn't have to worry that much about offending mainstream listeners because most of them were watching television.

Of course, the synthesis of blues and country spawned rock, a music form that was vigorously opposed by the mainstream. But by the end of the '50s, many stations were specializing in rock. And as the years went by, musical forms continued to subdivide, and each form had radio stations specializing in it. Today, in Los Angeles, one can find classic rock, progressive rock, country, salsa, ranchero, and rap sharing the radio dial with all-talk and all-news stations.

The history of television over the past 15 years has been remarkably similar to that of radio in the '50s and '60s. Not surprisingly, the first way that cable channels such as HBO tried to distinguish themselves from the networks was by offering more sexually explicit programming. The scheduled of HBO and Showtime were—and still are—full of unedited R-rated movies and original programming full of completely gratuitous nudity. This sort of programming cuts at the heart of network television by stealing away the demographic group most prized by advertisers: young urban viewers.

Filmmakers and television programmers have long known that young people tolerate—even demand—a greater degree of sexual explicitness and violence than other groups. As James Baughman notes in his book *The Republic of Mass Culture,* polls consistently show that young moviegoers want "vivid sex scenes." Young adults' taste for sex and violence has always been a problem for broadcast networks. Young urban professionals have always been the group most valued by advertisers. and young people's demand for sexy or hip programming has always been well-known. The problem for the networks has been how to attract these valued viewers without offending the larger audience.

Back in the '50s, ABC had no such problems. It wasn't attracting a larger audience anyway. The network was a distant third. NBC and CBS had all of the major stars locked up in big-money contracts. Further, because there weren't as many stations then, ABC had to share affiliates in some areas with one of the other two networks. The company gambled that by airing risky programming it could attract young viewers and make a name for itself.

The first of these series was *Maverick,* starting James Garner. The show looks rather tame by today's standards, but for 1957 it was revolutionary: The protagonist—Brett Maverick—was a coward, a con man, and a professional gambler, not the tall, straight-shootin' hero of the traditional western. Each week writer-producer Roy Huggins satirized all of those traditional values that the western held so dear. Honor, chivalry, integrity—Maverick would have none of that. And it worked. *Maverick* immediately grabbed the most-prized demographic groups and slowly gained a mass following, cracking the top 10 in its second season and remaining there for the next four years.

The next year, Huggins was back with *77 Sunset Strip,* the first of the sexy detective shows. Granted, this was still the '50s, so Stu Bailey and Jeff Spencer were never shown even kissing any of the girls they dated. But the audience was hip enough to figure out what they were doing with that seemingly endless procession of beautiful starlets that passed through their apartments. Later in the decade, ABC brought viewers *Ben Casey* (a young doctor who in each episode managed at least once angrily to defy the older doctors running his hospital and bare his very hairy, muscular chest) and *The Untouchables* (still one of the most violent series ever aired).

J. Fred MacDonald notes in his book *One Nation Under Television* that critics looked at these shows and accused ABC of dumping "garbage onto the rugs of the American people every night." But network executives could weather such criticism. By the '60s, ABC was still in third place, but thanks to sex and violence, it was turning a profit and was a viable network due to its relatively large number of young viewers.

In the early '70s, CBS found itself in a dilemma. It was the number-one network, but it was losing valuable younger viewers to shows such as *Laugh In* on NBC. So in the 1970 and 1971 seasons, CBS canceled a half dozen country comedies, including *The Beverly Hillbillies, Petticoat Junction, Hee Haw,* and *Green Acres.* Each of these shows was ranked in the top 20, but their viewers were too rural, too poor, and too old.

These shows were replaced on the week's schedule by daring shows such as *All in the Family* and *M\*A\*S\*H.* CBS gambled that if it could attract young viewers, the broader audience would follow. The new shows might offend older, more conservative viewers—certainly these shows were more likely to shock than *Green Acres.* But what were these viewers going to do—change the channel to *Laugh In?* In effect, market forces meant that the networks were always pushing the envelope ever so slightly. They needed shows that would titillate but not offend.

But in 1974 the dynamics of network programming changed. That year HBO put its signal on satellite, delivering the network to cable systems all over the United States. A little less than a year later, Ted Turner put his Atlanta television station WTBS on satellite.

The initial programming strategies of these two outlets represented the dilemma that cable would pose for the networks. If some viewers wanted daring, sexy programming, they could buy HBO (and later the Playboy Channel or Showtime) and see all of the bare boobs, raunchy comedians, or violent deaths they could stomach. If, on the other hand, a viewer wanted cleaner, more wholesome entertainment, he could turn to TBS and catch all of those rural comedies canceled a few year earlier by CBS.

Now the networks faced a new dilemma: If they made their programs sexy enough to compete with cable, they would drive away the family audience. If they made them more wholesome, they would lose young viewers to HBO.

The answer to this dilemma was provided by a novice to the American broadcasting world: Rupert Murdoch. In 1986, Murdoch started the Fox network, and he never had any illusions about getting a broad audience. He went after young urban viewers—the people most valued by advertisers. Fox's shows—*Married with Children, Studs, A Current Affair, The Simpsons*—pushed the envelope of good taste. The housewives of Minnesota were outraged, but they weren't Fox's viewers. A mere five years later, Fox was still the fourth-place network, but it was number one among the demographic groups it had targeted, and Fox was the second most profitable network.

At first, Fox's rise to prominence seems like ABC's rise to profitability in the '50s. But there is a difference. ABC planned to become, and eventually did become, a broad-based network, balancing the tastes of its young urban viewers against those of other, more conservative viewers. Fox shows no signs of reaching out to a broader audience. It has established an identity as the network of young people. If other viewers also happen to like its programs and turn them into mainstream hits—as they have done with *The Simpsons, Married with Children,* and *Beverly Hills 90210*—great. But the network still targets its programs solely at young people.

Narrowcasting isn't simply a recipe for more sex and violence, however. It can also give a voice to political, religious, or artistic views that are too *conservative* for the mainstream. Back when the networks dominated television they had to target their wares to the broadest market. If religion showed up at all, it tended to be safe, moderate, and mainstream; religious figures or views that were controversial or even just marginal had no place on the dial. ABC may have had a place in prime time for Bishop Fulton Sheen, but can one seriously imagine the network airing a show hosted by a Hasidic rabbi or a fundamentalist preacher? But today there are cable shows, and even entire networks, aimed at charismatic Christians, orthodox Jews, Buddhists, and probably some religions that I've never even heard of.

In the past, if television got too sexy, the only choice conservative viewers had was to watch programs that offended them or to give up television. Now if TV watchers find even network programming too sexy or irreverent, they can turn to Pat Robertson's Family Channel and see shows that are wholesome and family oriented.

Indeed, the Family Channel demonstrates the true strengths of cable. Originally, it was a vehicle for Pat Robertson's evangelism, but Robertson and his son Tim saw a market niche that they thought was underserved, so they began devoting more of their programming schedule to family-oriented entertainment. Today, the channel still has The 700 Club, but most of its schedule is filled with shows such as Maniac Mansion and Zorro that are, as Tim Robertson told The Wall Street Journal, "solid entertainment where good guys win, bad guys lose, people aren't engaging in gratuitous sex." (The schedule is not completely unobjectionable, the Family Channel's heavy lineup of westerns makes it one of the most violent spots on the TV dial.)

As people choose other forms of entertainment, the audience for the big three is being whittled to pieces. In 1978, the median rating for a top 20 show was 22.8 (each rating point represents a little more than three-quarters of a million viewers); by 1988 the median rating was 18.8. The numbers for network shows ranked even lower plummeted.

Oddly enough, this worries some on the political left. Ev Dennis, executive director of the Gannett Center for Media Studies argues, "We have shared values that are enhanced by three networks. For the same reason that we don't favor five hundred languages in the country. It does create a national consensus of values and what we think is important."

But America won't be speaking 500 languages. It will be speaking one language with a very expansive vocabulary. Each of these channels will be brought into the home through one medium, allowing viewers to sample a large variety of smaller cultures and add to their lives the elements that appeal to them. Most rap music is now bought by white suburban teens. It's unlikely they would ever have ventured into the Harlem clubs, where rap originated, but once MTV added the genre to its play list, whites fell in love with rap. In turn, Hollywood filmmakers eager to attract young people to their action films have made movie stars out of rappers such as Ice T and Ice Cube.

Meanwhile, the Nashville Network has brought country music into the homes of people who never would have tuned to country radio, fueling the biggest sales the genre has ever had. A new breed of country artists has attracted millions of new fans to the music. But each performer brings his own unique sound to the genre. Travis Tritt draws upon the Southern rock of bands like Lynyrd Skynyrd and the Marshall Tucker Band. Dwight Yoakum uses elements of Mexican-American ranchero music. Clint Black incorporates elements of the Southern California rock sound of the Eagles and Linda Ronstadt.

The result is that the "sound" of country music is bigger and more diverse than it has ever been. But even as country music absorbs other sounds, it has begun to divide. Already some radio stations have begun to specialize in different types of country—easy-listening format for stations serving Northern markets or ranchero-country formats for the South-West, for example.

Indeed, what is happening in country music is a paradigm for how television will shape the popular culture of the future. New channels will reach out to niche markets. Very often these markets will remain small, but in some cases, millions of viewers will be introduced to a genre of music or a type of filmmaking that they have never seen before. They will adopt it and make it part of the mainstream. But even as this new form of entertainment enters the mainstream, it will be transformed, and its audience will begin to fragment, beginning the cycle anew.

And if viewers aren't energetic enough to sample new forms of entertainment, artists eager for new inspiration and entrepreneurs searching for new products are. Few young girls have been in a transvestite bar, but they all learned how to vogue a few years ago when Madonna brought the dance out of New York after-hours clubs and into her videos.

And while few Americans patronize art-house theaters, they've all now been exposed to the peculiar vision of David Lynch thanks to *Twin Peaks*. As *Twin Peaks* demonstrated, particular shows still have the ability to transcend their target audiences and permanently alter mainstream sensibilities.

Of course, this really isn't a new process; it's simply the old story of how popular culture evolves. What is new is the speed at which it will happen. Previously, for example, people could only learn about new music forms by hearing them in nightclubs. Records changed all of that. But people still had to seek out the right records. Now television delivers the latest acts directly into the home, allowing people to absorb and assimilate new types of music more quickly. And easy channel surfing by remote control encourages far more cultural exploration than the radio dial ever produced.

This exploration will lead to an even greater variety of entertainment, as each artist draws upon an expanded universe for inspiration. It also means that fashions will pass much more quickly. Overnight, today's "hot" looks, sounds, and artists will become passé.

But their work will be preserved forever. Paradoxically, evolving video technology also makes it easier for people remain outside of popular culture when that culture changes in ways that they do not like. When network television entered its "jiggle" phase during the 1970s, with shows such as *Charlie's Angels* dominating the airwaves, most people had one choice: watch the shows or abandon television. Now if the networks are too sexy, one can turn to TBS or to the Family Channel to watch older, more wholesome TV shows, or one can rent older, more wholesome movies at Blockbuster.

Such alternatives act as a brake when culture begins to change too rapidly. They also act as a tie to our culture's past. Previously, after films had ended their theatrical runs, they could only be seen occasionally at revival houses or on late-night movies. Now, cable channels such as TNT and American Movie Classics deliver a steady stream of old movies into viewers homes, and the corner video store typically has hundreds of old movies on tape. Soon, cable systems will have the capability to provide true pay-per-view movies on demand, allowing subscribers to access any movie on video or any episode of any television series ever made anytime they want simply by picking up their phones.

Again, even if consumers don't actively seek out these choices, artists eager for inspiration will. Already, artists reach back into the past, whether it is Madonna copying the "looks" of Marlene Dietrich or Marilyn Monroe, or Brian de Palma copying visual passages from Alfred Hitchcock films, or Guns 'n' Roses doing remakes of songs by Paul McCartney and Bob Dylan. Making it easier for artists to access old works can only facilitate such sampling.

As America prepares for the 21st century, television's role as the dominant cultural force remains unchallenged. But the networks domination of television is over. In the future, Americans will not be united by a bland, one-size-fits-all culture. But they will not be divided into multitudes of tiny subcultures either. They will be united by a common cultural bazaar, where hundreds, perhaps thousands, of merchants compete for their attention, and in the end, we will all be tied together by the best that market has to offer.

## Themes, Issues, and Ideas

1. What do you think of Oliver's critique of his examples, such as Madonna or Guns 'n' Roses? Do they seem representative to you? Why or why not?

2. Does your experience of watching television corroborate Oliver's view? Do you find any of his assertions too optimistic? Too pessimistic? Why?

3. What do you think of Oliver's anologies with radio and the early days of television? Do you find them valid?

## Writing Strategies and Techniques

1. How would you characterize the way Oliver approaches television? What might be some other approaches?

2. Oliver starts his essay by talking about *Twin Peaks*. Does he gain credibility by doing so? What devices does Oliver use to identify himself as someone who knows what he's talking about?

## Suggestions for Writing

1. Compare Oliver's view of television with that of Mark Crispin Miller, in "Big Brother is You, Watching." What do the two have in common? Where do they depart from each other? Who is more convincing?

2. Write what a 21st-century *TV Guide* might look like if Oliver's view of the future is correct.

# MAKING CONNECTIONS

1.  Tom Wolfe sees the next century differently than do most other authors in this chapter. He says, "The twenty-first century, I predict, will confound the twentieth-century notion of the Future as something exciting, novel, unexpected, or radiant; as Progress, to use an old word." Write an essay comparing and contrasting Wolfe with the other authors on the issue of the future.

2.  Michael Kinsley and Barbara Ehrenreich both make valid arguments about Ice-T's lyrics. Will their arguments about free speech and social responsibility still be as valid in the world that Charles Oliver describes?

3.  Mark Crispin Miller makes the most radical critique of popular culture in this chapter. Do you find such a critique provocative? Compare Miller, as a social critic, with two of the other writers in this chapter.

4.  Tom Wolfe, who begins this chapter, claims that ideas create cultural innovations. Charles Oliver, on the other hand, seems to be saying that technology and business inform culture, not the other way around. Write an essay considering both sides of the question. Make sure to back up your statements with evidence and argument from the text as well as your own examples and experience.

5.  After finishing the other essays in this chapter, do you think they confound or bear out Tom Wolfe's remarks about America in the twentieth century? What are some cultural phenomena that you think should have been included in this chapter, and how might they have supported or undermined Wolfe's argument?

# CHAPTER SEVEN

## *Mortality and the Human Spirit*

### *Struggles of Belief and Doubt*

# THE PAST AS PROLOGUE

# A Defence of Skeletons

## G. K. Chesterton

*G. K. Chesterton (1874–1936) was one of the most prolific and original writers of the modern era. Although he began writing in an age that treasured progress and scientific enlightenment above all things, Chesterton took an opposite stance, standing up for old Europe, Christianity, and the medieval mind, and trying to persuade others to revere as he did "the teeming vitality of the dead." Although primarily a journalist, Chesterton wrote extensively in other genres, including literary criticism, biography, social policy, moral theology and apologetics, poetry, drama, detective stories (Father Brown was his most famous creation), novels, and children's books. He died in 1936, having seen his worst predictions for the modern world (world war, fascism, hopelessness, and worse) begin to come true, but having borne it all with his characteristic good humor.*

*In "A Defence of Skeletons," Chesterton turns his feverish attention to a typical image of death: the human skeleton. In this reading, he manages to encapsulate his own view of the universe into the space of a very few pages.*

The importance of the human skeleton is very great, and the horror with which it is commonly regarded is somewhat mysterious. Without claiming for the human skeleton a wholly conventional beauty, we may assert that he is certainly not uglier than a bull-dog, whose popularity never wanes, and that he has a vastly more cheerful and ingratiating expression. But just as man is mysteriously ashamed of the skeletons of the trees in winter, so he is mysteriously ashamed of the skeleton of himself in death. It is a singular thing altogether, this horror of the architecture of things. One would think it would be most unwise in a man to be afraid of a skeleton, since Nature has set curious and quite insuperable obstacles to his running away from it.

One ground exists for this terror: a strange idea has infected humanity that the skeleton is typical of death. A man might as well say that a factory chimney was typical of bankruptcy. The factory may be left naked after ruin, the skeleton may be left naked after bodily dissolution; but both of them have had a lively and workmanlike life of their own, all the pulleys creaking, all the wheels turning, in the House of Livelihood as in the House of Life. There is no reason why this creature (new, as I fancy, to art), the living skeleton, should not become the essential symbol of life.

The truth is that man's horror of the skeleton is not horror of death at all. It is man's eccentric glory that he has not, generally speaking, any objection to being dead, but has a very serious objection to being undignified. And the fundamental matter which troubles him in the skeleton is the reminder that the ground-plan of his appearance is shamelessly grotesque. I do not know why he should object to this. He contentedly takes his place in a world that does not pretend to be genteel—a laughing, working, jeering world. He sees millions of animals carrying, with quite a dandified levity, the most monstrous shapes and appendages, the most preposterous horns, wings, and legs, when they are necessary to utility. He sees the good temper of the frog, the unaccountable happiness of the hippopotamus. He sees a whole universe which is ridiculous, from the animalcule, with a head too big for its body, up to the comet, with a tail too big for its head. But when it comes to the delightful oddity of his own inside, his sense of humour rather abruptly deserts him.

In the Middle Ages and in the Renaissance (which was, in certain times and respects, a much gloomier period) this idea of the skeleton had a vast influence in freezing the pride out of all earthly pomps and the fragrance out of all fleeting pleasures. But it was not, surely, the mere dread of death that did this, for these were ages in which men went to meet death singing; it was the idea of the degradation of man in the grinning ugliness of his structure that withered the juvenile insolence of beauty and pride. And in this it almost assuredly did more good than harm. There is nothing so cold or so pitiless as youth, and youth in aristocratic stations and ages tended to impeccable dignity, an endless summer of success which needed to be very sharply reminded of the scorn of the stars. It was well that such flamboyant prigs should be convinced that one practical joke, at least, would bowl them over, that they would fall into one grinning man-trap, and not rise again. That the whole structure of their existence was as wholesomely ridiculous as that of a pig or a parrot they could not be expected to realize; that birth was humorous, coming of age humorous, drinking and fighting humorous, they were far too young and solemn to know. But at least they were taught that death was humorous.

There is a peculiar idea abroad that the value and fascination of what we call Nature lie in her beauty. But the fact that Nature is beautiful in the sense that a dado or a Liberty curtain is beautiful, is only one of her charms, and almost an accidental one. The highest and most valuable quality in Nature is not her beauty, but her generous and defiant ugliness. A hundred instances might be taken. The croaking noise of the rooks is, in itself, as hideous as the whole hell of sounds in a London railway tunnel. Yet it uplifts us like a trumpet with its coarse kindliness and honesty, and the lover in 'Maud' could actually persuade himself that this abominable noise resembled his lady-love's name. Has the poet, for whom Nature means only roses and lilies, ever heard a pig grunting? It is a noise that does a man good—a strong, snorting, imprisoned noise, breaking its way out of unfathomable dungeons through every possible outlet and organ. It might be the voice of the earth itself, snoring in its mighty sleep. This is the deepest, the oldest, the most wholesome and religious sense of the value of Nature—the value which comes from her immense babyishness. She is as top-heavy, as grotesque, as solemn and as happy as a child. The mood does come when we see all her shapes like shapes that a baby scrawls upon a slate—simple, rudimentary, a million years older and stronger than the whole disease that is called Art. The objects of earth and heaven seem to combine into a nursery tale, and our relation to things seems for a moment so simple that a dancing lunatic would be needed to do justice to its lucidity and levity. The tree above my head is flapping like some gigantic bird standing on one leg; the moon is like the eye of a cyclops. And, however much my face clouds with sombre vanity, or vulgar vengeance, or contemptible contempt, the bones of my skull beneath it are laughing for ever.

## Themes, Issues, and Ideas

1. What does Chesterton suggest is the primary value of skeletons?

2. Why do such things as skeletons and the grunts of pigs represent, to Chesterton, "the deepest, the oldest, the most wholesome and religious sense of the value of Nature?"

3. What is Chesterton assuming when he writes of the universe as humorous, top-heavy, etc.? Is such poetic language reconcilable with serious issues?

## Writing Strategies and Techniques

1. How would you describe the voice in which this essay is written? Is it one you would be inclined to admire or respect? Is it an attractive voice? A convincing one? Explain your answer.

2. G. K. Chesterton was famous for certain rhetorical techniques, such as the alliteration in the last sentence. Find another writing strategy Chesterton uses.

## Suggestions for Writing

1. Pretend you are G. K. Chesterton and write an editorial on a current topic that might appear in tomorrow's paper.

2. Write a response, in Chesterton's voice, to Camille Paglia's essay (see Chapter 2).

# The Need for Transcendence in the Modern World

## Václav Havel and Edward Cornish

*Václav Havel, the President of the Czech Republic, has as much claim as any person now living to represent the postmodern* zeitgeist. *His essay "The Power of the Powerless" helped to propel Soviet-bloc Europe out into the post–Cold War democracy, and his moral leadership as well as his plays and essays have continued to inspire people around the world. In this speech, originally given in Philadelphia's Independence Hall on the 4th of July, 1994, Havel discusses the spirituality of postmodern times, and what he sees as its most pressing needs. Edward Cornish, the President of the World Future Society and the editor of* The Futurist, *where the speech was first published, offers a rebuttal in the second part.*

## Václav Havel:

There are thinkers who claim that, if the modern age began with the discovery of America, it also ended in America. This is said to have occurred in the year 1969, when America sent the first men to the moon. From this historical moment, they say, a new age in the life of humanity can be dated.

I think there are good reasons for suggesting that the modern age has ended. Today, many things indicate that we are going through a transitional period, when it seems that something is on the way out and something else is painfully being born. It is as if something were crumbling, decaying, and exhausting itself, while something else, still indistinct, were arising from the rubble.

Periods of history when values undergo a fundamental shift are certainly not unprecedented. This happened in the Hellenistic period, when from the ruins of the classical world the Middle Ages were gradually born. It happened during the Renaissance, which opened the way to the modern era. The distinguishing features of such transitional periods are a mixing and blending of cultures and a plurality or parallelism of intellectual and spiritual worlds. These are periods when all consistent value systems collapse, when cultures distant in time and space are discovered or rediscovered. They are periods when there is a tendency to quote, to imitate, and to amplify, rather than to state with authority or integrate. New meaning is gradually born from the encounter, or the intersection, of many different elements.

Today, this state of mind or of the human world is called postmodernism. For me, a symbol of that state is a Bedouin mounted on a camel and clad in traditional robes under which he is wearing jeans, with a transistor radio in his hands and an ad for Coca-Cola on the camel's back. I am not ridiculing this, nor am I shedding an intellectual tear over the commercial expansion of the West that destroys alien cultures. I see it rather as a typical expression of this multicultural era, a signal that an amalgamation of cultures is taking place. I see it as proof that something is happening, something is being born, that we are in a phase when one age is succeeding another, when everything is possible. Yes, everything is possible, because our civilization does not have its own unified style, its own spirit, its own aesthetic.

## Science and Modern Civilization

This is related to the crisis, or to the transformation, of science as the basis of the modern conception of the world.

The dizzying development of this science, with its unconditional faith in objective reality and its complete dependency on general and rationally knowable laws, led to the birth of modem technological civilization. It is the first civilization in the history of the human race that spans the entire globe and firmly binds together all human societies, submitting them to a common global destiny. It was this science that enabled man, for the first time, to see Earth from space with his own eyes; that is, to see it as another star in the sky.

At the same time, however, the relationship to the world that modern science fostered and shaped now appears to have exhausted its potential. It is increasingly clear that, strangely, the relationship is missing something. It fails to connect with the most intrinsic nature of reality and with natural human experience. It is now more of a source of disintegration and doubt than a source of integration and meaning. It produces what amounts to a state of schizophrenia: Man as an observer is becoming completely alienated from himself as a being.

Classical modern science described only the surface of things, a single dimension of reality. And the more dogmatically science treated it as the only dimension, as the very essence of reality, the more misleading it became. Today, for instance, we may know immeasurably more about the universe than our ancestors did, and yet, it increasingly seems they knew something more essential about it than we do, something that escapes us. The same thing is true of nature and of ourselves. The more thoroughly all our organs and their functions, their internal structure, and the biochemical reactions that take place within them are described, the more we seem to fail to grasp the spirit, purpose, and meaning of the system that they create together and that we experience as our unique "self."

And thus today we find ourselves in a paradoxical situation. We enjoy all the achievements of modern civilization that have made our physical existence on this earth easier in so many important ways. Yet we do not know exactly what to do with ourselves, where to turn. The world of our experiences seems chaotic, disconnected, confusing. There appear to be no integrating forces, no unified meaning, no true inner understanding of phenomena in our experience of the world. Experts can explain anything in the objective world to us, yet we understand our own lives less and less. In short, we live in the postmodern world, where everything is possible and almost nothing is certain.

## When Nothing Is Certain

This state of affairs has its social and political consequences. The single planetary civilization to which we all belong confronts us with global challenges. We stand helpless before them because our civilization has essentially globalized only the surface of our lives. But our inner self continues to have a life of its own. And the fewer answers the era of rational knowledge provides to the basic questions of human

Being, the more deeply it would seem that people, behind its back as it were, cling to the ancient certainties of their tribe. Because of this, individual cultures, increasingly lumped together by contemporary civilization, are realizing with new urgency their own inner autonomy and the inner differences of others.

Cultural conflicts are increasing and are understandably more dangerous today than at any other time in history. The end of the era of rationalism has been catastrophic: Armed with the same supermodern weapons, often from the same suppliers, and followed by television cameras, the members of various tribal cults are at war with one another. By day, we work with statistics; in the evening, we consult astrologers and frighten ourselves with thrillers about vampires. The abyss between rational and the spiritual, the external and the internal, the objective and the subjective, the technical and the moral, the universal and the unique, constantly grows deeper.

Politicians are rightly worried by the problem of finding the key to ensure the survival of a civilization that is global and at the same time clearly multicultural. How can generally respected mechanisms of peaceful coexistence be set up, and on what set of principles are they to be established?

These questions have been highlighted with particular urgency by the two most important political events in the second half of the twentieth century: the collapse of colonial hegemony and the fall of communism. The artificial world order of the past decades has collapsed, and a new, more-just order has not yet emerged. The central political task of the final years of this century, then, is the creation of a new model of coexistence among the various cultures, peoples, races, and religious spheres within a single interconnected civilization. This task is all the more urgent because other threats to contemporary humanity brought about by one-dimensional development of civilization are growing more serious all the time.

Many believe this task can be accomplished through technical means. That is, they believe it can be accomplished through the invention of new organizational, political, and diplomatic instruments. Yes, it is clearly necessary to invent organizational structures appropriate to the present multicultural age. But such efforts are doomed to failure if they do not grow out of something deeper, out of generally held values.

This, too, is well known. And in searching for the most natural source for the creation of a new world order, we usually look to an area that is the traditional foundation of modern justice and a great achievement of the modern age: to a set of values meaningful to world order. Yet, I think it must be anchored in a different place, and in a different way, than has been the case so far. If it is to be more than just a slogan mocked by half the world, it cannot be expressed in the language of a departing era, and it must not be mere froth floating on the subsiding waters of faith in a purely scientific relationship to the world.

Paradoxically, inspiration for the renewal of this lost integrity can once again be found in science, in a science that is new—let us say post-modern—a science producing ideas that in a certain sense allow it to transcend its own limits. I will give two examples:

The first is the **Anthropic Cosmological Principle.** Its authors and adherents have pointed out that from the countless possible courses of its evolution the universe took the only one that enabled life to emerge. This is not yet proof that the aim of the universe has always been that it should one day see itself through our eyes. But how else can this matter be explained?

I think the Anthropic Cosmological Principle brings us to an idea perhaps as old as humanity itself: that we are not at all just an accidental anomaly, the microscopic caprice of a tiny particle whirling in the endless depths of the universe. Instead, we are mysteriously connected to the entire universe, we are mirrored in it, just as the entire evolution of the universe is mirrored in us.

Until recently, it might have seemed that we were an unhappy bit of mildew on a heavenly body whirling in space among many that have no mildew on them at all. This was something that classical science could explain, Yet, the moment it begins to appear that we are deeply connected to the entire universe, science reaches the outer limits of its powers. Because it is founded on the search for universal laws, it cannot deal with singularity, that is, with uniqueness. The universe is a unique event and a unique story, and so far we are the unique point of that story. But unique events and stories are the domain of poetry, not science. With the formulation of the Anthropic Cosmological Principle, science has found itself on the border between formula and story, between science and myth. In that, however, science has paradoxically returned, in roundabout way, to man, and offers him—in new clothing—his lost integrity. It does so by anchoring him once more in the cosmos.

The second example is the **Gaia Hypothesis.** This theory brings together proof that the dense network of mutual interactions between the organic and inorganic portions of the earth's surface form a single system, a kind of mega-organism, a living planet—Gaia—named after an ancient goddess who is recognizable as an archetype of the Earth Mother in perhaps all religions. According to the Gaia Hypothesis, we are parts of a greater whole. Our destiny is not dependent merely on what we do for ourselves but also on what we do for Gaia as a whole. If we endanger her, she will dispense with us in the interests of a higher value—that is, life itself.

## Toward Self-Transcendence

What makes the Anthropic Principle and the Gaia Hypothesis so inspiring? One simple thing: Both remind us, in modern language, of what we have long suspected, of what we have long projected into our forgotten myths and what perhaps has always lain dormant within us as archetypes. That is, the awareness of our being anchored in the earth and the universe, the awareness that we are not here alone nor for ourselves alone, but that we are an integral part of higher, mysterious entities against whom it is not advisable to blaspheme. This forgotten awareness is encoded in all religions. All cultures anticipate it in various forms. It is one of the things that form the basis of man's understanding of himself, of his place in the world, and ultimately of the world as such.

A modern philosopher once said: "Only a God can save us now."

Yes, the only real hope of people today is probably a renewal of our certainty that we are rooted in the earth and, at the same time, the cosmos. This awareness endows us with the capacity for self-transcendence. Politicians at international forums may reiterate a thousand times that the basis of the new world order must be universal respect for human rights, but it will mean nothing as long as this imperative does not derive from the respect of the miracle of Being, the miracle of the universe, the miracle of nature, the miracle of our own existence. Only someone who submits to the authority of the universal order and of creation, who values the right to be a part of it and a participant in it, can genuinely value himself and his neighbors, and thus honor their rights as well.

It logically follows that, in today's multicultural world, the truly reliable path to coexistence, to peaceful coexistence and creative cooperation, must start from what is at the root of all cultures and what lies infinitely deeper in human hearts and minds than political opinion, convictions, antipathies, or sympathies—it must be rooted in self-transcendence:

- Transcendence as a hand reached out to those close to us, to foreigners, to the human community, to all living creatures, to nature, to the universe.

- Transcendence as a deeply and joyously experienced need to be in harmony even with what we ourselves are not, what we do not understand, what seems distant from us in time and space, but with which we are nevertheless mysteriously linked because, together with us, all this constitutes a single world.

- Transcendence as the only real alternative to extinction.

The Declaration of independence states that the Creator gave man the right to liberty. It seems man can realize that liberty only if he does not forget the One who endowed him with it.

## Edward Cornish:

*The Futurist* broke a house rule to bring you the foregoing speech by Václav Havel. The rule is that we do not publish material that has previously appeared in another periodical. Havel's speech, made in a ceremony in Philadelphia in 1994, was carried by the *New York Times* and other media. However, many readers missed seeing Havel's remarkable statement, so we are reproducing it here.

Havel addresses some of the great issues of our time in a way that compels our thoughtful attention. (He is, after all, a dramatist.) So we hope readers will excuse us for giving them a text that some will have seen before. We also believe that Havel's statement deserves a more critical examination than it has received so far.

Havel rightly focuses attention on today's great political task: the governance of a multicultural world. Rapidly improving communications and transportation have largely nullified the natural barriers that once kept each of the world's tribes and communities apart from most other peoples who spoke different languages, practiced different religions, and had different skin colors and facial features. Now people everywhere are forced to live in an environment filled with alien peoples, languages, customs, governments, and ideas.

The sudden mixing of peoples and cultures—through migration, telecommunications, and soaring intercontinental trade—tends to devalue and destroy the familiar community and culture of the past. The customary order of society crumbles, and many individuals often find themselves disoriented and even lost, a phenomenon described by Émile Durkheim as *anomie* and by Alvin Toffler as "future shock." Amid this turbulence, some people seek salvation in a fervent reassertion of tribal beliefs and customs. This resurgent dedication to traditional values—or some aspects of them—often becomes a virulent force producing riots, bombings, and assassinations.

Havel suggests that responsibility for these modern troubles rests with science, but that exaggerates science's role in the technological progress that disrupts traditional practices and lifestyles. Many of the most significant technological developments were achieved with only modest input from scientists. The automobile and the airplane, for example, were developed principally by mechanics and engineers.

Exaggerating the role of science allows Havel to blame it for the modern malaise that worries him. He frets that the universe revealed by science does not accord well with ordinary human thinking and feeling: Science, he charges, has failed to enable us to understand our lives and live at peace with ourselves and our surroundings.

Most scientists would agree that science has not produced a satisfying religion or philosophy to assuage the pangs of the modern heart. The scientists would argue that the responsibility for that lies not with science but with religion, philosophy, or perhaps psychotherapy. However, Havel offers a more challenging idea: The rudiments of the desired spiritual renewal can be found in science itself—"a science producing ideas that in a certain sense allow it to transcend its own limits."

He offers two examples from this "self-transcending science"— the Anthropic Cosmological Principle and the Gaia Hypothesis. The Anthropic Principle suggests that the universe was expressly built for humans, and the Gaia Hypothesis portrays the world around us as a living Earth Mother. Both ideas appeal to people's desire for a more comfortable universe than the cold, weird, and unfeeling realm that scientific inquiry has revealed. But these ideas are more romantic than scientific. They reside in the misty regions of human thought where generally respected scientific findings and theories are conflated with poetic fantasies and mystical speculations.

The more basic issue, however, is this: Do the world's people really need to share a common metaphysical doctrine in order to have

world peace? And, if we believe we have a "suitable" doctrine to pro-
mulgate, how are we to persuade people to accept it? Humans have
always disagreed sharply on matters of faith, so world religious unity
implies a global system for teaching people the approved dogmas, monitoring people's beliefs, and punishing those whose thinking strays
from the Truth. Anyone who has spoken with many devout Christians,
Moslems, and other religionists will have reason to doubt that they will
quickly switch their allegiance to Gaia or Anthropic Cosmology.

History shows us that metaphysical doctrines have only too often
led to intense conflict rather than increased harmony. Indeed, Havel's
capital city, Prague, has been the scene of numerous savage religious
battles; in one celebrated incident in 1618, outraged Protestants threw
two Catholic councillors from the windows of Hradčany Castle, which
later became the residence of Czech presidents. Havel offers no reason
to believe that the worshipers of Gaia will not be subject to the same
fanaticism that has long afflicted the followers of the Prince of Peace.

Nonetheless, Havel's remarkable speech should stimulate us to
look harder for better solutions to the problems of governing our multicultural world.

Where should we look? Havel himself mentions the need "to
invent new organizational structures appropriate to the present multicultural age." Perhaps more can be done in that area than Havel seems
to think. We might start by reviewing the thoughtful articles by Harlan
Cleveland that have appeared in *The Futurist* ("Ten Keys to World
Peace," July-August 1994, and "The Limits to Cultural Diversity,"
March-April 1995). Cleveland suggests practical steps that can be taken
toward world harmony.

We can also do far more to encourage a healthy development of
the social sciences, which have given occasional demonstrations of
their power to help us understand more clearly our psychological and
institutional failings. Up to now, the social sciences have been poorly
supported and often corrupted by ideologies and special interests, but
that could change in the future. A reformed social science might show
us how to overcome many of the obstacles to cultural understanding
and global peace.

Lastly, the new electronic technologies offer enormous possibilities for helping people to communicate constructively across frontiers,
to access the most accurate and up-to-date information, and to understand each other better than at any time in the past. So there are reasons
for believing that we can eventually solve the urgent problems of gov-

erning a multicultural world. The belief that "Only a God can save us now" is, at bottom, only an excuse for doing little or nothing to save ourselves.

## Themes, Issues, and Ideas

1. What does Havel mean by "transcendence?" In what way does he define it? What are some other conceptions he uses to define it against?

2. What, at bottom, would you say the biggest difference is between Havel's and Cornish's perspectives?

3. Do Cornish's characterizations of Havel's arguments appear accurate to you? Why or why not?

## Writing, Strategies and Techniques

1. Compare and contrast Havel's and Cornish's ways of writing. Making allowances for the fact that one is a speech and one a text written in response to that speech, characterize both, giving examples.

2. In what ways might Havel have anticipated in his speech the criticisms made by Edward Cornish? What criticisms has he anticipated?

## Suggestions for Writing

1. Write a counterrefutation of Cornish, by Václav Havel.

2. Write an essay in which you discuss the conception of transcendence, and its advisability in something smaller than global affairs— say, in the educational process.

# Facing Up to Global Repentance

## Rosemary Ruether

*Most opinions about the future of our world have centered around questions of food, energy, politics, and other practical matters. But as Rosemary Ruether points out, without a transcendent faith, we cannot hope to make changes important enough to save our world. In Chapter 10, Al Gore, in his essay, "Ecology: the New Sacred Agenda" will put it into more secular terms; here, in an essay taken from* Christianity and Crisis, *Ruether looks on a troubled future from a distinctly Christian perspective.*

*Ruether is the author of over two dozen books, including* A Democratic Catholic Church *(1992) and* New Woman, New Earth: Sexist Ideologies and Human Liberation *(1975).*

The World Watch Institute reports that humanity has 40 years in which to make major changes if we are not to face extreme global disasters in the second quarter of the 21st century (*State of the World,* 1990). That statement is not extremist, but truthful, and the details add up to a daunting picture of the future. I am convinced that it will take a powerful faith—faith in God rather than only in ourselves and our own powers—to face this future, and to struggle for a more just and peaceful world.

Here is a sketch of the truths we must acknowledge.

- **We are facing the end of the petroleum age.** At present rates of consumption, without allowing for any expansion of use, accessible sources of petroleum will run out about 2030. If instead of moving toward conservation and alternative energy, the U.S. continues to make petroleum the centerpiece of our energy supply, the Gulf War will have been only the beginning of expensive high-tech wars fought to control oil, wars that will have a heavy cost for the whole world, and finally for ourselves.

- **The earth's ability to produce food is declining.** The doubling of the world's grain harvest as a result of petroleum-based fertilizers, pesticides, and mechanization during the Green Revolution hit its limits in the 1980s, and its adverse effects began to take their toll. In many areas food-producing capacity is declining due to drought and desertification, acid rain, and soil salination.

  Meanwhile, some 24 billion tons of topsoil are being lost each year from the world's croplands, and the U.S. continues to push agricultural methods that exaggerate these trends. The emphasis on the Western meat diet also means that a large percentage of the world's grain harvest is used to feed animals, rather than human beings.

- **The 1980s saw a shift from greater equalization of resources between rich and poor people to greater gaps.** Around the world, 90 to 99 percent of the wealth is concentrated in the hands of the top 10 percent of the population, particularly the top 1 percent, while a larger percentage of the population falls into dire poverty. The middle classes struggle to keep even.

  At the same time, the lion's share of each country's wealth, particularly in the last decade, has been used on armaments. In 1972, $197 billion was spent on armaments worldwide. In 1987 this figure had expanded five-fold to over $1000 billion (one trillion), some 5.5 percent of the aggregate global economic product.

- **The world's population is rapidly exploding.** In 1930 world population was two billion people. By 1975 it had doubled to four billion. By the year 2000 it may well reach six billion. Yet during the 1980s, the U.S., under pressure from conservative religious and social groups, cut funding for research and promotion of family planning worldwide. The issue here is a stark choice between voluntary population control, preferably before conception, and millions of infants and children dying in the first years of life. At present some 15 million children under the age of one die each year due to famine and disease.

## Imagine Life Anew

Can we face this almost apocalyptic scenario, or will we run away from it, seeking either to deny its possibility or else (if we can) wall ourselves into dwindling enclaves of privilege, while the rest of the world goes under?

The people of my generation, those born in the 1930s, stand responsible before the generation born in the 1970s, who must carry the burden of the world we have made. Whether we see ourselves as culpable or simply as actors in a drama we did not foresee or control, reality remains the same. We need ways of expressing our sorrow and working through our grief. We also need to be able to find the grace to stand up together and begin to imagine healing and new possibilities.

This is very much a matter of faith, of spirituality and soul-healing. New technologies and organizational strategies are crucial, but without a new vision, our technologies and organizations will only recycle toxicity, rather than generate renewed life.

Let us begin to imagine life—not as hoarding power by rendering our competitors powerless, not as feasting by starving children, not as going faster and faster in a system that is eating up its own foundations. No, let us cleave to a vision of life that is reciprocal and compassionate in the fullest sense: feeling the joys and wounds of others as one's own.

What does this mean? It means pulling our bomber pilots out of the sky and forcing them and us to stand before the people of Baghdad as they pick up the pieces of their lives. It means feeling the bombs that ripped through their flesh as tearing into our spirit as well. Loving your neighbor as yourself means acknowledging that we are all children of one earth, created by the same God, sustained by the same sun and earth under the same sky. Finally we cannot live through making others die. We cannot prosper by impoverishing others. This may appear to work for awhile, but in the end it is an illusion.

We need a profound global *metanoia,* a repentance that makes our interconnectedness a felt knowledge of our hearts and minds. I suspect that this must start by reaching out across those divides that we have raised the highest. Only a year ago that meant Americans and Russians reaching across the divide created by the Cold War.

Today, it also means reaching out to the Arab and Islamic worlds, which have been retooled as the new Satans. And to the poor of every land, the real casualties of every war. And finally, in our race to annihilate enemies, we meet ourselves coming around the corner, weapons in hand, and we recognize in our own face both aggressor and victim.

## Earth-healing

How do we begin to withdraw our projections of light and darkness, God and Satan, and recognize the mixture of both in each of us? How do we begin to think the earth-healing "we," of Americans and Russians, Anglos and Arabs, Israelis and Palestinians, white and black, East and West, North and South? How can we begin to understand a God who did not choose us against them, but created one universe in which all our manynesses converge and interconnect in one covenant of grace and hope?

With the world of life we can begin to reshape our ways of driving engines to produce, transport, cook, and heat, by drawing on renewable sources of energy. We can begin to relearn the ancient wisdoms of renewing the earth, even as we draw from it our daily bread. We can begin to imagine communities of livable proportions, and more just interdependencies.

The technological and organizational tools for such transformations can stimulate and delight the best creative abilities of this generation and the generations to come. Challenges aplenty exist for the next 40 years. What is wanting is not the skills, but the heart; a heart rooted in compassion, justice, and mercy, rather than envy and enmity. In the words of the ancient biblical author, "I set before you two ways, life and death. Choose life."

# Themes, Issues, and Ideas

1. What does Ruether say is most important to saving the world?

2. According to Ruether, our plans for the future too often involve either stark denial or a crafty plan that walls us in. Based on today's newspaper, do you believe this is true?

3. A question Ruether might be asked is "Why bring God into it?" How do you think she might answer? How has she anticipated this question?

# Writing Strategies and Techniques

1. Ruether's essay falls into two parts, a factual one and a homiletic one. Why do you think this is so? Why are the two parts in their particular order?

2. Who does Ruether mean by "our?" What is the effect on her essay of such broad terms as "our," "spirit," "global," and "faith?" As a reader, how do you respond to such terms?

# Suggestions for Writing

1. Write an essay criticizing such a plan for the future as the one Ruether proposes.

2. Write a critique of the moral approach to practical matters.

# Our Lost Heritage: New Facts on How God Became a Man

## Riane Eisler

*Throughout the twentieth century, modern feminist scholarship has continued to question basic tenets of our civilization. As the twenty-first century approaches, one of the most fundamental of all beliefs has come under the spotlight: the identity of the creator of the universe. Although all serious Christian, Jewish, and Islamic doctrines consider God to transcend human limitations such as gender, representations of God have traditionally been male. In "Our Lost Heritage: New Facts on How God Became a Man," Riane Eisler looks at the history of this idea, and the extent to which it has affected society.*

*Riane Eisler (b. 1931) is a leading feminist writer and codirector of the Center for Partnership Studies. She is also the author of such books as* Dissolutions: No Fault Divorce, Marriage, and the Future of Women, *and* The Chalice and the Blade: Our History, Our Future.

In the nineteenth century, archeological excavations began to confirm what scholars of myth had long maintained—that goddess worship preceded the worship of God. After reluctantly accepting what no longer could be ignored, religious historians proposed a number of explanations for why there had been this strange switch in divine gender. A long-standing favorite has been the so-called Big Discovery theory. This is the idea that, when men finally became aware that women did not bring forth children by themselves—in other words, when they discovered that it involved their sperm, their paternity—this inflamed them with such a new-found sense of importance that they not only enslaved women but also toppled the goddess.

Today, new archeological findings—particularly post–World War II excavations—are providing far more believable answers to this long-debated puzzle. For largely due to more scientific archeological methods, including infinitely more accurate archeological dating methods such as radiocarbon and dendrochronology,[1] there has been a veritable archeological revolution.

As James Mellaart of the London University Institute of Archeology writes, we now know that there were in fact many cradles of civilization, all of them thousands of years older than Sumer, where civilization was long said to have begun about five thousand years ago.[2] But the most fascinating discovery about these original cultural sites is that they were structured along very different lines from what we have been taught is the divinely, or naturally, ordained human order.

One of these ancient cradles of civilization is Catal Huyuk, the largest Neolithic site yet found. Located in the Anatolian plain of what is now Turkey, Catal Huyuk goes back approximately eight thousand years to about 6500 B.C.E.—three thousand years before Sumer. As Mellaart reports, this ancient civilization "is remarkable for its wall-paintings and plaster reliefs, its sculpture in stone and clay..., its advanced technology in the crafts of weaving, woodwork, metallurgy..., its advanced religion..., its advanced practices in agriculture and stockbreeding, and... a flourishing trade...."[3]

But undoubtedly the most remarkable thing about Catal Huyuk and other original sites for civilization is that they were *not* warlike, hierarchic, and male-dominated societies like ours. As Mellaart writes, over the many centuries of its existence, there were in Catal Huyuk no signs of violence or deliberate destruction, "no evidence for any sack or massacre." Moreover, while there was evidence of some social inequality, "this is never a glaring one." And most significantly—in the sharpest possible contrast to our type of social organization—"the position of

---

[1]Radiocarbon dating is a method of establishing the age of prehistoric artifacts by measuring the radioactivity of carbon; dendrochronology is a dating procedure based on counting the growth rings of trees.

[2]J. Mellaart, *The Neolithic of the Near East* (New York: Charles Scribner's Sons, 1975). [Au.]

[3]J. Mellaart, *Catal Huyuk* (New York: McGraw-Hill, 1967), p. 11. [Au.]

women was obviously an important one . . . with a fertility cult in which a goddess was the principal deity."[4]

Now it is hardly possible to believe that in this kind of society, where, besides all their other advances, people clearly understood the principles of stockbreeding, they would not have also had to understand that procreation involves the male. So the Big Discovery theory is not only founded on the fallacious assumption that men are naturally brutes, who were only deterred from forcefully enslaving women by fear of the female's "magical" powers of procreation; the Big Discovery theory is also founded on assumptions about what happened in prehistory that are no longer tenable in light of the *really* big discoveries we are now making about our lost human heritage—about societies that, while not ideal, were clearly more harmonious than ours.

But if the replacement of a Divine Mother with a Divine Father was not due to men's discovery of paternity, how did it come to pass that all our present world religions either have no female deity or generally present them as "consorts" or subservient wives of male gods?

To try to answer that question, let us look more carefully at the new archeological findings.

Logic would lead one to expect what ancient myths have long indicated and archeology has since confirmed: that since life issues from woman, not man, the first anthropomorphic deity was female rather than male. But logical or not, this position was hardly that of the first excavators of Paleolithic caves, some of whom were monks, such as the well-known Abbé Henri Breuil. They consistently refused to see in the many finds of twenty-five-thousand-year-old stylized female sculptures what they clearly were: representations of a female divinity, a Great Mother. Instead, the large-breasted, wide-hipped, bountiful, and often obviously pregnant women these men christened "Venus figurines" were described either as sex objects (products of men's erotic fantasies) or deformed, ugly women.[5] Moreover, in order to conform to their model of history as the story of "man the hunter" and "man the warrior," they refused to see what was actually in the famous cave

---

[4]Ibid., pp. 69, 225, 553. [Au.]

[5]See, for example, E. O. James, *The Cult of the Mother Goddess* (London: Thames and Hudson, 1959), and M. Gimbutas, "The Image of Woman in Prehistoric Art," *Quarterly Review of Archeology,* December 1981. [Au.]

paintings. As Alexander Marshack has now established, not only did they insist that stylized painting of tree branches and plants were weapons, they sometimes described these pictures as backward arrows or harpoons, chronically missing their mark![6] They also, as Andre Leroi-Gourhan noted in his major study of the Paleolithic, insisted on interpreting the already quite advanced art of the period as an expression of hunting magic, a view borrowed from extremely primitive contemporary societies like the Australian aborigines.[7]

Although Leroi-Gourhan's interpretation of the objects and paintings found in Paleolithic caves is in sexually stereotyped terms, he stresses that the art of the Paleolithic was first and foremost religious art, concerned with the mysteries of life, death, and regeneration.[8] And it is again this concern that is expressed in the rich art of the Neolithic, which, as Mellaart points out, not only shows a remarkable continuity with the Paleolithic,[9] but clearly foreshadows the great goddess of later Bronze Age civilizations in her various forms of Isis, Nut, and Maat in Egypt, Ishtar, Lillith, or Astarte in the Middle East, the sun-goddess Arinna of Anatolia, as well as such later goddesses as Demeter, Artemis, and Kore in Greece, Atargatis, Ceres, and Cybele in Rome, and even Sophia or Wisdom of the Christian Middle Ages, the Shekinah of Hebrew Kabalistic tradition, and, of course, the Virgin Mary or Holy Mother of the Catholic Church about whom we read in the Bible.[10]

This same prehistoric and historic continuity is stressed by UCLA archeologist Marija Gimbutas, whose monumental work, *The Goddesses and Gods of Old Europe,* brings to life yet another Neolithic civilization: the indigenous civilization that sprang up in the Balkans and Greece long, long before the rise of Indo-European Greece.[11] Once again, the archeological findings in what Gimbutas termed the civilizations of Old Europe not only demolish the old "truism" of the "warlike

[6]A. Marshack, *The Roots of Civilization* (New York: McGraw-Hill, 1972). [Au.]

[7]A. Leroi-Gourhan, *Prehistoire de l'Art Occidental* (Paris: Edition D'Art Lucien Mazenod, 1971). [Au.]

[8]Ibid. [Au.]

[9]J. Mellaart, *Catal Huyuk,* p. 11. [Au.]

[10]See, for example, R. Eisler, *The Chalice and the Blade: Our History, Our Future* (New York: Harper and Row, 1987); M. Stone, *When God Was a Woman* (New York: Harvest, 1976); E. Neumann, *The Great Mother* (Princeton, NJ: Princeton University Press, 1955). [Au.]

[11]M. Gimbutas, *The Goddesses and Gods of Old Europe* (Berkeley, CA: University of California Press, 1982). [Au.]

Neolithic" but also illuminate our true past, again showing that here, too, the original direction of human civilization was in some ways far more civilized than ours, with pre-Indo-Europeans living in far greater harmony with one another and the natural environment.

Moreover, excavations in Old Europe, like those unearthed in other parts of the ancient world, show that what brought about the onset of male dominance both in heaven and on earth was not some sudden male discovery. What ushered it in was the onslaught of barbarian hordes from the arid steppes and deserts on the fringe areas of our globe. It was wave after wave of these pastoral invaders who destroyed the civilizations of the first settled agrarian societies. And it was they who brought with them the gods—and men—of war that made so much of later or recorded history the bloodbath we are now taught was the *totality* of human history.

In Old Europe, as Gimbutas painstakingly documents, there were three major invasionary waves, as the Indo-European peoples she calls the Kurgans wiped out or "Kurganized" the European populations. "The Old European and Kurgan cultures were the antithesis of one another," writes Gimbutas. She continues:

> The Old Europeans were sedentary horticulturalists prone to live in large well-planned townships. The absence of fortifications and weapons attests the peaceful coexistence of this egalitarian civilization that was probably matrilinear and matrilocal. ... The Old European belief system focused on the agricultural cycle of birth, death, and regeneration, embodied in the feminine principle, a Mother Creatrix. The Kurgan ideology, as known from comparative Indo-European mythology, exalted virile, heroic warrior gods of the shining and thunderous sky. Weapons are nonexistent in Old European imagery; whereas the dagger and battle-axe are dominant symbols of the Kurgans, who, like all historically known Indo-Europeans, glorified the lethal power of the sharp blade.[12]

So while we are still commonly taught that it was to Indo-European invaders—such as the Aechaean warriors, celebrated by Homer, who eventually sacked Troy—that we owe our Western heritage, we

[12]M. Gimbutas, "The First Wave of Eurasian Steppe Pastoralists in Copper Age Europe," *Journal of Indo-European Studies,* 1977, p. 281. [Au.]

now know that they in fact did not bring us civilization. Rather, they destroyed, degraded, and brutalized a civilization already highly advanced along wholly different lines. And, just as the factuality of how these truly savage peoples demoted both women and goddesses to the subservient status of consort or wife has now been established, the fact [that] they brought in warfare with them is also confirmed.

Once again, as when Heinrich Schliemann defied the archeological establishment and proved that the city of Troy was not Homeric fantasy but prehistoric fact, new archeological findings verify ancient legends and myths. For instance, the Greek poet Hesiod, who wrote about the same time as Homer, tells us of a "golden race," who lived in "peaceful ease" in a time when "the fruitful earth poured forth her fruits." And he laments how they were eventually replaced by "a race of bronze" who "ate not grain" (in other words, were not farmers) and instead specialized in warfare ("the all-lamented sinful works of Ares were their chief care").[13]

Perhaps one of the most fascinating legends of ancient times is, of course, that of the lost civilization of Atlantis. And here again, as with the once only legendary city of Troy, archeological findings illuminate our true past. For what new findings suggest is what the eminent Greek scholar Spyridon Martinatos already suspected in 1939: that the legend of a great civilization which sank into the Atlantic is actually the garbled folk memory of the Minoan civilization of Crete and surrounding Mediterranean islands, portions of which did indeed disappear into the sea after unprecedented volcanic eruptions sometime after 1500 B.C.E.[14]

First discovered at the turn of this century, the once unknown Bronze Age civilization of ancient Crete has now been far more extensively excavated. As Nicolas Platon, former superintendent of antiquities in Crete and director of the Acropolis Museum, who excavated the island for over thirty years, writes, Minoan civilization was "an astonishing achievement." It reflected "a highly sophisticated art and way of life," indeed producing some of the most beautiful art the world has ever seen. Also in this remarkable society—the only place where the worship of the goddess and the influence of women in the public sphere

---

[13]Hesiod, quoted in J. M. Robinson, *An Introduction to Early Greek Philosophy* (Boston: Houghton Mifflin, 1968), pp. 12–14. [Au.]

[14]S. Martinatos, "The Volcanic Destruction of Minoan Crete," *Antiquity,* 1939, 13:425–439. [Au.]

survived into historic times, where "the whole of life was pervaded by an ardent faith in the goddess Nature, the source of all creation and harmony"—there was still "a love of peace, a horror of tyranny, and a respect for the law."[15]

And once again, it was not men's discovery of their biological role in paternity that led to the toppling of the goddess. It was another, final Indo-European invasion: the onslaught of the Dorians, who, with their weapons of iron, as Hesiod writes, brought death and destruction in their wake.[16]

So the revolution in norms that literally stood reality on its head— that established this seemingly fundamental and sacrosanct idea that we are the creations of a Divine Father, who all by Himself brought forth all forms of life—was in fact a relatively late event in the history of human culture. Moreover, this drastic change in direction of cultural evolution, which set us on the social course that in our nuclear age threatens to destroy all life, was certainly not predetermined or, by any stretch of the imagination, inevitable. Rather than being some mystical mystery, it was the substitution of a force-based model of social organization for one in which both the female and male halves of humanity viewed the supreme power in the universe not as the "masculine" power to destroy but rather as the "feminine" power to give and nurture life.

Another popular old idea about this change was that it was the replacement of matriarchy with patriarchy. But my research of many years shows that matriarchy is simply the flip side of the coin to the *dominator* model of society, based upon the dominance of men over women that we call patriarchy. The real alternative to patriarchy, already foreshadowed by the original direction of human civilization, is what I have called the *partnership* model of social relations.[17] Based upon the full and equal partnership between the female and male halves of our species, this model was already well-established a long time ago,

[15]N. Platon, *Crete* (Geneva: Nagel, 1966), pp. 48, 148. [Au.]

[16]Hesiod, see note 13. [Au.]

[17]See, for example, R. Eisler, *The Chalice and the Blade;* R. Eisler "Violence and Male-Dominance: The Ticking Time Bomb," *Humanities in Society,* Winter–Spring 1984, 7:1/2:3–18; R. Eisler and D. Loye, "The 'Failure' of Liberalism: A Reassessment of Ideology from a New Feminine-Masculine Perspective," *Political Psychology,* 1983, 4:2:375–391; R. Eisler, "Beyond Feminism: The Gylan Future," *Alternative Futures,* Spring–Summer 1981, 4:2/3:122–134. [Au.]

before, as the Bible has it, a male god decreed that woman be subservient to man.

The new knowledge about our true human heritage is still meeting enormous resistance, with traditional "experts" from both the religious and academic establishments crying heresy. But it is a knowledge that, in the long run, cannot be suppressed.

It is a knowledge that demolishes many old misconceptions about our past. It also raises many fascinating new questions. Is the real meaning of the legend of our fall from paradise that, rather than having transgressed in some horrible way, Eve should have obeyed the advice of the serpent (long associated with the oracular or prophetic powers of the goddess) and *continued* to eat from the tree of knowledge? Did the custom of sacrificing the first-born child develop after the destruction of this earlier world—as the Bible has it, after our expulsion from the Garden of Eden—when women had been turned into mere male-controlled technologies of reproduction, as insurance of a sort that conception had not occurred before the bride was handed over to her husband?

We may never have complete answers to such questions, since archeology only provides some of the data and ancient writings, such as the Old Testament, were rewritten so many times, each time to more firmly establish, and sanctify, male control.[18] But what we do have is far more critical in this time when the old patriarchal system is leading us ever closer to global holocaust. This is the knowledge that it was not always this way: there are viable alternatives that may not only offer us survival but also a far, far better world.

# Themes, Issues, and Ideas

1.  Would you describe Eisler's theory as feminist? Why or why not? How do ideas about gender work here?

2.  What are the religious implications of Eisler's theory?

3.  Eisler describes the earliest Mother Creatrix–worshipping societies as being peaceful and agrarian, but soon corrupted and overthrown by warrior tribes. What evidence does she offer for this view? What evidence does she offer for her views about prehistoric religion?

---

[18]Ibid. [Au.]

# Writing Strategies and Techniques

1. What does Eisler's approach to writing seem to be? Which writer in this book does she most remind you of? Why?

2. Where in her essay does Eisler suddenly shift styles, and why? Is it an effective transition?

# Suggestions for Writing

1. Using a variety of academic sources, write a description of one of the prehistoric societies Eisler discusses.

2. Write an essay outlining how a return to female-creation myths could enrich the world.

# The Never-ending Fight

## Isaac Asimov

*Isaac Asimov, scientist and science fiction writer, was one of the most prolific writers in the history of the printed word, the author of over 300 books. In an essay originally published in* The Humanist *magazine, Asimov's view of the future state of the human spirit is frankly at odds with some of the attitudes found in the previous essays in this chapter. Asimov claims to speak for reason and the scientific pursuit of truth, which he sees not only as the proudest achievement of the modern age but also as, in the words of his title,* The Never-ending Fight. *Asimov, however, does not underrate what he sees as the powers of unreason. He modestly concludes: "If we're still here a century from now, we'll know we're winning."*

*Isaac Asimov was born in Russia in 1920. His family came to New York when he was young and he was educated at Columbia University, taking B.A., M.A., and Ph.D. degrees in chemistry. When this essay was published, Asimov was president of the American Humanist Association. He died in 1992, at the age of 72.*

I was interviewed on television recently and, in answering the questions, I found myself expressing my contempt for the various superstitious beliefs that plague humanity.

The interviewer asked, "But since, by your own admission, most people believe this sort of thing and find solace or comfort in it, why do you want to deprive them of it?"

I answered as best I could in the brief time available to me before the camera. But I can do it better now with more space at my disposal. This, in essence, is what I said.

There are two reasons. In the first place, I have the call to do so, the call to point out the uselessness of superstition. Everyone is perfectly ready to believe theists when they say they have the call to preach their version of the word of God and to accord them a kind of humble respect for having such a noble mission. Why, then, should I be scorned because I have the call to preach my version of the word of reason?

I have my own notion of what it means to be rational and to look at the universe clearly. Unlike theists, I threaten no one with hellfire if they refuse to agree with every word I say; nor do I attempt to bribe them with tales of eternal bliss if only they accept my every syllable. Rather, I preach a universe in which there is neither threat nor bribe but merely something one strives to understand merely for the sake of understanding.

Unlike theists, I do not claim to have a pipeline to something supernatural. I do not claim to have absolute truth and an eternal answer to every problem past, present, or future. Rather, I offer the fallible human mind doing the best it can to improve its view somewhat from generation to generation.

And what I ask is merely that I be given a chance to express this rather modest and humble attitude without let or hindrance.

Secondly, it is no defense of superstition and pseudoscience to say that it brings solace and comfort to people and that therefore we "elitists" should not claim to know better and to take it away from the less sophisticated.

If solace and comfort are how we judge the worth of something, then consider that tobacco brings solace and comfort to smokers; alcohol brings it to drinkers; drugs of all kinds bring it to addicts; the fall of cards and the run of horses bring it to gamblers; cruelty and violence bring it to sociopaths. Judge by solace and comfort only and there is no behavior we ought to interfere with.

To be sure, it is easy to see that all these things bring harm to their practitioners, but can it not be argued that if some people get pleasure out of a practice that does harm to them it is nevertheless their body, their choice, their health, and their life to do with as they wish? Who are we to be the "big brother" who attempts to dictate our notion of a superior way of life to others against their will?

There is indeed something to this if it is *only* the practitioner's body and health and life that is involved and no one else's. But what of the smoker whose effluvium damages the lungs of nonsmokers forced to breathe his or her reek? What of the drinker who drives and kills? What of the addict who lures others into addiction? What of the sociopath who directly harms others as his or her path to joy?

By and large, then, society demands that these harmful physical practices be controlled insofar as it can be done humanely.

But, in that case, why should we not be at least as deeply concerned with the pernicious effects of superstition? Those who believe in magical methods of preventing or curing disease often do not turn to rational methods till it is too late. Those who believe that disasters are the work of inscrutable supernatural forces do not search for rational ways of preventing them or ameliorating their effects. Those who believe that humanity is under the beneficent control of supernatural forces that will see us through all our problems if we only "have faith" do not seek natural solutions to those problems.

We live in times when overpopulation, pollution, the greenhouse effect, the thinning of the ozone layer, the deterioration of the environment, the destruction of the forests and of wildlife, and the dangers of multiplying nuclear armaments all threaten us with the destruction of civilization and the radical reduction in the very viability of Earth. If our only answer to all this is a superstitious reliance on something outside ourselves as a solution to all those problems, we are making that destruction certain.

Yes, we will have our solace and comfort till the moment of the destruction, and we might console ourselves with the thoughts that we will all meet in a better world than this one and that indeed the Bible predicts the destruction of this world. But how many really believe that, even among those who say they do?

I notice little in the way of great joy at the death of friends and loved ones, little triumph in their having passed on to heavenly glory sooner than they might otherwise have done so. When an earthquake kills two thousand people at a blow, we do not rejoice that the innocent among them are now in heaven, but we raise powerful hosannahs if even *one* child is rescued alive from the ruins and is condemned to wait another sixty years, perhaps, before experiencing bliss.

I notice that all the people who are absolutely convinced that the United States is under the special protection of a powerful deity ("In God We Trust" it says on all our coins) are not at all certain that that deity is capable of protecting us unaided and insist that we have armed forces that are second to none. I myself feel safer if our defenses are strong, but I do not expect any supernatural force to help out. Why do the Falwells and the other television preachers feel the need?

And, as a matter of fact, average people living average lives, however much they may "believe" in God and in whatever religion they have been brought up to believe, act as though the world is in the grip of evil forces that must be held off in silly ways.

How many countless millions of people, even in "sophisticated" Western societies, place their faith not in God but in rabbits' feet, in horseshoes, in four-leaf clovers, in Saint Christopher medals, or in lucky pieces of an infinite number of shapes and forms? How many are terrified of black cats crossing their path, of ladders being walked under, of mirrors being broken, of aces of spades being turned up?

How many countless millions who explain that they are sure that God holds the key to the future and loves us all nevertheless feel much better consulting fortune-tellers, tea-leaf readers, crystal-ball gazers, and (especially if in high political office) astrologers, who apparently know the future just as well as God does and can give advice on what to do and not do that God (out of selfishness?) withholds?

Let us consider a small example of how the universe looks to the superstitious. August 8, 1988, is written "8/8/88" in brief form. The concatenation of eights looks somehow significant. It is based, of course, on the numbering of the days, months, and years according to a strictly human-arranged system that has no cosmic significance whatsoever. Nevertheless, uncounted people played the number 888 in lotteries on that day in the belief that the random fall of whatever system is used to choose the number is influenced by this strictly human convention. They lost, of course, for I'm told 888 turned up not on 8/8/88 but on the *next* day. Consequently, nothing was said. However, there was a one-in-one-thousand chance that 888 would indeed have appeared on 8/8/88, and, if it had, how many millions would have hailed it as "proof" of the truth of numerology?

Let us consider a large example of how the universe looks to the superstitious. Every once in a while, some region suffers a drought. In the summer of 1988, the United States suffered the worst drought in over fifty years. Presumably God has a divine plan for humanity, which seems inscrutable to us because our knowledge is finite and his is infinite and even a bad drought is for our long-term good. There may even be people who believe this and say this and are thankful there is a drought that may ruin them, because they know that it is all part of a marvelous plan for their long-term good. I suspect they are in the minority, though, for the more usual practice is to pray for rain—that is, to beg God over and over to abandon his plan, whatever it was, and do something for the short-term advantage of those praying. And if the rains do come, that proves the efficacy of prayer—and no one says that it rather proves the irresolution of God and his readiness to abandon his plan. And you know, if he was so ready to abandon his plan, he might just as well not have sent the drought in the first place. (You might argue that God's plan was to keep the drought going till humanity turned humbly to him and begged and begged and begged, so that he could demonstrate his power, but I've always thought that to be a rather petty interpretation of the ways of a supposedly infinitely beneficent deity.)

And, of course, there are many superstitions that have nothing to do with the dominant religion of the Western world. All sorts of peculiar beliefs arise about the Bermuda Triangle, about pyramid power, about flying saucers, about transmigration of souls, and all of them instantly attract the enthusiastic beliefs of millions.

The magazine *Science News* once questioned a number of scientific authorities on the Velikovskian theory of astronomical hopscotch that defies all the most elementary notions of celestial mechanics. All the authorities questioned gave reasoned refutations of this or that. I did not. I simply said, "There is no idea, however ridiculous on the very face of it, that some people won't instantly hug to their breasts and be ready to die for." Some issues later, the Velikovskians had their chance to reply, and every last one of them attacked my statement and left all the others alone. I had, quite obviously, struck a nerve.

Well, then, what do I expect of the next century? Assuming that we avoid destruction from the dogged adherence of humanity to superstition and its rejection of rationality, will we at least make a little progress in our cause?

I'm sorry. I don't think so. In addressing the humanists of 2089 (and I am sure there will be humanists in the world of 2089, if there should indeed be a world of 2089), I would have to say this.

Despite all the further advance of technology, despite the fact that we have computerized the world, despite the fact that robots are doing the menial work of humanity and that human beings are freed to work creatively at human tasks, despite the fact that we have expanded to the moon and beyond and are rapidly penetrating the solar system generally, and despite the fact that we understand the universe far better than we used to a century ago, the vast majority of human beings still take solace and comfort in their various superstitions and still follow any pied piper who fills their ears with notes of nonsense while filling his or her own pockets with money. And we are still in the minority and still struggling to convince people that, if, indeed, there were a god, he would in the end reject anyone who failed to make use of that one truly godlike gift.

But if that is so, and if we are engaged in a never-ending fight with no victory in sight, why continue?

Because we must. Because we have the call. Because it is nobler to fight for rationality without winning than to give up in the face of continued defeats. Because whatever true progress humanity makes is through the rationality of the occasional individual and because any one individual we may win for the cause may do more for humanity than a hundred thousand who hug their superstitions to their breast.

# Themes, Issues, and Ideas

1.  How does Asimov handle the objection that he and people like him are "elitists"? As a college student, have your views ever been objected to on this basis? How did you, or would you, respond? In what ways is Asimov's whole essay a kind of response?

2.  Asimov raises a question at the end of his essay: "If we are engaged in a never-ending fight with no victory in sight, why continue?" How does he answer his own question? What do you think of the answer? Does the beginning of his essay convince you that he believes in his conclusion? Why, or why not?

3.  Imagine a debate between a believer in the New Age and Isaac Asimov on the subject of the healing power of crystals. On what general matters might they agree—the need for evidence, for example? In what ways might they disagree on the same issues? For example, would they give the same weight to personal testimony?

# Writing Strategies and Techniques

1.  In what ways do the metaphors of "threat" and "bribe," as applied to his opponents, serve Asimov's argument at the beginning of his essay? What metaphors does he use to define his own manner of argumentation? How do they serve his purpose?

2. Asimov says, "I notice little in the way of great joy at the death of friends and loved ones, little triumph in their having passed on to heavenly glory sooner than they might otherwise have done so." How does Asimov's irony work? What point does it make for his argument? Rewrite the point in a way that does not use irony, but retains roughly the same meaning. What, if anything, has been lost by the change in tone?

# Suggestions for Writing

1. In his last paragraph, Asimov expresses his ultimate reasons for the position he takes using terms that include "call" and "nobler." Surely these terms are not among those employed in scientific proof. Citing and analyzing particular examples, write an essay in which you describe the nonscientific aspects of Asimov's argument in favor of science.

2. Suppose someone told Isaac Asimov, "You blame preachers for threatening their hearers with hellfire and bribing them with promises of heaven, but you implicitly threaten your audience with universal annihilation through the nuclear power invented by science and bribe the audience with thoughts of further scientifically produced material comforts, in order to make your audience worship your ideas of 'rationality.'" Write an essay in which you either come to Asimov's defense, or continue the attack. Be sure to use specific examples and reasoned arguments.

# The Code of the Universe

## James A. Haught

*The essays in this chapter have ranged in subject from religion to science, and almost all of the writers included have used religion and science as a pair of words with opposed meanings. Yet investigative reporter James Haught—winner of thirteen national awards for articles and editorials—finds that science offers him a religious sense of mystery, awe, and a key to understanding. Haught breaks down the usual dichotomy of the physical and the spiritual and suggests that phenomena like electrons and quarks, galaxies and black holes, electromagnetic radiation, DNA and cells, gravity, molecular bonds, the speed of light, and the power in the nucleus all contain a gospel more profound than any written by humans.*

*Haught was born in West Virginia in 1932, where he has spent almost his entire life. He has long worked for the* Charleston Gazette *in Charleston, West Virginia. This essay was originally published in* The Humanist *magazine.*

Did you know that Albert Einstein, although Jewish, went through a brief childhood phase of devout Christianity? In an autobiographical sketch written at age sixty-seven, he described his short-lived faith, planted in him by daily indoctrination at a Catholic school to which his parents had sent him:

> Thus I came—despite the fact that I was the son of entirely irreligious (Jewish) parents—to a deep religiosity, which, however, found

an abrupt ending at the age of twelve. Through the reading of popular scientific books I soon reached the conviction that much in the stories of the Bible could not be true. The consequence was a positively fanatic freethinking coupled with the impression that youth is intentionally being deceived by the state through lies; it was a crushing impression.

Suspicion against every kind of authority grew out of this experience, a skeptical attitude toward the convictions which were alive in any specific social environment—an attitude which has never left me, even though later on, because of a better insight into the causal concessions, it lost some of its original poignancy.

It is quite clear to me that the religious paradise of youth, which was thus lost, was a first attempt to free myself from the chains of the "merely personal," from an existence which is dominated by wishes, hopes, and primitive feelings. Out yonder there was this huge world, which exists independently of us human beings and which stands before us like a great, eternal riddle, at least partially accessible to our inspection and thinking. The contemplation of this world beckoned like a liberation. . . .

The road to this paradise was not as comfortable and alluring as the road to the religious paradise, but it has proved itself as trustworthy, and I have never regretted having chosen it.

Commenting on Einstein's reminiscence, physicist Heinz Pagels wrote:

What this passage reveals is a conversion from personal religion to the "cosmic religion" of science, an experience which changed him for the rest of his life. Einstein saw that the universe is governed by laws that can be known by us but that are independent of our thoughts and feelings.

The existence of this cosmic code—the laws of material reality as confirmed by experience—is the bedrock faith that moves the natural scientist. The scientist sees in that code the eternal structure of reality, not as imposed by man or tradition but as written into the very substance of the universe. This recognition of the nature of the universe can come as a profound and moving experience to the young mind.

Looking into the soul of the universe isn't just for world-class physicists. It can happen to anyone who ponders the awesome discoveries of science, from quarks to quasars.

When I was a farmboy in Wetzel County, West Virginia, my grandfather taught me the orbits of Earth and the moon, and I thought it was utterly amazing that these colossal balls weighing quintillions of tons were whirling and circling and rolling forever in open space—and that we live on one of them.

When I studied chemistry in high school and learned the combining valences of atoms, I thought it was utterly amazing that this hidden code governs virtually all matter—Earth and the moon, our bodies, trees, water, air. How could atoms lock together into substances because of gaps in their outer layers of electrons—electrons eternally streaking at nearly the speed of light?

*Why* do the mysterious electrical parts of atoms whirl forever, like the planets and stars?

*Why* do electrically neutral atoms seize onto each other, just because their outer electron layers lack the magic number of eight?

*Why* do they turn into remarkably different things as they combine? Hydrogen gas and oxygen gas are nothing like water, yet they constitute it. Some carbon atoms lock in tetrahedrons to become diamonds; others lock in layers of six-sided carbon rings to become graphite pencil lead.

*Why* do atoms link into carbon-based molecules that link into amino acids that link into proteins that link into living cells as complex as whole cities—and why does all this link into a thinking, feeling, loving, fearing, aging, dying human?

How can a combination of amino acids write a symphony or join the Republican party or commit stock fraud or feel patriotism for a section of Earth likewise composed of molecules?

The old "planetary" model of the atom was envisioned like a solar system—orbits around a nucleus. This raised a far-out theory that our solar system might be an atom in some stupefyingly larger universe and that our atoms might be tiny solar systems with people living on some of the particles. I first encountered this idea in a *Captain Marvel* comic book. The great astronomer Harlow Shapley once gave a talk at West Virginia State College. I hung around afterward and asked him, "What's the name of the theory that atoms might be solar systems?" He looked at me and said, "The name of it is damn nonsense." I later learned that it's called the subatomic universe theory—but Shapley's name probably is better.

During this period, when I was muddling over the boggling impossibilities that science revealed, I started reading books on Einstein and relativity and found that *his* scientific truth was even more astonishing. What our common sense tells us is real *can't* be real if space shrinks to nonexistence or time runs slower and stops under some conditions.

I hatched mental experiments that short-circuited my brain. For example, Einstein says the speed of light is the great constant of the universe—nothing can go faster. He also says all speeds are relative between moving objects. Well, if you strike a match, photons of visible light fly out in all directions. If one photon is going west at the speed of light and another is going east at the speed of light, how fast are they separating from each other?

It gets even worse when you read quantum physics. The more I studied, the more I developed an eerie sense that the world we think we inhabit and all existing things are some sort of fiction.

For example, take steel. It can be a one-hundred-foot bridge girder or it can be the coil of a bass piano string, a long wire spiraled into a hard spring. All the curves of that spring are composed of iron atoms locked rigidly to each other in a strong crystal lattice that is nearly unbreakable.

And yet, those atoms are an illusion of emptiness. They are a void of unknowable electrical charges. They are virtually a vacuum. They are as empty as the solar system. If you look at the night sky and see how remote the planets are, that's how remote the parts of an atom are from each other.

If an atom were the size of a fourteen-story building, the nucleus would be a grain of salt in the middle of the seventh floor, too tiny to be seen. Therefore, heavy, rigid steel doesn't exist the way we think it does. It's 99.999999 percent vacuum—as empty as the night sky.

Sometimes I picture atoms as soap bubbles: empty but bumping against each other and sticking together. The buzzing outer electrons are negative, and they repel the negative electron clouds of adjoining atoms; this holds the atoms apart and gives them an illusion of solidity. Yet, they are bound to each other by valence bonds and hydrogen bonds and Van der Waals bonds and other electrical links.

Atom emptiness is the key to white dwarfs, pulsars, and black holes.

At the end of their life cycles, stars explode. Then, what's left of them collapses, and gravity pulls the collapsing material into incredible density. If the residue is small, compressed electrons in the seething stellar plasma of crushed atoms push back fiercely and resist further collapse. This produces a white dwarf that is nearly impossible to comprehend.

The material of a white dwarf weighs around ten tons per thimbleful. How could something the size of a thimble be so heavy that one hundred strong men couldn't lift it? It might crush a house. A large crane would be required to pick it up.

But that's just the first step in removing the empty space inside atoms. A teenage genius, Subrahmanyan Chandrasekhar, computed that, if a collapsing star has 1.4 times the mass of our sun, its gravity would be too great to be stopped by the resistance of the electrons. He didn't know it, but he was predicting pulsars, or neutron stars, which later were discovered. Their enormous gravity squeezes the electrons into the nucleus of each atom, where they merge with protons to form a solid mass of neutrons. This material weighs about 10 million tons per cubic centimeter.

A cubic centimeter is the size of a bouillon cube. Can you imagine a bouillon cube weighing more than the World Trade Center? But that's what matter is when the empty space is removed between the nucleus and the electrons of atoms.

If 10 million tons of actual substance is the size of a bouillon cube, how much real material is in a 180-pound man or a 120-pound woman? Not as much as a dust speck. Not enough to see with a microscope. Our five-foot or six-foot bodies, like all material things, are an illusion made of vacuum and whirling electrical charges.

It gets worse. Even the packed neutrons in a pulsar are not basic material. They, too, are empty and compressible. If the remains of a collapsing star are 3.2 times larger than our sun, the gravity is too strong to be checked at the pulsar level. The collapse continues until it passes the point of no return—the Schwarzchild radius—and becomes a black hole, the ultimate pit of gravity, where everything is compressed to nothing.

If planet Earth were squeezed to its Schwarzchild radius, *it would be the size of a pearl.* Can anyone imagine the matter of the entire Earth being reduced to fingernail size—but retaining all its weight—and continuing to shrink beyond that point?

This isn't Captain Marvel comics. Pulsars are real. So are black holes, the astrophysicists say. If they are actuality, then what is our everyday world?

The nonreality of matter is just one of many enigmas that science reveals. Consider these:

- As we lie in bed, we are flying 67,000 miles an hour around the sun and 600,000 miles an hour around the Milky Way galaxy.

- When we see the North Star, we are looking back in time to the medieval era, because the light we see began traveling 680 years ago.

- Every second, the visible universe expands by a volume as large as the Milky Way.

- Peaceful atoms of rock, lying still for centuries, have a power in their nuclei that is beyond comprehension: Only as much matter as a *dime* was transformed into the energy that destroyed Hiroshima and killed 140,000 people.

- The smallness of atoms likewise is beyond grasping: A cubic inch of air contains 300 *billion billion* molecules, all moving at 1,000 miles an hour and hitting each other 5 billion times a second.

- Although atoms are generally indestructible, their electrons keep coming loose to produce lightning and the other electricity of the world.

- The light we see, the *sun warmth* we feel, the radio and television signals we receive, the X-rays we use—all of these come from electrons. Electromagnetic radiation is emitted by excited electrons oscillating or dropping to lower layers in atoms.

- All life on Earth comes from a tiny electric current: When sunlight hits chlorophyll molecules, excited outer electrons jump through a mosaic of molecules, and this energy drives plant processes.

- As for the DNA that conveys our genetic code, there is six feet of it inside each cell of our bodies. The body has more than 10 trillion cells, so every person contains *several billion miles* of DNA.

These are profoundly important topics, yet, when I try to discuss science with my chums in the news business or music circles or political groups, they look at me as if I'm babbling in the Unknown Tongue. They are highly educated people who know multitudes of facts, but they shrug at what I think are the most crucial facts of all.

If religion and philosophy are an attempt to comprehend the universe and the meaning of life, then science is the best portal. Every time I learn another rule of subatomic forces or cell behavior or galactic motion, I get an eerie sense of glimpsing the mysterious code underlying our existence. Physicists often apply the word *God* to this order, but they don't mean *God* in the church sense.

In a world of supernatural religions, mystical religions, guilt-based religions, violent religions, money-collecting religions, social club religions, and cult religions, grasping the code of the universe is the most religious experience I know.

## Themes, Issues, and Ideas

1.  Why do you think Haught begins his essay with an account of Einstein's early religious experience? Haught later reports his own wonder stimulated by *Captain Marvel* comics. Would that anecdote have made an equally effective beginning? Explain your answer.

2.  Haught apparently takes his title from a passage he quotes by Heinz Pagels on the laws of material reality: "The scientist sees in that code the eternal structure of reality, not as imposed by man or tradition but as written into the very substance of the universe." What do Haught and Pagels find attractive about the concept of a "code"? What does that metaphor imply about the nature of the universe that the metaphor of "natural laws" does not?

3.  Haught reports his own early belief in a theory that our solar system might be an atom in a larger universe, along with a scientist's response to that theory. Why do you think this experience did not disillusion Haught in his general tendency to speculate and wonder? What does the anecdote add to the essay? Would you feel differently were it not included?

## Writing Strategies and Techniques

1.  Is there any "plot" to the many examples of scientific phenomena that Haught includes? What connects the examples he uses and keeps them from being merely a random list?

2.  Haught is a reporter. Do you notice any journalistic techniques employed in his essay? How, if at all, does he modify his style for an educated rather than a general audience? Point to particular examples.

# Suggestions for Writing

1. In the beginning of his essay, Haught quotes Albert Einstein as saying that his early religiosity was an attempt to free himself from "the chains of the 'merely personal.'" How might the personal be seen as an imprisonment of the spirit? Write an essay comparing and contrasting science and religion as ways to transcend the self.

# MAKING CONNECTIONS

1. Write an essay comparing and contrasting G. K. Chesterton and Isaac Asimov. How are their styles different? How are their approaches different? Are both men addressing the same issues?

2. What might Asimov make of Rosemary Ruether's piece? What would Chesterton make of Riane Eisler's? If you were to make debate teams of these authors, who would be on which team, and why?

3. What beliefs bout the modern world does Václav Havel seem to have in common up Isaac Asimov? What does he have in common with James Haught? What could Haught and/or Asimov give to Havel in the latter's search of "transcendence?" What might Havel give to Asimov or Haught?

4. Different styles appear in these essays: humor in Chesterton; profundity in Asimov; scientific solemnity in Eisler. What other styles do you find in these selections? Which styles do you think work best for the topic of mortality? Which writer's style advances the writer's thought best?

5. Where does G. K. Chesterton's view of the world fit in with James Haught's? What does the answer to this question tell you about both writers?

# CHAPTER EIGHT

## *Science, Technology, and Human Life*

### *Some Issues of Modern Medicine*

# THE PAST AS PROLOGUE

# 1933 Medicine

## Lewis Thomas

*When Lewis Thomas (b. 1913) began the medical training described in his essay, medicine consisted largely of diagnosing a disease and predicting its probable course. By the time he finished medical school, however, science had created a technology that allowed medicine to cure diseases—a technology taken for granted today. Thomas himself played a part in some of the astounding triumphs of medicine since then. He has been a medical doctor, a research biologist, and a prolific writer on medicine both for technical and general audiences. Among his many books,* The Lives of a Cell *won the National Book Award in 1975. This essay is a chapter in* The Youngest Science: Notes of a Medicine Watcher *(1983).*

I was admitted to medical school under circumstances that would have been impossible today. There was not a lot of competition; not more than thirty of my four hundred classmates, most of these the sons of doctors, planned on medicine. There was no special curriculum; elementary physics and two courses in chemistry were the only fixed requirements; the term "premedical" had not yet been invented. My academic record at Princeton was middling fair; I had entered college at fifteen, having been a bright enough high-school student, but then I turned into a moult of dullness and laziness, average or below average in the courses requiring real work. It was not until my senior year, when I ventured a course in advanced biology under Professor Swingle, who had just discovered a hormone of the adrenal cortex, that I became a reasonably alert scholar, but by that time my grade averages had me solidly fixed in the dead center, the "gentlemen's third," of the class. Today, I would have been turned down by every place, except perhaps one of the proprietary medical schools in the Caribbean.

I got into Harvard, the hardest, by luck and also, I suspect, by pull. Hans Zinsser, the professor of bacteriology, had interned with my father at Roosevelt and had admired my mother, and when I went to Boston to be interviewed in the winter of 1933, I was instructed by the dean's secretary to go have a talk with Dr. Zinsser. It was the briefest of interviews, but satisfactory from my point of view. Zinsser looked at me carefully, as at a specimen, then informed me that my father and mother were good friends of his, and if I wanted to come to Harvard he would try to help, but because of them, not me; he was entirely good-natured, but clear on this point. It was favoritism, but not all that personal, I was to understand.

My medical education was, in principle, much like that of my father. The details had changed a lot since his time, especially in the fields of medical science relating to disease mechanisms; physiology and biochemistry had become far more complex and also more illuminating; microbiology and immunology had already, by the early 1930s, transformed our understanding of the causation of the major infectious diseases. But the *purpose* of the curriculum was, if anything, even more conservative than thirty years earlier. It was to teach the recognition of disease entities, their classification, their signs, symptoms, and laboratory manifestations, and how to make an accurate diagnosis. The treatment of disease was the most minor part of the curriculum, almost left out altogether. There was, to be sure, a course in pharmacology in the second year, mostly concerned with the mode of action of a handful of everyday drugs: aspirin, morphine, various cathartics, bromides, barbiturates, digitalis, a few others. Vitamin B was coming into fashion as a treatment for delirium tremens, later given up. We were provided with a thin pocket-size book called *Useful Drugs,* one hundred pages or so, and we carried this around in our white coats when we entered the teaching wards and clinics in the third year, but I cannot recall any of our instructors ever referring to this volume. Nor do I remember much talk about treating disease at any time in the four years of medical school except by the surgeons, and most of their discussions dealt with the management of injuries, the drainage or removal of infected organs and tissues, and, to a very limited extent, the excision of cancers.

The medicine we were trained to practice was, essentially, Osler's medicine. Our task for the future was to be diagnosis and explanation. Explanation was the real business of medicine. What the ill patient and his family wanted most was to know the name of the illness, and then, if possible, what had caused it, and finally, most important of all, how it was likely to turn out.

The successes possible in diagnosis and prognosis were regarded as the triumph of medical science, and so they were. It had taken long decades of careful, painstaking observation of many patients; the publication of countless papers describing the detailed aspects of one clinical syndrome after another; more science, in the correlation of the clinical features of disease with the gross and microscopic abnormalities, contributed by several generations of pathologists. By the 1930s we thought we knew as much as could ever be known about the dominant clinical problems of the time: syphilis, tuberculosis, lobar pneumonia, typhoid, rheumatic fever, erysipelas, poliomyelitis. Most of the known varieties of cancer had been meticulously classified, and estimates of the duration of life could be made with some accuracy. The electrocardiogram had arrived, adding to the fair precision already possible in the diagnosis of heart disease. Neurology possessed methods for the localization of disease processes anywhere in the nervous system. When we had learned all that, we were ready for our M.D. degrees, and it was expected that we would find out about the actual day-to-day management of illness during our internship and residency years.

During the third and fourth years of school we also began to learn something that worried us all, although it was not much talked about. On the wards of the great Boston teaching hospitals—the Peter Bent Brigham, the Massachusetts General, the Boston City Hospital, and Beth Israel—it gradually dawned on us that we didn't know much that was really useful, that we could do nothing to change the course of the great majority of the diseases we were so busy analyzing, that medicine, for all its facade as a learned profession, was in real life a profoundly ignorant occupation.

Some of this we were actually taught by our clinical professors, much more we learned from each other in late-night discussions. When I am asked, as happens occasionally, which member of the Harvard faculty had the greatest influence on my education in medicine, I no longer grope for a name on that distinguished roster. What I remember now, from this distance, is the influence of my classmates. We taught each other; we may even have set careers for each other without realizing at the time that so fundamental an educational process was even going on. I am not so troubled as I used to be by the need to reform the medical school curriculum. What worries me these days is that the curriculum, whatever its sequential arrangement, has become so crowded with lectures and seminars, with such masses of data to be learned, that the students may not be having enough time to instruct each other in what may lie ahead.

The most important period for discovering what medicine would be like was a three-month ward clerkship in internal medicine that was a required part of the fourth year of medical school. I applied for the clerkship at the Beth Israel Hospital, partly because of the reputation of Professor Hermann Blumgart and partly because several of my best friends were also going there. Ward rounds with Dr. Blumgart were an intellectual pleasure, also good for the soul. I became considerably less anxious about the scale of medical ignorance as we followed him from bed to bed around the open circular wards of the B.I. I've seen his match only three or four times since then. He was a tall, thin, quick-moving man, with a look of high intelligence, austerity, and warmth all at the same time. He had the special gift of perceiving, almost instantaneously, while still approaching the bedside of a new patient, whether the problem was a serious one or not. He seemed to do this by something like intuition; at times when there were no particular reasons for alarm that could be sensed by others in the retinue, Blumgart would become extremely alert and attentive, requiring the resident to present every last detail of the history, and then moving closer to the bedside, asking his own questions of the patient, finally performing his physical examination. To watch a master of physical diagnosis in the execution of a complete physical examination is something of an aesthetic experience, rather like observing a great ballet dancer or a concert cellist. Blumgart did all this swiftly, then asked a few more questions, then drew us away to the corridor outside the ward for his discussion, and then his diagnosis, sometimes a death sentence. Then back to the bedside for a brief private talk with the patient, inaudible to the rest of us, obviously reassuring to the patient, and on to the next bed. So far as I know, from that three months of close contact with Blumgart for three hours every morning, he was never wrong, not once. But I can recall only three or four patients for whom the diagnosis resulted in the possibility of doing something to change the course of the illness, and each of these involved calling in the surgeons to do the something—removal of a thyroid nodule, a gallbladder, an adrenal tumor. For the majority, the disease had to be left to run its own course, for better or worse.

There were other masters of medicine, each as unique in his way as Blumgart, surrounded every day by interns and medical students on the wards of the other Boston hospitals.

The Boston City Hospital, the city's largest, committed to the care of indigent Bostonians, was divided into five separate clinical services, two staffed by Harvard Medical School (officially designated as the Second and Fourth services), two by Tufts, and one by Boston University. The most spectacular chiefs on the Harvard faculty were aggregated on the City Hospital wards, drawn there in the 1920s by the creation of the Thorndike Memorial Laboratories, a separate research institute on the hospital grounds, directly attached by a series of ramps and tunnels to the buildings containing the teaching wards. The Thorndike was founded by Dr. Francis Weld Peabody, still remembered in Boston as perhaps the best of Harvard physicians. Peabody was convinced that the study of human disease should not be conducted solely by bedside observations, as had been largely the case for the research done by physicians up to that time, nor by pure bench research in the university laboratories; he believed that the installation of a fully equipped research institute, containing laboratories for investigations of any promising line of inquiry, directly in communication with the hospital wards, offered the best opportunity for moving the field forward.

Peabody was also responsible for the initial staffing of the Thorndike. By the time I arrived, in 1937, the array of talent was formidable: George Minot (who had already received his Nobel prize for the discovery of liver extract as a cure for pernicious anemia), William Castle (who discovered the underlying deficiency in pernicious anemia), Chester Keefer, Soma Weiss, Maxwell Finland, John Dingle, Eugene Stead—each of them running a laboratory, teaching on the wards, and providing research training for young doctors who came for two- or three-year fellowship stints from teaching hospitals across the country. The Thorndike was a marvelous experiment, a model for what were to become the major departments of medicine in other medical schools, matched at the time only by the hospital of the Rockefeller Institute in New York.

Max Finland built and then ran the infectious disease service. He and his associates had done most of the definitive work on antipneumococcal sera in the treatment of lobar pneumonia, testing each new preparation of rabbit antiserum as it arrived from the Lederle Laboratories. Later, Finland's laboratories were to become a national center for the clinical evaluation of penicillin, streptomycin, chloromycetin, and all the other antibiotics which followed during the 1950s and 1960s. As early as 1937, medicine was changing into a technology based on genuine science. The signs of change were there, hard to see because of the overwhelming numbers of patients for whom we could do nothing but stand by, but unmistakably there all the same. Syphilis could be treated in its early stages, and eventually cured, by Paul Ehrlich's arsphenamine; the treatment took a long time, many months, sometimes several years. If arsphenamine was started in the late stages of the disease, when the greatest damage was under way—in the central nervous system and the major arteries—the results were rarely satisfactory—but in the earliest stages, the chancre and then the rash of secondary syphilis, the spirochete could be killed off and the Wassermann reaction reversed. The treatment was difficult and hazardous, the side effects of the arsenical drugs were appalling, sometimes fatal (I cannot imagine such a therapy being introduced and accepted by any of today's FDA or other regulatory agencies), but it did work in many cases, and it carried a powerful message for the future: It was possible to destroy an invading microorganism, intimately embedded within the cells and tissues, without destroying the cells themselves. Chemotherapy for infectious disease in general lay somewhere ahead, and we should have known this.

Immunology was beginning to become an applied science. Thanks to the basic research launched twenty years earlier by Avery, Heidelberger, and Goebbel, it was known that pneumococci possessed specific carbohydrates in their capsules which gave rise to highly specific antibodies. By the mid-1930s, rabbit antipneumococcal sera were available for the treatment of the commonest forms of lobar pneumonia. The sera were difficult and expensive to prepare, and sometimes caused overwhelming anaphylactic reactions in patients already moribund from their infection, but they produced outright cures in many patients. Pernicious anemia, a uniformly fatal disease, was spectacularly reversed by liver extract (much later found to be due to the presence of vitamin $B_{12}$ in the extracts). Diabetes mellitus could be treated—at least to the extent of reducing the elevated blood sugar and correcting the acidosis that otherwise led to diabetic coma and death—by the insulin preparation isolated by Banting and Best. Pellagra, a common cause of death among the impoverished rural populations in the South, had become curable with Goldberger's discovery of the vitamin B complex and the subsequent identification of nicotinic acid. Diphtheria could be prevented by immunization against the toxin of diphtheria bacilli and, when it occurred, treated more or less effectively with diphtheria antitoxin.

All these things were known at the time of my internship at the Boston City Hospital, but they seemed small advances indeed. The major diseases, which filled the wards to overflowing during the long winter months, were infections for which there was no treatment at all.

The two great hazards to life were tuberculosis and tertiary syphilis. These were feared by everyone, in the same way that cancer is feared today. There was nothing to be done for tuberculosis except to wait it out, hoping that the body's own defense mechanisms would eventually hold the tubercle bacillus in check. Some patients were helped by collapsing the affected lung (by injecting air into the pleural space, or by removing the ribs overlying the lung), and any number of fads were introduced for therapy—mountain resorts, fresh air, sunshine, nutritious diets—but for most patients tuberculosis simply ran its own long debilitating course despite all efforts. Tertiary syphilis was even worse. The wards of insane asylums were filled with psychotic patients permanently incapacitated by this disease—"general paresis of the insane"; some benefit was claimed for fever therapy; but there were few real cures. Rheumatic fever, the commonest cause of fatal heart disease in children, was shown by Coburn to be the result of infection by hemolytic streptococci; aspirin, the only treatment available, relieved the painful arthritis in this disease but had no effect on the heart lesions. For most of the infectious diseases on the wards of the Boston City Hospital in 1937, there was nothing to be done beyond bed rest and good nursing care.

Then came the explosive news of sulfanilamide, and the start of the real revolution in medicine.

I remember the astonishment when the first cases of pneumococcal and streptococcal septicemia were treated in Boston in 1937. The phenomenon was almost beyond belief. Here were moribund patients, who would surely have died without treatment, improving in their appearance within a matter of hours of being given the medicine and feeling entirely well within the next day or so.

The professionals most deeply affected by these extraordinary events were, I think, the interns. The older physicians were equally surprised, but took the news in stride. For an intern, it was the opening of a whole new world. We had been raised to be ready for one kind of profession, and we sensed that the profession itself had changed at the moment of our entry. We knew that other molecular variations of sulfanilamide were on their way from industry, and we heard about the possibility of penicillin and other antibiotics; we became convinced, overnight, that nothing lay beyond reach for the future. Medicine was off and running.

## Themes, Issues, and Ideas

1. Thomas writes, "The treatment of disease was the most minor part of the curriculum, almost left out altogether." Why was this the case? What did his medical study mainly consist of in college?

2. By 1937, "the signs of change were there," writes Thomas. What were those signs, and what did they portend?

3. Thomas distinguishes between the responses of the interns and those of the older physicians to the new discoveries in medicine. What does he imply were the reasons for this difference? Do any additional reasons suggest themselves to you? Explain.

## Writing Strategies and Techniques

1. Thomas ends his essay with the metaphor of a race: "Medicine was off and running." What other sources of metaphor does Thomas employ? Pick some examples and explain how they contribute to his writing.

2. This essay is on science and medicine, but it is written for a generally educated audience. How does Thomas try to avoid technical language in his explanations? Point to some examples and show how they work to make technical content understandable to the nontechnical reader.

## Suggestions for Writing

1. Thomas praises his teacher Dr. Blumgart for his brilliant abilities in diagnosis and prediction, and for his manner with his patients. Write

an essay analyzing the manner of Lewis Thomas's strengths in exposition. How does he maintain the relationship he creates with his audience?

2. Pick a subject that you have studied (mathematics or art, for example) and write an essay on the history of your training. Include a sketch of at least one instructor who influenced you for better or for worse.

# Beyond Prozac

## Peter Jaret

*The discovery by the counterculture of mind-altering drugs in the 1960s led, cultural historians note, to their absorbtion by the mainstream in the 1970s. As neuropharmacology has developed, more sophisticated prescription medications such as the tranquilizer Valium or the anti-depressants Xanax and Halcion have become more widely known and used by ordinary patients. In this essay, Peter Jaret describes the latest and seemingly most promising of mind-altering drugs—an anti-depressant that seems to contain the promise to "design your own brains."*

It's been called the "pill of pills"—a small green-and-cream capsule that, six years after its introduction, has become one of the top ten best-selling drugs in the world. Ask around and you'll find at least one friend who's taking it and half a dozen who think they should.

Officially, Prozac is simply one in a series of antidepressants. But in his controversial paean to the pill, *Listening to Prozac*, on the best-seller list since May, psychiatrist Peter Kramer claims that Prozac offers nothing less than self-transformation, turning self-doubt into confidence, increasing sex appeal and energy, even improving one's business acumen.

In the pipeline, researchers say, are even better methods for fine-tuning personality: pills to cure shyness, improve memory, enhance creativity, defuse anger. Soon, one eminent research psychologist recently claimed, we will be able to design our own brains. But like so many widely touted scientific revolutions, the flurry over Prozac and the brave new world of "cosmic psychopharmacology" it purportedly heralds is beginning to look like much ado about surprisingly little.

In one sense, Prozac *is* genuinely remarkable. During the 1960s and 1970s, scientists began to identify specific chemicals that carry signals from one brain cell to another, including a neurotransmitter called serotonin. Studying the action of several commonly used antidepressant medications, neuroscientists came to suspect that abnormally low levels of serotonin might be at least one cause of serious depression.

Enter Prozac—the first "designer drug" deliberately created to alter the biochemistry of a single neurotransmitter. Normally, brain cells that produce serotonin quickly reabsorb the chemical and inactivate it, clearing the pathway for the next chemical signal. Prozac interferes with that reabsorption process, making more serotonin available in the brain. Officially dubbed a selective serotonin re-uptake inhibitor, or SSRI, Prozac was quickly joined by other SSRIs, including Zoloft, Paxil, and Effexor (which works on not one but two neurotransmitters).

More are certain to follow. Refinements in biochemistry continue to turn up new neurotransmitters that, like serotonin, exert important effects on thoughts and feelings. At the same time, cell biologists have begun to pinpoint tiny receptors on brain cells whose structure determines which neurotransmitters they can receive and respond to. Meanwhile, computer-assisted imaging techniques are revealing which parts of the brain become activated when we're feeling sad or happy, excited or sleepy, enabling researchers to chart the geography of the mind.

"Slowly but surely, we're learning more about the chemical language of thought and feeling and the complex circuitry of the brain," says Stuart Yudofsky, chairman of the psychiatry department at Baylor College of Medicine in Houston. Along the way, scientists are identifying—or designing from scratch—drugs that can alter the ebb and flow of brain chemistry far more precisely and subtly than ever before.

Consider shyness. Far from a simple character trait, some scientists now believe extreme shyness may be caused by too much of the neurotransmitter norepinephrine, which normally helps alert us to danger. Tinker with norepinephrine levels, the thinking goes, and shy children could become class clowns virtually overnight. Hypersensitivity to rejection also seems to have its basis in biochemistry, but instead of too much stimulation, the problem may be too little. Treating patients with a drug called Nardil, which raises levels of the brain's natural stimulants, psychiatrist Donald Klein of the New York State Psychiatric Institute and his colleagues have helped patients overcome this disabling hypersensitivity.

There are drugs under study that smooth out troublesome mood swings and others that promise to help teenagers weather the emotional storms of adolescence. Yudofsky, who specializes in the biochemical basis of aggression and violence, believes there may soon be drugs that will be able to short-circuit aggressive impulses.

Prozac itself may prove useful in treating men prone to domestic violence, some researchers believe. Family doctors are already prescribing it for women with symptoms of PMS. One prominent researcher, bemoaning the fact that Prozac takes several weeks to become effective, looks forward to the day when a quick-acting version is available that we can pop at the first sign of sadness—or anger, or listlessness, or whatever.

Ethicists have already begun to debate the issues raised by personality-altering drugs. If medications are found to quiet the urge to violence, they ask, will society have an excuse to ignore poverty and despair? With the power to alter personality, which traits will we value and which will we choose to suppress? Will we be in danger of producing legions of people whose temperaments conform to the latest fashion?

Surprisingly, it's not a worry that keeps many neuroscientists awake at night. "The reality is," says psychiatrist Donald Klein, one of the pioneers of psychopharmacology, "our grasp of the biochemical circuitry of the brain is still astonishingly sketchy." New receptors are being identified practically every week, he points out—but researchers still have a lot to learn about exactly what they do, not to mention how the vast circuitry of the brain works together.

Even Prozac, it seems, isn't all it's cracked up to be. Hype notwithstanding, Prozac and the other SSRIs are actually no more effective in treating depression than the previous generation of tricyclic antidepressants like Elavil and Tofranil. They all help 65 to 70 percent of patients. The real advantage of the SSRIs is that they produce fewer side effects. Tricyclics have a scattershot effect; at the same time that they increase serotonin levels, for instance, they interfere with chemical messages that control blood pressure, heart rate, even memory.

"Patients taking tricyclic antidepressants have had to put up with blurred vision, constipation, memory loss, confusion, dry mouth, and a host of other unpleasant side effects," says Robert J. Birnbaum, director of psychopharmacology and neuroscience training at Boston's Beth Israel Hospital. "Often the only people willing to suffer through were people with serious, really disabling depression."

Far more specific in their effect, SSRIs are much easier for most people to tolerate. That's great news for the estimated 17.6 million Americans who suffer from clinical depression, according to National Institute of Mental Health statistics—nearly two-thirds of whom now go untreated. But it's significant for another reason, as well. The relative lack of side effects has encouraged psychiatrists and family doctors to prescribe SSRIs more widely than previous antidepressants, not just for severe depression but for many milder complaints. "If a patient comes to me feeling unhappy or out of sorts, why not try Prozac?" as one leading psychiatrist puts it. "It's not going to do them any harm, and it just might help."

It's that attitude, skeptics say, that probably accounts for the highly touted "transformations." "Mostly what we're looking at I suspect, are subclinical cases of depression," says Klein—people who were umnotivated, lethargic, or pessimistic simply because they were mildly depressed and didn't know it. Prozac lifted the veil of depression and, voilà, patients felt their lives transformed. "The truth is, the same sort of transformations occurred with earlier antidepressants. But because the side effects were so troublesome, psychiatrists were far less likely to prescribe them and patients far less willing to take them."

Moreover, treating bona fide chemical imbalances in the brain, Klein insists, is a far cry from tinkering with otherwise healthy personalities. "What we're learning is that the brain is self-regulating. Receptors can up-regulate if they're not getting enough of a given neurotransmitter, and they can down-regulate if they're getting too much. There's a built-in balancing mechanism. That means it's always going to be much easier to treat abnormal brain chemistry than it is to boost healthy brain function." Klein likens the effect to aspirin, which lowers body temperature only if you're running a fever, not when body temperature is normal.

And even when SSRIs work wonders, they still carry the risk of side effects that have turned some patients off—including jumpiness, nausea, insomnia, unwanted weight gain, and loss of sexual interest or inability to achieve orgasm. Although initial studies concluded that sexual problems plagued only about 2 percent of SSRI users, more recent reports suggest that as many as one in five people may have trouble achieving orgasm. And one study found that upwards of 75 percent of men on Prozac reported difficulty maintaining erections. Now there's Wellbutrin, the latest antidepressant to hit the pharmacists' shelves, which, the manufacturer claims, won't upset users' sex lives. But it does cause seizures in a small number of patients, and if history is any guide, other bothersome side effects may arise as the drug is more widely used.

The better our understanding of the biochemistry of the brain, the more precisely targeted new generations of psychoactive medications will be. Still, given the extraordinary complexity of the brain, even the best drugs are likely to have some unwanted side effects. Those can be dampened by other drugs, of course. But prescribe too many drugs and clinicians begin to worry about interactions. Something like half of all prescription drugs aren't taken as directed as it is. Designing our own brains, it seems, will be no easy task.

In the end, our current infatuation with Prozac is likely to prove more interesting as a cultural phenomenon than as a medical breakthrough. The hype that surrounds Prozac promises nothing less than a spiritual reawakening—and even that's nothing new. As Yale professor Sherwin B. Nuland points out in a recent issue of *The New York Review of Books,* the idea of being reborn, purified of one's defects, has been repeated throughout history "in folklore, fantasy, and the beliefs of those who seek it in religious faith." Peter Kramer begins as a psychiatrist Nuland notes, but by the end of *Listening to Prozac* he has become something like a messiah.

It's a sobering measure of our diminished prospects that we've come to look for salvation in a squirt of serotonin. No doubt the latest advances in psychopharmacology will help those among us overburdened by depression, anxiety, and other mental disorders. But just as certainly, the task of realizing our best and most embracing selves will remain the complicated work of a lifetime.

# Themes, Issues, and Ideas

1. Does the concept of "designing your own brain" appeal to you? Why or why not? How would you design your brain—other than making yourself a genius, that is.

2. What are some of the reasons Jaret doubts some of the more exalted claims made for Prozac? Do they seem valid to you?

3. Have you ever known anyone who took medication for emotional or mental problems of any kind? Did their experience fit with what Jaret has written? Explain your answer.

# Writing Strategies and Techniques

1. Why does Jaret begin with the most enticing descriptions of Prozac in the beginning of his essay and then go on to debunk them in the end?

2. How would Jaret's essay be different if his strategy were reversed— if he started out with the skeptical scientific perspective, and then went on to describe Prozac's more exciting, poetic possibilities?

# Suggestions for Writing

1. Write a story in which everyone in the world has access to designer pharmaceuticals and can in effect "design their own brains."

2. Write an essay arguing the issue of whether people without serious disorders should be able to take medicines such as Prozac.

# The Gene Dream

## Natalie Angier

*Scientists are now attempting to map the complete human genetic code, a goal whose achievement will revolutionize science and will have enormous effects on scientific ethics. Those involved in the Human Genome Initiative use some of the same biological techniques described by Peter Jaret in the preceding essay, but they attack similar problems on a vastly more ambitious scale. Unlocking the human gene code may be science's greatest dream—or nightmare—in the twenty-first century.*

*In this essay, which first appeared in* American Health *magazine, science writer Natalie Angier focuses on health as a point of view that organizes her exploration of a problem whose implications extend well beyond medicine. Angier, a free-lance writer based in New York City and author of* Natural Obsession: The Search for the Oncogene *(1988), draws on her expert knowledge of this essay's subject.*

At first glance, the Petersons* of Utah seem like a dream family, the kind you see only on television. They're devout, traditional and very, very loving. Bob Peterson works at a hospital near home to support the family while he finishes up a master's program in electrical engineering. Diane, who studied home economics at Brigham Young University, is a full-time wife and mother. And her time is certainly full: The Petersons have five sons and two daughters, ranging in age from two to thirteen. (As Mormons, the parents don't practice birth control.)

The children are towheaded, saucer-eyed, and subject to infectious fits of laughter. During the summer months, the backyard pool is

---

*Not their real name.

as cheerily deafening as the local Y. Says Diane, "Our kids really like just spending time together."

Yet for all the intimacy and joy, the Petersons' story is threaded with tragedy. One of the daughters has cerebral palsy, a nerve- and muscle-cell disorder. The malady isn't fatal, but the girl walks with great difficulty, and she's slightly retarded. Three of the other children suffer from cystic fibrosis, a devastating genetic disease in which the lungs become clogged with mucus, the pancreas fails, malnutrition sets in, and breathing becomes ever more labored. Thus far, their children's symptoms have been relatively mild, but Bob and Diane know the awful truth: Although a person with cystic fibrosis may live to be twenty or even thirty, the disease is inevitably fatal.

"Right now, the kids don't act sick," says Bob. "They go on thinking, 'I have a normal life,'" But, he admits softly, "We know it won't last forever. If they do get bad, then we won't have a choice. We'll have to put them in a hospital."

The Petersons realize their children's ailments aren't likely to be cured in the immediate future, but they're battling back the best way possible. Bob, Diane, and their seven children, as well as the three surviving grandparents, have all donated blood samples to biologist Ray White and his team at the University of Utah in Salt Lake City. Scientists are combing through the DNA in the blood, checking for the distinctive chemical patterns present only in cystic fibrosis patients.

Their work is part of a vast biomedical venture recently launched by the government to understand all the genes that either cause us harm or keep us healthy. It's medicine's grandest dream: By comprehending the genome—the complete set of genetic information that makes us who we are—in minute detail, scientists hope to answer the most enigmatic puzzles of human nature. The effort is so immense in its scale and goals that some have called it biology's equivalent of the Apollo moonshot, or the atom bomb's Manhattan project.

In fact, it's the most ambitious scientific project ever undertaken; it will cost a whopping $3 billion and take at least fifteen years to complete. By the time researchers are through, they will have deciphered the complete genome. They'll have drawn up a detailed genetic "map," with the size, position, and role of all 100,000 human genes clearly marked. And they'll have figured out each gene's particular sequence of chemical components, called nucleotides.

Though there are only four types of nucleotides, represented by the letters A, T, C, and G, spelling out all the combinations that make up our total genetic heritage will fill the equivalent of one million pages of text. "What we'll have," says Dr. Leroy Hood, a biologist at the California Institute of Technology in Pasadena, "is a fabulous 500-volume 'encyclopedia' of how to construct a human being." Nobel laureate Walter Gilbert goes so far as to describe the human genome as "the Holy Grail of biology."

Some scientists, however, think their colleagues are chasing a will-o'-the-wisp. Current genetic engineering techniques, say critics, are too embryonic to attempt anything as massive as sequencing the entire genome. Dr. Robert Weinberg of the Whitehead Institute in Cambridge, MA, calls the whole project "misguided" and doubts that scientists will gain major insights even if they can sequence it.

Still, researchers involved in the Human Genome Initiative insist the knowledge will revolutionize the fields of medicine, biology, health, psychology and sociology, and offer a bounty of applications. Using advanced recombinant DNA techniques, scientists will pluck out the genes that cause the 4,000 known hereditary diseases, including childhood brain cancer, familial colon cancer, manic depression, Huntington's disease—the neurological disorder that killed folk singer Woody Guthrie—and neurofibromatosis, or Elephant Man's disease. Beyond analyzing rare inherited disorders, researchers will glean fresh insights into the more common and complicated human plagues, such as heart disease, hypertension, Alzheimer's, schizophrenia, and lung and breast cancer. Those studies will enable scientists to develop new drugs to combat human disease.

But the Genome Initiative is not restricted to the study of sickness. As biologists decode the complete "text" of our genetic legacy, they'll be asking some profound questions: Are there genes for happiness, anger, the capacity to fall in love? Why are some people able to gorge themselves and still stay slim, while others have trouble losing weight no matter how hard they diet? What genetic advantages turn certain individuals into math prodigies, or Olympic athletes? "The information will be fundamental to us *forever*," says Hood, "because that's what we are."

The most imaginative scientists foresee a day when a physician will be able to send a patient's DNA to a lab for scanning to detect any genetic mutations that might jeopardize the patient's health. Nobel laureate Paul Berg, a biochemistry professor at Stanford, paints a scenario in which we'll each have a genome "credit card" with all our genetic liabilities listed on it. We'll go to a doctor and insert the card into a machine. Instantly reading the medical record, the computer will help the doctor to put together a diagnosis, prognosis, and treatment course. Says Caltech's Hood, "It's going to be a brave new world."

Coping with that new world will demand some bravery of our own. Once our genetic heritage has been analyzed in painstaking detail, we'll have to make hard choices about who is entitled to that information, and how the knowledge should be used. This technology is proceeding at an incredible rate, and we have to be sure that it doesn't lead to a discrimination in jobs, health insurance or even basic rights, says Dr. Jonathan Beckwith, a geneticist at Harvard Medical School. "We don't want a rerun of eugenics, where certain people were assumed to be genetically inferior, or born criminals."

For better or worse, politicians are convinced that the knowledge is worth seeking. This year, Congress has earmarked almost $50 million for genome studies and, if current trends continue, by 1992 the government should be spending about $200 million annually. Opponents worry the price tag could leave other worthy biomedical projects in the lurch.

Even at that level of funding, the genome project could be beyond the resources of any single country. That's why research teams from Europe, Asia, North America, and New Zealand have joined to form the Human Genome Organization. Among other goals, the newly created consortium plans to distribute money for worthwhile projects worldwide. Meanwhile, the Paris-based Center for the Study of Human Polymorphism distributes cell samples to researchers and shares their findings through an international data bank.

In this country, Nobel laureate James Watson, the co-discoverer of the molecular structure of DNA, is in charge of human genome research at the National Institutes of Health. And Dr. Charles Cantor, a highly respected geneticist from New York's Columbia University, has accepted the top spot at the Department of Energy's Human Genome Center.

## The Genetic Haystack

The Genome Initiative is sure to affect everybody. Doctors estimate that each of us carries an average of four to five severe genetic defects in our DNA. The majority of those mutations are silent: They don't affect you. However, if you were to marry someone who carries the same defect, you could have a child who inherits both bad genes and is stricken with the disease.

Most genetic flaws are so rare that your chances of encountering another silent carrier are slim—let alone marrying and conceiving a child with such a person. But some defects are widespread. For example, five out of one hundred harbor the mutant cystic fibrosis gene; seven out of one hundred blacks carry the trait for sickle cell anemia. Bob and Diane Peterson are both cystic fibrosis carriers—but they didn't realize their predicament until they gave birth to afflicted children.

For all the improvements of the last ten years, prenatal diagnosis techniques remain limited. Doctors can screen fetuses for evidence of about 220 genetic disorders, but most of the tests are so time-consuming and expensive they won't be done unless family history suggests the child may have a disease.

One reason it's difficult to screen for birth defects is that most genes are devilishly hard to find. The 50,000 to 100,000 genes packed into every cell of your body are arrayed on 23 pairs of tiny, sausage-shaped chromosomes, which means that each chromosome holds a higgledy-piggledy collection of up to 4,400 genes. Scientists cannot look under a microscope to see the individual genes for cystic fibrosis, Down's syndrome, or any other birth defect; instead, they must do elaborate chemical operations to distinguish one human gene from another. So daunting is the task of identifying individual genes that scientists have determined the chromosomal "address" of only about 2 percent of all human genes. "It's like finding a needle in a haystack," says Utah's Ray White.

Scientists must first chop up the twenty-three pairs of human chromosomes into identifiable pieces of genetic material and then study each fragment separately. To make the cuts, they use restriction enzymes—chemicals that break the bonds between particular sequences of nucleotides, the chemical components of genes.

Normally, restriction enzymes snip genetic material at predictable points, as precisely as a good seamstress cuts a swatch of fabric. But scientists have found that the enzymes also cut some fragments at unexpected places, yielding snippets that are longer than normal. It turns out that these variations are inherited, and many have been linked to certain genetic abnormalities. The fragments even serve as reference points for map-making efforts. The DNA segments produced by this technique are nicknamed "riff-lips," for restriction fragment length polymorphisms (RFLPs).

In the past three years, DNA sleuths have used the technique to isolate the genes for Duchenne's muscular dystrophy, one of the most common genetic diseases; a grizzly childhood eye cancer; and a hereditary white-blood-cell disease commonly called CGD. But the technique remains labor-intensive and in some ways old-fashioned. Armies of graduate students and postdoctoral fellows do the bulk of the work, using tedious, error-prone methods.

Scientists everywhere are racing to build superfast computers to sort through chromosome samples and analyze RFLP patterns. Until they're devised, researchers are learning to make do. At White's lab, for instance, researchers have jerry-rigged a device that automatically dispenses exceedingly small samples of DNA into rows of test tubes. "It can do in two days what used to take a researcher two weeks," says a technician.

## The Hapgoods Become Immortal

Despite all the technology, the genome project remains deeply human—even folksy. That's because the people donating their blood and genes are from ordinary families who happen to have something extraordinary to offer. They're families like the Petersons, whose DNA may contain clues to cystic fibrosis.

Or they're families like the Hapgoods, whose greatest claim to fame may be the ability to live long and multiply. Brenda and Sam Hapgood,* a Mormon couple in their early fifties, are plump and boisterous, and love to be surrounded by people. That may explain why, although they have five girls, four boys, three sons-in-law, two daughters-in-law and five grandchildren, they wouldn't mind having a few more kids around. Says Brenda, "I almost wish I hadn't stopped at nine!"

The Hapgoods are one of forty Utah families helping White construct a so-called linkage map of human DNA. He's trying to find chemical markers in the genome that are "linked" with certain genes. The markers will serve as bright signposts, dividing the snarl of genes into identifiable neighborhoods—just as road signs allow a traveler to pin down his location. Finding those markers is a crucial first step toward identifying the genes themselves, and for providing researchers with a decent chart of the terrain.

---

*Not their real name.

That's where the Hapgoods come in. To detect those tiny patches in the DNA that stand out from the background of surrounding genetic material, White must be able to compare the genomes of many related people over several generations. Mormon families are large, and they don't tend to move around much, so it's easy for White to get blood samples from many generations of a given family.

"The researchers told us there are lots of big families around," says Brenda. "What made us special was that all the grandparents were still with us."

In 1984, Brenda, Sam, their parents, and nine children all donated blood to White's researchers. Lab technicians then used a special process to keep the blood cells alive and dividing forever—ensuring an infinite supply of Hapgood DNA for study. "Our linkage families are becoming more and more important as we go to the next stage of mapping," says Mark Leppert, one of White's colleagues. "Hundreds of researchers from all over will be using the information from their DNA."

"We're going to go down in medical history!" Brenda says excitedly. "But you know what I'm really worried about?" one son-in-law teases her. "They might decide to clone you!"

Another reason the Hapgoods were chosen for the linkage study is because, in contrast to the Petersons, they didn't seem to have any major hereditary diseases. White wanted his general-purpose map to be a chart of normal human DNA. Ironically, however, two years after the Hapgoods first donated blood, one of the daughters gave birth to a son with a serious genetic defect known as Menkes' disease, a copper deficiency.

The child is two years old but looks like a deformed six-month-old. He has one hundred or more seizures a day. Half his brain and most of his immune system have been destroyed. Cradled in his mother Carol's arms, he moans steadily and sadly. "This is as big as he'll get," says Carol. "He'll only live to be four at the very most."

Carol and Brenda hope that the genome project will someday bring relief for Menkes victims. "We originally volunteered for the study to help the scientists out, to help their research," says Brenda. "But now we see that it could be important for people like us."

## The Big Payoff

"You don't need to have the whole project done before you start learning something," says Dr. Daniel Nathans, a Nobel laureate and professor of molecular biology and genetics at Johns Hopkins University in Baltimore. "There are things to be learned every step of the way." The first spin-offs are likely to be new tests for hereditary diseases. Within one to three years, biologists hope to have cheap and accurate probes to detect illnesses known to be caused by defects in a single gene, such as susceptibility to certain kinds of cancers.

Another inherited ailment that could quickly yield to genome research is manic depression, which is also thought to be caused by an error in any one of several genes. The psychiatric disorder afflicts 1 percent of the population—2.5 million people in the United States alone—yet it's often difficult to diagnose. With the gene isolated, experts will be better able to distinguish between the disease and other mood disorders, explains Dr. Helen Donis-Keller, a professor of genetics at Washington University in St. Louis.

Of even greater relevance to the public, the Genome Initiative will give investigators their first handle on widespread disorders such as cancer, high blood pressure, and heart disease. Researchers are reasonably certain that multiple DNA mutations share much of the blame for these adult plagues, but as yet they don't know which genes are involved. Only when biologists have an itemized map of the genome will they be able to detect complex DNA patterns that signal trouble in many genes simultaneously.

As the quest proceeds, surprises are sure to follow. "There are probably hundreds or thousands of important hormones yet to be isolated," says Dr. David Kingsbury, a molecular biologist at George Washington University. Among them, he believes, are novel proteins that help nerve cells grow, or *stop* growing. Such hormones could be made into new cancer drugs that target tumors while leaving the rest of the body unscathed.

"I have an intuitive feeling that this is going to open up all sorts of things we couldn't have anticipated," says Donis-Keller. "Even mundane things like obesity and baldness—imagine the implications of having new therapies for them!"

The human genome also holds keys to personality and the emotions. Department of Energy gene chief Charles Cantor says it's estimated that half of our 100,000 genes are believed to be active only in brain cells, indicating that much of our DNA evolved to orchestrate the subtle dance of thought, feeling, memory, and desire. "There are genes that are very important in determining our personality, how we think, how we act, what we feel," says Cantor. "I'd like to know how these genes work." Donis-Keller is also curious. "Is panic disorder inherited? Is autism?" she wonders. "These are controversial questions we can start to clarify."

Like the first Apollo rocket, the Human Genome Initiative has cleared the launch pad in a noisy flame of promise. Its crew is international, and so too will be the fruits of exploration. When the human genome is sequenced from tip to tail, the DNA of many people is likely to be represented—perhaps that of the Hapgoods and the Petersons, perhaps that of a Venezuelan peasant family. "It's going to be a genetic composite," predicts Yale professor of genetics Frank Ruddle. "The Indians will work on their genomes, the Russians on theirs, the Europeans on theirs. We'll pool the data and have one great patchwork quilt.

"I get a lot of pleasure out of thinking of this as a world project. No one single person will be immortalized by the research. But it will immortalize us all."

# Themes, Issues, and Ideas

1. In speculating on the possible significance of the information acquired from the Genome Initiative, Dr. Donis-Keller says, "Even mundane things like obesity and baldness—imagine the implications of having new therapies for them!" List some of the implications you imagine, both positive and negative, of the ability to alter relatively minor imperfections in appearance or behavior.

2. What are the basic elements of the genetic "map?" According to researchers, how will a knowledge of the size, position, and role of these elements be useful?

3. As Angier suggests, the information contained in an individual's genome could be abused. In what ways might this happen?

# Writing Strategies and Techniques

1. Does the essay's title strike you as an effective one? In what ways do you imagine Angier hopes it will affect her audience? What effect does the rhyme create?

2. Do the scientists quoted *sound* like the conventional idea of how you think a scientist should sound? Stylistically speaking, what do the

speeches in Angier's sources have in common? Do you think the quotations add to the essay? Explain.

# Suggestions for Writing

1. Angier stresses the usefulness and desirability of knowing your genetic profile. Can you think of a situation in which you might not want to know certain features? What attitude might be elicited by the knowledge of your genetic limitations? Write an essay giving your reasons for or against knowing your entire genetic makeup.

2. This essay focuses largely on health, but as Angier herself acknowledges, issues beyond health may also be involved. Write an essay speculating on the possible uses and abuses caused by greater knowledge of the human genetic code.

# When Is a Mother Not a Mother?

## Katha Pollitt

*As some of the essays in this book suggest, ethics and law are not keeping up with medical technology. Dilemmas and disputes that would have been unimaginable only a generation ago are commonplace today, and the effects of genetic engineering and advanced eugenics in the future remain a mystery. In the present day, however, the problems we face are not insoluble. Katha Pollitt addresses one of them in "When Is a Mother Not a Mother?"*

*Pollitt was born in 1949 and attended Radcliffe College. She became associate editor of* The Nation, *where this essay was first published, in 1991.*

T o the small and curious class of English words that have double and contradictory meanings—"moot," for example, and "cleave"—the word "mother" can now be added. Within the space of a single dazzling week this fall, this hoary old noun was redefined so thoroughly, in such mutually exclusive ways, that what it means now depends on which edition of the newspaper you read.

On October 23 in Orange County, California, Superior Court Judge Richard Parslow decided that the rightful mother of Baby Boy Johnson was not Anna Johnson, the black "gestational surrogate" who, for $10,000, carried him and birthed him, but Crispina Calvert, the wombless Asian-born woman who provided the egg from which, after in vitro fertilization with her (white) husband's sperm and implantation in Ms. Johnson, the baby grew. Declining, he said, to play Solomon and put the baby in the "crazy-making" position of having "two mothers"—

or to follow California law, which defines the mother as the woman who gives birth to the child—Judge Parslow ruled that genes make the mom, as they do the dad. Anna Johnson was merely a kind of foster mother, a "home," an "environment."

One wonders what Judge Parslow would make of a headline two days later. "Menopause Is Found No Bar to Pregnancy" announced *The New York Times,* reporting that doctors had succeeded in making six prematurely menopausal women pregnant by implanting them with donated eggs fertilized in vitro with their husband's sperm. By Judge Parslow's reasoning, of course, those women are merely foster mothers, homes and environments, but so far no one has suggested this, much less called for a re-evaluation of Johnson's claim in the light of new information about the value women place on pregnancy and childbirth and the persistent (if apparently erroneous) belief that the resultant babies belong to them.

To their credit, commentators have not regarded these developments with unalloyed rapture. Perhaps they learned something from the Baby M fracas [see Pollitt, "The Strange Case of Baby M," May 23, 1987]. In that dispute, you will remember, many intelligent people persuaded themselves that the baby's rightful mother was a woman who had no biological connection to it, and that its real mother, Mary Beth Whitehead, was a grasping madwoman because she did not think she was, as child psychologist Lee Salk put it, a "surrogate uterus." The New Jersey Supreme Court disagreed and, lo and behold, none of the confidently predicted dire consequences ensued. Women are not regarded as too emotional to make binding contracts, as some feminists feared, nor has motherhood been more deeply consigned to the realm of instinct and mystification. The child, now a toddler, has not been destroyed or corrupted by contact with her mother: Mary Beth Whitehead, the supposed Medea of the Meadowlands, turns out to be such a good mom, in fact that *New York Times* columnist Anna Quindlen, who observed one of the child's visits, felt moved to recant her earlier anti-Whitehead position. Indeed, the only consequences have been positive: The child knows both her parents; paid Baby M–style surrogacy has been outlawed in two states, the contracts declared unenforceable in three; Noel Keane, the infamous baby broker who boasted that he had made $300,000 in fees the year of the Baby M contract, has found another métier.

As our Eastern European friends are now reminding us, however, markets must be served. The New Jersey Supreme Court put a damper on Baby M–style contract motherhood—now commonly referred to as "traditional surrogacy," as though it came over with the Pilgrims—but it seems to have spurred science and commerce on to more ingenious devices. And so we have Baby Boy Johnson. Thanks to Baby M, we are a little sheepish, a little wiser. Ellen Goodman has called for the banning of gestational surrogacy for pay; like millions of other middle-aging moms, she wonders if being able to bear a child in one's 50s is really an unmitigated blessing. But we have not yet, as a society, begun to face the underlying ideas about class, race, children and, above all, women that the new maternities rely on.

Take class. By upholding the Johnson-Calvert contract, Judge Parslow opens the door to the sale of poor women's bodies to well-off couples. It is disingenuous to claim, as does Polly Craig of the Los Angeles Center for Surrogate Parenting, that $10,000 is not enough money to motivate a woman to sell her womb, and that gestational surrogates simply enjoy being pregnant, want to help others, or wish to atone for a past abortion. Why offer payment at all, if it serves no function? And why, if gestational surrogacy is such an occasion for pleasure, altruism and moral purification, don't prosperous women line up for it? The Calverts—she a nurse, he an insurance broker—presumably possess a wide female acquaintanceship in their own income bracket, none of whom felt friendship required of them that they turn over their bodies to the Calvertian zygote. Instead the couple approached Johnson, a sometime welfare recipient, single mother and low-paid worker at Crispina Calvert's hospital.

No, money is the motivator here. Ten thousand dollars may not seem like a lot to Craig and her clients, but it's a poor person's idea of major cash—as much as 25 percent of American women earn in a whole year of full-time employment. It's quite enough to becloud good judgment. "You wave $10,000 in front of someone's face," said Anna Johnson, "and they are going to jump for it." By "someone," Johnson meant women like herself, shuttling between welfare and dead-end jobs, single, already supporting a child, with a drawerful of bills and not much hope for the future.

In a particularly nasty wrinkle, gestational surrogacy invites the singling out of black women for exploitation. It's not just that blacks are disproportionately poor and desperate, more likely to be single mothers and more likely to lack the resources to sue. It's that their visible lack of genetic connection with the baby will argue powerfully against them in court. (Indeed, about the Baby Boy Johnson case hovers the suggestion that the Calverts chose Johnson for precisely this reason.) Judge Parslow's comparison of Johnson to a foster mother is interesting in view of the fact that foster mothers who grow attached to their charges and try to keep them are regarded with much popular sympathy and sometimes even succeed. But it is safe to say that few American judges are going to take seriously the claims of a black woman to a nonblack child. Black women have, after all, always raised white children without acquiring any rights to them. Now they can breed them, too.

There are those who worry about the social implications of gestational surrogacy but who still think Judge Parslow made the right choice of homes for Baby Boy Johnson. Be that as it may, Anna Johnson wasn't suing for custody but for visitation. She wanted to be a small part of the child's life, for him to know her and for her to know him. Why would that be so terrible? As Dr. Michelle Harrison, who testified for Johnson, wrote in *The Wall Street Journal,* Judge Parslow wasn't being asked to divide the child between three parents; the Calverts had in fact so divided him when they chose to produce a baby with Johnson's help. Recent court decisions (not to mention social customs like open adoption, blended families and gay and lesbian co-parenting) have tended to respect a widening circle of adult relationships with children. Every state, for instance, gives grandparents access to grandchildren in the case of a divorce, regardless of the wishes of the custodial parent. Stepparents and lesbian co-parents are demanding their day in court. In 1986 California state courts upheld the right of a sperm donor to sue for parental rights when the artificial insemination did not involve a doctor (the old turkey baster method). Why isn't *that* prospect too "crazy-making" for California? Or, for that matter, mandatory joint custody, an innovation that California pioneered? Given the increasing number of children living outside the classic nuclear-family arrangement, and the equanimity with which the courts divide them up between competing adults, it seems rather late in the day to get all stuffy about Anna Johnson.

The most important and distressing aspect of Judge Parslow's decision, however, is that it defines, or redefines, maternity in a way that is thoroughly degrading to women. By equating motherhood with fatherhood—that is, defining it solely as the contribution of genetic material—he has downgraded the mother's other contributions (carrying the fetus to term and giving birth) to services rather than integral components of parenthood. Under this legal definition, a normally pregnant women is now baby-sitting for a fetus that happens to be her own. "In a debate over nature vs. nurture, the winner is nature," read the *New York Times* pull-quote. But why define "nature" as DNA rather than as the physiological events of pregnancy and birth? There's nothing "natural" about egg donation, which involves the hormonal priming of an infertile woman, the extraction of an egg by delicate technology, fertilization in a dish with masturbated sperm and implantation of the zygote in another. And to call pregnancy and childbirth "nurture" seems a feeble way to describe the sharing of the body and the risking of health, well-being and even life itself that is required to bring another life into existence. Like "parenting," another fashionable buzzword, "nurture" is a bland social-sciency word that belittles a profound relationship and masks the role of women in gender-neutral language.

The picture of pregnancy as biological baby-sitting has many sources. It's as old as Aeschylus, who had Athena acquit Orestes of matricide in *The Eumenides* on the ground that mothers are merely "nurses" of men's seed, and as new as those ubiquitous photos of fetuses seeming to float in empty space. But its major proponents today are the anti-abortionists. In order to maximize the claims of the fetus to personhood, they must obscure the unique status of the pregnant woman: She is not making a person, because the fertilized egg already *is* a person; she's only caring for it, or housing it, or even (as one imaginative federal judge wrote), holding it captive. Ironically, the movement that claims to celebrate motherhood is led by its own logic to devalue the physical, emotional and social experience of pregnancy. If unwanted pregnancy is just an "inconvenience," how serious an occasion can a *wanted* pregnancy be? If mass adoption is the answer to 1.6 million annual abortions, how strong can the ties be between mother and newborn? When ethicists fret that professional women may resort to gestational surrogacy to avoid "putting their careers on hold," they betray more than antiquated views about the capacities of pregnant women to get out of bed in the morning. They reveal their own assumption that pregnancy is a trivial, empty experience with nothing positive about it except the end product, the genetically connected baby. They then compound the insult by attributing this view to a demonized fantasy of working women—cold, materialistic, selfish, corrupted by "male values"—that is, those held by the ethicists themselves. Is there any evidence that working women—even MBAs, even lawyers—see pregnancy this way? Who do the pundits think are mobbing infertility clinics and signing on for donated eggs? A couple needs two incomes just to pay the doctors.

Why is the primacy of genetics so attractive? At the moment, genetic determinism is having one of its periods of scientific fashion, fueling the fear that an adopted baby will never "really" be yours. At the same time, hardening class distinctions make the poor, who provide most adoptive babies, seem scary and doomed: What if junior took after his birth parents? It's not an accident that sperm donors and now egg donors are largely recruited among middle-class professionals—they're not just white, they're successful and smart—and that the commercial aspects of the transaction ($50 for sperm, $1,500 for an egg) are disguised by calling it a "donation." You can buy a womb because wombs don't really matter, but if the all-important DNA must come from a third party, it should come as a gift between equals.

The main reason for our love affair with genes, though, is that men have them. We can't get all the way back to Aeschylus, with man as seed sower and woman as flowerpot (although we acknowledge it in our language, when we call women "fertile" or "infertile," like farmland). Women, we now know, have seeds too. But we can discount the aspects of procreation that women, and only women, perform. As the sociologist Barbara Katz Rothman has noted, Judge Parslow's decision follows the general pattern of our society, in which women's experiences are recognized to the extent that they are identical with men's, and devalued or ignored to the extent that they are different. Thus, Mary Beth Whitehead won back her parental rights because the New Jersey Supreme Court acknowledged her *genetic* contribution: Baby M was half hers. And the postmenopausally pregnant, egg-donated women achieve parental rights by being married to their babies' fathers, not through their own contributions.

Of the two practices—actually a single practice with two social constructions—gestational surrogacy is clearly the more repellent, but to see its real meaning it must be looked at with egg donation as its flip side. Taken together they bring pregnancy into line with other domestic tasks traditionally performed by women—housework, child care, sex. Performed within marriage, for no pay, these activities are slathered with sentimentality and declared beyond price, the cornerstone of female self-worth, family happiness and civilization itself. That is the world inhabited by prosperous married women now able to undergo pregnancy thanks to egg donation. That the egg is not their own is a detail; what counts is that they are able to have a profound and transforming life experience, to bond prenatally with their baby and to reproduce the genes of their husband. But look what happens when the checkbook and the marriage certificate are in the other hand: Now the egg is the central concern, pregnancy and childbirth merely a chore, prenatal bonding a myth. Like all domestic labor performed for pay—housecleaning, baby-sitting, prostitution—childbearing in the marketplace becomes disreputable work performed by suspect, marginal people. The priceless task turns out to have a price after all: about $1.50 an hour.

What should happen now? Some suggest that new methods of parenthood require a new legal principle: pre-conception intent. Instead of socio-bio-ethical headaches—Who is the mother? Who is the father? What's best for the child? What's best for society?—we could have a simple rule of thumb: Let the seller beware. But at what cost to economic fairness, to principles of bodily integrity, to the nonmarketplace values that shape intimate life? Why not let the *buyer* beware? We cannot settle thorny questions by simply refusing to ask them.

A doctrine of pre-conception intent could, moreover, turn ordinary family law into fruit salad. Most pregnancies in the United States, after all, are not intended by either partner. They occur for dozens of reasons: birth-control failure, passion, ignorance, mixed messages, fear. The law wisely overlooks these sorry facts. Instead, it says Here is a child, here are the parents, next case. Do we really want to threaten a philosophy aimed, however clumsily, at protecting children from pauperism and abandonment? If pre-conception intent caught on with the general public, no single mother would be able to win child support; no single father could win parental rights. A woman's right to abortion could be conditioned on her pre-conception intent as evidenced, for example, by her use or neglect of birth control. In fact, in several states, laws have already been proposed that would restrict abortion to women who could prove contraceptive failure (a near impossibility, if you think about it, which is probably the point).

Perhaps the biggest problem with pre-conception intent, however, is that it ignores almost everything about the actual experience of becoming a parent of either sex. Planning to have a baby is not the same as being pregnant and giving birth, any more than putting on sexy underwear is like making love. The long months of pregnancy and the intense struggle of childbirth are part of forming a relationship with the child-to-be, part of the social and emotional task of parenthood. Not the only part, or even a necessary part—I am not suggesting that adoptive parents do not "really" become mothers and fathers. But is there a woman who feels exactly the same about the baby in the ninth month, or during delivery or immediately after, as she did when she threw away her diaphragm? When friends and relatives assure ambivalent parents-to-be not to worry, they'll feel differently about the baby when they feel it kick, or go through Lamaze together, or first hold their newborn in their arms, are they only talking through their hats? Whether or not there is a purely biological maternal instinct, more mothers, and more fathers, fall in love with their babies than ever thought they would. Indeed, if they did not, most babies would die of neglect in their cribs. How can we respect this emotional and psychological process—indeed, rely on it—and at the same time forbid it to the Mary Beth Whiteheads and the Anna Johnsons? I don't think we can.

Pre-conception intent would wreak havoc on everyone—men, women and children—and for what? To give couples like the Calverts a risk-free shot at a genetically connected baby. It makes more sense to assimilate surrogacy to already existing values and legal principles. In my view, doing so would make payment illegal and pre-birth contracts unenforceable. We don't let people sell their organs or work at slave wages; we don't hold new mothers to pre-delivery adoption arrangements; we don't permit the sale of children; we don't enforce contracts that violate human dignity and human rights. We respect the role of emotion and change and second thoughts in private life: We let people jilt their fiancés, and we let them divorce their spouses. True, we uphold prenuptial agreements (a mistake, in my opinion), but they're about property. If someone signed a premarital contract never to see his children again in the case of a divorce, what judge would uphold it? Those children weren't even conceived when that contract was signed, the judge would point out—and furthermore they have rights that cannot be waived by others, such as the right to contact with both parents after divorce. The children of surrogates—even nongenetic surrogates like Anna Johnson—have the right to know the woman through whose body and through whose efforts they came into the world. We don't need any more disposable relationships in the world of children. They have quite enough of those already.

In order to benefit a very small number of people—prosperous womb-infertile couples who shun adoption—paid surrogacy does a great deal of harm to the rest of us. It degrades women by devaluing pregnancy and childbirth; it degrades children by commercializing their creation; it degrades the poor by offering them a devil's bargain at bargain prices. It creates a whole new class of emotionally injured children rarely mentioned in the debate: the ones the surrogate has already given birth to, who see their mother give away a newborn, or fight not to.

It is hard for Americans to see why they shouldn't have what they want if they can pay for it. We would much rather talk about individual freedoms and property rights, rational self-interest and the supposed sanctity of contracts, than about the common good or human dignity, or the depths below which no person should be allowed to sink. But even we have to call it quits somewhere. As we decided 130 years ago, the buying and selling of people is a very good place to draw the line.

## Themes, Issues, and Ideas

1. Much of Pollitt's analysis hinges on the differing definitions of "motherhood." What are the various ones she mentions? Which seems most reasonable to you? Why?

2. Pollitt brings up slavery several times in the course of her argument. How far do you think the analogy between slavery and surrogate motherhood should go?

3. Pollitt's perspective is obviously a feminist one. Or is it? Give your opinion, and back it up with examples from the essay.

## Writing Strategies and Techniques

1. "We cannot settle thorny questions by simply refusing to ask them," says Pollitt. How is this statement reflected in her style? What does that style accomplish for the reader?

2. Pollitt is very good at punctuating an argument with an effective, direct statement. How does this technique further her argument? Give examples.

## Suggestions for Writing

1. Write an essay discussing another biomedical ethics issue from Katha Pollitt's point of view.

2. Is it fair to compare biomedical ethics with slavery? Write an essay that uses quotations from Pollitt's piece to support your opinion.

# A Modern Inquisition

## Jack Kevorkian

*Retired Michigan pathologist Jack Kevorkian has become the center of a legal and ethical firestorm in recent years as America's foremost advocate of physician-assisted suicide. Having gone from an obscure Midwestern practictioner to the spokesman for voluntary euthanasia changed Kevorkian in many ways: from a private citizen helping hopelessly ill patients to an icon for a national controversy; from a person to an "ism"; and, as he reminded the American Humanist Association in this speech, from a free and respected citizen to the subject of multiple indictments for first-degree murder.*

This is probably the first time that this august body [the American Humanist Association] has been addressed by someone under indictment on two counts of first-degree murder.

The Inquisition is still alive and well. The only difference is that today it's much more dangerous and subtle. The inquisitors don't burn you at the stake anymore; they slowly sizzle you. They make sure you pay dearly for what you do. In fact, they kill you often in a subtle way. My situation is a perfect example of it.

This is not self-pity, understand. I don't regret the position I'm in. I'm not a hero, either—by my definition, anyway. To me, anyone who does what *should* be done is not a hero. And I still feel that I'm only doing what I, as a physician, should do. A license has nothing to do with it; I am a physician and therefore I will act like a physician whenever I can. That doesn't mean that I'm more compassionate than anyone else, but there is one thing I am that many aren't and that's honest.

The biggest deficiency today and the biggest problem with society is dishonesty. It underlies almost every crisis and every problem you can name. It's almost inevitable; in fact, it's unavoidable as you mature.

We feel that a little dishonesty greases the wheels of society, that it makes things easier for everybody if we lie a little to each other. But all this dishonesty becomes cumulative after a while. If everyone were perfectly honest at all times, if human nature could stand that, you would find many fewer problems in the world.

When we (my lawyers, sisters, medical technologist, and myself) first started this work [physician-assisted voluntary euthanasia], we didn't expect the explosion of publicity that followed. The mainstream media tried to make my work look very negative—they tried to make me look negative—so that they could denigrate the concept we're working on. They said I should not be identified with the concept, yet they strived to do just that. They insulted and denigrated me and then hoped that it would spill over onto the concept. It didn't work, however; according to the poll people may be split 50–50 on what they think of me, but they are three-to-one in favor of the concept, and that's never changed.

Now isn't it strange that on a controversial subject of this magnitude—one that cuts across many disciplines—the entire editorial policy of the country is on one side? Even on a contentious issue like abortion, there is editorial support for both sides. And our issue—death with dignity—as far as we're concerned, is simpler than abortion. So why is every mainstream editorial writer and newspaper in the country against us on this? Not one has come out in wholehearted support of us, even though public opinion is on our side.

As I surmise it, they're in a conspiracy, which is not a revelation to many people. But with whom? Well, let's take a look at who's against this: organized religion, organized medicine, and organized big money. That's a lot of power.

Why is organized medicine against this? For a couple of reasons, I think. First, because the so-called profession—which is no longer a profession; it's really a commercial enterprise and has been for a long time—is permeated with religious overtones. The basis of so-called medical ethics is religious ethics. The Hippocratic oath is a religious manifesto. It is not medical. Hippocrates didn't write it; we don't know who did, but we think it's from the Pythagoreans. So if you meet a physician who says "Life is sacred," be careful. We didn't study sanctity in medical school. You are talking to a theologian first, probably a businessperson second, and a physician third.

The second reason that organized medicine is against physician-assisted voluntary euthanasia is the money involved. If a patient's suffering is curtailed by three weeks, can you imagine how much that adds

338 SCIENCE, TECHNOLOGY, AND HUMAN LIFE

up to in medical care? And a lot of drugs are used in the last several months and years of life, which add up to billions of dollars for the pharmaceutical industry.

This is what is so dismaying to me, what makes me cynical. You have to be cynical in life when you read about a situation that's so terrible and so incorrigible. There are certain ways to deal with it: you can go along with it, which is hard to do; you can go insane, which is a refuge (and some do that); or you can face it with deep cynicism. I've opted for cynicism.

In responding to the religious issues, I ask this: Why not let all the religious underpinnings of medicine apply only to the ethics of religious hospitals and leave the secular hospitals alone? The doctors who work in religious hospitals can refuse to do abortions, they can refuse assisted suicide or euthanasia, they can do anything they want. But they have no right to impose what *they* call a universal medical ethic on secular institutions.

Besides, what is ethics? Can you define it? My definition is simple: Ethics is saying and doing what is right, at the time. And that changes. Seventy-five years ago, if I told you that for Christmas I was going to have a truck deliver 10 tons of coal to your house, you would have been delighted. If I told you that today, you would be insulted. Doing the right thing changes with time.

That's true of human society also. There is a primitive society—I don't know which one exactly—whose members were shocked to learn that we embalm our dead, place them in boxes, and then bury them in the ground. Do you know what they do? They eat them. To them, it's ethical and moral and honorable to devour the corpse of your loved one. We're shocked at that, right? It's all a matter of acculturation, time, where you are, and who you are. If I visited this primitive society and I was a real humanist, I'd say, "Oh, that's interesting." And if the so-called savage in turn said "Gee, that's interesting what you do," then he or she would be a humanist. I used to define maturity as the inability to be shocked. So I guess in some ways we're still immature. But if you're truly mature, and a true humanist, you can never be shocked. If they eat their dead, so be it—that's their culture. But you know what our missionaries did, don't you? That's immoral action.

I think you get the gist of my position.

# Themes, Issues, and Ideas

1. Do you agree with Kevorkian's definition of ethics? What do you think of the example he gives? Does it go along with everything else he says?

2. How would you sum up Kevorkian's main arguments in this speech?

3. What do you think of Kevorkian's theory about a "conspiracy" preventing anyone from coming out with "wholehearted support" of him? Do you find his reasons convincing? Why or why not?

# Writing Strategies and Techniques

1. Are there any passages in this essay that come off the page differently than their author may have intended? Can you give an example?

2. Why does Kevorkian go out of his way to say "I'm not a hero"?

# Suggestions for Writing

1. Write an essay discussing the subject of voluntary suicide. Do you consider it an ethical issue? Should it be legalized? How might it be change society? Make sure to discuss its implications in the future, using material from Kevorkian's essay.

2. Write an essay describing the position you would take if you were Dr. Kevorkian's lawyer in his murder trial.

# The Frontier Within

## J. Madeline Nash

*Medical progress has raised a host of questions about the twenty-first century: What developments will genetic engineering bring? Will fetal tissue be used in medicine? Will AIDS and cancer ever be cured? But of all medical frontiers, neurology is the most mysterious. What is the brain? Is there a physical cause for every mental, moral, and spiritual state? What does a more advanced neuroscience bode for human life?*

*In the following reading, J. Madeline Nash looks at some of the possibilities being raised about the brain. This essay originally appeared in a special issue of* Time *magazine dealing with the future.*

Contemplate for a moment a tangle of seaweed tossed up on the shore. This is what a neuron looks like, surrounded by a thicket of tiny tendrils that serve as communications channels. Now multiply that neuron 100 billion times. Crammed into the skull of every human individual are as many neurons as there are stars in the Milky Way. Each one of these receives inputs from about 10,000 other neurons in the brain and sends messages to a thousand more. The combinatorial possibilities are staggering. The cerebral cortex alone boasts 1 million billion connections, a number so large, marvels neuroscientist Gerald Edelman in his recent book about the brain, *Bright Air, Brilliant Fire,* that "if you were to count them, one connection per second, you would finish counting some 32 million years after you began."

Assembled by nature and honed by evolution, the convoluted 3-lb. organ positioned between our ears represents a triumph of bioengineering, one that continues to elude comprehension and defy imitation. "The brain," declares molecular biologist James Watson, co-discoverer of the physical structure of DNA, "is the most complex thing we have yet discovered in our universe." The quest to understand the biology of intelligence is likely to occupy the minds of the world's best scientists for centuries to come. The task may prove more challenging than those alive today suppose, requiring perhaps new breakthroughs in physics and chemistry. Meanwhile, the knowledge spawned by this search promises to transform society. Here is what lies ahead:

## Computers Will Emulate the Brain But Not Replace It

From the wheeled cart to the printing press, from the telephone to the airplane, inventions have enormously expanded the repertoire of human capabilities, and this trend will continue, even accelerate. In this century computers have provided instant access to awesome number-crunching power and a vast storehouse of information. In coming centuries they will augment and amplify human skills in far more astounding ways. Thus, while the brains will not undergo much in the way of biological evolution, humans, assisted by ever more powerful computers, will become capable of far greater intellectual feats. "We won't recognize any difference in brains themselves," emphasizes Maxwell Cowan, chief scientific officer of the Howard Hughes Medical Institute in Bethesda, Maryland. "But we will recognize enormous differences in what brains know and understand."

Intriguingly, the brain's expanding knowledge of itself has begun to suggest radical new approaches to computer design. Like the brain, the computers of the future will not execute tasks in serial lockstep but will be capable of doing a million things in parallel. The chips of which they are composed may well be silicon, but they will mimic biological systems in almost every other way. A tantalizing hint of what the future holds comes from a type of computer known as a neural network. Employing the time-tested tactic of trial and error, these assemblages of artificial neurons have already "learned" to recognize scribbled handwriting, deduce principles of grammar and even mimic the acoustic sensitivity of the barn owl. By cobbling several of these sensory systems together, scientists will certainly be able to create, say, a robot that combines a barn owl's hearing with the ability to track moving objects and issue an ear-piercing hoot. Home gardeners may well employ an artificial owl to chase away rabbits and deer, but they will hardly consider it an intellectual equal. "Let me put it this way," laughs Caltech physicist Carver Mead, a legendary designer of computer chips, "Two hundred years from now, I will not be having this conversation with a piece of silicon."

## The Deaf Will Hear, the Blind See, the Lame Walk

By the end of the century, if not before, scientific insight into the perceptual centers of the human brain should vanquish these ancient afflictions. Already scientists have developed a cochlear implant that bypasses nonfunctioning hair cells in the ear and stimulates the nerve leading to the auditory cortex of the brain. Says Michael Merzenich, a neurophysiologist at the University of California, San Francisco: "We know that these inputs to the brain are distorted, yet the patients who have worn them for a while insist that what they hear sounds perfectly normal." What appears to occur, says Merzenich, is that the brain somehow manages to adjust its connections to make sense of the distortions it receives. This clear demonstration of the plasticity inherent in the adult brain lends hope that scientists of the future will succeed in performing other similar feats. One of these might well be the ability to equip artificial limbs with electronic "neurons" that can respond to signals relayed by the brain. These circuits might even include the equivalents of the axons and dendrites that link one neuron to another.

Almost certainly, scientists will master techniques for stimulating injured neurons to regenerate themselves. The brains and spinal columns of adult mammals do not possess this ability, at least not yet. A clue that this should be possible comes from frogs and salamanders, whose central nervous systems miraculously regrow following injury. Scientists have discovered several proteins that may eventually be deployed to rejuvenate broken spinal cords and damaged optic nerves. "I don't hold out too much hope for bionic man." says Michael Stryker, a colleague of Merzenich's who specializes in vision. "I think we will get there faster using biological techniques."

## Genetic Engineering Will Extend to Mental Traits

Scientists are currently absorbed in tracking down genes believed to be responsible for such mental illnesses as manic depression and schizophrenia. Eventually, they can be expected to broaden their goals and seek out the genetic tool kit for building such intellectual traits as musical talent, mathematical genius and, above all, personality. Shyness, for instance, appears to have a genetic basis; assertiveness and hair-trigger anger probably do as well. Like it or not, predicts Dr. Lewis Judd, chairman of the psychiatry department at the University of California at San Diego, "We are going to find that the attitudes we take, the choices we make, are far more influenced by heredity than we ever thought."

For the next century or two, if not beyond, schemes for improving the brain through genetic tinkering are likely to be confounded by a combination of social taboos, legal restrictions and sheer biological ignorance. But when the genes that underlie personality and behavior are isolated and understood, society will reach a critical ethical divide. A Pandora's box of options that were not available in centuries past will suddenly pop wide open. Should would-be parents who learn a fetus has inherited a strong likelihood of developing a serious but treatable mental illness opt for an abortion? Should they choose gene therapy to replace the defective DNA in their newborn child's brain cells? And while they're contemplating all this, might they not consider conferring on their offspring desirable traits like intelligence?

## Mind Reading Will Be More Than a Parlor Game

The machines that make images of the brain today are large, expensive contraptions that only major medical centers can afford. But just as computers have become ever smaller, cheaper and more powerful, so will the ultrafast successors to present-day positron-emission tomography and magnetic-resonance imaging scanners. Washington University neurologist Marcus Raichle predicts, in fact, that the "brain scopes" of the future will make a big splash at Disneyland and other theme parks. One can imagine lines of vacationers waiting to have their thoughts and emotions imaged in garish hues.

But these machines will also be put to serious purpose. Consider, for example, the tantalizing evidence that certain patterns of brain activity correlate with higher achievement levels. Competing educational strategies might someday be judged by whether they stimulate specific areas of the brain and how strongly. "Is phonics really the best way to teach reading?" muses Dr. Raichle. "Or is it just another silly idea? By looking at the brain, I think we'll discover the answer to that question." And to others as well. Many mothers-to-be have wondered whether playing music and reciting poetry can influence embryonic brain development in desirable ways. Someday they may be able to judge for themselves.

More important, tomorrow's brain scanners will be able to assess intellectual strengths and weaknesses in preschool children. A wide spectrum of mental weaknesses will become targets for early intervention. Dyslexia could be diagnosed in infancy, the time when brain plasticity is highest. Therapies could then be monitored by charting changes in neuronal firing patterns.

## Brains Will Be Healthier, Happier

Prominent mainstays of the pharmacopoeia of the future will be compounds that prevent nerve cells from dying. Much of the devastation caused by stroke is believed to occur because the directly injured neurons release massive quantities of the neurotransmitter glutamate. Normally, tiny bursts of glutamate act as signals between one neuron and another, triggering the brief opening of minuscule channels that allow calcium to pass through the cell's protective membrane. Too much glutamate, however, causes the channels to remain open too long, permitting an abnormal, and lethal, influx of calcium. Soon drugs that mop up excess glutamate or block its action may make this sort of stroke-related brain damage as preventable as tissue damage from gangrene. Similar strategies should likewise succeed in protecting neurons from the ravages of Alzheimer's disease.

Needless to say, expanding knowledge of the brain's complex biochemistry and how it goes awry will bring about more effective treatments for depression and schizophrenia, panic attacks and obsessive compulsions, alcoholism and drug addiction. Along the way, scientists will gain profound insights into the biochemical signals that create the astounding range of human emotions. "Which peptides make you sad, which ones make you happy, and which ones make you feel just grand?" wonders Columbia University neuroscientist Eric Kandel. That knowledge could conceivably translate into an ability to fine-tune those states at will—through either pharmacology or sophisticated biofeedback techniques.

Certainly nothing in the past 100,000 years of cultural evolution can prepare future generations for the moment when science lays bare, as it most certainly will, the secrets of the human mind. "We will be rendered naked," predicts Tufts University philosophy professor Daniel Dennett, "in a way that we've never been naked before. The mind boggles at the varieties of voyeurism, eavesdropping, and intrusion that will become possible." Concepts like good and evil, free will and individual responsibility, will presumably survive the upheaval, but not before being shaken to their deepest foundations. Imagine, for a moment, that a psychiatrist could peer into the psyche of a serial killer. Could the doctor see what was wrong? If he could, would he know how to fix it?

The great adventure on which modern neuroscience has embarked will end up challenging our most cherished concepts of who we are. "In the end, we will even figure out how this tissue in our skulls produces the states of self-awareness we refer to as consciousness," ventures John Searle, a philosopher of science at the University of California, Berkeley. But just as understanding the Big Bang has not permitted humans to create new universes at will, understanding consciousness will probably not allow us to construct an artificial brain. Besides, says University of Iowa neurologist Dr. Antonio Damasio, "a brain is not likely to work without a body." At the very least, a disembodied brain would be extremely disoriented and terribly unhappy.

In the coming centuries, one imagines, the desire to create monstrous caricatures of ourselves will dissipate. At long last, we will reclaim the awe and wonder our predecessors reserved for machines and turn them back toward our biological selves. Like Narcissus, we will behold the image of our minds and lose ourselves in endless admiration.

## Themes, Issues, and Ideas

1. Is it fair to say that Nash has an optimistic attitude toward the future? Are there any points in her piece when you sense that the future might not be so bright?

2. "Like Narcissus, we will behold the image of our minds and lose ourselves in endless admiration." Does this sound like a particularly healthy destiny?

3. According to Nash, "[c]oncepts like good and evil, free will, and individual responsibility will presumably survive the upheaval..." Why? And what would a world be like without these things? Is such a world compatible with the rosy view of the future Nash describes?

# Writing Strategies and Techniques

1. What do you think of the "experts" Nash quotes? Are they the best judges of the future and the consequences of neuroscience? Give your opinion of scientists as futurists.

2. What is the basic structure of Nash's piece? What moves it forward? How is Nash's tone partially achieved through this structure?

# Suggestions for Writing

1. Write about a day in the life of a person in the twenty-first century, based on the assumption that all of Nash's predictions came true.

2. Write a horror story that includes at least four of Nash's predictions.

# MAKING CONNECTIONS

1. One constant throughout these essays has been the place of the doctor as chief medical practitioner. What do these essays suggest about the evolution of the profession?

2. Write a response to J. Madeline Nash's rosy view of science, using some of the perspectives gleaned from Katha Pollitt and Peter Jaret.

3. In their respective essays, Peter Jaret and Natalie Angier address similar topics. Compare and contrast their respective attitudes to (a) science; (b) the future; (c) nature and technology.

4. It might be said that the medical profession of Lewis Thomas's youth was most concerned with understanding and predicting death, while modern advances have the luxury of being concerned with life. Yet, as some of the other authors here point out, medical tinkering with human life is not always such a blessing. Using the evidence and arguments available to you from the essays in this chapter, write an essay in which you argue for your point of view of the proper limits of medical intervention.

5. What are some future biomedical debates that might be in an anthology called *Readings for the 22nd Century*?

# CHAPTER
# NINE

## *Science, Technology, and Human Living*

### *Adapting to a Changing World*

# THE
# PAST AS
# PROLOGUE

## Liberty, Quality, Machinery

### Aldous Huxley

*Technology is usually defined as "applied science,"
or as the realization in practical terms of the power of the
knowledge produced by scientific inquiry into the workings of the natural world. But what are the results of technology when it is applied to human life? And how will the
ceaseless advances of technology enhance (or inhibit)
human life in the future?*

*These questions about technology and its role in the
future have been frequently raised in modern times.
Aldous Huxley (1894–1963), one of the twentieth century's most prominent novelists, prophets, and social critics, addressed the issue of technology throughout his
career. A prolific writer, he is most widely known as the
author of* Brave New World *(1932), a science-fiction version of a deplorable future that became a famous symbol
in itself like Thomas More's* Utopia *and George Orwell's*
1984. *In this essay, from his collection* Tomorrow and
Tomorrow and Tomorrow *(1956), Huxley finds hope in
the fact that the do-it-yourselfer—of all people—can
escape the oppressiveness of technology.*

J ohn Ruskin deplored the railway engine. It might be useful; but why, why did it have to *look* like a railway engine? Why couldn't it be dressed up as a fiery dragon, breathing flames as it rushed along, and flapping iron wings? Machines, Ruskin thought, and all their productions are intrinsically hideous. If we must have them, let it be with Gothic trimmings.

To William Morris, power-driven contraptions were odious, even in fancy dress, even when disguised as wiverns or basilisks. He objected to them on aesthetic grounds, and, as a sociologist, he loathed them. In the process of creating ugliness and multiplying monotony, machines had destroyed the old order and were turning the men and women who tended them into brutes and automata. Morris's ideal was the Middle Ages. Not, it goes without saying, the real Middle Ages, but an improved Victorian version of Merrie England—clean, kindly, and sensible, free from bad smells and religious dogmas, from bubonic plague and papal indulgences and periodic famines. A snug little world of healthy, virtuous craftsmen, craftswomen, and craftschildren, producing not for somebody else's profit but for their own use and for the greater glory of God, and having, in the process, a really wonderful time.

Today we like to think of applied science as a kind of domesticated djinn, indentured to the service of the no-longer-toiling masses. Half a century ago Tolstoy saw in applied science the greatest threat to liberty, the most powerful instrument of oppression in the hands of tyrants. "If the arrangement of society is bad (as is ours) and if a small number of people have power over the majority and oppress them, every victory over Nature will inevitably serve to increase that power and that oppression. This is what is actually happening." It was for this reason (among others) that Tolstoy advocated a return to handicraft production within village communities, which were to be, as nearly as possible, self-sufficient. His greatest disciple, Mahatma Gandhi, preached the same doctrine—and lived long enough to see the nation, whose independence he had won, adopt a policy of all-out industrialization.

It is easy enough to detect the flaws in these classical arguments against machinery and in favor of a return to handicraft production. All of them fail to take into account the most important single fact of modern history—the rapid, the almost explosive increase in human numbers. Within the combined life spans of Tolstoy and Gandhi the population of the planet was more than trebled. Let us consider a few of the aesthetic, psychological, and political consequences of this unprecedented event in human history.

By no means all the ugliness of which Ruskin and Morris complained was due to the substitution of machine production for handicrafts. Much of it was simply the result of there being, every year, more and more people. Beyond a certain point, human beings cannot multiply without producing an environment which, at the best, is predominantly dreary, soul-stultifying, and hideous, at the worst foul and squalid into the bargain. There have been beautiful cities of as many as two or three hundred thousand inhabitants. There has never been a beautiful city of a million or over. The old, unindustrialized parts of Cairo or Bombay are worse than fully industrialized London, or New York, or the Ruhr. Man cannot live satisfactorily by bricks and mortar alone. This would be true even if the bricks and mortar were put together in decent houses. In actual practice a little good architecture has always been surrounded, in the world's great capitals, by vast expanses of mean and dreary squalor. In the small cities of earlier centuries, filth and ugliness surrounded the splendid churches and palaces; but these slums were to be measured in acres, not in square miles. Small quantities of man-made squalor can be taken with impunity, particularly when associated with the woods and fields which surrounded the small city on every side, endowing it, as an urban unit, with a kind of over-all beauty of its own. This kind of over-all urban beauty has never existed in a great metropolis, most of which must always seem, by the mere fact that it goes on and on, unutterably dull, hideous and soul-destroying. What Ruskin and William Morris were really objecting to was the consequence, not of machinery, but of Victorian fertility combined with improved sanitation and cheap food from the New World. Families were large and, for the first time in history, most of their members survived infancy and grew up to produce large families of their own—and, in the process, to create hundreds of monster cities, tens of thousands of square miles of squalor and ugliness.

Thanks to the advanced technology of which Tolstoy and Gandhi so passionately disapproved, one-third, more or less, of the earth's twenty-five hundred million inhabitants enjoy unprecedented prosperity and longevity, and the remaining two-thirds contrive, however miserably, to remain alive, on the average, for thirty years or so. A return to handicraft production would entail the outright liquidation, within a few years, of at least a billion men, women, and children. Moreover, if, while returning to handicraft production, we were to maintain our present standards of cleanliness and public health, numbers would tend once more to increase, and within half a century the liquidated billion would be back again, and ripe for new famines and another liquidation. Where Nature kills the majority of human beings in childhood, the practice of contraception is suicidal. But where human beings understand the principles of sanitation and where, consequently, most of the members of large families survive to become parents in their turn, it is unrestricted fertility that threatens to destroy not merely happiness and liberty, but, as numbers outrun resources, life itself. Generalized death control imposes the duty of generalized birth control. Gandhi was aware of the population problem and hoped (he can hardly have believed) that it could be solved by the inculcation of sexual continence among young married couples. In actual fact it is unlikely to be solved until such time as the physiologists and pharmacologists can provide the Asiatic and African masses with a contraceptive pill that can be swallowed, every few weeks, like an aspirin tablet. Within a generation of the discovery of such a pill, world population may be stabilized—somewhere, let us hope, on this side of five thousand millions. After which it may be possible to raise the standard of Far Eastern, Middle Eastern, Near Eastern, African, and Caribbean living to levels somewhat less subhuman than those now prevailing—a feat which will require all man's good will, all his best intelligence and (far from a return to handicraft production) a yet more advanced technology.

But the fact that man cannot now survive without advanced technology does not mean that Tolstoy was entirely wrong. Every victory over Nature does unquestionably strengthen the position of the ruling minority. Modern oligarchs are incomparably better equipped than were their predecessors. Thanks to fingerprinting, punched cards, and IBM machines, they know practically everything about practically everyone. Thanks to radios, planes, automobiles, and the whole huge armory of modern weapons, they can apply force wherever it is called for, almost instantaneously. Thanks to the media of mass communication, they can browbeat, persuade, hypnotize, tell lies, and suppress truth on a national, even a global scale. Thanks to hidden microphones and the arts of wire tapping, their spies are omnipresent. Thanks to their control of production and distribution, they can reward the faithful with jobs and sustenance, punish malcontents with unemployment and starvation. Reading the history, for example, of the French Revolution and Napoleon's dictatorship, one is constantly amazed at the easy-going ineptitude of earlier governmental procedures. Until very recent times such liberties as existed were assured, not by constitutional guarantees, but by the backwardness of technology and the blessed inefficiency of the ruling minority.

In the West our hard-won guarantees of personal liberty have not, so far, been offset by the political consequences of advancing technology. Applied science has put more power into the hands of the ruling few; but the many have been protected by law and, to make assurance doubly sure, have created (in the form of trade unions, cooperatives, political machines, and lobbies) great systems of power to counterbalance the power systems of the industrialists, government officials, and soldiers, who own or can command the resources of modern technology. Where, as in Russia or in Nazi Germany, the masses have not been protected by law and have been unable to create or maintain their own defensive power systems, Tolstoy's predictions have been fulfilled to the letter. Every victory over Nature has been at the same time a victory of the few over the many. And all the while the machinery of mass production is growing larger, more elaborate, increasingly expensive. In consequence its possession is coming to be confined more and more exclusively to the wielders of financial power and the wielders of political power—to big business, in a word, and big government. Never was there a greater need for the old Eternal Vigilance than exists today.

But here let us note a development entirely unforeseen by Ruskin and Morris, by Tolstoy, Gandhi, and most even of the more recent philosophers and sociologists who have viewed with alarm man's increasing dependence on the machine as producer of necessities and luxuries, the dispenser of entertainment and distractions, the fabricator of synthetic works of art, of tin or plastic surrogates for the immemorial products of manual skill. While big machines have been growing spectacularly bigger, new races of dwarf machines have quietly come into existence and, at least in America, are now proliferating like rabbits. These little machines are for private individuals, not for the great organizations directed by the wielders of financial and political power. They are produced by big business; but their purpose, paradoxically enough, is to restore to the individual consumer some, at least, of that independence of big business which was his in that not-too-distant past, when there was no big business to depend on. Small power tools, in conjunction with new gadgets of every variety, new synthetic raw materials, new paints and putties, new solders and adhesives, have called into existence (and at the same time have been called into existence by) a new breed of artisans. These new artisans pass their working hours in a factory that turns out mass-produced goods, in an office that arranges for their distribution, in a store that sells them, a truck or train that delivers them to their destination. But in their spare time—and a forty-hour week leaves a good deal of spare time—they become craftsmen, using the tools and materials supplied by the mass producers, but working for themselves, either for the sheer fun of it, or because they cannot afford to pay someone else to do the job, or else (deriving pleasure from what they are forced to do by economic necessity) for both reasons at once.

The "do-it-yourself" movement has its comic aspects. But then so does almost everything else in this strange vale of tears and guffaws, which is the scene of our earthly pilgrimages. The important fact is not that amateur plumbing is a fruitful subject for the cartoonist, but that something is actually being done to solve, at least partially, some of the problems created by a technology rapidly advancing, in industry after industry, toward complete automation. Millions of persons have grown tired of being merely spectators or listeners, and have decided to fill their leisure with some kind of constructive activity. Most of this activity is utilitarian in character; but there are also many cases in which these new handicraft workers of the machine age supplement their utilitarian hobbies with the practice of one of the fine arts. There is a countless host, not only of amateur plumbers, but also of amateur sculptors, painters, ceramists. Never before has there been so general an interest in art (you can buy books on Picasso and Modigliani at the five-and-ten), and never before have there been so many wielders of paintbrushes and modelers of clay. Are we then (in spite of all that Ruskin and Morris and their followers said about machinery) on the threshhold of a new Golden Age of creative achievement? I wonder. . . .

Art is not one thing, but many. Metaphysically speaking, it is a device for making sense of the chaos of experience, for imposing order, meaning, and a measure of permanence on the incomprehensible flux of our perpetual perishing. The nature of the order imposed, of the significance discovered and expressed, depends upon the native endowments and the social heredity of the person who does the imposing, discovering, and expressing. And this brings us to art as communication, art as the means whereby exceptionally gifted individuals convey to others their reactions to events, their insights into the nature of man and the universe, their visions of ideal order. All of us have such visions and insights; but whereas ours are commonplace, *theirs* are unique and enlightening. Art-as-communication is pretty pointless, unless the things communicated are worth communicating. But even in cases where they are not worth communicating, art is still valuable—if not to the persons who look at it, at least to those who produce it. For art is also a method of self-discovery and self-expression; an untier of knots, an unscrambler of confusions; a safety valve for blowing off emotional steam; a cathartic (the medical metaphor is as old as Aristotle) for purging the system of the products of the ego's constant auto-intoxication. Art-as-therapy is good for everybody—for children and the aged, for imbeciles and alcoholics, for neurotic adolescents and tired businessmen, for prime ministers on weekends and monarchs on the sly (Queen Victoria, for example, took drawing lessons from Edward Lear, the author of *The Book of Nonsense*). Art-as-therapy is even good for great artists.

> To me alone there came a thought of grief;
> A timely utterance gave that thought relief,
> And I again am strong.

Besides being a masterpiece of art-as-communication, Wordsworth's great Ode was also a (to him) most salutary dose of art-as-therapy. Involving, as they do, the highest manual skill, sculpture, painting, and ceramics are more effective as therapy than is poetry, at any rate Western poetry. In China writing is a branch of painting—or perhaps it would be truer to say that painting is a branch of the fine art of writing. In the West the writing even of the noblest poem is a purely mechanical act and so can never afford psychological relief comparable to that which we obtain from an art involving manual skill.

The spread of amateur housebuilding, of amateur painting and sculpture, will soothe many tempers and prevent the onset of a host of neuroses, but it will not add appreciably to the sum of architectural, pictorial, and plastic masterpieces. At every period of history the number of good artists has been very small, the number of bad and indifferent artists very great. Because immense numbers of people now practice art as therapy, it does not follow that there will be any noticeable increase in the output of masterpieces. Because I feel better for having expressed my feelings in a daub, it does not follow that you will feel better for looking at my daub. On the contrary, you may feel considerably worse. So let us practice art-as-therapy, but never exhibit the stuff as though it were art-as-communication.

We should not even expect to see an increase in the amount of good craftsmanship. In the past good craftsmanship has been contingent on two factors—intense and prolonged specialization in a single field, and ignorance of every style but that which happens to be locally dominant. Before the invention of foolproof machines nobody became an acknowledged master of his craft without going through a long apprenticeship. Moreover, the Jack-of-All-Trades was, proverbially and almost by definition, the master of none. If you wanted to have your house thatched, you went to the thatcher; if you needed a table, you applied to the joiner. And so on. Specialization in the crafts and arts goes back to remotest antiquity. Archaeologists assure us that the great paleolithic cave paintings were executed, in all probability, by teams of traveling artists, whose native skill had been increased by constant practice. As for flint arrowheads, these were manufactured in places where the raw material was plentiful and distributed to consumers over enormous areas.

Our new artisans, with their power tools and amazingly diversified raw materials, are essentially Jacks-of-All-Trades, and their work consequently is never likely to exhibit the kind of excellence which distinguishes the work of highly trained specialists in a single craft. Moreover, the older craftsmen took for granted the style in which they had been brought up and reproduced the old models with only the slightest modification. When they departed from the traditional style, their work was apt to be eccentric or even downright bad. Today we know too much to be willing to follow any single style. Scholarship and photography have placed the whole of human culture within our reach. The modern amateur craftsman or amateur artist finds himself solicited by a thousand different and incompatible models. Shall he imitate Phidias or the Melanesians? Miró or van Eyck? Being under no cultural compulsion to adopt any particular line, he selects, combines, and blends. The result, in terms of art-as-significant-communication, is either negligible or monstrous, either an insipid hash or the most horrifying kind of raspberry, sardine, and chocolate sundae. Never mind! As a piece of occupational therapy, as a guarantee against boredom and an antidote to television and the other forms of passive entertainment, the thing is altogether admirable.

# Themes, Issues, and Ideas

1. What does technology have to do with what Huxley calls "the most important single fact of modern history—the rapid, the almost explosive increase in human numbers?" According to Huxley, what has been the cause of these numbers and what are their potential results?

2. With what reasoning does Huxley support this contention: "Every victory over Nature does unquestionably strengthen the position of the ruling minority?" Do you agree? Why, or why not?

3. What, according to Huxley, is the reason for technology's failure in the West to tyrannize its inhabitants?

# Writing Strategies and Techniques

1. After discussing the "do-it-yourself" movement, Huxley ends his paragraph with ellipsis marks (...). What is the effect of this technique?

2. By the end of a paragraph that begins with a discussion of metaphysics, Huxley has cited Aristotle, Queen Victoria, and Edward Lear as examples. What is the effect of the mixture in this list of intellectual status? Does Huxley use this same device elsewhere?

# Suggestions for Writing

1. Huxley says that art gives meaning to the chaos of experience and can act as an antidote to combat technology's potential evils. Do you agree with him? Write an essay in which you attack, support, or modify Huxley's views about the relations between art and technology.

2. Huxley claims that liberty was formerly ensured "not by constitutional guarantees, but by the backwardness of technology and the blessed inefficiency of the ruling minority." Write an essay analyzing the ways in which Huxley tries to show that advanced technology is a danger to human liberty.

# Old News Is Good News

## Bill Moyers

*Bill Moyers is the host of a long-running interview series on public television. Over the past 15 years, Moyers has interviewed leading thinkers, politicians, writers, and scholars in America. A conscientious critic of the press in this essay, he writes about the danger of mixing "hard news" and entertainment. As a journalist and producer as well as an interviewer, Moyers has seen many changes in American mass media, and it is these changes he addresses here.*

*This piece was originally published in* New Perspectives Quarterly.

Mine is the reporter's perspective—one small fish in that vast ocean we call the media. I want to put in a word for the craft, for reporting, the old-fashioned kind.

When I began working for *Harper's* in 1970, I thought I understood what the word "news" meant, where information stopped and entertainment began; what newspapers did that was different from television. Since then, we have witnessed a media explosion, the effect of which is like standing at ground zero seconds after the explosion of the atomic bomb. Walter Lippmann told us that journalism is a picture of reality people can act upon. What we see today is a society acting upon reality refracted a thousand different ways.

Where is America's mind today? It's in the organs, for one thing. Now folks can turn on a series called *Real Sex* and watch a home striptease class; its premier was HBO's highest-rated documentary for the year. Or they can flip over to NBC News and get *I Witness Video*. There they can see a policeman's murder recorded in his cruiser's camcorder, watch it replayed and relived in interviews, complete with ominous music. Or they can see the video of a pregnant woman plunging from a blazing building's window, can see it several times, at least once in slow motion. Yeats was right: "We have fed the heart of our fantasies, and the heart's grown brutal from the fare."

I wonder if *Real Sex* and *I Witness Video* take us deeper into reality or insanity? How does a reporter tell the difference anymore in world where Oliver Stone can be praised for his "journalistic instincts" when he has Lyndon Johnson tell a cabal of generals and admirals: "Get me elected and I'll get you your war."

*Rolling Stone* dubs all this the "New News." Straight news—the Old News by *Rolling Stone's* definition—is "pooped, confused, and broke." In its place a new culture of information is evolving—"a heady concoction, part Hollywood film and TV, part pop music and pop art, mixed with popular culture and celebrity magazines, tabloid telecasts, cable and home video." Increasingly, says the magazine, the New News is seizing the function of mainstream journalism, sparking conversation and setting the country's social and political agenda. So it is that we first learn from Bruce Springsteen that the jobs aren't coming back. So it is that inner-city parents who don't subscribe to daily newspapers are taking their children to see the movie *Juice* to educate them about the consequences of street violence; that young people think Bart Simpson's analysis of America more trenchant than many newspaper columnists; that we learn just how violent, brutal and desperate society is, not from the establishment press, but from Spike Lee, Public Enemy, the Geto Boys and Guns N' Roses.

I don't want to seem a moralist. The public often knows what's new before we professionals do. But there's a problem. In this vast pounding ocean of media, newspapers are in danger of extinction. I don't mean that they're going to disappear altogether—but I do feel that we are in danger of losing the central role the great newspapers have historically played in the functioning of our political system.

Once newspapers drew people to the public square. They provided a culture of community conversation. The purpose of news was not just to represent and inform, "but to signal, tell a story and activate inquiry." When the press abandons that function, it no longer stimulates what the American philosopher John Dewey termed "the vital habits" of democracy—"the ability to follow an argument, grasp the point of view of another, expand the boundaries of understanding, debate the alternative purposes that might be pursued."

I know times have changed, and so must the newspapers. I know that while it's harder these days to be a reporter, it's also harder to be a publisher, caught between *Sesame Street* and Wall Street—between the entertainment imperatives that are nurtured in the cradle and survival economics that can send a good paper to the grave.

Taken together, these assumptions and developments foreshadow the catastrophe of social and political paralysis. But what's truly astonishing about this civic disease is that it exists in America just as a series of powerful democratic movements have been toppling autocratic regimes elsewhere in the world. While people around the globe are clamoring for self-government, millions of Americans are feeling as if they have been locked out of their homes and are unable to regain their rightful place in the operation of democracy. On the other hand, those same millions want to believe that it is still in their power to change America.

The Center for Citizen Politics at the University of Minnesota reports that beneath America's troubled view of politics "is a public that cares very deeply about public life. This concern is a strong foundation for building healthy democratic practices and new traditions of public participation in politics."

People want to know what is happening to them, and what they can do about it. Listening to America, you realize that millions of people are not apathetic; they want to signify; and they will respond to a press that stimulates community without pandering to it; that inspires people to embrace their responsibilities without lecturing or hectoring them; and that engages their better natures without sugarcoating ugly realities or patronizing their foibles.

I sense we're approaching Gettysburg, the moment of truth, the decisive ground for this cultural war—for publishers especially. Americans say they no longer trust journalists to tell them the truth about their world. Young people have difficulty finding anything of relevance to their lives in the daily newspaper. Non-tabloid newspapers are viewed as increasingly elitist, self-important, and corrupt on the one hand; on the other, they are increasingly lumped together with the tabloids as readers perceive the increasing desperation with which papers are now trying to reach "down-market" in order to replace the young readers who are not replacing their elders.

Meanwhile, a study by the Kettering Foundation confirms that our political institutions are fast losing their legitimacy; that increasing numbers of Americans believe they are being dislodged from their rightful place in democracy by politicians, powerful lobbyists and the media—three groups they see as an autonomous political class impervious to the long-term interests of the country and manipulating the democratic discourse so that people are treated only as consumers to be entertained rather than citizens to be engaged.

## Themes, Issues, and Ideas

1. Moyers quotes a number of experts—philosophers, scientists, etc.—in his essay. Do you find these authorities convincing? Does Moyers himself come across, or qualify, as an "expert"?

2. "I wonder," Moyers writes, "if *Real Sex* and *I Witness Video* take us deeper into reality or insanity?" Is this a fair question? Why or why not? Compare shows like the ones Moyers mentions to public broadcasting shows like Moyers's own.

## Writing Strategies and Techniques

1. The author of this essay takes a very cautious, modest tone throughout. What effect does this have on the reader? How does he create this tone? Give examples.

2. "I don't want to seem a moralist," says Moyers. Why not? *Is* Moyers a moralist?

## Suggestions for Writing

1. Write an essay refuting Bill Moyers, copying his style as closely as possible.

2. Write a transcript of a Bill Moyers interview show on which you discuss television with Moyers. Or, write a transcript in which Bart Simpson is the interview guest.

# The Politics of Culture

## Jan Wenner

*Jan Wenner was the founder and editor of* Rolling
Stone, *the first major countercultural magazine of the
1960s to go mainstream. As the editor of* Rolling Stone,
*Wenner had a guiding influence on American mass cul-
ture for twenty-five years. Culture is not just a sidelight,
Wenner maintains; "hard news" gets late what "culture
news" gets early. Since his magazine was directly
attacked by Bill Moyers in his essay "Old News is Good
News," Wenner was invited by* New Perspectives Quarterly *to respond.*

$A$round the world and in our own country, the battles
being waged have more to do with culture than with politics. Mainstream media in the U.S. ignored cultural news throughout the 1960s
and '70s, yet it has been the cultural events of those years—changing
sexual and family values, growing cynicism and alienation among the
young, ethnic and cultural tensions, etc.—that have come to define the
political values of the '90s in the U.S.

The so-called "entertainment media" have been following these
changes all along. In fact, *Rolling Stone* was founded on the premise
that cultural news was important political news. We saw early on that
cultural, artistic and, ultimately, political styles all take shape in the
popular-culture cauldron.

People can debate high-brow versus low-brow culture, or rail
against the entertainment media's frivolity. But the fact remains that
though rap and riots, sexual roles and family values are finally being
covered in the traditional press, all these issues were explored much
earlier, in much greater depth and with more feeling in the entertainment media.

The mainstream press is now having to play catch-up, and it's going to be an uphill battle because it has for so long misinformed the public by misreading what's really on people's minds. Worse, they have repeated the most fallacious remarks by politicians about what's really at stake in this country, without examining those remarks—which, by the way, is the role the great newspapers *used* to play so well.

In a way, the traditional press is coming full circle. After years and years of missing the story and losing its readership, this political season—particularly *The New York Times* and *Newsweek*—have really focused on the issues. They have gone into great depth on economic issues and they are no longer allowing politicians to make statements that are merely repeated and left unchallenged.

Television coverage, on the other hand, continues to be abysmal. With regard to the Democratic and Republican conventions this summer, the television anchors and reporters simply stood in the way of what TV does best, which is to present the news unfiltered. During both conventions, talking heads focused on the technicalities of speeches and how they were delivered rather than what was said. A very limited number of people actually had anything valuable to add to the political proceedings. Certainly no one needed a pompous Dan Rather telling them what was going on. These "personalities" need to get out of the way and let Americans see and judge the political process for themselves.

## De-massifying the Media

No one should lament the fact that a decentralization and defusion of news has taken place. Such a change does not mean that we will now depend on *Us Magazine* to tell us about economic issues, or Bart Simpson to enlighten us about foreign affairs. It's not an either/or proposition. Pure political reporting is extremely important and cannot be replaced. But I daresay that these days Bart Simpson is more attuned to the American people's cynicism about the values and priorities of this country than any number of other programs that are on the air.

As news outlets have decentralized—through cable and alternative press publications—there has also been an integration of cultural and political news. It seems that the mainstream media have finally realized that they cannot understand the workings of this country unless they understand the politics of culture. This integration of cultural and political news—the trend so many journalistic purists lament—is a welcome change, as far as I'm concerned. Such admixing—think of *Murphy*

*Brown,* Ice T, or Oliver Stone's *JFK* on the "entertainment" side—has given access to those whose voices and perspectives were rarely heard in the traditional press but whose critiques of American values and priorities are shared by millions of people. Whether the issue is police brutality, single-parenthood or government coverups, it has often been the "entertainment media" that has pushed the debate onto America's political agenda.

# Themes, Issues, and Ideas

1.  Wenner makes the case that hard news that does not recognize popular culture is narrow and behind the times. Do you agree? How might the "politics of culture" work with regard to an issue currently in the press?

2.  Wenner defends Bart Simpson, calling him "more attuned" than many other TV characters to American moods. What is the advantage of being so attuned? How might traditional journalism benefit from such knowledge?

# Writing Strategies and Techniques

1.  Compare Jan Wenner's style to Bill Moyers's. Which is more convincing? Why? Give examples.

2.  Wenner uses the words "culture" and "cultural" often in his essay. Just what do these words mean as Wenner uses them? Compare a dictionary definition of these terms to the way Wenner and other writers use them. What are the advantages and disadvantages of a term as broad and flexible as "culture?"

# Suggestions for Writing

1.  Write an essay examining a piece of popular culture such as a TV show, a recording, or a magazine such as *Rolling Stone;* then write a news story from five years in the future describing its political effects.

2.  Write an essay comparing Jan Wenner's view of popular culture with Mark Crispin Miller's. Use Bart Simpson as an example.

# The Evolutionary Future of Man

## Richard Dawkins

*Oxford zoologist Richard Dawkins is one of the foremost experts on evolution in the world, as he has demonstrated in books such as* The Blind Watchmaker, River Out of Eden, *and* The Selfish Gene. *In this essay, he looks at a question that has plagued biologists since the time of Darwin: To what extent can trends in human life be traced to evolutionary causes and effects? In this essay, Dawkins discusses the idea of "progress" and how that concept functions in the long-term world of evolutionary biology.*

Evolution is widely regarded as a progressive force thrusting inexorably towards racial improvement, which may be seen as offering some tangible hope for our troubled species. Unfortunately this way of thinking is based on two misunderstandings. First, it is by no means clear that evolution is necessarily progressive. Second, even when it is progressive, significant change proceeds on a time-scale many orders of magnitude longer than the scale of tens or hundreds of years with which historians feel at home.

We can define evolutionary progress either in a value-laden or value-neutral way—ie, either with or without building in notions of what is good or bad. A value-laden definition specifies whether the factor being monitored, be it brain-size, intelligence, artistic ability, physical strength or whatever, is desirable or undesirable. If a desirable factor increases, that is progress. But on a value-neutral definition, any change at all counts as progress, just so long as it continues on its course. Such a definition simply takes three entities in a time sequence—think of them as a series of ancestral fossils and call them Early, Middle and Late—and asks whether the change from Early to Middle is in the same direction as the change from middle to late. If the answer is yes, that is a progressive change. This definition is value-neutral because the factor which we discover to be "progressive" could be something which we regard as bad—say idleness or stupidity. In this value-neutral sense, a continued trend towards decreased brain size would be progressive, just as much as a trend towards increased brain size would be. The only thing that would not be progressive would be a reversal of the trend.

It was once fashionable for biologists to believe in something called orthogenesis. This was the theory that trends in evolution constitute a driving force and continue under their own momentum. The Irish Elk was thought to have been driven extinct by its huge antlers, which in turn were thought to have grown bigger under the influence of an orthogenetic force. Perhaps initially there was some advantage in larger antlers and this was how the trend started. But, once started, the trend had its own internal unstoppability, and, as the generations went by, the antlers continued inexorably to grow until they drove the species extinct.

We now think that the theory of orthogenesis is wrong. If a trend is seen towards increasing antler size, this is because natural selection favours larger antlers. Individual stags with large antlers have more offspring than stags with average-sized antlers, either because they survive better (unlikely) or attract females (probably irrelevant) or because they are better at intimidating rivals (likely) If the trend appears to persist for a long time in the fossil record, this indicates that natural selection was pushing in that direction for all that time. Metaphors like "inherent force" and "inexorable momentum" have no validity.

It seems to follow that there is no general reason to expect evolution to be progressive—even in the weak, value-neutral sense. There will be times when increased size of some organ is favoured and other times when decreased size is favoured. Most of the time, average-sized individuals will be favoured in the population and both extremes will be penalised. During these times the population exhibits evolutionary stasis (ie, no change) with respect to the factor being measured. If we had a complete fossil record and looked for the trends in some particular dimension, such as leg length, we would expect to see periods of no change alternating with fitful continuations or reversals in direction—like a weathervane in changeable, gusty weather.

It is all the more intriguing to find that sometimes long, progressive trends in one direction do turn up. When an organ is used for intimidation (like a stag's antlers) or for attraction (like a peacock's tail), it may be that the best size to have—from the point of view of intimidation or attraction—is always slightly larger than the average in the population. Even when the average gets bigger, the optimum is always one step ahead. It is possible that such "moving-target selection" did drive the Irish Elk extinct after all: by pushing the "intimidation optimum" too far ahead of what would have been the overall "utilitarian optimum." Peacocks and male birds of paradise also seem to have been pushed, in this case by female-taste selection, far from the utilitarian optimum of an efficient flying and surviving machine (though they have not been driven over the edge into extinction).

Another force diving progressive evolution is the so-called "arms race." Prey animals evolve faster running speeds because predators do. Consequently predators have to evolve even faster running speeds, and so on, in an escalating spiral. Such arms races probably account for the spectacularly advanced engineering of eyes, ears, brains, bat "radar" and all the other high-tech weaponry that animals display. Arms races are a special case of "co-evolution." Co-evolution occurs whenever the environment in which creatures evolve is itself evolving. From an antelope's point of view, lions are part of the environment like the weather—with the important difference that lions evolve.

## Virtual Progress

I want to suggest a new kind of co-evolution which, I believe, may have been responsible for one of the most spectacular examples of progressive evolution: the enlargement of the human brain. At some point in the evolution of brains, they acquired the ability to simulate models of the outside world. In its advanced forms we call this ability "imagination." It may be compared to the virtual-reality software that runs on some computers. Now here is the point I want to make. The internal "virtual world" in which animals live may in effect become a part of the environment, of comparable importance to the climate, vegetation, predators and so on outside. If so, a co-evolutionary spiral may take off, with hardware—especially brain hardware—evolving to meet improvements in the internal "virtual environment." The changes in hardware then stimulate improvements in the virtual environment, and the spiral continues.

The progressive spiral is likely to advance even faster if the virtual environment is put together as a shared enterprise involving many individuals. And it is likely to reach breakneck speeds if it can accumulate progressively over generations. Language and other aspects of human culture provide a mechanism whereby such accumulation can occur. It may be that brain hardware has co-evolved with the internal virtual worlds that it creates. This can be called hardware-software co-evolution. Language could be both a vehicle of this co-evolution and its most spectacular product. We know almost nothing of how language originated, since it started to fossilise only very recently, in the form of writing. Hardware has been fossilising for much longer—at least the brain's bony outer casing has. Its steadily increasing size, indicating a corresponding increase in the size of the brain itself, is what I want to turn to next.

It is almost certain that modern *Homo sapiens* (which dates only from about 100,000 years ago) is descended from a similar species, *H. erectus,* which first appeared a little before 1.6m years ago. It is thought that *H. erectus,* in turn, was descended from some form of *Australopithecus.* A possible candidate which lived about 3m years ago is *Australopithecus afarensis,* represented by the famous "Lucy." These creatures, which are often described as upright-walking apes, had brains about the size of a chimpanzee's. Presumably the change from *Australopithecus* to *erectus* was gradual. This is not to say that it took 1½m years to accomplish at a uniform rate. It could easily have occurred in fits and starts. The same goes for the change from *erectus* to *sapiens.* By about 300,000 years ago, we start to find fossils that are called "archaic *H. sapiens",* largish-brained people like ourselves but with heavy brow ridges more like *H. erectus.*

It looks, in a general way, as though there are some progressive changes running through this series. Our braincase is nearly twice the size of *erectus*'s; and *erectus*'s braincase, in turn, is about twice the size of that of *Australopithecus afarensis.* This impression is vividly illustrated using a program called Morph.

To use Morph, you supply it with a starting picture and an ending picture, ant tell it which points on the starting picture correspond to which opposite-number points on the ending picture. Morph then computes a series of mathematical intermediates between the two pictures. The series may be viewed as a ciné film on the computer screen, but for printing it is necessary to extract a series of still frames—arranged in a spiral. The spiral includes two concatenated sequences: *Australopithecus* to *H. erectus* and *H. erectus* to *H. sapiens.* Conveniently the two time intervals separating these three landmark fossils are approximately the same, about 1.5m years. The three labelled landmark skulls constitute the data supplied to Morph. All the others are computed intermediates (ignore *H. futuris* for the moment).

Swirl your eye around the spiral looking for trends. It is broadly true that any trends you find before *H. erectus* continue after him. The film version show this much more dramatically, so much so that it is hard, as you watch the film, to detect any discontinuity as you pass through *H. erectus*. We have made similar films for a number of probable evolutionary transitions in human ancestry. More often than not, trends show reversals of direction. The relatively smoother continuity around *H. erectus* is quite unusual.

We can say that there has been a long, progressive—and by evolutionary standards very rapid—trend over the past 3m years of human skull evolution. I am speaking of progress in a value-neutral sense here. As it happens, anybody who thinks increased brain size has positive value can also claim this trend as value-laden progress too. This is because the dominant trend, flowing both before and after *H. erectus,* is the spectacular ballooning of the brain.

What of the future? Can we extrapolate the trend from *H. erectus* through and beyond *H. sapiens,* and predict the skull shape of *H. futuris* 3m years hence? Only an orthogeneticist would take it seriously; but, for what it is worth, we have made an extrapolation with the aid of Morph, and it is appended at the end of the spiral diagram. It shows a continuation of the trend to inflate the balloon of the braincase; the chin continues to move forward and sharpen into a silly little goatee point, while the jaw itself looks too small to chew anything but baby pap. Indeed the whole cranium is quite reminiscent of a baby's skull. It was long ago suggested that human evolution is an example of "paedomorphosis": the retention of juvenile characteristics into adulthood. The adult human skull looks more like a baby chimp's than like an adult chimp's.

## Don't Bank on *H. futuris*

Is there any likelihood that something like this hypothetical large-brained *H. futuris* will evolve? I'd put very little money on it, one way or the other. Certainly the mere fact that brain inflation has been the dominant trend over the past 3m years says almost nothing about probable trends in the next 3m. Brains will continue to inflate only if natural selection continues to favour large-brained individuals. This means, when you come down to it, if large-brained individuals manage to have, on average, more children than small-brained ones.

It is not unreasonable to assume that large brains go with intelligence, and that intelligence, in our wild ancestors, was associated with the ability to survive, ability to attract mates or ability to outwit rivals. Not unreasonable—but both these clauses would find their critics. It is an article of passionate faith among "politically correct" biologists and anthropologists that brain size has no connection with intelligence; that intelligence has nothing to do with genes; and that genes are probably nasty fascist things anyway.

Leaving this to one side, problems with the idea remain. In the days when most individuals died young, the main qualification for reproduction was survival into adulthood. But in our western civilisation few die young, most adults choose to have fewer children than they are physically and economically capable of, and it is by no means clear that people with the largest families are the most intelligent. Anybody viewing future human evolution from the perspective of advanced western civilsation is unlikely to make confident predictions about brain size continuing to evolve.

In any case, all these ways of viewing the matter are far too short-term. Socially important phenomena such as contraception and education exert their influences over the timescale of human historians, over decades and centuries. Evolutionary trends—at least those that last long enough to deserve the title progressive—are so slow that they are all but totally insensitive to the vagaries of social and historical time. If we could assume that something like our advanced scientific civilisation was going to last for 1m, or even 100,000, years, it might be worth thinking about the undercurrents of natural-selection pressure in these civilised conditions. But the likelihood is that, in 100,000 years time, we shall either have reverted to wild barbarism, or else civilisation will have advanced beyond all recognition—into colonies in outer space, for instance. In either case, evolutionary extrapolations from present conditions are likely to be highly misleading.

Evolutionists are usually pretty coy about predicting the future. Our species is a particularly hard one to predict because human culture, at least for the past few thousand years and speeding up all the time, changes in ways that mimic evolutionary change, only thousands to hundreds of thousands of times faster. This is most clearly seen when we look at technical hardware. It is almost cliché to point out that the wheeled vehicle, the aeroplane, and the electronic computer, to say nothing of more frivolous examples such as dress fashions, evolve in ways strikingly reminiscent of biological evolution. My formal definitions of value-laden and value-neutral progress, although designed for fossil bones, can be applied, without modification, to cultural and technological trends.

Prevailing skirt and hair lengths in western society are progressive—value-neutrally, because they are too trivial to anything else—for short periods if at all. Viewed over the timescale of decades, the average lengths fritters up and down like yo-yos. Weapons improve (at what they are designed to do, which may be of positive or negative value depending on your point of view) consistently and progressively, at least partly to counter improvements in the weaponry of enemies. But mostly, like any other technology, they improve because inventions build on earlier ones and inventors in any age benefit from the ideas, efforts and experiences of their predecessors. This principle is most spectacularly demonstrated by the evolution of the digital computer. The late Christopher Evans, a psychologist and author, calculated that if the motor car had evolved as fast as the computer, and over the same time period, "Today you would be able to buy a Rolls-Royce for £135, it would do three million miles to the gallon, and it would deliver enough power to drive the QE2. And if you were interested in miniaturisation, you could place half a dozen of them on a pinhead."

Science and the technology that it inspires can, of course, be used for backward ends. Continued trends in, say, aeroplane or computers speed, are undoubtedly progressive in a value-neutral sense. It would be easy to see them also as progressive in various value-laden senses. But such progress could also turn out to be laden with deeply negative value if the technologies fall into the hands of, say, religious fundamentalists bent on the destruction of rival sects who face a different point of the compass in order to pray, or some equally insufferable habit. Much may depend on whether the societies with the scientific know-how and the civilised values necessary to develop the technologies keep control of them; or whether they allow them to spread to educationally and scientifically backward societies which happen to have the money to buy them.

Scientific and technological progress themselves are value-neutral. They are just very good at doing what they do. If you want to do selfish, greedy, intolerant and violent things, scientific technology will provide you with by far the most efficient way of doing so. But if you want to do good, to solve the world's problems, to progress in the best value-laden sense, once again, there is not better means to those ends than the scientific way. For good or ill, I expect scientific knowledge and technical invention to develop progressively over the next 150 years, and at an accelerating rate.

## Themes, Issues, and Ideas

1. Why, according to Dawkins, does evolution not offer a sure-fire model for thinking about human progress?

2. What is the difference between "value-laden" and "value-neutral" biology? What might some examples be of "value-laden" and "value-neutral" ways of thinking about other subjects?

3. What do you suspect is Dawkins's view of divine providence? Or for that matter, what do you think would be his view of Havel's "Gaia Hypothesis"?

## Writing Strategies and Techniques

1. Describe the tone that Dawkins's takes in this essay. How is it different from the tone taken by other experts in this book? How is it alike? What is its effect on you as a reader?

2. Do you find Dawkins's way of talking about nature and biology satisfying? Explain your answer.

## Suggestions for Writing

1. Write an essay, complete with a chart, in which you show how a trend has gone and predict it into the future.

2. "If we could assume that something like our advanced scientific civilization was going to last for 1m or even 100,000 years, it might be worth thinking about the undercurrents of natural selection pressure." Write an essay that makes that assumption.

# Automated Fabrication: Creating Ultracustomized Products

## Marshall Burns

*Most predictions about the technology of the coming century have, in general, tended to project current technologies into more and more advanced forms—videophones, for example, or electric cars. But according to Marshall Burns, a far more radical departure might be in store if automated fabrication or "autofab" comes into being. Marshall Burns is the president of a leading autofabrication firm, and the author of the book* Automated Fabrication: Improving Productivity in Manufacturing *(1993), His can be reached via e-mail at autofab @ennex.com.*

Imagine sitting in a car showroom, putting together your dream car on the computer screen, and, later that week, having that car—constructed exactly to your specifications—delivered to you. Such an accomplishment may be possible early next century through a process known as automated fabrication.

Automated fabrication, or "autofab," is a set of technologies that automate the processes for building three-dimensional solid objects from raw materials. This growing industry uses controlled solidification of polymers, powders, and other raw materials, guided by designs drawn on ordinary desktop computers. Autofab allows designers to make quick design changes, construct an object to precise dimensions, and create products with complex geometric surfaces.

Autofab could have an even more fundamental impact on society and economics than computers have had. The introduction and growth of computers have been heralded by some as a new era of human history, the so-called "Information Age." This idea supposes that the greatest value in our society is now placed on information and on the tools and skills for storing and manipulating it. But it is possible that the Information Age will be short-lived, superseded by a new age in which humans acquire untold powers to manipulate the properties of matter in much the same way that computers manipulate information.

## Customers and Co-construction

Autofab, along with computer-aided design and simulations, is now creating opportunities for manufacturers to satisfy the unique needs of customers. But to satisfy these needs, a manufacturer has to work with the customer to establish what those needs are. This is not always clear, even to the customer. Inviting the customer into the design, development, and production processes will likely lead to unexpected new products of which the customer is then a "co-constructor."

In co-construction, the customer does more than just give the manufacturer a list of specifications; rather, he or she actually participates in the ongoing experimentation with prototypes. The relationship between manufacturer and customer becomes longer term, and customer loyalty increases (as long as the quality of service is maintained). Product liability and other risks may be shared, along with patent rights to new technology. Instead of promoting their individual products, manufacturers market their "process prowess."

Customer co-construction represents a major change in the manufacturer's function in relation to customers. But it is only the tip of the iceberg of the coming Autofab Revolution.

## The Autofab Society

Automated fabrication will have dramatic impacts on society.

- **Entrepreneurial opportunities.** The rise of autofab brings opportunities for entrepreneurs and small manufacturers—even individual consumers—to participate in the development, manufacturing, distribution, use, and repair of fabricators and related hardware and software.

- **Reduced demand for skilled labor.** Fabrication facilities are already realizing hundredfold and thousandfold increases in productivity. While this influence has been resisted by large American manufacturers and their unions, there is under way a relentless decline in the amount of human effort needed to produce manufactured goods. The ultimate effect of this trend is yet to be determined.

- **The return of the "village crafts worker."** If mass production loses its economic advantage, huge centralized factories could disappear and be replaced by smaller, community-based facilities. In a co-construction environment, the customer may be served better by a local owner and operator of a manufacturing shop. Thus, factories will become decentralized. For marketing purposes, these jobs shops may be united into chains or franchises, but the facilities and expertise will be distributed widely to meet local needs.

- **Better product quality.** The automation of fabrication processes, together with automated methods of inspection and assembly, are improving the quality and durability of products. One effect is that cars, televisions, refrigerators, and many other products are lasting much longer than earlier models. The unfortunate irony for manufacturers is the resulting decline in need for replacement goods.

- **More recycling.** Instead of buying the latest model of a car or toaster and throwing away the old one, customers will return their older models to fabrication devices that will use them to build a new model. Fabricators that build up objects from melted or reprocessed plastics and metals will make the recycling of these materials practical in new ways.

- **Process-based commerce.** Instead of going into a store to buy goods, the customer of the future will probably select designs from a computer simulation. For more complex and larger jobs, such as a new body style for the family car or a computer keyboard with customized keys, a local fabricator shop or contractor may be called in.

- **New medical treatments.** As the scale of autofab shrinks to the nanostructure level, companies will be able to manufacture medical instruments that are no bigger than a drug molecule. These nanoinstruments will permit noninvasive investigation and treatment of diseases, reversal of natural tissue decay, and even artificial reconstruction of tissue contrary to the ingrained genetic design of an individual. The extension of the human life-span will continue and accelerate, the health of old people will improve, and people will gain the ability to painlessly redesign their bodies.

The combined effect of such changes could be dramatic. It is conceivable that, at some point in the twenty-first century, a small mountaintop community could be self-sufficient with a collection of fabricators and a solar-powered generator. While economically independent, it would be linked by satellite, jet, and rocket to other such villages around the world and on the moon.

## The Fabrication Revolution

After 45 years of development, the autofab industry is just now beginning to bloom. Off on the horizon, one can see autofab technologies being refined in accuracy to become the kind of machines that are being prophesied for nanotechnology—machines that could build things one atom or molecule at a time.

When the methods are advanced to such a level, the form of the raw materials used will be unimportant. Such machines will be capable of rearranging molecular structures in order to generate almost any conceivable object from them. Plastic milk jugs and last night's ruined casserole could be molecularly rearranged to form, for example, a new table lamp. This will not only be the ultimate style of manufacturing, but solve our recycling problems as well.

Many fabrication services would no doubt arise, ready to manufacture locally on a contract basis. They could be like old-fashioned machine shops or perhaps, more likely, arise in the form of chains or franchises. A "Fabricators-R-Us" shop could join the 7-Eleven, Kinko's Copies, and McDonald's now in every town.

However, with such widespread, easy use of this technology, problems are bound to develop. Just as computer software can now be illegally copied and distributed with a dizzying efficiency, it will one day be possible to fabricate unauthorized copies of a Rolex watch, a Panasonic fax machine, a Cadillac automobile, or even fabricators themselves. This may bring about the need for various restrictions and licensing. Fabrication software and devices may end up being allowed for one-time use only, or else royalty payments may be structured into their sale.

Eventually, personal fabricators may become available to anyone. These tabletop devices would fabricate everything from guest-customized dinner plates to replacement dishwasher parts and will cost about the same as a car.

As autofab technology improves, perhaps meeting most of our material desires, the resulting freedom from need might usher in a new golden age of art, music, and scientific discovery. But the open question is whether people want such freedom and will rejoice in it. In life, it is often found that the greatest satisfaction comes not from getting what one wants, but from working for it. The greatest challenge facing humanity as we proceed into the age of automated fabrication is to find a meaningful use for ourselves as we allow our machines to take over the satisfaction of our material needs and desires.

## Themes, Issues, and Ideas

1. What, according to Burns, will be the biggest change brought about by autofab?

2. What do find most questionable of the various claims Burns makes for autofab? Which the most persuasive? Why?

3. What might be some unexpected implications of the "autofab revolution" for 21st-century society, based on other essays you have read in this book?

## Writing Strategies and Techniques

1. Does Burns impress you with his understanding of technology? Does he impress you as an authority on technology and social change? Explain why or why not, and give examples.

2. What do you think were some of the major problems confronting Burns when he sat down to write this essay? How did he solve them?

## Suggestions for Writing

1. Write a scenario describing the life of Burns's "city on a hill."

2. Write an essay entitled "Autofab and the American Way."

# Is Progress Obsolete?

## Christopher Lasch

*Christopher Lasch was one of the most provocative and insightful of American cultural historians. Throughout his career, he angered both the left and the right with his critiques of American society, most notably in* The Culture of Narcissism *(1979) and* The True and Only Heaven *(1991). A professor of history at the University of Rochester, Lasch died in 1995.*

*In this essay, written for a special issue of* Time *magazine on the coming century, Lasch argues that progress, the pride of American society for so long, has finally run up against the wall.*

Progress and democracy, we assume, go hand in hand. Progress means abundance; more labor-saving machines, more comforts, more choices. It means a rich life for everyone, not for the privileged classes alone. Or so we used to believe, until recent events began to suggest that progress may have limits after all.

Compared with the rest of the world, industrial nations enjoy a lavish standard of living. The affluence generated by industrialism looks even more impressive when compared with living standards that prevailed throughout most of the millennium now drawing to a close. Goods that would once have been considered luxuries have become staples of everyday consumption. Medicine has reduced infant mortality and conquered many of the diseases that formerly struck down people in their prime. A vast increase in life expectancy dramatizes the contrast between our world and that of our ancestors in the distant past.

To be sure, we pay a price for progress. Constant change gives rise to widespread nervousness and anxiety. In solving old problems, we often create new ones in their place. Improvements in life expectancy make possible an aging population that puts a growing strain on the health-care system. Private cars give us unprecedented mobility but swell the volume of traffic to the point of gridlock. In the course of enjoying the delights of consumption, we generate so much garbage that we are running out of places to dump it.

Yet none of this destroys our faith in progress. The benefits, we think, outweigh the costs. As long as the question of progress is posed in this way, the question answers itself. The price may be high, but few would seriously choose not to pay it. Progress is an offer we have been unable to refuse.

The real question today is whether progress has built-in limits. Environmentalists argue that the earth will not support indefinite economic expansion along the old lines. Reports of global warming, damage to the ozone layer and long-term atmospheric shifts caused by deforestation raise further doubts about unlimited growth. Even though much of this evidence remains controversial, it has already transformed the debate about progress. For the first time we find ourselves asking not whether endless progress is desirable but whether it is even possible, as we have known it in the past.

The global distribution of wealth raises the same question in a more urgent form. If we consider the effect of extending Western patterns of consumption to the rest of the world, the potential impact on the earth is truly staggering. Imagine the populations of India and China equipped with two cars to a family, air conditioning in private homes and appliances galore, participating fully in a consumer economy that already makes heavy demands on the world's environment even when it is confined to a mere fraction of the world's population. It is obvious that the wasteful, heedless life now enjoyed by the West cannot be made available to everyone without stretching the energy resources of the earth, as well as its adaptive capacity, beyond the breaking point.

The idea of progress loses all meaning if progress no longer implies the democratization of affluence. It was the prospect of universal abundance that made progress a morally compelling ideology in the past. According to the old way of thinking, the productive forces unleashed by industrialism generated a steadily rising level of demand. Even humble men and women could now see the possibility of bettering their condition. The desire for a full life, formerly restricted to the rich, would spread to the masses. The expansion of desire—the motor of progress—would assure the expansion of the economic machinery necessary to satisfy it. Economic development would thus continue indefinitely in a self-generating upward spiral, without any foreseeable end or limit.

But affluence for all now appears unlikely, even in the distant future. The emergence of a global economy, far from eliminating poverty, has widened the gap between rich and poor nations. The revolution of rising expectations may not be self-generating, as we had thought. It may even be reversible. Famine and plague have returned to large parts of the world. Poverty is spilling over into the developed nations from the Third World. Desperate migrants pour into our cities, swelling the vast army of the homeless, unemployed, illiterate, drug-ridden, derelict and effectively disenfranchised. Their presence strains existing resources to the limit. Medical and educational facilities, law-enforcement agencies and the supply of available jobs—not to mention the supply of racial and ethnic goodwill, never abundant to begin with—all appear inadequate to the enormous task of assimilating what is essentially a surplus population.

The well-being of democracy, a political system that implies equality as well as liberty, hangs in the balance. A continually rising standard of living for the rich, it is clear, means a falling standard of living for everyone else. Forcible redistribution of income on a massive scale is an equally unattractive alternative. The best hope of reducing the gap between rich and poor lies in the gradual emergence of a new consensus, a common understanding about the material prerequisites of a good life. Hard questions will have to be asked. Just how much do we need to live comfortably? How much is enough?

Such questions implicitly challenge the notion of progress, which is usually taken to mean there is no such thing as enough. The prospect of a world in which people voluntarily agree to set limits on their acquisitive appetite bears little resemblance to what is conventionally understood as progress. But then neither does the prospect of a world in which unparalleled affluence coexists with frightful depths of misery and squalor.

# Themes, Issues, and Ideas

1. Is it true, as Lasch says, that "none of [our problems] destroys our faith in progress"? Give examples both supporting and refuting this statement.

2. The dynamic Lasch explains in the paragraph beginning "The idea of progress..." is somewhat complex. Give an example that might demonstrate it.

3. "How much is enough?" Lasch asks. What is your answer to this question? Using Lasch's test, could the earth support "enough" for everyone in China and India?

# Writing Strategies and Techniques

1. Lasch's style of writing, here as elsewhere, is objective and forceful, like that of a wise judge. Does this style appeal to you? Does it tend to persuade you?

2. Lasch, like all the authors in this book, makes certain assumptions about the world and about his reader. Identify five of each type of assertion.

# Suggestions for Writing

1. Write an essay in which you apply Lasch's thesis to progress in your hometown.

2. Write an essay defending the idea of progress that specifically addresses Lasch's argument.

# MAKING CONNECTIONS

1. In "Old News Is Good News," Bill Moyers talks about the dangers of too much public information. Describe how even trivial and distracting information can be easily dangerous.

2. Compare Jan Wenner's idea of popular culture in "The Politics of Culture" to Mark Crispin Miller's "Big Brother Is You, Watching" (Chapter 6). What does each writer think is the source of popular culture? Write an essay explaining each writer's assumptions about the nature and dynamics of American mass culture.

3. The fears and the hopes brought about by technology are two of the themes that run through the essays in this chapter. Describe the relationship between the two, and, using information from as many readings as you wish, write an essay stating and supporting your opinions on what we have to expect from technology now and in the near future.

4. Richard Dawkins seems to take a much longer point of view than the other authors in this chapter. Partially, this is due to the fact that he is the only scientist. Does this change his view of technology's effect on human life? What would be Dawkins's responses to the claims of the other authors in this chapter? Do any of those authors offer models which might be analogous to the evolutionary ones in Dawkins's essay? Explain.

5. What in Aldous Huxley's argument would Christopher Lasch most agree with?

# CHAPTER
## TEN

# *Science, Technology, and the Human Environment*

*You and the Earth of Tomorrow*

# THE PAST AS PROLOGUE

## Silent Spring
### A Fable for Our Time

Rachel Carson

*Rachel Carson (1907–1964) studied at the Johns Hopkins University and the Marine Biological Laboratory at Woods Hole, Massachusetts. Her books about the natural world* Under the Sea Wind *(1951) and* The Sea Around Us *(1954) were enormous bestsellers, and as a nature writer she is remembered as a pioneer.*

*It is her book* Silent Spring *(1962) for which she is best remembered.* Silent Spring, *from which this excerpt is taken, first sounded the alarm about the damaging effects of chemical pesticides and fertilizers. President John F. Kennedy took notice of the book and ordered a federal investigation whose aftereffects are still being felt today. As an environmental advocate and as a woman, Rachel Carson was a model who will be followed far into the twenty-first century.*

T here was once a town in the heart of America where all life seemed to live in harmony with its surroundings. The town lay in the midst of a checkerboard of prosperous farms, with fields of grain and hillsides of orchards where, in spring, white clouds of bloom drifted above the green fields. In autumn, oak and maple and birch set up a blaze of color that flamed and flickered across a backdrop of pines. Then foxes barked in the hills and deer silently crossed the fields, half hidden in the mists of the tall mornings.

Along the roads, laurel, viburnum and alder, great ferns and wild-flowers delighted the traveler's eyes through much of the year. Even in winter the roadsides were places of beauty, where countless birds came to feed on the berries and on the seed heads of the dried weeds rising above the snow. The countryside was, in fact, famous for the abundance and variety of its bird life, and when the flood of migrants was pouring through in spring and fall people traveled from great distances to observe them. Others came to fish the streams, which flowed clear and cold out of the hills and contained shady pools where trout lay. So it had been from the days many years ago when the first settlers raised their houses, sank their wells, and built their barns.

Then a strange blight crept over the area and everything began to change. Some evil spell had settled on the community: mysterious maladies swept the flocks of chickens; the cattle and sheep sickened and died. Everywhere was a shadow of death. The farmers spoke of much illness among their families. In the town the doctors had become more and more puzzled by new kinds of sickness appearing among their patients. There had been several sudden and unexplained deaths, not only among adults but even among children, who would be stricken suddenly while at play and die within a few hours.

There was a strange stillness. The birds, for example—where had they gone? Many people spoke of them, puzzled and disturbed. The feeding stations in the backyards were deserted. The few birds seen anywhere were moribund; they trembled violently and could not fly. It was a spring without voices. On the mornings that had once throbbed with the dawn chorus of robins, catbirds, doves, jays, wrens, and scores of other bird voices there was now no sound; only silence lay over the fields and woods and marsh.

On the farms the hens brooded, but no chicks hatched. The farmers complained that they were unable to raise any pigs—the litters were small and the young survived only a few days. The apple trees were coming into bloom but no bees droned among the blossoms, so there was no pollination and there would be no fruit.

The roadsides, once so attractive, were now lined with browned and withered vegetation as though swept by fire. These, too, were silent, deserted by all living things. Even the streams were now lifeless. Anglers no longer visited them, for all the fish had died.

In the gutters under the eaves and between the shingles of the roofs, a white granular powder still showed a few patches; some weeks before it had fallen like snow upon the roofs and the lawns, the fields and streams.

No witchcraft, no enemy action had silenced the rebirth of new life in this stricken world. The people had done it themselves.

This town does not actually exist, but it might easily have a thousand counterparts in American or elsewhere in the world. I know of no community that has experienced all the misfortunes I describe. Yet every one of these disasters has actually happened somewhere, and many real communities have already suffered a substantial number of them. A grim specter has crept upon us almost unnoticed, and this imagined tragedy may easily become a stark reality we all shall know.

# Themes, Issues, and Ideas

1. Does Carson's image of environmental devastation seem characteristic of her time? Why or why not?

2. What are some of the gifts of nature to the town? Which are most important among these? Why?

3. What other scenes of lifelessness and desolation does Carson's fable remind you of?

# Writing Strategies and Techniques

1. Why is this essay called "a fable"? How is it like or unlike other fables?

2. When Carson speaks about "evil spells" and "strange blights" she is not using the language of science. What language is she using? Why?

# Suggestions for Writing

1.  Write a fable, similar to Carson's, but about a city.

2.  Write an essay considering nature as you have experienced it. How has it been threatened? What changes have you seen that seemed mysterious at the time?

# Ecology: The New Sacred Agenda

## Albert Gore, Jr.

*Al Gore has long been an advocate on environmental issues, first as a senator from Tennessee, and currently in his position as Vice-President of the United States. His 1992 book* Earth in the Balance *was a bestseller nationwide, and helped many thousands of Americans understand the environmental issues that Gore felt most needed addressing.*

*The reading below was taken from an issue of* New Perspectives Quarterly *in which Gore, then a senator, established a moral footing for his environmental crusade. Here, Gore goes beyond statistics and puts forth the idea of environmental responsibility as the last gasp of faith by a secular, consumption-based society. Whether or not Gore's position changes with his job as Vice-President is something any reader of the following essay will certainly want to pursue.*

I fear that we are on a downslope toward a future catastrophic event that will dim history. At a gut level, people throughout the world realize that the environment is the issue of our time. In the not too distant future, there will be a new "sacred agenda" in international affairs: policies that enable the rescue of the global environment. I agree with the Spring 1989 issue of *NPQ* that this task will one day join, and then perhaps supplant, efforts to prevent the world's incineration through nuclear war as the principal test of statecraft.

When we consider the relationship of the human species to the planet Earth, not much change is visible in a single year, in a single nation. Yet, if we look at the entire pattern of that relationship from the emergence of the species until today, a distinctive contrast in very recent times clearly conveys the danger to which we must respond. It took ten thousand human lifetimes for the population to reach two billion. Now, in the course of a single human lifetime the world population is rocketing from two billion toward ten billion, and is already halfway there.

Startling graphs showing the loss of forest land, topsoil, stratospheric ozone, and species all follow the same pattern of sudden, unprecedented acceleration in the latter half of the 20th century. And yet, so far, the pattern of our politics remains remarkably unchanged. To date, we have tolerated self-destructive behavior and environmental vandalism on a global scale.

Even with top-level political focus, the pervasive nature of all the activities that cumulatively create the greenhouse effect make the global solutions almost unimaginably difficult. Therefore, our first task is to expand the circumference of what is imaginable. It is not now imaginable, for example, to radically reduce $CO_2$ emissions. Even if all other elements of the problem are solved, a major threat is still posed by emissions of carbon dioxide, the exhaling breath of the industrial culture upon which our civilization rests. Yet, emissions must be curbed. We can make that task imaginable by building our confidence with successful assaults on more easily achievable targets, like elimination of CFCs and reversing the practice of deforesting the earth.

The cross-cut between the imperatives of growth and the imperatives of environmental management represents a supreme test for modern industrial civilization. Can we devise dynamic new strategies that will accommodate economic growth within a stabilized environmental framework?

The effort to solve the global environmental problem will be complicated not only by blind assertions that more and more environmental manipulation and more and more resource extraction are essential for economic growth. It will also be complicated by the emergence of simplistic demands that development, or technology itself, must be stopped. This is a crisis of confidence that must be addressed.

There is no assurance that a balance can be struck. Nevertheless, the effort must be made. And because of the urgency, scope and even the improbability of complete success in such an endeavor, I will borrow from military terminology: To deal with the global environment, we will need the environmental equivalent of the Strategic Defense Initiative—a Strategic Environment Initiative. Even opponents of SDI, of which I am one, recognize that this effort has been remarkably success-ful in drawing together previously disconnected government programs, in stimulating development of new technologies, and in forcing a new wave of intense analysis of subjects previously thought to have been exhausted.

I have likened our newfound awareness of ozone depletion and the greenhouse effect to the Kristallnacht which forewarned the holo-caust. The logic of this analogy can be extended, as *NPQ* editor Nathan Gardels did in his foreword to the Spring 1989 issue on the ecology, to include Hannah Arendt's memorable notion of "the banality of evil" which emerged from her reflections on Hitler's lieutenants at the Eich-mann trial.

My own religious faith teaches me that we are given dominion over the earth, but that we are also required to be good stewards. If, dur-ing our lifetimes, we witness the destruction of half the living species God put on this earth, we will have failed in our responsibility as stew-ards. Are those actions, because of their result, "evil?" The answer depends upon our knowledge of their consequences. The individual actions that collectively produce the world's environmental crisis are indeed banal when they are looked at one by one—the cutting of a tree, the air conditioning of a car. The willingness to trace the line of respon-sibility from individual action to collective effect is a challenge that we as a civilization have not yet learned to master.

"Evil" and "good" are terms not frequently used by politicians. And, yes, we know from historical experience the dangers of mixing public policy and religion. but, in my own view, while we must avoid zealotry, this ecological crisis cannot be met without reference to spiri-tual values.

In truth, as a civilization, we don't have much faith left. The idea that we can totally abandon any but the secular values comes perilously close to saying that nothing has worth unless it can be consumed in our lifetimes.

The word "faith" need not be defined in conventional religious terms. Whether or not an individual has faith in life after death, they must have faith that life on earth continues after their death. If we are so far gone as a civilization that such a belief system cannot be put together, then nothing can save this species.

Ultimately, I believe that the ecological solution will be found in a new faith in the future of life on earth after our own, a faith in the future that sacrifices in the present, a new moral courage to choose higher values in the conduct of human affairs, and a new reverence for absolute principles that can serve as guiding stars by which to map the future course of our species.

## Themes, Issues, and Ideas

1. What, according to Gore, are our best reasons for preserving the environment?

2. Gore states that, "as a civilization we don't have much faith left." Do you agree with this statement? Can you provide some evidence for both sides of the question?

3. At the end of his essay, Gore calls for a "new reverence for absolute principles that can serve as guiding stars. . . ." What might some of those principles be?

## Writing Strategies and Techniques

1. The Vice-President has often been criticized for the stilted, wooden character of his speeches. Based on this essay, would you say that is a fair assessment? Give examples from the reading to support your view.

2. In what ways is the style of this essay much like the positions that it advocates?

## Suggestions for Writing

1. Write an essay in which you describe your feelings toward subsequent generations, possibly in the form of a letter to your grandchildren.

2. "The idea that we can totally abandon any but the most secular values comes perilously close to saying that nothing has worth unless it can be consumed in our lifetimes." Write an essay affirming or denying this statement of Gore's, using examples from your own experience as well as from this and other reading selections.

# In the Jungle

## Annie Dillard

*As the South American rain forests continue to disappear, they become an ever-more precious resource for industrialized peoples like ourselves. At least Annie Dillard, in visiting the Napo River in the Ecuadorian jungle, found it so. To Dillard, the rain forest is not so much a corner of the world, but a part of the world's real self. In this selection from her book* Teaching a Stone to Talk *(1988), Dillard describes a place so remote that it seems to be at the center of everything.*

*Dillard first sprang to prominence as a nature writer in 1974, when her first book,* Pilgrim at Tinker Creek, *won that year's Pulitzer prize. Her most recent books include* The Writing Life *(1991) and* An American Childhood *(1987).*

Like any out-of-the-way place, the Napo River in the Ecuadorian jungle seems real enough when you are there, even central. Out of the way of *what?* I was sitting on a stump at the edge of a bankside palm-thatch village, in the middle of the night, on the headwaters of the Amazon. Out of the way of human life, tenderness, or the glance of heaven?

A nightjar in deep-leaved shadow called three long notes, and hushed. The men with me talked softly in clumps: three North Americans, four Ecuadorians who were showing us the jungle. We were holding cool drinks and idly watching a hand-sized tarantula seize moths that came to the lone bulb on the generator shed beside us.

It was February, the middle of summer. Green fireflies spattered lights across the air and illumined for seconds, now here, now there, the pale trunks of enormous, solitary trees. Beneath us the brown Napo River was rising, in all silence; it coiled up the sandy bank and tangled its foam in vines that trailed from the forest and roots that looped the shore.

Each breath of night smelled sweet, more moistened and sweet than any kitchen, or garden, or cradle. Each star in Orion seemed to tremble and stir with my breath. All at once, in the thatch house across the clearing behind us, one of the village's Jesuit priests began playing an alto recorder, playing a wordless song, lyric, in a minor key, that twined over the village clearing, that caught in the big trees' canopies, muted our talk on the bankside, and wandered over the river, dissolving downstream.

This will do, I thought. This will do, for a weekend, or a season, or a home.

Later that night I loosed my hair from its braids and combed it smooth—not for myself, but so the village girls could play with it in the morning.

We had disembarked at the village that afternoon, and I had slumped on some shaded steps, wishing I knew some Spanish or some Quechua so I could speak with the ring of little girls who were alternately staring at me and smiling at their toes. I spoke anyway, and fooled with my hair, which they were obviously dying to get their hands on, and laughed, and soon they were all braiding my hair, all five of them, all fifty fingers, all my hair, even my bangs. And then they took it apart and did it again, laughing, and teaching me Spanish nouns, and meeting my eyes and each other's with open delight, while their small brothers in blue jeans climbed down from the trees and began kicking a volleyball with one of the North American men.

Now, as I combed my hair in the little tent, another of the men, a free-lance writer from Manhattan, was talking quietly. He was telling us the tale of his life, describing his work in Hollywood, his apartment in Manhattan, his house in Paris.... "It makes me wonder," he said, "what I'm doing in a tent under a tree in the village of Pompeya, on the Napo River, in the jungle of Ecuador." After a pause he added, "It makes me wonder why I'm going *back*."

The point of going somewhere like the Napo River in Ecuador is not to see the most spectacular anything. It is simply to see what is there. We are here on the planet only once, and might as well get a feel for the place. We might as well get a feel for the fringes and hollows in which life is lived, for the Amazon basin, which covers half a continent,

and for the life that—there, like anywhere else—is always and necessarily lived in detail: on the tributaries, in the riverside villages, sucking
this particular white-fleshed guava in this particular pattern of shade.

What is there is interesting. The Napo River itself is wide (I mean
wider than the Mississippi at Davenport) and brown, opaque, and
smeared with floating foam and logs and branches from the jungle.
White egrets hunch on shoreline deadfalls and parrots in flocks dart in
and out of the light. Under the water in the river, unseen, are anacon-
das—which are reputed to take a few village toddlers every year—and
water boas, stingrays, crocodiles, manatees, and sweet-meated fish.

Low water bares gray strips of sandbar on which the natives build
tiny palm-thatch shelters, arched, the size of pup tents, for overnight
fishing trips. You see these extraordinarily clean people (who bathe
twice a day in the river, and whose straight black hair is always freshly
washed) paddling down the river in dugout canoes, hugging the banks.

Some of the Indians of this region, earlier in the century, used to
sleep naked in hammocks. The nights are cold. Gordon MacCreach, an
American explorer in these Amazon tributaries, reported that he was
startled to hear the Indians get up at three in the morning. He was even
more startled, night after night, to hear them walk down the river
slowly, half asleep, and bathe in the water. Only later did he learn what
they were doing: they were getting warm. The cold woke them; they
warmed their skins in the river, which was always ninety degrees; then
they returned to their hammocks and slept through the rest of the night.

The riverbanks are low, and from the river you see an unbroken
wall of dark forest in every direction, from the Andes to the Atlantic.
You get a taste for looking at trees; trees hung with the swinging nests
of yellow troupials, trees from which ant nests the size of grain sacks
hang like black goiters, trees from which seven-colored tanagers flutter,
coral trees, teak, balsa and breadfruit, enormous emergent silk-cotton
trees, and the pale-barked *samona* palms.

When you are inside the jungle, away from the river, the trees
vault out of sight. It is hard to remember to look up the long trunks and
see the fans, strips, fronds, and sprays of glossy leaves. Inside the jungle you are more likely to notice the snarl of climbers and creepers
round the trees' boles, the flowering bromeliads and epiphytes in every
bough's crook, and the fantastic silk-cotton tree trunks thirty or forty
feet across, trunks buttressed in flanges of wood whose curves can
make three high walls of a room—a shady, loamy-aired room where
you would gladly live, or die. Butterflies, iridescent blue, striped, or

clear-winged, thread the jungle paths at eye level. And at your feet is a swath of ants bearing triangular bits of green leaf. The ants with their leaves look like a wide fleet of sailing dinghies—but they don't quit. In either direction they wobble over the jungle floor as far as the eye can see. I followed them off the path as far as I dared, and never saw an end to ants or to those luffing chips of green they bore.

Unseen in the jungle, but present, are tapirs, jaguars, many species of snake and lizard, ocelots, armadillos, marmosets, howler monkeys, toucans and macaws and a hundred other birds, deer, bats, peccaries, capybaras, agoutis, and sloths. Also present in this jungle, but variously distant, are Texaco derricks and pipelines, and some of the wildest Indians in the world, blowgun-using Indians, who killed missionaries in 1956 and ate them.

Long lakes shine in the jungle. We traveled one of these in dugout canoes, canoes with two inches of freeboard, canoes paddled with machete-hewn oars chopped from buttresses of silk-cotton trees, or poled in the shallows with peeled cane or bamboo. Our part-Indian guide had cleared the path to the lake the day before; when we walked the path we saw where he had impaled the lopped head of a boa, open-mouthed, on a pointed stick by the canoes, for decoration.

This lake was wonderful. Herons, egrets, and ibises plodded the sawgrass shores, kingfishers and cuckoos clattered from sunlight to shade, great turkeylike birds fussed in dead branches, and hawks lolled overhead. There was all the time in the world. A turtle slid into the water. The boy in the bow of my canoe slapped stones at birds with a simple sling, a rubber thong and a leather pad. He aimed brilliantly at moving targets, always, and always missed; the birds were out of range. He stuffed his sling back in his shirt. I looked around.

The lake and river waters were as opaque as rain-forest leaves; they are veils, blinds, painted screens. You see things only by their effects. I saw the shoreline water roil and the sawgrass heave above a thrashing *paichi*, an enormous black fish of these waters; one had been caught the previous week weighing 430 pounds. Piranha fish live in the lakes, and electric eels. I dangled my fingers in the water, figuring it would be worth it.

We would eat chicken that night in the village, and rice, yucca, onions, beets, and heaps of fruit. The sun would ring down, pulling darkness after it like a curtain. Twilight is short, and the unseen birds of twilight wistful, uncanny, catching the heart. The two nuns in their dazzling white habits—the beautiful-boned young nun and the warm-faced old—would glide to the open cane-and-thatch schoolrooms in darkness, and start the children singing. The children would sing in piping Spanish, high-pitched and pure; they would sing "Nearer My God to Thee" in Quechua, very fast. (To reciprocate, we sang for them "Old MacDonald Had a Farm"; I thought they might recognize the animal sounds. Of course they thought we were out of our minds.) As the children became excited by their own singing, they left their log benches and swarmed around the nuns, hopping, smiling at us, everyone smiling, the nuns' faces bursting in their cowls, and the clear-voiced children still singing, and the palm-leafed roofing stirred.

The Napo River: it is not out of the way. It is *in* the way, catching sunlight the way a cup catches poured water; it is a bowl of sweet air, a basin of greenness, and of grace, and, it would seem, of peace.

## Themes, Issues, and Ideas

1. Judging by this essay, where do you think Annie Dillard is from? What might this essay be like if she had stayed on the Napo River for a year?

2. "Out of the way of *what*?" asks Dillard. Make a list of ten things the Napo River is, and is not, out of the way of.

3. Compare Dillard's river to Carson's town. Which seems a better example of "harmony"? Explain why.

## Writing Strategies and Techniques

1. How does Dillard combine physical detail and narrative exposition to describe the Napo River?

2. How would it affect Dillard's piece if: (1) the little girls had pulled her hair; (2) the little boy hit and killed the birds he was shooting at; and (3) Dillard's hand *had* been bitten by a piranha and become infected?

# Suggestions for Writing

1. Write a parody of "In the Jungle" in which the situations described in Writing Strategies and Techniques, question 2, occur.

2. Write a parody of "In the Jungle" about a shopping mall or other local place.

# Seven Doomsday Myths About the Environment

## Ronald Bailey

*The global environmental crisis is not a crisis at all, say some critics. Global warming, pollution, the overuse of nonrenewable resources, and many of the other issues are actually just illusory, summoned up by overanxious environmentalists. One such critic is Ronald Bailey, a former science writer for* Forbes Magazine, *and a 1993 Fellow in Environmental Journalism at the Competitive Enterprise Institute, a prominent Washington think tank. Bailey is also the author of* Eco-Scam: The False Prophets of Ecological Apocalypse *(1993)*

As the author of *Eco-Scam: The False Prophets of Ecological Apocalypse,* I know by surprising experience that what I am about to say is going to make many people angry. But here goes.

THE END IS NOT NIGH! That's right—the Apocalypse has been postponed for the foreseeable future, despite the gloomy prognostications by the likes of Paul Ehrlich, Lester Brown, Al Gore, Stephen Schneider, and Carl Sagan. There is no scientific evidence to support the often heard claim that there is a global ecological crisis threatening humanity and life on the entire Planet Earth.

There are local environmental problems, of course, but no global threats. Instead, there is a record of enormous environmental progress and much to be optimistic about. As far as the global environment is concerned, there is a brilliant future for humanity and Planet Earth.

Of course, millions of people believe that we have only a few more years before the end, and no doubt some such doomsters are among the readers of this article. But I would like to remind them of seven false doomsday predictions—many of which are still being peddled by unscrupulous activists—and take a hard look at what actually happened.

## False Doomsday Prediction No. 1

**Global Famine** "The battle to feed all of humanity is over. In the 1970s the world will undergo famines—hundreds of millions of people are going to starve to death in spite of any crash programs embarked upon now," predicted population alarmist Paul Ehrlich in his book *The Population Bomb* (1968).

Two years later Ehrlich upped the ante by also painting a gruesome scenario in the Earth Day 1970 issue of *The Progressive,* in which *65 million* Americans would die of famine and a total of *4 billion* people worldwide would perish in "the Great Die-Off" between the years 1980 and 1989.

**What Really Happened?** While the world's population *doubled* since World War II, food production *tripled.* The real price of wheat and corn dropped by 60%, while the price of rice was cut in half. Worldwide life expectancy rose from 47.5 years in 1950 to 63.9 years in 1990, while the world infant mortality rate dropped from 155 to 70 per 1,000 live births. Even in the poorest countries, those with per capita incomes under $400, average life expectancy rose spectacularly from 35 years in 1960 to 60 years in 1990.

And there's even more good news—for the last decade, grain output rose 5% per year in the developing world, while population growth has slowed from 2.3% to 1.9% and continues to fall. These figures strongly bolster University of Chicago agricultural economist Gale Johnson when he claims, "The scourge of famine due to natural causes has been almost conquered and could be entirely eliminated by the end of the century."

## False Doomsday Prediction No. 2

**Exhaustion of Nonrenewable Resources** In 1972, the Club of Rome's notorious report, *The Limits to Growth,* predicted that at exponential growth rates the world would run out of raw materials—gold by 1981, mercury by 1985, tin by 1987, zinc by 1990, oil by 1992, and copper, lead, and natural gas by 1993.

**What Really Happened?** Humanity hasn't come close to running out of any mineral resource. Even the World Resources Institute estimates that the average price of all metals and minerals *fell* by more than 40% between 1970 and 1988. As we all know, falling prices mean that goods are becoming more abundant, not more scarce. The U.S. Bureau of Mines estimates that, at 1990 production rates, world reserves of gold will last 24 years, mercury 40 years, tin 28 years, zinc 40 years, copper 65 years, and lead 35 years. Proven reserves of petroleum will last 44 years and natural gas 63 years.

Now don't worry about the number of years left for any of these reserves. Just as a family replenishes its larder when it begins to empty, so, too, does humanity look for new mineral reserves only when supplies begin to run low. Even the alarmist Worldwatch Institute admits that "recent trends in price and availability suggest that for most minerals we are a long way from running out."

## False Doomsday Prediction No. 3

**Skyrocketing Pollution** In 1972, *The Limits to Growth* also predicted that pollution would skyrocket as population and industry increased: "Virtually every pollutant that has been measured as a function of time appears to be increasing exponentially."

In 1969, Paul Ehrlich outlined a future "eco-catastrophe" in which he prophesied that 200,000 people would die in 1973 in "smog disasters" in New York and Los Angeles.

**What Really Happened?** Since the publication of *The Limits to Growth,* U.S. population has risen 22% and the economy has grown by more than 58%. Yet, instead of increasing as predicted, air pollutants have dramatically declined.

Sulfur-dioxide emissions are down 25% and carbon monoxide down 41%. Volatile organic compounds—chief contributors to smog formation—have been reduced by 31%, and total particulates like smoke, soot, and dust have fallen by 59%. Smog dropped by 50% in Los Angeles over the last decade.

Water quality deteriorated until the 1960s; now, water pollution is abating. Experts estimate that up to 95% of America's rivers, 92% of its lakes, and 86% of its estuaries are fishable and swimmable. These favorable pollution trends are being mirrored in both western Europe and Japan.

But what about the developing countries and former communist countries? It is true that industrial pollution continues to rise in some poorer countries. But a recent study by two Princeton University economists, Gene Grossman and Alan Krueger, using World Health Organization data, concluded that air pollution typically increases in a city until the average per capita income of its citizens reaches $4,000–$5,000, at which point pollution levels begin to fall. This is what happened in the developed nations and will happen as developing nations cross that threshold. In other words, economic growth leads to less pollution—not more, as asserted by the doomsters.

## False Doomsday Prediction No. 4

**The Coming Ice Age** The public has forgotten that the chief climatological threat being hyped by the eco-doomsters in the 1970s was the beginning of a new ice age. The new ice age was allegedly the result of mankind's polluting haze, which was blocking sunlight. "The threat of a new ice age must now stand alongside nuclear war as a likely source of wholesale death and misery for mankind," declared Nigel Calder, former editor of *New Scientist,* in 1975.

**What Really Happened?** Global temperatures, after declining for 40 years, rebounded in the late 1970s, averting the feared new ice age. But was this cause for rejoicing? NO! Now we are supposed to fear global warming. Freeze or fry, the problem is always viewed as industrial capitalism, and the solution, international socialism.

## False Doomsday Prediction No. 5

**The Antarctic Ozone Hole** There have been widespread fears that the hole in the ozone layer of the earth's atmosphere will wipe out life all over the world. John Lynch, program manager of polar aeronomy at the

National Science Foundation, declared in 1989, "It's terrifying. If these ozone holes keep growing like this, they'll eventually eat the world."

**What Really Happened?** In 1985, British scientists detected reduced levels of stratospheric ozone over Antarctica. Could the Antarctic ozone hole "eventually eat the world"? No. "It is a purely localized phenomenon," according to Guy Brasseur at the National Center for Atmospheric Research. It is thought that the "ozone hole" results from catalytic reactions of some chlorine-based chemicals, which can take place only in high, very cold (below −80° C, or −176° F) clouds in the presence of sunlight. It is a transitory phenomenon enduring only a bit more than a month in the austral spring. The polar vortex—that is, the constant winds that swirl around the margins of the ice continent—tightly confine the hole over Antarctica.

What about the southern ecosystems? Isn't the increased ultraviolet light threatening plants and animals there? U.S. Vice President Albert Gore credulously reports in his book that hunters are finding rabbits and fish blinded by ultraviolet light in Patagonia.

This is sheer nonsense. Scientists have found not one example of animals being blinded by excess ultraviolet light in the Southern Hemisphere.

What about the phytoplankton in the seas around Antarctica? Osmond Holm-Hartsen, a marine ecologist at Scripps Institute of Oceanography, has been studying the effects of ultraviolet light on Antarctica's ecosystems since 1988. He found that the extra ultraviolet-B light reduces phytoplankton by less than 4%–5%, which is well within the natural variations for the region. Holm-Hansen concludes, "Unlike the scare stories you hear some scientists spreading, the Antarctic ecosystem is absolutely not on the verge of collapse due to increased ultraviolet light."

## False Doomsay Prediction No. 6

**Ozone Hole Over America** In 1992, NASA spooked Americans by declaring that an ozone hole like the one over Antarctica could open up over the United States. *Time* magazine showcased the story on its front cover (February 16, 1992), warning that "danger is shining through the sky.... No longer is the threat just to our future; the threat is here and now." Then-Senator Albert Gore thundered in Congress: "We have to tell our children that they must redefine their relationship to the sky, and they must begin to think of the sky as a threatening part of their environment."

**What Really Happened?** On April 30,1992, NASA sheepishly admitted that no ozone hole had opened up over the United States. *Time,* far from trumpeting the news on its cover, buried the admission in four lines of text in its May 11 issue. It's no wonder the American public is frightened.

But let's stipulate that there have been minor reductions in ozone over the United States due to chlorofluorocarbons in the stratosphere. So what?

Reduced stratospheric ozone over the United States was never going to be a disaster or a catastrophe. At most, it might have become an environmental nuisance in the next century.

But doesn't reduced stratospheric ozone severely injure crops and natural ecosystems? The answer is no. Ultraviolet levels vary naturally by as much as 50% over the United States. The farther south you go, the higher the ultraviolet exposure a person or plant receives. For example, an average 5% reduction in the ozone layer over the United States would increase ultraviolet exposure by about as much as moving a mere 60 miles south—the distance from Palm Beach to Miami. How many people worry about getting skin cancer as a result of moving 60 miles? Not many, I bet.

Alan Teramura, who is perhaps the world's leading expert on the effects of ultraviolet light on plants, says, "There is no question that terrestrial life is adapted to ultraviolet." His experiments have shown that many varieties of crops would be unaffected by reductions in the ozone layer. In fact, corn, wheat, rice, and oats all grow in a wide variety of ultraviolet environments now.

## False Doomsday Prediction No. 7

**Global Warming** Global warming is "the Mother of all environmental scares," according to the late political scientist Aaron Wildavsky. Based on climate computer models, eco-doomsters predict that the earth's average temperature will increase by 4°–9°F over the next century due to the "greenhouse effect": Burning fossil fuels boosts atmospheric carbon dioxide, which traps the sun's heat.

**What Is Really Happening?** The earth's average temperature has apparently increased by less than a degree (0.9) Fahrenheit in the last century. Unfortunately for the global-warming alarmists, most of that temperature rise occurred before World War II, when greenhouse gases had not yet accumulated to any great extent in the atmosphere.

And here's more bad news for doomsters: Fifteen years of very precise satellite data show that the planet has actually cooled by 0.13° C. Some years are warmer while others are cooler, according to NASA space scientist Roy Spencer, but the global temperature trend has been slightly downward. The satellites can measure temperature differences as small as 0.01° C. By contrast, the computer models of the doomsters predict that temperatures should have risen by an easily detectable 0.3° C per decade. They have not.

Even more bad news for the global-warming doomsters: One of the more robust predictions of the climate computer models is that global warming should be strongest and start first in the Arctic. Indeed, Albert Gore says in his book: "Global warming is expected to push temperatures up much more rapidly in the polar regions than in the rest of the world."

However, scientists did a recent comprehensive analysis of 40 years of arctic temperature data from the United States and the former Soviet Union. In an article in the prestigious scientific journal *Nature,* the scientists reported, "We do not observe the large surface warming trends predicted by the models; indeed, we detect significant surface cooling trends over the western Arctic Ocean during the winter and autumn." This is the exact opposite of what the doomsters are predicting is happening; the Arctic is becoming *cooler.*

Climate doomsters also predict that the ice caps of Antarctica and Greenland will melt, drastically raising sea levels and inundating New York, London, Bangladesh, and Washington, D.C. Recent scientific evidence shows that in fact the glaciers in both Antarctica and Greenland are accumulating ice, which means that sea levels will drop, not rise. Another false apocalypse averted.

Furthermore, over the past 100 years, winters in the Northern Hemisphere have become warmer, Why? Because the world is becoming cloudier. Cloud blankets warm long winter nights while long summer days are shaded by their cloud shields, This means longer growing seasons and fewer droughts for crops. This is decidedly not a recipe for a climate disaster.

Given the dismal record of the environmental doomsayers, why do so many people think the world is coming to an end? I think it's pretty clear. People are afraid because so many interest groups have a stake in making them afraid. "Global emergencies" and "worldwide crises" keep hundreds of millions of dollars in donations flowing into the coffers of environmental organizations. As environmental writer Bill McKibben admitted in *The End of Nature,* "The ecological movement has always had its greatest success in convincing people that we are threatened by some looming problem." That success is now measured at the cash register for many leading environmental groups. For example, in 1990, the 10 largest environmental organizations raised $400 million from donors. That pays for a lot of trips to international environmental conferences, furnishes some nice headquarters, and buys a lot of influence on Capitol Hill.

Crises also advance the careers of certain politicians and bureaucrats, attract funds to scientists' laboratories, and sell newspapers and TV air time. The approach of inevitable doom is now the conventional wisdom of the late twentieth century.

But despite the relentless drumbeat of environmental doomsaying, people have to want to believe that the end is nigh. How do we account for the acquiescence of such a large part of the public to a gloomy view of the future?

I conclude that the psychological attraction of the apocalyptic imagination is strong. Eric Zencey, a self-described survivor of apocalyptic environmentalism, wrote about his experience in the *North American Review* (June 1988): There is a seduction in apocalyptic thinking. If one lives in the Last Days, one's actions, one's very life, take on historical meaning and no small measure of poignance.... Apocalypticism fulfills a desire to escape the flow of real and ordinary time, to fix the flow of history into a single moment of overwhelming importance."

To counteract the seduction of the apocalypse, scientists, policy makers, intellectuals, and businessmen must work to restore people's faith in themselves and in the fact of human progress. History clearly shows that our energy and creativity will surmount whatever difficulties we encounter. Life and progress will always be a struggle and humanity will never lack for new challenges, but as the last 50 years of solid achievement show, there is nothing out there that we cannot handle.

So what's the moral of the story? Please don't listen to the doomsters' urgent siren calls to drastically reorganize society and radically transform the world's economy to counter imaginary ecological apocalypses. The relevant motto is not "He who hesitates is lost," but rather, "Look before you leap."

## Themes, Issues, and Ideas

1. Bailey has an original expression to describe people who are alarmed about the environment, namely "doomsters." Later in his essay he imputes their concern to escapism. Does this strike you as a fair assessment? What is Bailey's evidence for this view? How is it like Bailey's other evidences?

2. At the end of his essay, Bailey quotes Bill McKibben. After you read Bill McKibben on environmental optimism of exactly Bailey's brand, do you think this is an accurate quotation? What does it tell you about other quotations Bailey uses?

3. "Another false apocalypse averted," Bailey concludes at the end of a paragraph on global warming. Are you reassured by his certitude?

## Writing Strategies and Techniques

1. Why do you think Bailey is so fond of statistics?

2. Why does Bailey break his essay into seven discrete "doomsday myths," and each of these into a myth section and a "What really happened" section?

## Suggestions for Writing

1. Rewrite a section of Bailey's essay, using the fiery intemperate language of a radical militiaman or talk radio host.

2. Look up the sources Bailey quotes from, and write an essay critiquing his accuracy in using them.

# Not So Fast

## Bill McKibben

*As the twentieth century draws to a close, the cause
of conservation that Rachel Carson did so much to bring
to public consciousness in the sixties has undergone an
unexpected turn: many "environmental optimists" are
declaring the war is largely won, and that America has
turned back from the environmental precipice toward
which we seemed headed. Naturalist Bill McKibben
believes otherwise, however, as he explains in "Not So
Fast." McKibben is a writer whose previous books,* The
End of Nature *and* The Age of Missing Information *have
earned great critical praise.*

Here's a short chemistry lesson. Grasp it and you will
grasp the reason the environmental era has barely begun; perhaps you
will grasp the history of the next 50 years.

Put a gallon of gasoline in the tank of your car and go out for a
drive. Assuming your engine's well tuned, burning that gallon of petroleum should put about half a pound of carbon in the form of carbon
monoxide—CO—into the air. A generation ago that number was closer
to one pound; by decade's end, as new technologies clean the exhaust,
it should drop to barely a tenth of a pound. The steady decrease in CO
emissions, as well as in those of nitrous oxide and particulates, is the
reason the air is clearer and safer now in Los Angeles than it was a generation ago.

On the same drive, however, that gallon of gas will transmute
itself into almost five and a half pounds of carbon in the form of carbon
*di*oxide. Long considered proof that gas was burning cleanly, invisible
and odorless $CO_2$ is the inevitable byproduct of fossil fuel consumption. It doesn't matter if your car's old or new, there's no filter you can
stick on the exhaust to reduce $CO_2$ production. And if the wide interna-

tional consensus of scientists is correct, this carbon dioxide is now warming the planet more quickly and to higher temperatures than ever in human history.

CO versus $CO_2$. One damn oxygen atom, and all the difference in the world.

If you focus on carbon *mon*oxide, then you can count yourself among the currently fashionable environmental optimists. Pollution, from their perspective, is an unfortunate byproduct of an essentially sound system. Since smog and its many analogues (river pollution, acid rain, crowded landfills) are precisely the sorts of things that can be tamed with filters and scrubbers, or with small changes in human behavior like recycling, the optimists are in some ways right. Though Congress is even now gutting the laws that have begun to clean America, and though there are plenty of poor and minority communities that never began to get cleaned in the first place, the technology exists to diminish smog, to purify drinking water. It's merely a matter of finding the will to pay for it—there's no reason for rivers to catch fire. (And every poll suggests that the will is there, that after a quarter-century of hard-fought environmental campaigns the American people are far more convinced than their congressmen that the environment is worth cleaning up.) So if CO turns out to be the real issue, then its just a systems problem. Environmentalism is a success story, and the world we die in will resemble the one we were born into, albeit with more computers.

That's the conventional wisdom of the moment, best expressed by Gregg Easterbrook in his recent book, *A Moment on the Earth.* And yet there are those of us who are not soothed—who grow more worried with each passing month, and not simply by the fact of a Republican Congress. Those in this second camp tend to be focused on problems like widespread extinction, growing populations, dying fisheries and dwindling wilderness—signals like the ever-expanding cloud of $CO_2$, indicating that our societies and their appetites have simply grown too large. Signals still all but ignored.

Since the environmental movement began, all these crises have been lumped together. The same people who worried about clean air worried about recycling and species extinction, about dirty rivers and the press of population. All these causes are important—now more than ever as the right attempts to undermine environmental protection—but acting as if they were all essentially the same crisis carries risks as well as benefits. While it's certainly easier to focus on things like smog, which people see around them every day, the logic of focusing on the most visible pollution cuts both ways. Such a narrowly pragmatic vision is potentially paralyzing precisely because you *can* clean urban air, you *can* return fish to the Great Lakes, you *can* recycle enough to keep landfills from overflowing.

Unfortunately, you can do all these quite vital things without having any real effect on the more systematic troubles. The progress we've made in solving environmental problems is deceptive: we're making no progress at all on the deeper problems, *because they do not spring from the same sources.* One set stems from a defect in the car; the other set comes from the very existence of the car. And in an odd way, solving the first kind of problem makes the deeper ones ever more intractable— if visible air pollution starts to decline, then the push for better mass transit dwindles, and with it the chances of cutting the invisible $CO_2$.

The environmental movement, in other words, has reached a diagnostic crisis. To use a medical analogy: The world has presented itself, complaining of chest pains. After three decades of examination, there are still those who insist it's indigestion and want to prescribe some Bromo. Others say arteriosclerosis, which means our most basic behaviors must change. Most people—not just C.E.O.'s—badly want to find out that our problems are not related to our life styles. Change frightens us: we've come to believe, for instance, that our well-being is lashed to constant economic growth. "It's the economy, stupid."

And yet the basic laws of chemistry may soon demand that we give up such fixations. The Inter-governmental Panel on Climate Change, a group of scientists assembled by the United Nations, has calculated that an immediate *60 percent* reduction in fossil fuel use is necessary to stabilize global climate. This could not happen in a world that closely resembles ours. Addicted to growth, busily spreading our vision of the good life around the globe, we are sprinting in the opposite direction. The growth in our economies and populations wipes out our incremental gains in energy efficiency: from 1983 to 1993, despite a tremendous push toward efficiency by power companies, Americans increased their per capita power usage by more than 22 percent. Electric utilities offered rebates for installing compact fluorescent bulbs, and, indeed, between 1986 and 1991 the typical household added one such light. But as Andrew Rudin pointed out recently in *Public Power* magazine, the typical household also added more than seven incandescent lamps.

Since the greenhouse effect and other consequences of our civilization's basic momentum have yet to hit us full-on, no mass movement has developed to challenge that momentum. "We are in an unusual predicament as a global civilization," Al Gore said when I interviewed him early in his Vice Presidency. "The maximum that is politically feasible, even the maximum that is politically *imaginable* right now, still falls short of the minimum that is scientifically and ecologically necessary." And that was *before* Newt Gingrich.

But this state of affairs may not last. According to the most accurate computer models of global climate, for instance, increased global temperatures may be obvious to the man in the street by decade's end. For all the right-wing bluster about taming the environmental movement, for all the happy-talk books about our ecological triumphs, it will take only a hot summer or two, a string of crop failures or some similar catastrophe to bring these issues center stage once more. A spate of recent studies has begun to make clear that an average temperature increase of only a few degrees hides tremendous heat waves, droughts and storms; the insurance industry has actually begun to worry publicly about the greenhouse effect and the losses it will cause.

If and when such stresses really show themselves, though, we will need an environmental movement that understands what is happening—that understands that more recycling is not the main answer, that is willing to advocate the unpopular and the disturbing. Partly this means a stepped-up political campaign—continual pressure on governments around the world to sign and fulfill treaties, share renewable technologies and pass steep new taxes on the use of fossil fuels and other polluters. Already a small segment of the environmental movement has begun to focus on such issues.

But remember the numbers. A 60 percent reduction in fossil fuel use? Even under the most hopeful technological scenarios, it won't happen if we're simultaneously doubling or tripling our economies. More money makes reducing smog easier, because you can afford to build *better* cars; more money makes dealing with the greenhouse effect harder, because you can afford to buy *more* cars. So the sweet dream that we'll all grow rich enough to turn green is simply that—a dream, and one that will turn into a nightmare if we try to follow it.

We face tough choices. The most pragmatic realism, rooted in the molecular structure of $CO_2$, demands electric cars. It also demands nothing less than heresy: an all-out drive for deep thrift, for self-restraint, for smaller families. Brute objectivity requires new ideas about what constitutes sufficiency: smaller homes, more food grown locally, repair instead of replacement. Environmental visionaries have always talked about simplicity and community, but now atmospheric chemists are starting to say the same things. Not for esthetic and moral reasons, but for eminently practical ones. The world can't support a population of five and a half billion people living like middle-class Americans, much less the eight or nine billion that will soon share the planet with us. That's the crux of the issue—that and the fact that as long as we go on living the way we do everyone else will want to as well. We need China to stop burning so much fossil fuel—the developing world *now* produces as much $CO_2$ as the developed—but China will pay no attention until we start cutting back too.

Clearly, it's as immoral as it is impractical for us to demand that underdeveloped countries remain underdeveloped—those countries passionately want to develop. But it's terrifying to imagine Asians owning cars in the same numbers as we do. The only way out of this dilemma is to rethink what we mean by "development"—and to do it here first. We've exported our passion for democracy, our devotion to human rights. But that's not all we've exported. More than a billion humans, one in five of us, watch "Baywatch" every week. If the good life whose pictures we flash around the world doesn't change, then all the treaties on earth won't do the job. We need bicycles and we need buses, and we need to make them seem as marvelous as Miatas.

Rush Limbaugh has it right when he denounces environmentalists as a threat to current ways of life. The systemic environmentalism he fears has one question to ask: "How much is enough?" How much convenience, how many people, how much money? It's a question that won't go away. It's a question with a time limit, too: either we make these changes soon, or it won't be worth the bother.

# Themes, Issues, and Ideas

1. Are you familiar with arguments such as the one McKibben makes here? Where does McKibben fit in your sense of the camps in the environmental debate?

2. Patterns of economic growth which Americans take for granted, McKibben says, cannot be supported by the environment. Why not? Do you see any are flaws in McKibben's argument? Why can't nine billion people live like middle-class Americans? Give examples from the text.

3. Why does McKibben ignore the political atmosphere of the time in which he writes—one in which, it will be remembered, economic legislation was in grave peril?

# Writing Strategies and Techniques

1. What are some different ways McKibben has of concentrating the reader's attention on a key point?

2. What are the most commonly repeated themes in this essay, and how does McKibben vary their presentation?

# Suggestions for Writing

1. Write an essay describing what such a reformed lifestyle as McKibben describes might entail.

2. Describe your response to "Not So Fast." Did you find McKibben's essay persuasive? Alarming? Annoying? Boring? Make an effort to describe your encounter with an essay whose basic purpose is to change commonly held beliefs.

# Voting Green

## Carol Grunewald

> *The following essay combines two trends that seem to be increasing as the twenty-first century approaches; first, our growing consciousness of environmental risk, and second, more active, grassroots interactive democracy. As Vice President Al Gore has said on numerous occasions, "The environment will become the central organizing principle of the twenty-first century."*
>
> *Carol Grunewald is a longtime environmental advocate from whose book (cowritten with her husband Jeremy Rifkin)* Voting Green *this selection is based on. She is among the most visible of a new wave of environmentalists looking for change in the very near future.*

"*Global warming doesn't exist.*"
"*People are more important than owls and forests.*"
"*All the scares about the environment—it's a big lie.*"
"*You environmentalists are destroying everything we've worked for in this country.*"

If you're a defender of the environment, you're probably familiar with comments like these. In the past few months, I, along with my husband, Jeremy Rifkin, have been on dozens of call-in radio shows across the country talking about *Voting Green—Your Complete Environmental Guide to Making Political Choices in the 1990s,* a new book we co-authored. Each time we go on the air we are prepared to talk about what people can do to save the environment; and each time we are confronted by a series of callers who challenge us to prove that there is

This article was adapted from a book, *Voting Green—Your Complete Environmental Guide to Making Political Choices in the 1990s,* by Jeremy Rifkin and Carol Grunewald, 1992, Doubleday, 390 pages.

anything wrong with the environment in the first place. These callers are among the more vocal representatives of the backlash against environmentalism that is sweeping the country.

Now that the Cold War is over, it appears that some Americans are searching for a new scapegoat to blame for the current chaos in the economy. Environmentalists have quickly become the new target of the right. Although it is dispiriting to be assailed as the destroyer of the American way of life, the backlash is not necessarily a reason to despair. More than anything, the ferocious antagonism now being directed toward environmentalists proves that the environmental movement has made major inroads into the public psyche.

Conservatives are now reacting to the environmental movement as if it were a formidable political opponent. While they may be overestimating the current power of the environmental community, there are encouraging signs that the movement is indeed being transformed into what right-wingers fear most: a broadly based political force capable of challenging the corporate status quo.

The Democratic Party, as well, has wisely recognized the emerging power of the environmental movement. Democratic presidential candidate Gov. Bill Clinton picked Sen. Al Gore (D-Tenn.) as his running mate precisely because Gore is an environmental champion and would appeal to the growing number of Americans who are concerned about the environment. Indeed, in his nomination acceptance speech, Gore forecast the potential power of the environmental movement when he said, "The environment will become the central organizing principle of the 21st century."

One can sense in many places across the country the rising energy of green politics—an emerging political philosophy that broadens the focus of environmentalism to include peace, community, justice technology, and animal rights issues. Despite the noisy clamoring of the environmental backlash, green politics is making itself felt in three slowly evolving trends, each of which seems to be setting the stage for a significant break from politics-as-usual in years to come.

First, the environmental movement is broadening to include other constituencies. Activists from beyond the typical white, middle-class constituency of environmentalism have begun to view a healthy environment as central to their own concerns and have begun to work closely with environmentalists.

Hundreds of African-Americans, Hispanics, Native Americans, and Asians assembled in Washington last fall for the first National People of Color Environmental Leadership Summit. Representing communities not traditionally active in environmental causes, delegates came to this meeting to organize against the environmental assaults experienced disproportionately by minority, poor, and working-class people—threats like toxic waste dumps, hazardous waste incinerators, lead poisoning, poor air quality, and lack of access to healthy food. Conference participants argued that the struggle for a healthy environment is part of the struggle for social justice and that only a healthy environment can provide the basis for a healthy and just economy.

Feminists are also broadening their politics to encompass the environment. Last fall, the Women's Foreign Policy Council, chaired by former U.S. Rep. Bella Abzug, sponsored the first World Women's Congress for a Just and Healthy Planet. More than 1,500 activist women from 83 countries attended this unprecedented conference to discuss the effect of environmental degradation on women and families worldwide.

Even labor leaders have begun to talk seriously about how they might align themselves with environmentalists while at the same time devising strategies to provide an economic safety net for workers who lose jobs as a result of environmental protection measures.

There is more good news. At the state and local level, Green parties are being organized, and hundreds of independent, green-oriented (although they seldom use this phrase to describe themselves) legislators across the country are becoming increasingly successful at passing environmental-protection legislation in their communities. For example, in 1990 alone, 140 recycling laws were passed by state legislatures.

This year, California became the second state, following Alaska, to officially recognize the Greens as a political party. More than 83,000 Californians registered with the Green Party, qualifying the party to have its candidates on the November 3 election ballot. The Green Party has also been working to gain official recognition in Arizona, Hawaii, Missouri, and Pennsylvania.

In many areas of the country where Green parties have not yet made inroads, scores of state and local legislators have been working with national progressive policy groups such as the Center for Policy Alternatives and Renew America, in Washington, D.C., and smaller, more localized groups, such as Local Solutions to Global Pollution in

Berkeley, California, to develop environmental protection legislation and strategies for its passage in their communities.

A third hopeful development is occurring, of all places, on Capitol Hill. Green politics is quietly emerging as a distinct new political presence in the U.S. Congress. In researching *Voting Green,* we sifted through a couple of thousand pieces of proposed federal legislation (covering issues ranging from transportation to foreign policy to animal rights to agriculture) in search of evidence of green thinking about the problems America faces. To our surprise, we found nearly 300 bills proposed between January 1989 and June 1991 that fit our criteria. We tracked and graded all 535 members of Congress, marking on a "report card" whether they had supported each of these bills or not. Because much of this legislation is far-sighted and visionary, little of it has made it out of committee to the floor of the House or Senate for a vote. We therefore decided to track support for these innovative bills by noting which legislators were sponsoring and co-sponsoring the legislation.

We ended up with an intriguing finding: A small but solid group of U.S. legislators, a good 10 percent of the Congress, is proposing and supporting radical new solutions for America. Ten years ago, there was no trace of a "green contingent" in Congress, but now a discernible group can be identified. Foremost among these congressional greens is Al Gore, whose presence on the Democratic ticket this fall is another sign of growing interest in green politics.

The bills introduced and supported by these legislators prescribe nearly everything that environmentalists have advocated and fought for in areas ranging from agriculture to animal rights to foreign policy. Taken together, their bills provide a virtual "greenprint" for a new green society. They are the bridge between idealistic green visions and the complex realities of modern society.

These three new trends are still in their infancy, but they are the seeds of a national political movement. If these trends continue to flourish, they could produce a powerful new political force. At the core of these trends is a revolutionary concept: the idea of placing the environment at the center of public life and then planning economic, social, and other policies around it.

While the environmental movement has made considerable gains over the past two decades, especially in raising the public's consciousness, the movement as it is presently constituted is reaching the limit of what it can accomplish. Environmentalism as it is practiced in this country is too narrow, which has made it vulnerable to charges of elitism. The environmental movement now faces the challenge of transforming itself into something deeper and broader. Green politics is based on the recognition that we can't have a healthy economy, peace among nations, or a satisfying quality of life if we are trying to live and work within a degraded environment.

American politics has always revolved around the economy—with disastrous results for the environment and human welfare. Most Republicans and Democrats view the environment as just another issue—a special interest, one among many. As a result, the environment is ignored whenever it is politically expedient—which is most of the time. Conventional political analysts often claim that concern about the environment evaporates in the face of a nation's economic and other stresses.

But an intricate, delicate natural system cannot regularly be shunted aside without suffering considerable, even permanent damage. The earth's biological system supports our economy; it is literally our life-support system—hardly a special interest! With further bad news about global warming, the ozone hole, extinction of species, and toxic waste horrors, more and more people are beginning to realize this.

The seemingly insoluble nature of the country's economic and other problems has catalyzed many people's search for a more holistic, commonsensical approach to politics. This new thinking may begin to make itself felt at the polls in November—if not in the presidential election, then in many congressional, state, and local races. In the increasingly stale political atmosphere of 1992, these visionary green ideas coming from all corners of the nation as well as from Capitol Hill are a breath of fresh air.

In our study of proposed federal legislation, we uncovered bills that present a whole new way of seeing and relating to the world—ideas that challenge conventional notions of global security, economics, progress, science and technology, and community.

For example, some members of Congress are beginning to sense that an increasingly weakened biosphere poses a more serious threat to our individual and national security than the relative military and economic strength of other nations. Some of the legislation they have proposed reflects this shift in thinking. The bills range from those that would protect and preserve the global commons—rain forests, the atmosphere, outer space, Antarctica, and even the gene pool of the planet—to those that would begin to dismantle the U. S. military-industrial complex and move toward an equitable, sustainable peacetime economy.

In 1990, a number of legislators—including Gore, Sen. John Kerry (D-Mass.) and Rep. Wayne Owens (D-Utah)—proposed and pushed through legislation to "fully protect Antarctica as a global ecological commons." In 1991, President Bush, under heavy pressure, was eventually forced to sign this legislation as well as a global treaty banning commercial activity on the continent for another 50 years.

Far-reaching legislation to counter global warming and deterioration of the ozone layer, and to dramatically limit the gas emissions that are responsible for these potentially cataclysmic environmental effects, has been submitted by a handful of legislators including Gore and former Republican Rep. Claudine Schneider of Rhode Island.

Protecting the planet's gene pool has also gained the attention of Congress. Legislation has been introduced by Sen. Mark Hatfield (R-Ore.) that challenges the right of corporations and individuals to genetically engineer, patent, and own plants, animals, and microbes.

Legislation to rein in the U.S. military-industrial complex includes a congressional resolution to cut U.S. military spending by at least 50 percent by the year 2000 and dramatically cut U.S. military assistance and arms sales to developing nations. Bills introduced by Reps. Barbara Boxer (D-Calif.), Ted Weiss (D-N.Y.), Sam Gejdenson (D-Conn.), and Nicholas Mavroules (D-Mass.) would ease the economic transition for companies, workers, and communities in the wake of cutbacks in military spending by requiring military contractors to establish special committees to plan for the transition, and by providing workers with economic assistance and retraining.

A bill sponsored by Hatfield and Rep. Andrew Jacobs (D-Ind.) would create a "peace tax fund" into which citizens who are conscientiously opposed to the military could pay their federal taxes; such funds would be used only to fund social and environmental protection programs.

In other areas too, the range and depth of green legislation being proposed is extraordinary and provocative and based on radical green values and ideas. In the area of animal rights, for example, one bill would allow any citizen or organization to file suit against the federal government on behalf of an individual animal in order to compel enforcement of the Animal Welfare Act, an animal-protection law. Implicit in the legislation is the revolutionary idea that individual animals have intrinsic value and inherent rights to exist and not be harmed.

At one point, the bill had more than 68 co-sponsors in the House. Another animal-rights bill would require all federally funded school lunch programs to provide optional meatless meals for all students and teachers who are conscientiously opposed to eating meat.

In the area of foreign development aid, one green bill would require the U.S. government to dramatically increase the number of cash loans of between $50 and $300 to women and the poorest of the poor in developing nations to enable them to set up their own self-sustaining and environmentally sustainable businesses. Another bill would require the United States to promote and defend the rights of indigenous and tribal peoples throughout the world. These two pieces of green legislation represent radical departures from the goals and methods of current U.S. foreign aid programs and policies, which do not encourage self-reliance and sustainability.

These are just a few of the green ideas and practical approaches being discussed among legislators on Capitol Hill. Make no mistake—these lawmakers are not dyed-in-the-wool, self-conscious, ideological greens; but they are experimenting with new ideas about what constitutes security and quality of life. Unfortunately, green initiatives and progressive legislation are almost always ignored or go down to defeat in Congress because of a lack of broad-based support. Such legislation is usually supported by and lobbied for almost exclusively by the constituency group that is considered the "closest" to the issue at hand.

But as the idea of a comprehensive green politics—one that places the environment at the center of public life and plans economic and other activities around it—takes root among voters and elected officials, we are likely to see less fragmentation and more cooperation among various constituencies. Advocates of the environment, social justice, workers, women, family farmers, animal rights, peace, community empowerment, and numerous other groups and issues can find common ground in a green agenda.

Perhaps the only ingredient that's now missing for a national green movement is a sense of urgency. The forces of environmental backlash continue to press for the exploitation of the steadily weakening natural environment. So far, they are winning. The various constituencies that would make up the new green movement are acting as though they have all the time in the world to mobilize themselves.

Meanwhile, the short-lived presidential "candidacy" of H. Ross Perot gained surprising support among an increasingly alienated electorate in search of a new vision for the country. For these and millions of other Americans, the old political labels of "Republican/Democrat," "conservative/liberal," "right/left" that have long been used to define political debate are becoming increasingly irrelevant. That's because many issues of interest to American voters (and non-voters) transcend these old forms of classification.

A new, more relevant political spectrum is beginning to emerge. At one end are those who view their fellow human beings, other species, and the environment in strictly utilitarian terms—as resources to exploit for short-term material gain. At the opposite end of the spectrum are those who view all life on the earth as an interrelated community to which we are all indebted and for which we are all responsible.

Increasingly, political debate will be defined and shaped by looming global environmental threats and resource shortages; as a result we will see growing polarization between these two camps.

Among some groups in Congress, there is evidence that traditional political boundaries are becoming blurred and are beginning to reorganize around this new value system. For example, members of the two-year-old animal-rights caucus, Congressional Friends of Animals, which provides a base of support for animal-protection legislation in Congress, is bipartisan and includes a significant number of conservative Republicans as well as liberal Democrats.

If we act now to join forces under the green banner, support those legislators at all levels—federal, state, and local—who are trying to think green, aggressively lobby for the green legislation that is being proposed, and vote more greens (including ourselves) into public office, we could spawn a powerful new political force—one that could have a major impact on the nation and the world by the time another presidential election rolls around in 1996.

# Themes, Issues, and Ideas

1. How would you describe Grunewald's perspective? Is she a convincing advocate of green politics? Why or why not?

2. What sort of person does Grunewald seem to be? Is she like anyone you know? How would you describe her politically?

3. How would you describe the moral tone of Grunewald's essay?

# Writing Strategies and Techniques

1. Why does Grunewald begin her essay with quotations? Why are the quotes from anti-environmental voices?

2. Compare Grunewald's style with Hillary Rodham Clinton's (Chapter 4). Who is the better writer? Who is more persuasive? Why? Defend both the "policy-paper" style of Clinton and the journalistic style of Grunewald.

# Suggestions for Writing

1. Write an essay predicting what a twenty-first century election would be like, given Grunewald's predictions.

2. Write an essay advocating the traditional two-party system as the best avenue for change.

# Reforest the Earth!

## Norman Myers

*Suppose that those scientists are correct who sus-
pect global disasters to be the result of the greenhouse
effect described in previous essays. What can be done to
avoid or to limit those disasters? Norman Myers, a senior
fellow for the World Wildlife Fund and an expert on environment and development, suggests a plan: "A worldwide campaign to reforest the earth... will improve the
quality of our lives, stabilize rising temperatures, and buy
time until we find solutions to the greenhouse effect."
Myers proposes that for an average cost of $160 per acre
we could undertake a program of reforestation that would
greatly counter the negative symptoms of an "ailing
world." Though the total costs are very high, Myers
argues that the costs of not reforesting are even higher.
This essay was first published in* Omni *magazine, under
the title "First Word."*

Throughout the drought-ridden summer of 1988, the
world heard much about how the burning of fossil fuels causes the
greenhouse effect (the rapid warming of the earth's atmosphere). We
heard little about how the burning of tropical rain forests also contributes to the greenhouse effect. And still less do we hear about how reforestation of these tropics could help heal an ailing world.

The earth constantly maintains 700 billion metric tons of carbon
dioxide ($CO_2$) in the atmosphere. Fossil fuels emit another 5.2 billion
metric tons of $CO_2$ into the air each year, while the burning of tropical
forests emits roughly 1.8 billion metric tons of $CO_2$—both contributing
to a buildup of carbon dioxide that will soon trigger the greenhouse
effect. The $CO_2$ gases trap the heat of the sun in the same way the glass
of a greenhouse controls temperature for plants. If the gases become too
concentrated, too much heat will collect, resulting in rising temperatures.

Of all the carbon dioxide spewed into the atmosphere, only about half accumulates in the skies while the rest disappears into oceans and lakes, vegetation and soil. So out of the 5.2 billion metric tons of $CO_2$ emitted from the burning of fossil fuels and the 1.8 billion metric tons released from the burning of rain forests each year, only 3.5 billion metric tons contributes to global warming.

In 1980, 36,000 square miles of forest were burned in the tropics. In 1987, 33,000 square miles of rain forest were burned in Brazilian Amazonia alone. By the year 2020 the figure for tropical-forest emissions of $CO_2$ could climb to another 5 billion metric tons. As a result, the $CO_2$ released into the atmosphere each year would rise to approximately 10.2 billion metric tons.

Replanting trees in the tropics could eventually offer a solution to the greenhouse effect. A tree absorbs carbon dioxide through photosynthesis. Plant enough trees (as many as 250 billion) and we could remove much of the additional $CO_2$ building up in the atmosphere. Nowhere in the world are conditions better for growing trees than in the tropics, where year-round warmth and moisture encourage rapid growth. To embark on a grand-scale tree-growing project in the tropics, however, would require as many as 20 governments in Latin America, Africa, and Asia to stop the rapid destruction of rain forests.

How many trees would we need to reforest the earth and stabilize the damage produced by global warming? One acre of a tropical plantation can absorb an annual average of four metric tons of atmospheric carbon. In order to soak up 1 billion metric tons of $CO_2$, we would have to plant 400,000 square miles of new tropical forests. To eliminate the buildup of 3.5 billion metric tons would require planting trees on 1.2 million square miles, an expanse roughly equivalent to all states east of the Mississippi.

Where can we find enough space to replant what isn't being otherwise utilized? In the humid tropics forests have been cut down in watershed regions where replanting is urgently needed to stop topsoil from eroding and to prevent flooding. Last year flooding devastated regions in Bangladesh, India, the Sudan, and Thailand. In lowland Southeast Asia deforested lands have degenerated into poor-quality scrub and brush or coarse grasslands, good for little apart from reforestation. In addition, tropical countries urgently need to increase forest cover to adequately expand their fuelwood and commercial timber supplies.

At an average cost of $160 per acre, reforesting the tropics would cost $120 billion. This may seem like a high figure, but the global community would be spared much higher greenhouse costs. According to the Environmental Protection Agency, a rise in sea level (just through heating of the ocean surface) would threaten the developed coastal regions of the eastern United States. To protect these shorelines, sea-walls and tidal dams would have to be built at a cost of $110 billion. To revamp dams and irrigation systems in the United States could cost an additional $23 billion. In comparison, the Department of Agriculture currently spends $200 million a year on flood-prevention programs. Further costs related to sealevel rise and disrupted agriculture in other parts of the world (lush, fertile cropland may turn into desert) would surely turn out to be similarly great.

The consequences of the greenhouse effect will be far-reaching and possibly even devastating. If the projections of experts come to pass in the next 50 years, the earth's temperatures will rise between 3° and 9°F. (In polar regions the temperatures may rise as much as 20°F). After a look at the consequences we face as a result of the greenhouse effect, reforesting the earth doesn't seem as outrageous as it might have at first. In fact, a program to plant billions of trees throughout the tropics now seems like a very sensible action.

Reforesting the earth is not the definitive solution to the warming trend of the greenhouse effect. It is only one way to bring the rising levels of carbon in the atmosphere under control. A worldwide campaign to reforest the earth, however, will improve the quality of our lives, stabilize rising temperatures, and buy time until we find additional solutions to the greenhouse effect.

# Themes, Issues, and Ideas

1. Myers deals in staggering figures and, since the essay is not a formal scientific presentation, he does not list all the sources of those figures. But educated readers should try to avoid being staggered. Try to check his numbers—do they add up and divide properly? How else might they be presented? For example, how much per *tree* would Myers's program cost?

2. Why does Myers focus on the tropics for the location of his plan? Surely trees grow the world over. According to Myers, what makes the tropics such an attractive place for reforestation?

3. Myers says that the cooperation of twenty governments would be needed to stop the destruction of tropical rain forests. How and why might these governments argue *against* Myers's proposals?

# Writing Strategies and Techniques

1. Myers alludes to experts, but does not quote any as the sources for his statistics. When do you think it is necessary to give precise citations in your writing, and when is it not? Explain your reasoning.

2. Alternative sources of fuel (for example, nuclear, solar) are not mentioned in the essay. Do you find this appropriate, given the nature of the essay?

# Suggestions for Writing

1. When first reading the title, a reader might think Myers's program to be irrational, yet Myers himself concludes that "reforesting the earth doesn't seem as outrageous as it might have at first." Do you agree? Write a brief essay in which you analyze and demonstrate the strengths and weaknesses of Myers's essay as you see them.

2. How does one properly make a global proposal that includes such immense costs? Write an essay in which you argue the appropriateness of Myers's style to the importance of his context by analyzing particular examples.

# MAKING CONNECTIONS

1. If the purpose of an essay is to persuade, who in this chapter does the best job? Does a descriptive, personal essay like Annie Dillard's "In the Jungle" affect you more than a formal statement like Al Gore's "Ecology: The New Sacred Agenda?"

2. Bill McKibben's essay was written precisely with someone like Ronald Bailey in mind. Does he get the better of the exchange? Why or why not? To what extent do both authors marshall the facts available to them? Which one seems better informed? How do both deal with a subject that neither can be absolutely sure about, but which one believes requires urgent attention, and which the other believes can be safely ignored?

3. Norman Myers takes a somewhat different approach to environmental change than does Gore or, for that matter, Grunewald. Evaluate each of these authors on the practicality, sincerity, and potential usefulness of their ideas.

4. Many environmental problems have dramatic effects but obscure origins. Which of the authors in this chapter give you the best grasp on where environmental crises come from, as opposed to how they may be cured?

5. Many environmental problems are raised in this chapter, but which author seems to you the best at presenting a problem clearly and forcefully? Who is next best? Write an essay comparing the writers' expository strengths.

# RHETORICAL
# INDEX

## ANALOGY AND METAPHOR

## PROCESS ANALYSIS

## CAUSE AND EFFECT

## DEFINITION

## DESCRIPTION

# INDEX
# OF AUTHORS
# AND TITLES